HOW JOHN WORKS

RESOURCES FOR BIBLICAL STUDY

Editor
Tom Thatcher, New Testament

Number 86

HOW JOHN WORKS

Storytelling in the Fourth Gospel

Edited by

Douglas Estes and Ruth Sheridan

SBL PRESS

SBL PRESS

Atlanta

Library of Congress Cataloging-in-Publication Data

Names: Estes, Douglas, editor.
Title: How John works : storytelling in the fourth gospel / edited by Douglas Estes and Ruth Sheridan.
Description: Atlanta : SBL Press, 2016. | Series: Resources for biblical study ; Number 86 | Includes bibliographical references and index.
Identifiers: LCCN 2016023462 (print) | LCCN 2016024439 (ebook) | ISBN 9781628371314 (pbk. : alk. paper) | ISBN 9780884141488 (hardback : alk. paper) | ISBN 9780884141471 (ebook)
Subjects: LCSH: Bible. John—Criticism, Narrative.
Classification: LCC BS2615.52 .H69 2016 (print) | LCC BS2615.52 (ebook) | DDC 226.5/066—2dc23
LC record available at https://lccn.loc.gov/2016023462

Printed on acid-free paper.

Contents

ABBREVIATIONS

Primary Sources

1 Apol.	Justin, *Apologia i*
Acts John	Acts of John
Adv. Jud.	Tertullian, *Adversus Judaeos*
Ag.	Aeschylus, *Agamemnon*
A.J.	Josephus, *Antiquitates judaicae*
Alex.	Plutarch, *Alexander*
Ant.	Sophocles, *Antigone*; Josephus, *Antiquties*
Ars.	Horace, *Ars poetica*
Bapt.	Tertullian, *De baptismo*
Cels.	Origen, *Contra Celsum*
Comm. Jo.	Origen, *Commentarii in evangelium Joannis*
Comm. Matt.	Origen, *Commentarii in evangelium Matthaei*
Conf.	Augustine, *Confessionum libri XIII*
Corp. herm.	Corpus hermeticum
Dem.	Dionysius of Halicarnassus, *De Demosthene*
De or.	Cicero, *De oratore*
Dial.	Justin, *Dialogus cum Tryphone*
Doct. chr.	Augustine, *De doctrina christiana*
Eloc.	Demetrius, *De elocutione* (*Peri hermēneias*)
Ep. Apos.	Epistle of the Apostles
Ep. Diog.	Epistle to Diognetus
Epist.	Jerome, *Epistulae*
Eth. nic.	Aristotle, *Ethica nicomachea*
Haer.	Irenaeus, *Adversus haereses* (*Elenchos*)
Hist.	Polybius, *Histories*
Hist. conscr.	Lucian, *Quomodo historia conscribenda sit* (*How to Write History*)
Hist. eccl.	Eusebius, *Historia ecclesiastica*

Inst.	Quintilian, *Institutio oratoria*
J. W.	Josephus, *Jewish War*
Lib ed.	Pseudo-Plutarch, *De liberis educandis*
Mon.	Tertullian, *De monogamia*
Nat. d.	Cicero, *De natura deorum*
Noet.	Hippolytus, *Contra haeresin Noeti*
Or. Brut.	Cicero, *Orator ad M. Brutum*
Or. Graec.	Tatian, *Oratio ad Graecos* (*Pros Hellēnas*)
Paed.	Clement of Alexandria, *Paedagogus*
Phil.	Sophocles, *Philoctetes*
Phld.	Ignatius, *To the Philadelphians*
Phys.	Aristotle, *Physica*
Poet.	Aristotle, *Poetica*
Pomp.	Dionysius of Halicarnassus, *Epistula ad Pompeium Geminum*
Probl.	Pseudo-Aristotle, *Problemata*
Prog.	Aelius Theon, *Progymnasmata*
Protr.	Clement of Alexandria, *Protrepticus*
Pud.	Tertullian, *De pudicitia*
Resp.	Plato, *Respublica*
Rhet.	Aristotle, *Rhetorica*
Rhet. Her.	Rhetorica ad Herennium
Rom.	Ignatius, *To the Romans*
Strom.	Clement of Alexandria, *Stromateis*
Thuc.	Dionysius of Halicarnassus, *De Thucydide*
Top.	Cicero, *Topica*
Tro.	Euripides, *Daughters of Troy*
Vid.	Ambrose, *De viduis*

Secondary Resources

AB	Anchor Bible
ABG	Arbeit zur Bibel und ihrer Geschichte
ABR	*Australian Biblical Review*
ABRL	Anchor Bible Reference Library
AcBib	Academia Biblica
ACW	Ancient Christian Writers
AJEC	Ancient Judaism and Early Christianity
AnBib	Analecta Biblica

ANF	*The Ante-Nicene Fathers.* Edited by Alexander Roberts and James Donaldson. 1885–1887. 10 vols. Repr., Peabody, MA: Hendrickson, 1994.
ATANT	Abhandlungen zur Theologie des Alten und Neuen Testaments
AUS	American University Studies
BBB	Bonner biblische Beiträge
BBR	*Bulletin for Biblical Research*
BCNHSE	Bibliothèque Copte de Nag Hammadi Section
BDAG	Danker, Frederick W., Walter Bauer, William F. Arndt, and F. Wilbur Gingrich. *A Greek-English Lexicon of the New Testament and Other Early Christian Literature.* 3rd ed. Chicago: University of Chicago Press, 2000.
BDF	Blass, Friedrich, Albert Debrunner, and Robert W. Funk. *A Greek Grammar of the New Testament and Other Early Christian Literature.* Chicago: University of Chicago Press, 1961.
BETL	Bibliotheca Ephemeridum Theologicarum Lovaniensium
BibInt	*Biblical Interpretation*
BibInt	Biblical Interpretation Series
BJRL	*Bulletin of the John Rylands University Library of Manchester*
BNTC	Black's New Testament Commentaries
BTB	*Biblical Theology Bulletin*
BZNW	Beihefte zur Zeitschrift fur die neutestamentliche Wissenschaft
CBET	Contributions to Biblical Exegesis and Theology
CurBR	*Currents in Biblical Research*
CBQ	*Catholic Biblical Quarterly*
CCS	Cambridge Classical Studies
CI	*Critical Inquiry*
CRINT	Compendia Rerum Iudaicarum ad Novum Testamentum
DRev	*Downside Review*
DSD	*Dead Sea Discoveries*
ECC	Eerdmans Critical Commentary
ECL	Early Christianity and Its Literature

ELS	Edinburgh Leventis Studies
ESCO	European Studies on Christian Origins
ESEC	Emory Studies in Early Christianity
ETL	*Ephemerides Theologicae Lovanienses*
ExpTim	*Expository Times*
FRLANT	Forschungen zur Religion und Literatur des Alten und Neuen Testaments
GBS	Guides to Biblical Scholarship
GRBS	*Greek, Roman, and Byzantine Studies*
HDR	Harvard Dissertations in Religion
HNT	Handbuch zum Neuen Testament
HTR	*Harvard Theological Review*
HUCA	*Hebrew Union College Annual*
Int	*Interpretation*
ITQ	*Irish Theological Quarterly*
JBL	*Journal of Biblical Literature*
JGRChJ	*Journal of Greco-Roman Christianity and Judaism*
JLS	*Journal of Literary Semantics*
JR	*Journal of Religion*
JSNT	*Journal for the Study of the New Testament*
JSNTSup	Journal for the Study of the New Testament Supplement Series
JSOTSup	Journal for the Study of the Old Testament Supplement Series
JTS	*Journal of Theological Studies*
JTI	*Journal of Theological Interpretation*
LCL	Loeb Classical Library
LD	Lectio Divina
LNTS	Library of New Testament Studies
LSTS	Library of Second Temple Studies
LTPM	Louvain Theological and Pastoral Monographs
MARG	*Mitteilungen für Anthropologie und Religionsgeschichte*
MnSup	Mnemosyne Supplements
NCB	New Century Bible
NHMS	Nag Hammadi and Manichaean Studies
NLH	*New Literary History*
NovT	*Novum Testamentum*
NovTSup	Supplements to Novum Testamentum

NTL	New Testament Library
NTS	*New Testament Studies*
NTSCE	New Testament Studies in Contextual Exegesis
NTTS	New Testament Tools and Studies
PBTM	Paternoster Biblical and Theological Monographs
PCNT	Paideia: Commentaries on the New Testament
PMLA	*Proceedings of the Modern Language Association*
PRSt	*Perspectives in Religious Studies*
PTMS	Princeton Theological Monograph Series
RBS	Resources for Biblical Study
REL	Routledge Engagements with Literature
SAC	Studies in Antiquity and Christianity
SANt	Studia Aarhusiana Neotestamentica
SBLDS	Society of Biblical Literature Dissertation Series
SBLMS	Society of Biblical Literature Monograph Series
SBS	Stuttgarter Bibelstudien
SBT	Studies in Biblical Theology
SCL	Sather Classical Lectures
Semeia	*Semeia*
SemeiaSt	Semeia Studies
SHR	Studies in the History of Religions
SIJD	Schriften des Institutum Judaicum Delitzschianum
SLJ	*Southern Literary Journal*
SNTSMS	Society for New Testament Studies Monograph Series
SNTW	Studies of the New Testament and Its World
SP	Sacra Pagina
SR	*Studies in Religion*
SSEJC	Studies in Scripture in Early Judaism and Christianity
STAC	Studien und Texte zu Antike und Christentum
StBibLit	Studies in Biblical Literature (Lang)
STDJ	Studies on the Texts of the Desert of Judah
SubBi	Subsidia Biblica
SVTQ	*St. Vladimir's Theological Quarterly*
SymS	Symposium Series
Them	*Themelios*
TrinJ	*Trinity Journal*
TS	Texts and Studies

VC	*Vigiliae Christianae*
WBC	Word Biblical Commentary
WGRW	Writings from the Greco-Roman World
WMANT	Wissenschaftliche Monographien zum Alten und Neuen Testament
WUNT	Wissenschaftliche Untersuchungen zum Neuen Testament
ZECNT	Zondervan Exegetical Commentary on the New Testament
ZKT	*Zeitschrift für katholische Theologie*
ZNT	*Zeitschrift für Neues Testament*
ZNW	*Zeitschrift für die neutestamentliche Wissenschaft*

Introduction

Douglas Estes

The Gospel of John is arguably the most read book of the New Testament. So prominent is this gospel that it would be difficult to overstate its impact on world culture. We only need to consider a particular snippet of Jesus's speech in John—what we today refer to as John 3:16—to see how great an impact the *words* of John have had on our world. Yet below these words exists a powerful *story* that has had a similar, incalculable impact. Just saying the phrase "water into wine" draws all hearers within range of Western tradition to reference the story of the miracle at Cana (John 2:1–11). These two examples are simply the tip of the proverbial iceberg when it comes to John: there is the "Word," the raising of Lazarus, the call to eat Jesus's flesh and drink his blood, Mary Magdalene wiping Jesus's nard-anointed feet with her hair, the rumor of John living on earth until Jesus's return, the "signs" and "I am" statements, the resurrection, the mystery of the Beloved Disciple, and much, much more that have left indelible marks on our world. John has made these indelible marks because of the power of the story that people have read.

At this point a reader may protest, "But it is not the story of John that has made such impact—it is the events and the testimony and the words of Jesus that make it what it is." However, the very first words of John, "In the beginning…," stop this protest cold. John could have taken the words and events and testimony and transcribed it into a list of what Jesus did and said. He did not, and he did not for a reason.[1] John created a story that would make powerful connections between the real world and the world of his story. John's story connects each of these words and events and tes-

---

1. Plus, there is the cryptic explanation by Papias for John's writing, which he describes as a "spiritual gospel" created by John, since the "outward [literally, *bodily*] facts" were already known (Eusebius, *Hist. eccl.* 6.14.7).

timonies in such a way as to build meaning through the arc of their story. In contrast, bald statements and colorless lists do not make for much use in the larger world. They are not connective. They also are not natural to people, as human beings are fundamentally storytellers (not transcribers or list makers). Therefore, it is the shaping of the raw materials that John had that makes for the real meaning of his life of Jesus. It is this shaping that is the subject of this book: how John works; how storytelling succeeds in the Fourth Gospel.

Narrative Dynamics in the Gospel of John

Interest in how John tells his story continues to be a fruitful discussion some forty or fifty years after the "narrative turn" in biblical studies.[2] Without discounting the importance of historical investigation, literary critical approaches to John have established themselves as worthwhile avenues for defining how certain events from history became world-changing stories.[3] This transformation of raw material to stories about Jesus is, in itself, its own "narrative turn," of which literary-critical studies of the gospels have only begun to scratch the surface. Literary critical approaches to John show that there is a "meaning" in the text—in the sense that raw materials have been transfigured into powerful stories that affect readers even today.

This transfiguration (or narrativization) of events and words and testimonies into a communicable story is both a natural outgrowth of being human and an intentional plan to add meaning to these raw materials. When studying the transfiguration of an ancient story, one has to start with the features or aspects of the story that we have at hand. We work back through the narrative process. This is because there is no way to go back to the raw material and work forward.[4] The result is that we may

---

2. For a history of this turn, see, e.g., Mark W. G. Stibbe, *John as Storyteller: Narrative Criticism and the Fourth Gospel*, SNTSMS 73 (Cambridge: Cambridge University Press, 1992), 5–13.

3. For a recent evaluation of literary criticism of John, including possible new directions, see Stanley E. Porter, "Study of John's Gospel: New Directions or the Same Old Paths?" in *Linguistic Analysis of the Greek New Testament: Studies in Tools, Methods, and Practice* (Grand Rapids: Baker Academic, 2015), 277–306.

4. This is true even if scholars had a sayings source; this source would not be the same thing as all the raw materials that went into the creation of the gospels. For

create an "anatomy" of the story, showing its different parts and how these parts are connected.[5] Yet this book looks to take this approach a step further by looking a little less at parts (static) and a little more at process and action (dynamic). These processes and actions within narrative—movements that actually *make* narrative—are what we call *narrative dynamics*.

Thus, in one sense narrative dynamics concern "the movement of a narrative from its opening to its end."[6] But the various aspects and features of narrative are not easily isolatable in stories; they all work together to create the ups and downs of story. Thrice now I have used the word "powerful" in this introduction. Readers may assume that the "power" I am referring to is John's frequent challenge(s) to believe in Jesus that create moving religious experiences within readers. Though it is true that this occurs and that John can do this (after all, it is the point of the story, John 20:31), here I am using the word "powerful" for a slightly different reason. I use it to indicate that, when stories are told, there is an activity or action that must animate the telling of the story. Not the reading, necessarily, but in the story itself. As Paul Ricoeur points out, from the beginning of Aristotle's writing on *Poetics*, an intentional regard for the *power* of story is required for it to complete itself and become a meaningful story. To put it another way, it is not the parts that make a story but how the parts are put together that make a story. Ricoeur goes one step further and explains that Aristotle (and, by extension, the literary tradition from Aristotle to John to us today) is not interested in the *structure* of a story but in the *structuration* of a story.[7] This gets us to the heart of how a story is told.

---

example, the writer of John had access to cultural insights—a raw material—that we no longer possess.

5. Intentional allusion to the original work of R. Alan Culpepper, *Anatomy of the Fourth Gospel: A Study in Literary Design* (Philadelphia: Fortress, 1983); and cf. Tom Thatcher and Stephen D. Moore, eds., *Anatomies of Narrative Criticism: The Past, Present and Futures of the Fourth Gospel as Literature*, RBS 55 (Atlanta: Society of Biblical Literature, 2008).

6. Brian Richardson, "General Introduction," in *Narrative Dynamics: Essays on Time, Plot, Closure, and Frames*, ed. Brian Richardson (Columbus: Ohio State University Press, 2002), 1.

7. Paul Ricoeur, *Time and Narrative*, trans. Kathleen McLaughlin and David Pellauer, 3 vols. (Chicago: University of Chicago Press, 1984–1988), 1:48; and cf. Holly E. Hearon, "The Storytelling World of the First Century and the Gospels," in *The Bible*

The Thing about Powerful Stories

There are two things that we can say about powerful stories. First, powerful stories are created from powerful raw materials. Powerful stories are not typically created out of the mundane or the uninspired; they are often about love, or war, or hope, or similar great ideas and great themes. It will be no surprise to anyone that many stories are written about the military habits of Julius Caesar (battles and victories), but few are written about the dietary habits of Julius Caesar (what he had for dinner on a typical kalends). Second, and less often noted, powerful stories tend toward more intense scrutiny and questioning from later readers. For example, the *Iliad* is one of the greatest stories in the Western tradition. Yet readers have studied it and criticized it and picked at it from antiquity to the present day.[8] In fact, powerful stories with powerful themes *invite* an increase in scrutiny. When readers read a powerful story, they naturally want to know how such a powerful story came about, what it means, and what makes it tick. Therefore, "the earliest writing that we might call 'literary theory' comes from trying to figure out how stories work."[9] We may call an investigation of the narrative of John's Gospel "literary critical," but in the end it is mostly about figuring out how John's story works.

From this we should not be surprised that readers have put the Gospel of John to the test. As the title *How John Works: Storytelling in the Fourth Gospel* suggests, this book invites readers to do just that through the looking glass of fifteen different narrative features that "powerfully" imbue the story of the Fourth Gospel.[10] With contributions from a group of international scholars who are distinct in social location and reading perspectives but who share a commitment to a scholarly guild, the intent of this volume is not only to show "how John works" but how these different narrative dynamics are related and tied to one another. Like nar-

---

in Ancient and Modern Media: Story and Performance, ed. Holly E. Hearon and Philip Ruge-Jones (Eugene, OR: Cascade, 2009), 34.

8. René Nünlist, "Some Ancient Views on Narrative, Its Structure and Working," in *Defining Greek Narrative*, ed. Douglas Cairns and Ruth Scodel, ELS 7 (Edinburgh: Edinburgh University Press, 2014), 158.

9. Janine Utell, *Engagements with Narrative*, REL (London: Routledge, 2016), 2.

10. In most cases, previous attempts to point out narrative features of the gospel either focused on one feature (or a few features) or drifted further towards a traditional commentary. While we could fill many books with the narrative dynamics of John, our present situation required a compromise: selecting the top fifteen features.

ratives in general, sometimes there is a great deal of continuity and, in a few places, notes of divergences, but the essays work together to help the reader understand the movement of story in the Gospel of John. This, then, is how John works.

1

Genre

Harold W. Attridge

Crafting a literary work does not happen in isolation. Imitation and creative adaptation of extant models are regular parts of the creative process. Imitation and adaptation result in the formation of literary "genres" or types that conform to certain patterns, generating expectations on the part of readers.[1] Genres are thus inevitable wherever literature is created.[2] In some contexts, generic patterns may be more formally recognized and described by theorists, but genres are operating whether formally recognized or not.

Genres in Classical Literature

The development of well-defined genres played an important role in the history of classical literature. Reflecting on how these literary types functioned is useful for understanding how genre works in John.[3] Genres with ideal norms governing literary production are found in Athens of the fifth

---

1. On issues of genre in general, see John Frow, *Genre: The New Critical Idiom* (London: Routledge, 2006); Alastair Fowler, *Kinds of Literature: An Introduction to the Theory of Genres and Modes* (Oxford: Clarendon, 1982); and Adena Rosmarin, *The Power of Genre* (Minneapolis: University of Minnesota Press, 1985), who suggests a "pragmatic" approach to the process by which genres are defined in the reading process.

2. Mikail M. Bakhtin, *Speech Genres and Other Late Essays*, ed. Caryle Emerson and Michael Holquist, trans. Vern W. McGee (Austin: University of Texas Press, 1986); Tzvetan Todorov, "The Origin of Genres," *NLH* 8 (1976): 159–70, see esp. 163 for genres as "horizons of expectations" and "models of writing" for authors. Such horizon-defining models come about through a continual process of transforming various speech acts and subsequently established forms (167, 169).

3. Joseph Farrell, "Classical Genre in Theory and Practice," *NLH* 34 (2003): 383–408.

century BCE, where dramatists had to conform to institutionalized expectations to see their works performed. Ancient theorists, particularly Aristotle (384–322 BCE), built on that practice in understanding genres, and his theory formed the foundation of the study of genre from antiquity to the modern period. As Joseph Farrell points out, however, the archetypical paradigms did *not* in fact always govern the ways in which ancient authors actually worked. As he puts it:

> With time one finds an ever greater sense of adventure until, by the Hellenistic and Roman periods, it comes to seem that testing and even violating generic boundaries was not merely an inevitable and accidental consequence of writing in any genre, but an important aspect of the poet's craft.[4]

Poetic play on genre is visible in the work of artists such as Horace (65–8 BCE). The Roman poet theorizes about the purity of genres that ought not be mixed, but he does so within the context of a didactic poem, the *Ars poetica*, that does that very thing. In the world of Hellenistic and Roman literature, as Jacques Derrida long ago noted, genres were regularly mixed, or, as I have suggested, "bent."[5] Genre bending may be the way that creative literary figures always work; it was certainly the way they worked in first-century Greek and Latin literature.

Genres in Second Temple Jewish Literature

What is true of the world of classical literature is also true of contemporary Jewish literature. While there is no Hebrew or Aramaic *Poetics* or *Ars poetica*, there are observable commonalities in Jewish literary products of the Second Temple period. Though theoretical discussion of genre was absent, mimetic plays on literary models within a literary tradition was common.[6]

---

4. Ibid., 388.

5. Jacques Derrida, "The Law of Genre," *CI* 7 (1980): 55–81. On genre "bending," see Harold W. Attridge, "Genre Bending in the Fourth Gospel," *JBL* 121 (2002): 3–21.

6. See Carol Newsom, "Pairing Research Questions and Theories of Genre: A Case Study of the Hodayot," *DSD* 17 (2010): 270–88; Newsom, "Spying Out the Land: A Report from Genology," in *Seeking Out the Wisdom of the Ancients: Essays Offered to Honor Michael V. Fox on the Occasion of His Sixty-Fifth Birthday*, ed. Ronald L. Troxel, Kelvin G. Friebel, and Dennis R. Margy (Winona Lake, IN: Eisenbrauns, 2005), 437–50; Benjamin Wright, "Joining the Club: A Suggestion about Genre in Jewish Texts,"

One way of describing the phenomenon is that authors worked with an "idealized cognitive model," a pattern of literary production that would be widely recognized. Thus a genre would be a paradigm "conventionalized, though not institutionalized," as were classical genres.[7]

Even when there are not putatively normative genres at play, there may well be literary models with some expected features with which authors of a particular work could interact, in much the same way as classical poets and Hellenistic novelists interacted with the genres that theoretically governed their literary worlds.[8]

AN EXAMPLE OF GENRE ADAPTATION

One example of genre adaptation or "bending" comes from ancient historiography, where actual "genres" were not as clearly defined as in classical poetry but where recognized models defined types of historiogra-

DSD 17 (2010): 288–313; Robert Williamson Jr., "Pesher: A Cognitive Model of the Genre," DSD 17 (2010): 336–60. In his useful study of the genre of rewritten Bible or pesher, George J. Brooke, "Genre Theory, Rewritten Bible and Pesher," DSD 17 (2010): 361–86, usefully appeals to Derrida ("Law of Genre," 65) that "every text participates in one or several genres, there is no genreless text; there is always a genre and genres, yet such participation never amounts to belonging. And not because of an abundant overflowing or a free, anarchic, and unclassifiable productivity, but because of the trait of participation itself" (370). In other words, playing with generic conventions is a fact of literary life.

7. For the terminology, inspired by Wittgenstein's theory of universals, see Hindy Najman, "The Idea of Biblical Genre: From Discourse to Constellation," in *Prayer and Poetry in the Dead Sea Scrolls and Related Literature: Essays in Honor of Eileen Schuller on the Occasion of Her 65th Birthday*, ed. Jeremy Penner, Ken M. Penner, and Cecilia Wassen, STDJ 98 (Leiden: Brill, 2012), 307–22. Her approach is applied in George J. Brooke, "Reading, Searching and Blessing: A Functional Approach to the Genres of Scriptural Interpretation in the Yahad," in *The Temple in Text and Tradition: A Festschrift in Honour of Robert Hayward*, ed. R. Timothy McLay, LSTS 83 (London: Bloomsbury, 2014), 140–56.

8. Other examples of creative appropriation of generic conventions appear, for example, in "apocalypses" and "testaments." On the former, see the discussion by John J. Collins, *The Apocalyptic Imagination: An Introduction to Jewish Apocalyptic Literature*, 2nd ed. (Grand Rapids: Eerdmans, 1998), 6–11. On testaments, which have a long history in Jewish and Christian traditions, see Vered Hillel, *Testaments of the Twelve Patriarchs: Structure, Source, Composition* (Lewiston, NY: Mellen, 2013), which highlights the "paradigmatic" (48–86) as well the "modified" (87–125) and "deviant" (125–64) structures found in the texts.

phy.[9] One ideal type was the work of Thucydides (455–400 BCE), who wrote about contemporary political and military events, tested eyewitness sources, and strove for accuracy in reporting the facts of historical events, while making allowances for creativity in reporting speeches. In the Hellenistic period, Polybius (ca. 200–118 BCE) followed that model in recounting the rise of Roman hegemony over the eastern Mediterranean. The satirist Lucian (ca. 120–180 CE) later defended the model in *How to Write History*, which criticized the imperialistic historiography about the Parthian war of 162–165 CE.

Another model, ultimately derived from Herodotus (ca. 484–420 BCE), explored not contemporary political and military affairs but broader history and culture. The model found echoes in the early imperial period in the works of Diodorus Siculus (first century BCE), whose *Bibliotheca historica* compiled ancient myths and legends, and Dionysius of Halicarnassus (first century BCE), whose twenty-volume *Roman Antiquities* offered a Greek alternative to the Latin celebration of Rome's past in Livy.

The Jewish historian Josephus (b. 37/38 CE) shaped the programmatic statements of his *Jewish War* to conform to the Thucydidean-Polybian model. His preface claims that this is the *only* way to write history.[10] Some twenty years later, his *Jewish Antiquities* clearly imitated the work of Dionysius of Halicarnassus. That there were different subgenres of historiographical writing with different expectations is evident. Polybius, for example, defines his kind of history over and against a despised other, tragic drama. Criticizing his contemporary Phylarchus, Polybius writes:

> The object of tragedy [i.e., the kind of thing that, according to Polybius, Phylarchus was up to] is not the same as that of history, but quite the opposite. The tragic poet should thrill and charm his audience for

---

9. See Harold W. Attridge, *The Interpretation of Biblical History in the* Antiquitates Judaicae *of Flavius Josephus*, HDR 7 (Missoula, MT: Scholars, 1976); Attridge, "Historiography," in *Jewish Writings of the Second Temple: Apocrypha, Pseudepigrapha, Qumran Sectarian Writings, Philo, Josephus*, ed. Michael E. Stone, CRINT 2.2 (Philadelphia: Fortress, 1984), 157–84; and Attridge, "Josephus and His Works," in Stone, *Jewish Writings of the Second Temple*, 185–232. More recently, see John Marincola, *Authority and Tradition in Ancient Historiography* (Cambridge: Cambridge University Press, 1997), and Roberto Nicolai, *La storiografia nell' educazione antica*, Biblioteca di materiali e discussioni per l'analisi dei testi classici 10 (Pisa: Giardini, 1992).

10. Josephus, *J.W.* 1.13–16, where Josephus castigates the Greeks as untrustworthy while articulating as his own the principles of Thucydidean-Polybian historiography.

the moment by the verisimilitude of the words he puts in his characters mouths, but it is the task of the historian to instruct. (*Hist.* 2.56.11
[Paton])

These cases enshrine a discourse about history as a genre. Authors felt free
not only to write things in different subgenres, as Josephus did, but also to
"bend" or "tweak" the models to which they paid allegiance. Both Polybius
and Josephus admit doing so, when they introduce into their political and
military accounts "tragic" elements like lamenting the fate of the peoples
conquered by Rome. Historical genres, like poetry, also could be transformed even while being celebrated and affirmed. From the way "genre"
works in the first century CE, one should probably expect that any creative
author would be engaged in "bending" whatever genre he was employing.

A GENERIC MODEL?

The Fourth Gospel undoubtedly had some literary model, an account of
the deeds of Jesus, such as a "signs source" or the Synoptic Gospels supple-
mented with other traditional materials.[11] In either case, the model was
probably something like the classic definition of Mark, "a passion narrative with an extended introduction."[12] In reworking the model, the evangelist also exploited other "idealized cognitive models," drawing on them
precisely as other contemporary authors did in adapting their genres.

John is clearly not dependent on any of the gospels in the way that Matthew and Luke, according to the usual two-source theory, are dependent
on Mark. The evangelist probably used other sources, and, insofar as he
appropriated anything, he did so with considerable freedom. Yet there is
persuasive evidence that John did indeed know the Synoptics.[13] Particularly

---

11. For a history of this hypothesis, see Gilbert Van Belle, *The Signs Source in
the Fourth Gospel: Historical Survey and Critical Evaluation of the Semeia Hypothesis*,
BETL 116 (Leuven: Peeters, 1994). For a recent defense, see Volker Siegert, *Das Evangelium des Johannes in seiner ursprünglichen Gestalt: Wiederherstellung und Kommentar*, SIJD 7 (Göttingen: Vandenhoeck & Ruprecht, 2008).

12. Martin Kähler, *The So-Called Historical Jesus and the Historic, Biblical Christ*,
trans. Carl E. Braaten (Philadelphia: Fortress, 1964), 80. For a reflection on the application of Kähler's summary, coined for the Gospel of Mark, to John, see Raymond
F. Collins, *These Things Have Been Written: Studies on the Fourth Gospel*, LTPM 2
(Leuven: Peeters; Grand Rapids: Eerdmans, 1990), 87–88.

13. On the history of the issue, see D. Moody Smith, *John among the Gospels:*

telling are the connections in the passion and resurrection narratives. Decisive is the connection between John and Luke in the appearance stories, where the two appearance accounts of John 20:19–29 are clearly built on pieces of the one Easter appearance story in Luke 24:6–43, which the evangelist has deconstructed and recomposed, a technique he uses elsewhere.[14] It is highly likely that the evangelist knows Mark and Luke and may well know Matthew.[15]

The Synoptic Gospels do not offer a simple generic model. Defining their genre usually appeals to some form of Hellenistic literature, particularly biographies. Some scholars argue that all the gospels are in some sense *bioi*, or "lives."[16] Others nuance that judgment and find particular gospels displaying features of other literature, including Jewish novels, manifestos, and others.[17] However the gospels related to ancient *bioi*, other literary elements were also at play, as is surely the case with the Fourth Gospel.

The Relationship in Twentieth-Century Research (Minneapolis: Fortress, 1992); for the recent scholarly debate, see Michael Labahn and Manfred Lang, "Johannes und die Synoptiker: Positionen und Impulse seit 1990," in *Kontexte des Johannesevangeliums: Das vierte Evangelium in religions- und traditionsgeschichtlicher Perspektive*, ed. Jörg Frey and Udo Schnelle, WUNT 175 (Tübingen: Mohr Siebeck, 2004), 443–516; Roland Bergmeier, "Die Bedeutung der Synoptiker für das johanneische Zeugnisthema: Mit einem Anhang zum Perfekt-Gebrauch im vierten Evangelium," NTS 52 (2006): 458–83.

14. See especially Manfred Lang, *Johannes und die Synoptiker: Eine redaktionsgeschichtliche Analyse von Joh 18–20 vor dem markinischen und lukanischen Hintergrund*, FRLANT 182 (Göttingen: Vandenhoeck & Ruprecht, 1999).

15. Recent commentators arguing for the dependence of John on the Synoptics include Hartwig Thyen, "Johannes und die Synoptiker: Auf der Suche nach einem neuen Paradigma zur Beschreibung ihrer Beziehungen anhand von Beobachtungen an Passions-und Ostererzählungen," in *John and the Synoptics*, ed. Adelbert Denaux, BETL 101 (Leuven: Leuven University Press, 1992), 81–108, and Thyen, *Das Johannesevangelium*, HNT 6 (Tübingen: Mohr Siebeck, 2005). Arguing for mutual influence between John and the Synoptics is Paul N. Anderson, "Aspects of Interfluentiality between John and the Synoptics: John 18–19 as a Case Study," in *The Death of Jesus in the Fourth Gospel*, ed. Gilbert van Belle, BETL 200 (Leuven: Peeters, 2007), 711–28.

16. Richard Burridge, *What Are the Gospels? A Comparison with Greco-Roman Biography*, 2nd rev. ed. (Grand Rapids: Eerdmans, 2004); Burridge, "Gospels," in *The Oxford Handbook of Biblical Studies*, ed. J. W. Rogerson and Judith M. Lieu (Oxford: Oxford University Press, 2006), 432–44. On the complexity of the genre, see Thomas Hägg, *The Art of Biography in Antiquity* (Cambridge: Cambridge University Press, 2012).

17. For novel, see Michael E. Vines, *The Problem of Markan Genre: The Gospel*

While the evangelist might find attractive Mark's element of mystery or Luke's dramatic encounters, he is not satisfied that any earlier narrative achieves what it should. In departing from his predecessors, the evangelist apparently does what Farrell suggested classical genre benders regularly did: they defined the Y that they were writing as a non-X. The X that the Fourth evangelist had in his sights was most likely the Gospel of Luke. The Third Gospel is, to be sure, a complex literary work but one with literary pretentions that at least evoke the ideals of historiography. The language of Luke's prefaces is not quite at the level of sophisticated historiography.[18] The narratives of the Gospel of Luke and Acts, whatever their precise relationship,[19] is not exactly the work of critical historiography,[20] although scholars still defend the historical value of Luke's two volumes.[21] Whatever the final judgment on Luke's effort, it is hard to ignore the gesture toward historiography in the claim to "set down an orderly account [*diēgēsis*] of the events that have been fulfilled among us" (Luke 1:1).[22] The tone of Luke's preface is echoed in the efforts to synchronize the story of Jesus with imperial and local history (Luke 1:5; 2:1–2; 3:1–2). Whatever it may in fact be doing, Luke-Acts presents itself as an effort to tell a historical tale accurately. Serious historians, as noted above, ought not be writers of

---

of Mark and the Jewish Novel, AcBib 3 (Leiden: Brill, 2002). For manifesto, see Adela Yarbro Collins, *Is Mark's Gospel a Life of Jesus? The Question of Genre* (Milwaukee: Marquette University Press, 1990); Collins, *Mark: A Commentary*, Hermeneia (Minneapolis: Fortress, 2007), 15–44.

18. Loveday Alexander, *The Preface to Luke's Gospel: Literary Convention and Social Context in Luke 1.1–4 and Acts 1.1*, SNTSMS 78 (Cambridge: Cambridge University Press, 1993), and more recently, Alexander, *Acts in Its Ancient Literary Context: A Classicist Looks at the Acts of the Apostles*, LNTS 298 (Edinburgh: T&T Clark, 2005).

19. Mikeal Parsons and Richard I. Pervo, *Rethinking the Unity of Luke and Acts* (Minneapolis: Fortress, 1993), and, for another perspective, Andrew F. Gregory and C. Kavin Rowe, *Rethinking the Unity and the Reception of Luke and Acts* (Columbia: University of South Carolina Press, 2010).

20. So Richard I. Pervo, *Profit with Delight: The Literary Genre of the Acts of the Apostles* (Philadelphia: Fortress, 1987), and Pervo, *Acts*, Hermeneia (Minneapolis: Fortress, 2009). For a critique of the comparison of Acts with ancient novels, see Craig Keener, *Introduction and 1:1–2:47*, vol. 1 of *Acts: An Exegetical Commentary* (Grand Rapids: Baker, 2012), 62–83.

21. See, e.g., Colin J. Hemer, *The Book of Acts in the Setting of Hellenistic History*, WUNT 49 (Tübingen: Mohr Siebeck, 1989), and the nuanced treatment by Keener, *Acts*, 1:166–220, in a section entitled "Approaching Acts as a Historical Source."

22. Unless otherwise stated, all translations of biblical texts are my own.

drama. The Fourth Evangelist, by contrast, frames his account of Jesus as
something quite different from a simple *diēgēsis*.[23]

Objectifying Narrative or Dramatic Encounter

Scholars often describe the Fourth Gospel as "dramatic," and some have
made a more formal case for the term.[24] Four elements bend the narrative in the direction of drama. The first is the Prologue, with its cadenced
celebration of the Word. Unlike anything in Mark or Matthew, this introduction has a parallel in Luke's prefaces. But, apart from the similarity in
the general function, the Lukan prefaces are remarkably different. They
are a prosaic, and somewhat apologetic, appeal to the reader, similar to
the prefaces found in historiography[25] and in specialized technical manu-
als.[26] John's quasi-poetic Prologue hints at many elements of the gospel's
thematic world: the contrast between light and darkness, the relationship
between Father and Son, the stark juxtaposition of those who accept the
Word and those who do not, the contrast between what Jesus offers and
what Moses provided, the emphasis on the presence of the Word in flesh,
and the resultant experience of seeing and understanding flowing from
encounter with the Word. Not an afterthought, the Prologue belongs

---

23. Plato, *Resp.* 392d, frames the distinction between "narrative" (*diēgēsis*) and
"imitation" (*mimēsis*). Aristotle classifies tragedy, with epic poetry, as a mode of "imitation" (*Poet.* 1.1447a15) and argues that a tragedy works *drōntōn kai ou di' apangelias*
(*Poet.* 6.1449b27). I. Bywater usefully translates this as "in a dramatic, not a narrative
form" in Aristotle, *The Complete Works of Aristotle: The Revised Oxford Translation*,
ed. Jonathan Barnes, 2 vols., Bollingen Series 71.2 (Princeton: Princeton University
Press, 1984), 2:2320.

24. Ben Witherington III, *John's Wisdom: A Commentary on the Fourth Gospel*
(Louisville: Westminster John Knox, 1995), 4–5, labels it a "dramatic biography," list-
ing as dramatic elements: initial hymn, irony, magnitude of main character, dualisms,
crescendo effect, self-contained scenes, rhetoric at key points, on stage triads, surprising revelations. See also Mark W. G. Stibbe, *John as Storyteller: Narrative Criticism and
the Fourth Gospel*, SNTSMS 73 (Cambridge: Cambridge University Press, 1992), and
Stibbe, *The Gospel of John as Literature: An Anthology of Twentieth-Century Perspectives*, NTTS 17 (Leiden: Brill, 1993); G. Rochais, "Jean 7: Une construction littéraire
dramatique, à la manière d'un scénario," *NTS* 39 (1993): 355–78; Jo-Ann A. Brant,
Dialogue and Drama: Elements of Greek Tragedy in the Fourth Gospel (Peabody, MA:
Hendrickson, 2004).

25. See above, n. 18.

26. As argued by Loveday Alexander. See n. 16 above.

where it stands, at the beginning of the gospel in its final form. There it functions precisely as does the "hypothesis" of a Greek drama, telling the audience what to expect.

Another trope has received considerable recent attention, the gospel's pervasive irony.[27] The gospel displays many kinds of irony, but the first and most obvious is "dramatic" in the technical sense. Irony in general is the trope of saying one thing and meaning another. Dramatic irony is the kind that occurs "on stage," when a clueless character says something true, which the audience understands. Or a character may deny the truth of something that the audience knows to be true. The dramatist and his audience know something that the characters do not, a situation exemplified in unmistakable form in Euripides's *Bacchae*.[28]

The characters interacting with Jesus in the Fourth Gospel strongly resemble Pentheus in the *Bacchae*. They resist the presence of the divine in their midst; they deny truths that the audience knows, as does Nicodemus's question about rebirth (3:4). They articulate a truth that they do not grasp, as do the "Judaeans,"[29] who, as the narrator suggests, believe that Jesus was "making himself equal to God" (5:18). The opponents of Jesus ironically describe themselves when they say that no one will know of the messiah's origin (7:27). The incredulous question of the crowds about going to the Greek diaspora (7:35) points to events that begin to unfold in chapter 12. An ironic gem is the statement of Caiaphas, "It is better for you to have one man to die for the people" (11:50).

Also richly ironic is the gospel's central claim that in being "lifted up" (Greek, *hypsoō*) on the shameful tree of the cross, Jesus is "lifted up in glory" (Greek, *doxazō*), which evokes awe and wonder. Irony is not a

27. See Paul D. Duke, *Irony in the Fourth Gospel* (Atlanta: John Knox, 1985), and Gail R. O'Day, *Revelation in the Fourth Gospel: Narrative Mode and Theological Claim* (Philadelphia: Fortress, 1986).

28. See George W. MacRae, "Theology and Irony in the Fourth Gospel," in *The Word in the World: Essays in Honour of Frederick. L. Moriarty, S.J.*, ed. Richard J. Clifford and George W. MacRae (Cambridge, MA: Weston College, 1973), 83–96.

29. Translating *hoi Ioudaioi* is controversial. The most common rendering, "the Jews," which nourished a long history of Christian anti-Judaism, probably reflects the polemical situation of the evangelist in opposition to the Jews of his day held responsible for the expulsion of his community from "the synagogue" (John 9:22; 12:42; 16:2). Yet, within the narrative the term usually refers to the leadership of the Jerusalem community and may have a more narrow connotation than the usual translation suggests. This ambivalent use of the term connects the audience to the dramatic situation.

casual literary device embellishing dramatic encounters, it is a conceptual
device at the heart of the narrative.

Both a prologue as "hypothesis" and pervasive irony are very much
at home in a drama. A third element, the "delayed exit" of Jesus in the
last supper discourses, explains a discontinuity in the narrative.[30] After
announcing that it is time to go to Gethsemane (14:31), Jesus continues
teaching for two chapters about abiding in the vine, the Paraclete, and the
coming persecution. He then offers a prayer (ch. 17) before finally moving
to the garden. In drama, such delayed exits often occur when a leading
character is on the verge of death, which conventionally takes place offstage. The protagonist hints at that conclusion but then pauses and continues speaking, offering reflections on the significance of the coming separa-
tion.[31] What happens in John 15–17 conforms to that technique.

Dramatic conventions are not the only generic features of the Farewell Discourse. The evangelist combines in John 13–17 elements of many
generic types, including "testaments" of patriarchs, philosophical or rhetorical messages of consolation, and symposia.[32] Yet whatever else is present, a dramatic device plays a major role.

Another regular part of the dramatist's toolkit, the recognition scene,
shapes the Fourth Gospel in significant ways.[33] The Samaritan woman in
John 4 through her dialogue with Jesus comes to recognize that he might
indeed be the messiah (4:29). However tentative, she experiences a moment

30. The dramatic parallels are pointed out by George L. Parsenios, *Departure and Consolation: The Johannine Farewell Discourses in Light of Greco-Roman Literature*, NovTSup 117 (Leiden: Brill, 2005).

31. For examples, noted by Parsenios, see the delay of Cassandra in Aeschylus, *Ag.*, lines 1290–1331; Sophocles, *Phil.* 1402–1415; *Ant.* 883–930; Euripides, *Tro.* 294–461.

32. See Harold W. Attridge, "Plato, Plutarch, and John: Three Symposia about Love," in *Beyond the Gnostic Gospels: Studies Building on the Work of Elaine Pagels*, ed. Eduard Iricinschi et al., STAC 82 (Tübingen: Mohr Siebeck, 2013), 367–78. Important analyses of the Farewell Discourse include Johannes Beutler, *Do Not Be Afraid: The First Farewell Discourse in John's Gospel*, NTSCE 6 (Frankfurt am Main: Lang, 2011); trans. of *Habt keine Angst: Die erste johanneische Abschiedsrede (Joh 14)*, SBS 116 (Stuttgart: Katholisches Bibelwerk, 1984); Fernando F. Segovia, *The Farewell of the Word: The Johannine Call to Abide* (Minneapolis: Fortress, 1991); D. Francois Tolmie, *Jesus' Farewell to the Disciples: John 13:1–17:26 in Narratological Perspective*, BibInt 12 (Leiden: Brill, 1995).

33. On this device, see Kasper Bro Larsen, *Recognizing the Stranger: Recognition Scenes in the Gospel of John*, BibInt 93 (Leiden: Brill, 2008).

of recognition, an *anagnoresis*, which leads to that of other Samaritans (4:42). Mary Magdalene, weeping outside Jesus's tomb and wondering what has become of his body, recognizes, at the sound of the voice calling her name, that her beloved Lord is present. She, too, at the verbal signal that recalls the sheep and their shepherd (10:27) experiences a moment of *anagnoresis*. Thomas, the famous doubter, comes to faith through the very tangible sign of a scarred but resurrected body that enables him to confess his recognition, "My Lord and my God!" (20:28).

<h2 style="text-align:center">Stimulating a Dramatic Encounter
through Identification with a Character</h2>

The Fourth Gospel is a particularly "dramatic" narrative of a special life and death. The generic adaptation seems designed above all to ensure that the reader/hearer has the possibility of an encounter with the resurrected Christ himself. Creation of a vivid "drama" illustrating encounters between Christ and various characters provided potent images, but such adaptation might not suffice to engage a reader or audience. Accounts of encounters could easily be historicized and vacated of their allure to foster a similar encounter with the resurrected Christ. To achieve that, the evangelist further "tweaked" the gospel paradigm by playing with the category of "eyewitness," a term that played an important role in historiographical literature.[34] In doing so, he challenges antiquarians like Luke or Papias, who valued such testimony.

Essential to the appeal to an eyewitness in ancient legal transactions is that the witness be identifiable.[35] It is hardly the case that the identity of the Beloved Disciple, obliquely identified as the eyewitness to the events of the gospel (19:35), is readily available. Rather, the gospel systematically precludes an identification.[36] Instead, it returns the reader to

<hr>

34. On eyewitnesses in general, see Samuel Byrskog, *Story as History—History as Story: The Gospel Tradition in the Context of Ancient Oral History*, WUNT 123 (Tübingen: Mohr Siebeck, 2000).

35. See Howard M. Jackson, "Ancient Self-Referential Conventions and Their Implications for the Authorship and Integrity of the Gospel of John," *JTS* 50 (1999): 1–34.

36. On anonymity, see David R. Beck, "The Narrative Function of Anonymity in Fourth Gospel Characterization," *Semeia* 63 (1993): 143–58, and Beck, *The Discipleship Paradigm: Readers and Anonymous Characters in the Fourth Gospel*, BibInt 27 (Leiden: Brill, 1997); Adele Reinhartz, "Anonymity and Character in the Books of

the text, searching for the identity of the eyewitness only to encounter the one who bears witness to the truth (18:37).[37] When the reader encounters and accepts him, she becomes another beloved disciple and witness to his truth. The trope effects the kind of "identification" that Aristotle identified as a feature of drama,[38] not with the protagonist, but with one as close to the protagonist as any ordinary mortal may be (13:23; 19:26; 20:8). The gospel thus enables the kind of dramatic encounter that it describes.

DRAMA'S CONCEPTUAL FOUNDATION: A RIDDLING ARABESQUE

Two other features make the Fourth Gospel a distinctive kind of drama: its engagement with conceptual issues and its vivid imagery. Despite its simple Greek, the gospel is replete with tensions, in Christology, eschatology, soteriology, and much more. In the past, these tensions have often generated theories of source and redaction. More recent Johannine scholarship instead has explored their function as deliberate "riddles."[39]

The phenomenon of paradoxes or riddles used as a literary device is not confined to the Fourth Gospel. Riddles appear in Jewish literature such as 4 Ezra, where an angel leads the seer to comprehend theodicy (see, e.g., 4 Ezra 4:5–7, 50; 5:36). Riddling is a key element in the Nag Hammadi text Thunder: Perfect Mind (NHC VI 2).[40] Riddling is

---

Samuel," *Semeia* 63 (1993): 117–41, and Reinhartz, *"Why Ask My Name?": Anonymity and Identity in Biblical Narrative* (New York: Oxford University Press, 1998).

37. See Harold W. Attridge, "The Restless Quest for the Beloved Disciple," in *Early Christian Voices: In Texts, Traditions, and Symbols; Essays in Honor of François Bovon*, ed. David H. Warren, Ann Graham Brock, and David W. Pao, BibInt 66 (Leiden: Brill, 2003), 71–80.

38. For Aristotle, the aim of tragedy is "catharsis" of pity and fear (*Poet.* 6.1449b28) achieved primarily through a well-designed plot but also through characters who were morally attractive and realistic (*Poet.* 15.1454a16–1454b14).

39. Herbert Leroy, *Rätsel und Missverständnis: Ein Beitrag zur Formgeschichte des Johannesevangeliums*, BBB 30 (Bonn: Hanstein, 1968); Tom Thatcher, *The Riddles of Jesus in John: A Study in Tradition and Folklore*, SBLMS 53 (Atlanta: Society of Biblical Literature, 2000); Thatcher, "Riddles, Repetitions, and the Literary Unity of the Johannine Discourses," in *Repetitions and Variations in the Fourth Gospel: Style, Text, Interpretation*, ed. Gilbert Van Belle, Michael Labahn, and Petrus Maritz, BETL 223 (Leuven: Peeters, 2009), 357–77; Paul N. Anderson, *The Riddles of the Fourth Gospel: An Introduction to John* (Minneapolis: Fortress, 2011).

40. Bentley Layton, *The Gnostic Scriptures: A New Translation with Annotations and Introductions* (Garden City, NY: Doubleday, 1983), 77–78. This is also noted by

also a psychagogic technique in a Hermetic tractate resembling John 3, Corp. herm. 13,[41] where Hermes instructs a befuddled Tat about rebirth (*palingenesia*).[42] Clement of Alexandria treated riddles at length (*Strom.* 5),[43] and Origen calls attention to the importance of such language, citing standard Stoic paradoxes about the sage (*Comm. Jo.* 2.10). Despite differences in content, the basic point is clear: riddling and paradoxical statements can play a significant educational role.

The Fourth Gospel deploys its riddles not as discrete units but as interconnected chains.[44] One might think of this phenomenon as the Johannine "arabesque," a pattern of interwoven vines found in ancient and medieval art. The presence of these reflective strands suggests that this dramatic narrative was meant for use in a Christian "study group." The gospel facilitates an encounter with the resurrected Christ but in a context where theoretical issues arising from that encounter are of concern. It offers suggestions about resolving those theoretical issues but does not provide a definitive resolution. It is not, therefore, a work of systematic or philosophical theology, although it displays acquaintance with theoretical discourse.[45] While it does not argue a case, it leads read-

---

Pheme Perkins, *Gnosticism and the New Testament* (Minneapolis: Fortress, 1993), 124–34.

41. See C. H. Dodd, *The Interpretation of the Fourth Gospel* (Cambridge: Cambridge University Press, 1953), and more recently, M. Eugene Boring, Klaus Berger, and Carsten Colpe, eds., *Hellenistic Commentary to the New Testament* (Nashville: Abingdon, 1995), 254–55.

42. See Brian Copenhaver, *Hermetica: The Corpus Hermeticum and the Latin Asclepius in a New English Translation* (Cambridge: Cambridge University Press, 1992), cited in Boring, Berger, and Colpe, *Hellenistic Commentary*, 254.

43. See Guy G. Stroumsa, *Hidden Wisdom: Esoteric Traditions and the Roots of Christian Mysticism*, 2nd ed., SHR 70 (Leiden: Brill, 2005), particularly his treatment of "Mosaic Riddles," 92–108.

44. On the phenomenon, see Wayne A. Meeks, "The Man from Heaven in Johannine Sectarianism," *JBL* 91 (1972): 64, who comments on "the elucidation of themes by progressive repetition"; Jörg Frey, "Love-Relations in the Fourth Gospel: Establishing a Semantic Network," in Van Belle, Labahn, and Martiz, *Repetitions and Variations*, 171–98; Ruben Zimmermann, "Metaphoric Networks as Hermeneutic Keys in the Gospel of John: Using the Example of the Mission Imagery," in Van Belle, Labahn, and Martiz, *Repetitions and Variations*, 381–402; and on "glory," Nicole Chibici-Revneanu, *Die Herrlichkeit des Verherrlichten*, WUNT 2/231 (Tübingen: Mohr Siebeck, 2007), esp. 325–30.

45. See Harold W. Attridge, "An Emotional Jesus and Stoic Traditions," in *Stoicism*

ers to consider complex issues and thus serves as a psychagogic program,[46] always keeping the theoretical questions subordinated to the encounter with Christ.

The theme of judgment is an important strand of the "arabesque." The theme's tensions, which have long attracted attention,[47] begin with the first declaration of John 3:16–17 that God did not send the Son to judge the world, a notion repeated frequently (5:22; 8:15; 12:47). Alongside these affirmations is the insistence that judgment does take place, brought about by the action of Jesus (3:18; 5:30; 8:16; 8:26). These apparently contradictory affirmations find some degree of resolution in 12:48–49, when Jesus speaks of a judgment by the word that he has spoken. The implicit resolution is confirmed in 16:11, which assigns a judgmental role to the Paraclete.[48] In short, judgment happens but not in the manner of traditional eschatological or apocalyptic scenarios, such as Matt 25:31–46. Jesus brings judgment but not from the bench of a great assize. He proclaims the word given him by the Father; reaction to that word, belief or rejection, determines the verdict.

Intertwined with the sequence about "judgment" is another strand of tensive reflection concerning the relationship between divine sovereignty and human responsibility in the salvific process. Some readers find here a rigidly determinist scheme; others a space for human responsibility. Some are content to affirm that the gospel, perhaps like other Jewish sources,

in *Early Christianity*, ed. Tuomas Rasimus, Troels Engberg-Pedersen, and Ismo Dunderberg (Peabody, MA: Hendrickson, 2010), 77–92.

46. On psychagogy in general, see Clarence E. Glad, *Paul and Philodemus: Adaptability in Epicurean and Early Christian Psychagogy*, NovTSup 81 (Leiden: Brill, 1995). For a more theoretical approach, see Hugo Lundhaug, *Images of Rebirth: Cognitive Poetics and Transformational Soteriology in the* Gospel of Philip *and the* Exegesis on the Soul, NHMS 73 (Leiden: Brill, 2010).

47. The classic treatment is Josef Blank, *Krisis: Untersuchungen zur johanneischen Christologie und Eschatologie* (Freiburg: Lambertus, 1964).

48. The language (*elenxei*) is clearly forensic, as is the title Paraclete, whatever its precise connotations. See Michel Gourgues, "Le paraclet, l'esprit de vérité: Deux désignations, deux fonctions," in *Theology and Christology in the Fourth Gospel: Essays by the Members of the SNTS Johannine Writings Seminar*, ed. Gilbert Van Belle, Jan G. van der Watt, and P. Maritz, BETL 184 (Leuven: Leuven University Press, 2005), 83–108; David Pastorelli, *Le Paraclet dans le corpus johannique*, BZNW 142 (Berlin: de Gruyter, 2006); Lochlan Schelfer, "The Legal Precision of the Term 'παράκλητος,'" *JSNT* 32 (2009): 131–50.

holds that the two principles are mysteriously compatible.[49] Yet others relate the tensive principles to the gospel's social circumstances.[50] The variety of interpretations attests the presence of another riddle.

From chapter 3 on, the gospel juxtaposes two principles: that origins are determinative and that one can reset the point of origin and be "born *anōthen*." Feints in one direction or another entice a reader, wondering how the tension is to be resolved. Finally, in chapter 12, in combination with the resolution of the "judgment" theme, the reader learns that what one loves determines whether one will accept the opportunity to accept or reject the revealer (12:43). The evangelist concludes with an implied account of divine sovereignty and human responsibility not unlike that of classical Stoicism. The divine will exercise a strong influence, inviting belief, making it possible and attractive, but God does not force a decision. There is room for the individual to assent or reject the invitation to believe. The latter move is simply "sin."[51]

DRAMA'S VISUAL EMBELLISHMENT

Deploying riddles is one way that the evangelist bends the dramatic narrative. It grounds the term "theologian" that tradition applied to him, but it is only one part of the "arabesque." In addition to the Fourth Gospel's riddles, usually revolving around important faith claims, another thematic strand weaves through the story of Jesus: a complex array of visual images—visual flowers, as it were—on the conceptual tendrils of the arabesque. Johannine imagery has received much attention,[52] and the

49. So, e.g., Craig Keener, *The Gospel of John: A Commentary*, 2 vols. (Peabody, MA: Hendrickson, 2003), 1:571–74, discussing John 12:37–45.

50. See, e.g., Enno Ezard Popkes, "Exkurs: Die sukzessive Entfaltung des Prädestinationsgedankens im Erzählverlauf des Johannesevangeliums," in *Die Theologie der Liebe Gottes in den johanneischen Schriften: Zur Semantik der Liebe und zum Motivkreis des Dualismus*, WUNT 2/197 (Tübingen: Mohr Siebeck, 2005), 204–11, with reference to other literature.

51. Harold W. Attridge, "Divine Sovereignty and Human Responsibility in the Fourth Gospel," in *Revealed Wisdom: Studies in Apocalyptic in Honour of Christopher Rowland*, ed. John Ashton, AJEC 88 (Leiden: Brill, 2014), 183–99.

52. See, e.g., Craig Koester, *Symbolism in the Fourth Gospel: Meaning, Mystery, Community*, 2nd ed. (Minneapolis: Fortress, 2003); Dorothy A. Lee, *Flesh and Glory: Symbol, Gender, and Theology in the Gospel of John* (New York: Crossroad, 2002); Jörg Frey, Jan G. van der Watt, and Ruben Zimmermann, *Imagery in the Gospel of John:*

Johannine treatment of imagery, working like cubist art, formally resembles the play on generic features. Life, light, shepherds, vines, blood, and water flow through the text in interwoven streams, emanating from and refracting the central image of the cross, that ironic symbol at the gospel's center.[53] If the arabesque's riddles appeal to the mind, its images appeal to the senses, but they do the same kind of work as the whole of the dramatic enterprise; they facilitate an encounter with the living Christ.

CONCLUSION

Ancient literary practice sheds light on how "genre works" in the Fourth Gospel. Ancient literature of all stripes developed genres, but even when they were explicitly theorized, as in the Greek and Roman traditions, they were regularly the subjects of literary play, often by defining one's own version of a genre against another. Our evangelist was writing in an environment in which historicizing impulses were at work. The story of Jesus's life, death, and resurrection was a way of connecting people to him. Our evangelist shared the rhetorical goal, but for him, mere historicizing narrative was inadequate to do the job. The story of Jesus had to be reconceived along the lines of other types of literary production. Most importantly and most clearly, the story needed to be dramatized, to display and to invite transformative encounters with the crucified and resurrected Way, Truth, and Life. But neither would a simple dramatized narrative suffice. Drama offered the possibility of encounter, through identification of the reader with a character in the story, but other dimensions of experience required other tools. The dramatic narrative was further bent toward a bit of conceptual artistry that would at the same time bedazzle and perplex but ultimately transform the attentive reader.

Terms, Forms, Themes and Theology of Johannine Figurative Language, WUNT 200 (Tübingen: Mohr Siebeck, 2006).

53. Harold W. Attridge, "The Cubist Principle in Johannine Imagery: John and the Reading of Images in Contemporary Platonism," in Frey, van der Watt, and Zimmermann, *Imagery in the Gospel of John*, 47–60.

2

STYLE

Dan Nässelqvist

Style has been a feature of the study of the Fourth Gospel for a long time. It has rarely been examined on its own terms, however; primarily, it has been used in a supporting function within source-critical research. This application of style focuses upon identifying and demarcating sources in and behind the text in its current form. The idea is that some parts of the Fourth Gospel exhibit a style that is inconsistent with the prevalent style of the Fourth Evangelist. In the history of source criticism, stylistic features have thus been used to prove (or, by critics, to disprove) sources and redaction, rather than to understand how the style affects the interpretation of the gospel.[1]

This chapter introduces another perspective on style, one that is based upon the presentation and analysis of stylistic features found in ancient writings on rhetoric and literary criticism. This perspective is also evident in some early Christian authors. The fourth-century CE theologian Augustine spends a considerable portion of his *Christian Instruction* on style. He also applies considerations of style to his reading of several biblical texts from both the Old and the New Testaments (Augustine, *Doctr. chr.* 4, esp. 4.12.27–4.26.58). Although this ancient perspective on style may well aid in delimiting possible sources and redactional layers in the Fourth Gospel, this chapter will focus upon how style and stylistic features affect how the gospel is understood. As we shall see, stylistic features

---

1. Tom Felton and Tom Thatcher, "Stylometry and the Signs Gospel," in *Jesus in Johannine Tradition*, ed. Robert T. Fortna and Tom Thatcher (Louisville: Westminster John Knox, 2001), 209–18; Gilbert Van Belle, "Style Criticism and the Fourth Gospel," in *One Text, A Thousand Methods: Studies in Memory of Sjef van Tilborg*, ed. Patrick Chatelion Counet and Ulrich Berges, BibInt 71 (Leiden: Brill, 2005), 291–316.

conveyed information about the mood, focus, and interpretation of the gospel to a number of ancient text users: readers who studied the gospel privately, lectors who prepared to read publicly from it, and listeners who heard it read aloud.

STYLE IN ANTIQUITY

Although discussions of style abound in writings by ancient rhetoricians and literary critics, especially in the first centuries BCE and CE, they do not give us a clear definition of style. Nor has modern research come to any consensus as to how style should be defined. Nevertheless, a few things can be confidently stated about style in general. First, style involves a choice on the part of the author, as specific content can be expressed in a number of ways. An author repeatedly makes choices between different linguistic elements on several levels (phonemes, words, clauses, sentences, etc.). These choices give us an impression of his or her style. Scholars have predominantly focused upon a single linguistic element, the word. Saeed Hami-Khani even states that "style is the way an author uses words."[2] As I will discuss below, however, ancient authors did not focus only on, or even primarily upon, the choice and use of words. They also gave much attention to how the content was expressed through stylistic features such as ornamentation, sound, and rhythm. This was especially important since only a small minority of the population could read and most text users thus experienced literary writings by hearing them read aloud by someone else.

Second, style concerns the expression of ideas—how a message is conveyed through a text. This involves how the message is embodied and expressed in the text but also how readers understand such information and convey it in oral delivery to listeners. Style in antiquity thus cannot be reduced to literary composition and the stylistic choices made by authors. It also involves how readers and listeners interpret stylistic features (regardless of whether or not these are intentionally chosen by the author) according to the conventions of the time.

Thus, at the very least, style involves choice, expression of ideas, and interpretation. It is important to remember, however, that style did not

---

2. Saeed Hamid-Khani, *Revelation and Concealment of Christ: A Theological Inquiry into the Elusive Language of the Fourth Gospel*, WUNT 2/120 (Tübingen: Mohr Siebeck, 2000), 145.

have the same connotations in antiquity as it does today. We may think of style as something that expresses the unique characteristics of a person, and we use it in metaphorical expressions such as "lifestyle," "hairstyle," and "leadership style." In antiquity, the Greek and Latin terms for style were regularly related to speaking, and they did not have the type of metaphorical extension found in modern expressions.[3] Ancient rhetoricians and literary critics occasionally commented upon unique features of an author's style, yet they primarily focused upon how well the author approached one of several ideal patterns or models. Style in antiquity thus had more to do with archetypes than with expressing an author's individuality.[4] This fact provided the conventions of style that readers and listeners used to identify and interpret stylistic features as something that affected their interpretation of the content of a literary writing.

The archetypes according to which literary writings were assessed changed with the passing of time. During the first centuries BCE and CE, however, a single system with three levels of style predominated. This system endured at least until late antiquity, although it was eventually outrivalled by other classifications with more levels and an evaluation of varying quality between them. Though more research needs to be conducted before we can fully understand the development and character of these systems, it is clear that Augustine continued to use the three levels of style in the fourth century CE.[5]

LEVELS OF STYLE

The three levels of style represent increasing stylistic intensity, from "plain" to "middle" to "grand," each with its own function and characteristics. All

---

3. For example, four of the most common terms for style also have to do with speaking: *lexis* ("saying" or "something spoken"), *frasis* ("speech" or "enunciation"), *dictio* ("saying" or "speaking"), and *elocutio* ("expression" or "oratorical delivery").

4. Described in sociolinguistic terms, ancient conceptions of style focused rather on *sociolect* (how a group uses and interprets language) than on *idiolect* (an individual's unique use of language).

5. For a brief introduction to the history of different systems for understanding style, see D. A. Russell, *Criticism in Antiquity* (London: Duckworth, 1981), 129–47. An interpretation of how this development affects the New Testament is found in Craig A. Smith, "The Development of Style (Fifth Century BCE to Second Century CE) and the Consequences for Understanding the Style of the New Testament," *JGRChJ* 7 (2010): 9–31.

levels of style employ the same stylistic features but in different ways and to various extent. The level can thus be decided by examining the combination of stylistic features used in a text.

Ancient rhetoricians described the basic difference in function between the three levels of style as follows: the plain style informs the readers/listeners and proves arguments to them; the middle style charms and conciliates them; and the grand style stirs and sways them by evoking their emotions. The function of each style is thus connected to the fundamental functions of an orator: to be able to prove, please, and sway the audience.[6] These, in turn, are linked to the modes of persuasion—the three most basic rhetorical strategies that were described already by the philosopher Aristotle in the fourth century BCE: *logos* (appeal to argument), *ethos* (appeal to credibility), and *pathos* (appeal to emotions) (Aristotle, *Rhet.* 1.2.3–6; 2.1.1–4). The system with three levels of style is thus connected to well-known and established rhetorical principles. This probably explains its success throughout the first few centuries CE, even as it was relativized by the need for more levels.

An important aspect of the three stylistic levels is that they are all considered agreeable. Later systems added more levels and differentiated between ones that were suitable and ones that should be avoided. In the three-level system, however, the different and indispensable functions of the stylistic levels rendered them all necessary, even though several rhetoricians and literary critics favored a particular level of style (usually the middle or grand).

The indispensable nature of each stylistic level is also indicated by the fact that one should not solely employ one of them, but rather one ought to choose between them according to the function of each section of a text. This means that most literary writings, if not all, contain more than one level of style. Augustine states: "No one should suppose that it is against the rule to mingle these styles. On the contrary, as far as it can properly be done, one should vary one's diction by using all three" (*Doctr. chr.* 4.22.51). He proves the point by citing examples of both the middle and grand levels of style in Romans and by stating that although most of Galatians is written in plain style, it also includes portions in middle style (4.20.40–44).

---

6. The functions of stylistic levels and orators are combined by the first-century BCE rhetorician Cicero (*De or.* 2.128–129; *Or. Brut.* 69), the first-century CE rhetorician Quintilian (*Inst.* 12.10.59.), and Augustine (*Doctr. chr.* 4.12.27; 4.17.34).

The descriptions of the three levels of style vary between authors, although they regularly present them as increasing in stylistic intensity from plain to grand. The major differences are found in the presentations of the middle style, which is either described as a true mean between the two other (and older) levels or as a third style with unique characteristics, sometimes called the "florid" style.

Plain style is most often connected with explaining, teaching, and presenting information and proofs. It uses a concise and restrained mode of expression, which is stripped of most ornaments, such as elaborate rhetorical figures. The term "rhetorical figure [*schema*]" will recur throughout this chapter; it is one of the most important stylistic features as it occurs in all levels of style.[7] The term refers to an expression that is used to achieve an effect beyond simply conveying information through the literal meaning of the words found in it. As such, it includes a wide variety of structures with various effects, such as metaphor (an expression that refers to something that it does not literally signify), antithesis (an expression which contains two contrasting ideas), anaphora (the repetition of a sound, word, or phrase at the beginning of several successive clauses), and alliteration (the repetition of similar sounds at the beginning of several words in close proximity). Ancient rhetorical handbooks and treatises include extensive lists and descriptions of such figures, which should be integrated with the content of a passage to emphasize, embellish, and clearly express the point.[8]

The plain style focuses more upon making things clear than impressive. Plain-style passages therefore frequently use a clear and simple (although not unsophisticated) language, while they at the same time avoid almost all aspects of a more intense style (or apply these with restraint). One achieves required variation by alternating with sections written in middle or grand style or by applying stylistic features that are allowed in plain style, such as sayings, maxims, humor, and irony.

The grand style is the most intense of the three levels, and it is often described as the opposite of the plain style, since it makes ample use of

---

7. In ancient Greek and Latin literature, rhetorical figures are often divided into figures of speech (*schēmata lexeōs* or *figurae dictionis*) and figures of thought (*schēmata dianoias* or *figurae sententiarum*).

8. The most extensive description in a text roughly from the same time period as the New Testament is found in book four of the anonymous first-century BCE handbook Rhetorica ad Herennium.

rhetorical figures and embellishments in order to make the text powerful. Grand style is connected with forcefulness, persuasion, and especially
with evoking and appealing to the emotions. It employs bold and impressive language, which includes new, rare, and metaphorical words, and it
often achieves an approximate rhythm in oral delivery. It can come across
as rather artificial in its remoteness from ordinary speech.

The first-century CE historian and literary critic Dionysius of Halicarnassus accentuates the obvious differences between plain and grand
style. He compares and opposes the two stylistic levels in terms of shape
and effect. According to him, the grand style is daring and original with
its elaborate rhetorical figures, whereas plain style is conventional and
appears to be unstudied. While grand style produces tension and emotion,
plain style soothes and relaxes the listener. The effects can even be violent
emotion and compulsion in grand-style writing, whereas the plain style
may deceive the listeners and conceal facts from them (*Dem.* 2).

The middle style is occasionally described as a true mean between
plain and grand style. In such cases, it exhibits few distinctive features. It
is more often presented, however, as an intermediate level with a distinct
character of its own. Its most fundamental qualities are smoothness and
charm. It differs from the plain style primarily by being far more stylisti-
cally intense, since it employs numerous rhetorical figures. Although it has
this in common with grand style, middle-style writing employs embellishments to create a smooth effect; grand style uses them in order to build up
force or a strong emotional appeal. The combination and effect of embellishments (such as rhetorical figures) thus distinguishes between middle
and grand style.

Middle style is often connected with charm, pleasing, conciliating,
and winning the listeners' favor. The smooth, polished, and ornamented
character of this stylistic level style led some ancient authors to call it the
"florid" style. Such a label better captures the calm procession and beautiful embellishment of some middle-style passages. The effect can be quite
different from the intellectual appeal of the plain style and the emotional
force of the grand style.

In practice, however, there is constant overlap between the stylistic
levels, as authors struggle to express different ideas and make stylistic
choices that fit them. We should not expect to find numerous clear-cut
examples of each stylistic level in the Fourth Gospel but rather passages
that approximate to one of the levels. Indeed, several of the ancient literary
critics that analyzed style found faults even in the best authors. Despite

this, they still interpreted their literary writings according to the existing system for describing levels of style, even if these writings were composed centuries before the system was established. We have seen a similar attitude in Augustine, who interpreted Old and New Testament writings (as well as passages by contemporary theologians, such as Ambrose) according to the three levels of style.

STYLE IN THE FOURTH GOSPEL

The style of the Fourth Gospel is regularly described with a focus upon the author's use of words. I will go beyond this and describe how other stylistic features, primarily sound quality and the employment of periods, affect the composition. The use of words in the Fourth Gospel does display some distinctive features, however, and I will begin with this aspect of style.

Use of Words

As mentioned above, ancient rhetoricians and literary critics analyzed style both in terms of an author's unique features and of how well he or she approached stylistic archetypes. The use of words in the Fourth Gospel falls into both of these categories. Some of the well-known ways the Fourth Evangelist uses words are as double entendres, repetition, a limited vocabulary, and polar opposites. These features are often described as the author's unique style, yet further consideration of them from the perspective of ancient discussions of style reveals that only the double entendres are undoubtedly idiosyncratic. The other features are frequently used to affect the stylistic intensity of a literary writing. For example, grand-style passages may contain constant repetition of key words, since this creates emphasis and force, which can be used to evoke the emotions of the listeners. Similarly, the use of polar opposites, such as love-hate and light-darkness, corresponds to the rhetorical figure *antithesis*. Antithesis is employed as an ornament that creates distinction and intensity in passages of middle or grand style (see Rhet. Her. 4.15.21).[9] Such stylistic features are thus

---

9. Note also that ancient rhetoricians and literary critics used "ornament" to refer not only to embellishment on the surface of a writing (as we may think of it), but also to those features of a text (for example, rhetorical figures) that bring out its essence. Cicero states that ornaments can be used "not only to increase the importance of a

used in most literary writings to affect the stylistic intensity of individual passages or sections.

The double entendres found in the Fourth Gospel function differently, however. One of the most basic characteristics of good style, as presented by ancient rhetoricians and literary critics, is clarity. A double entendre consists of a word that is employed in such a way that it could have any of two distinctly different meanings. This creates ambiguity rather than clarity. Nevertheless, the Fourth Evangelist frequently and deliberately employs double entendres. For example, in the discourse with Nicodemus, Jesus uses several double entendres. In 3:3, he states that no one can see the kingdom of God without being born *anōthen*, "again" or "from above."[10] Shortly thereafter, in 3:8, he combines two double entendres as he seemingly describes the wind: "The wind [*pneuma*] blows where it chooses and you hear its sound [*phōnē*]." Since *pneuma* also means "spirit" and *phōnē* "voice," the readers/listeners, who are in a privileged position compared to the characters in the story, can hear what Jesus is really saying: "The *Spirit* blows where it chooses and you hear its *voice*."[11]

How, then, do the author's use of words affect the reader's understanding of the Fourth Gospel? It accomplishes several things at once on multiple levels. It creates misunderstandings for characters within the story, which in turn produces irony and stimulates readers/listeners to reflect upon what the proper understanding of what is stated may be. Such a reaction is reinforced by multiple examples of how characters in the story misunderstand the sayings and actions of Jesus. The privileged position of the readers/listeners aids their search for deeper meanings, yet it also challenges them and keeps them attentive and ready for what follows. They are thus likely to be attentive to other stylistic features, such as the use of sound quality to convey information about how an encounter should be interpreted.

Already on the level of word usage, however, the story draws them in and induces them to accept the dichotomous view of the world presented in the gospel, which is strongly accentuated by the polar opposites used by the author. Readers/listeners are thus faced with a choice, to accept or to

---

subject and raise it to the highest level, but also to diminish and disparage it" (*De or.* 3.104).

10. Unless otherwise stated, all translations of biblical texts are my own.

11. This privileged position is due both to the introduction given in the Prologue and the multiple comments given by the narrator throughout the gospel.

refute what is stated about Jesus. The narrator or Jesus himself invalidates all other positions, and the stylistic features heighten the intensity and rule out the option of passively regarding the story from a distance. The stylistic fashioning of the text thus interacts with its content (the story)—in accordance with the instructions of ancient rhetoricians and literary critics—and forces the readers/listeners to make a decision if what is stated about Jesus is true or false.

Sound Quality

Style in antiquity involved much more than the use of words, however. We now turn into territory where not much research has been conducted.[12] Conclusions are thus tentative, yet compelling enough to indicate that the reading of the Fourth Gospel will be much enriched by including aspects of style. I will focus upon two features of style that are rarely studied in the context of the Fourth Gospel: sound quality and periods.

Sound quality comprises the aural effects of a text as it is read aloud. It involves features such as euphonious and dissonant sounds, which affect the smoothness of a passage, and clashes of letters between words, which impact the rhythm. Instances of euphony, dissonance, and clashes between words also attract the attention of listeners and influence their impression of the passage in question. The use of distinctive sound quality also intensifies the style and thus often raises the stylistic level of the passage. In the case of middle (or florid) style, additional affects apply due to the smooth and flowing nature of this stylistic level. Euphonious sounds strengthen this requisite smoothness, whereas dissonant sounds hamper it. Let us turn to a few examples of distinctive euphony and dissonance in the Fourth Gospel and see how the sound quality of passages interact with its content and thus influence those who hear the (Greek) text read aloud.

One feature that generates euphony is repeated use of the same type of vowel in a passage. The harmony increases if the vowel is long or found in especially noticeable positions, namely, at the beginning or the end of a word. The fact that long vowels in noticeable positions constitute the most euphonious sounds is not an objective truth for all languages, of course,

---

12. A rare example is found in the analysis of John 20 in the excellent introduction to sound analysis of New Testament writings: Margaret Ellen Lee and Bernard Brandon Scott, *Sound Mapping the New Testament* (Salem, OR: Polebridge, 2009), 247–82.

but expresses the aural aesthetics of ancient Greek.[13] Two examples of euphony caused by high concentrations of long vowels can be found in 15:9–10 and 1:4. Jesus's discourse on the true vine at the beginning of chapter 15 contains several euphonious passages. The most noticeable of these is found in his exhortation about abiding in his love (15:9–10). Almost one in three syllables in this passage comprises a long e-sound, the Greek letter *ēta*:

> Abide in my love [*tē agapē tē emē*].
> If you keep [*tērēsēte*] my commandments,
> you will abide in my love [*tē agapē mou*].

The repetition of e-sounds, which in the Greek are found at the end of each line and predominantly at the end of the words, renders Jesus's exhortation euphonious and attracts the attention of listeners. Considered in their totality, the stylistic features in the section about the true vine (I will return to this passage below) turn the attention of readers and listeners to Jesus's exhortation about abiding in his love in 15:9–10. This passage includes more and stronger attention-attracting features than, for example, Jesus's commandment about loving one another in 15:12. Analysis of style thus highlights points of emphasis in the text as well as passages that were particularly noticeable to ancient readers and listeners.

It is no coincidence that euphony is found in passages with significant statements that influence both the story and the listeners, such as 15:9–10. This is also the case in the Prologue, which—similarly to the discourse on the true vine—contains several euphonious passages (for example, 1:1–2, 4, 7, 9). One of these, 1:4, includes repeated long vowels (the Greek letters *ēta* and *ōmega*) in more than two thirds of the syllables. A transcription of the Greek discloses the constant repetitions:

> *en autō zōē ēn kai hē zōē ēn to phōs tōn anthrōpōn*
> In him was life and the life was the light of humankind.

---

13. Evidence of such aural aesthetics can be found not only in works of ancient literary criticism (such as the ones by Dionysius of Halicarnassus and Pseudo-Demetrius), but also in the most commonly used grammar of the ancient world by the second-century BCE grammarian Dionysius Thrax.

As a result of this assonance, the passage produces a strong and noticeable euphony. Similar to 15:9–10, this passage combines euphony with important content, in what is the Fourth Gospel's first allusion to the eternal life promised to believers in Christ (see, e.g., 3:15, 16; 5:24; 6:40; 10:28; 17:2). Euphony is thus one of the ways in which the Fourth Evangelist directs the attention of readers/listeners to significant statements with which they can interpret and evaluate the story.

Like euphonious sounds, dissonant sounds also attract the attention of listeners, guide it to certain passages, and affect the listeners' interpretation of them. The sounds that produce dissonance include some harsh consonants, such as *thēta* and *phi*,[14] and letters that comprise s-sounds, such as *sigma*, *xi*, and *psi*, which cause a hissing sound when they are pronounced. Only frequent repetition of such harsh or hissing letters in a limited passage will cause noticeable dissonance. An example of this is found in 13:31–32.

The second half of the Fourth Gospel, which is regularly referred to as the "Book of Glory," begins in chapter 13. From that point, Jesus turns to his own disciples and teaches them in private about himself. After having commanded Judas Iscariot to leave and betray him (13:27), he picks up the theme of glorification in a strongly repetitious and aurally noticeable passage (13:31–32):

Now the Son of Man has been glorified [*edoxasthē ho huios*],
and God has been glorified [*theos edoxasthē*] in him.
If God has been glorified [*theos edoxasthē*] in him,
God will also glorify [*theos doxasei*] him in himself,
and he will glorify [*euthys doxasei*] him at once

The passage not only involves frequent repetitions of the verb "glorify" (*doxazein*), but it combines these with other words (*huios* ["son"], *theos* ["God"], *euthys* ["at once"]) in such a way that each short line contains three hissing consonants in close proximity.[15] These hissing sounds produce a

---

14. Such aspirated consonants are considered harsh, since they cannot be pronounced without a strong release of breath. Compare, for example, the difference in pronunciation between *thick* and *tick*.

15. Note that *doxazein* in the present tense comprises one hissing consonant (*sigma*) as well as one euphonious consonant (*zēta*). This verb is therefore not dissonant in the present tense, yet the conjugated forms used in 13:31–32 (the aorist

dissonant aural impression, which affects how listeners interpret it. The stylistic fashioning of the passage imparts critical information about the glorification of Jesus. Through creative use of dissonance, the author communicates that glorification is an ambiguous concept and not something to simply delight in. It will soon become clear to the listeners that the glorification of Jesus indeed involves suffering and death.

Another stylistic feature that produces dissonance consists of frequent clashes of letters between words. Such clashes produce a rough aural impression and affect the rhythm. Clashes between consonants—when one words ends with a consonant and the next begins with one—are quite common and only result in dissonance if the frequency of the clashes is considerably higher than in surrounding passages or if the clashing consonants are harsh or hissing (such as *thēta*, *phi*, *sigma* or *psi*).[16] Clashes between vowels (often called *hiatus*) are not as common as clashes between consonants, but they produce more dissonance. The first-century CE rhetorician Quintilian describes the nature of the dissonance: "When a clash of vowels occurs, the speech gapes, pauses, and is afflicted" (*Inst.* 9.4.33).[17] The two vowels thus force the reader to make a short pause between the words, which affects the sound quality and the smoothness of the passage.

An example of how clashes between letters affect the impression of a passage is found in 21:5. The preceding verses, which describe how (after the death and resurrection of Jesus) several of the disciples go fishing in the Sea of Tiberias, contain slightly more clashes than what is normal in the Fourth Gospel. Several of these are also dissonant, such as the two clashes between hissing s-sounds in 21:3 (*autois Simōn* and *hēmeis sun*). This pattern continues into 21:5 and includes its opening phrase, "Jesus said to them." At this point, however, the clashes disappear altogether, and the question posed by Jesus flows without any interruptions, clashes, or dissonance: "Children, you have no fish, have you?" Immediately following

---

edoxasthē and the future *doxasei*) do not include the euphonious letter, but rather two hissing s-sounds (*sigma* and *xi*) as well as a harsh consonant (*thēta*; only found in the aorist form).

16. Thus the phrase *gynaikos Samaritidos* ["a Samaritan woman"] in John 4:9 produces a dissonant consonant clash, since the first word ends with the same hissing consonant with which the second begins (*sigma*). The phrase *Simōn Petros* ["Simon Peter"] in John 21:2 includes a consonant clash, yet it is not dissonant, since the consonants are not identical, harsh, or hissing. In these and the following examples, I indicate clashes of letters between words with underlining at the point of the clash.

17. Quintilian then goes on and describes which types of hiatus sound worst.

this question, the clashes resume and the disciples' brief answer includes a dissonant clash of vowels (*autō̲ ̲ou*). The rest of the gospel continues in much the same manner.

The words of Jesus in 21:5 comprise the only sentence in chapter 21 that is free from clashes. It seems as though the author may have arranged it to be noticeably smooth. In the context of the story, in which the disciples have not yet realized that they are talking to Jesus, the change in sound quality creates irony. The listeners know that it is Jesus (they can even hear it!), whereas the disciples, once again, act with less than perfect insight.[18] The euphonious nature of Jesus's address also matches the fact that the difficulties between Jesus and his disciples have now been resolved; in the preceding chapter, the disciples received the Spirit and were commissioned for their mission as apostles (20:21–23). The Fourth Evangelist makes ample use of irony and other stylistic features such as distinctive sound quality, a fact that aids us in identifying veiled or previously unknown instances of irony.

Analysis of style proves especially useful for guiding the interpretation of questions posed by characters in the gospel. For example, the comparative smoothness of Jesus's question in 21:5 affects not only the style of the passage, but also the listeners' interpretation of it. That style in general and sound quality in particular affects how questions are understood is confirmed by a study of leading questions in the Fourth Gospel.

Leading questions are posed in such a manner that they indicate which answer is expected.[19] Most leading questions in the Fourth Gospel have no distinctive sound quality. When they do, however, the type of sound quality (euphonious or dissonant) almost always fits the expected answer (euphonious sounds for an expected positive answer and dissonant sounds for a negative). These cases not only confirm that sound quality guides the interpretation of questions, but also that it amplifies the impression of them. For example, the question posed by the Samaritan woman to her neighbors in Sychar about the identity of Jesus (4:29) is leading in such a way that a negative answer is expected: "Surely, he is not the Messiah?" The dissonant sounds accompanying the question, mainly due to frequent hissing consonants, reinforce and confirm the expected negative

---

18. Jesus more often than any other character in the Fourth Gospel speaks in memorable and well-turned sentences.

19. This is easily accomplished in Greek with the help of varying negative particles at the beginning of the question.

answer. They even imply a skeptical attitude towards Jesus on the part of
the Samaritan woman. This impression is strengthened by the sound quality of a question that she poses directly to Jesus: "How can you, a Jew, ask
me, a Samaritan woman, for a drink?" (4:9). This question, which is not
leading, produces a strongly dissonant sound quality when it is read aloud,
due to frequent clashes of both consonants and vowels.[20] The already skeptical question is thus rendered even less friendly by the dissonant sounds.
Ancient listeners may well have perceived it as an intentional insult.

Periods

A period is a sophisticated arrangement of clauses that ends with a round-
ing, which connects the end to the beginning. Occasionally, especially
elaborate periods also include a *clausula*, a rhythmic ending. The use of
periods fits the florid (or middle) style especially well, but it is also found
in writings of the grand style and, albeit to a much lesser degree, in the
plain style. Periods regularly comprise a single sentence and according to
the literary critic Pseudo-Demetrius, they bring "the underlying thought
to a conclusion with a well-turned ending" (*Eloc.* 10). When read aloud,
a period is followed by a brief pause, in which listeners can reflect over or
react to what they have heard (see Quintilian, *Inst.* 9.4.61).

The Fourth Gospel contains a surprisingly large number of periods.
Almost each chapter includes at least one period. Even the unadorned
second chapter, which is characterized by plain style and few rhetorical
figures, contains a brief period. Not surprisingly, however, it is found in
2:19, in the momentous statement by Jesus about the temple (or, as it will
be revealed, about his body): "Destroy this temple, and in three days I will
raise it up." The arrangement of clauses into a period does not always translate well into English, which indicates the necessity of studying the gospel
in Greek if we want to identify stylistic features beyond the use of words.

According to which criteria can we identify periods? The fundamental
requirement is that the clauses "bend back" at the end, in the sense that
the ending relates to the beginning and thus creates a circuit (the Greek
term *periodos* means "circle"). Additionally, authors regularly signal the

---

20. The question and its introductory formula ("The Samaritan woman says to
him") include several dissonant vowel clashes (due to long vowels at the end and
beginning of adjoining words) and two dissonant consonant clashes (as hissing consonants collide between words).

existence of a period through the use of at least one other periodic feature, such as symmetry (repetition of sounds or words in parallel position), *hyperbaton* (inversion of the regular word order), elongation (a longer long final line or clause), or a *clausula* (a rhythmic ending). An example of a well-turned period that is discernible in English can be found in 3:17:

> For God did not send the Son to the world [*ton kosmon*]
> in order to [*hina*] condemn the world [*ton kosmon*],
> but to [*hina*] save the world [*ho kosmos*] through him.

This sentence contains three periodic features: the requisite bending back at the end, symmetry, and a *clausula*. The bending back is recognizable even in translation. The final word of the period ("him") connects with the first line, since "him" refers to "the Son." The reference to the Son at the end of the period thus integrates the three lines and produces the necessary circuital structure, which in turn makes the period well-turned. Symmetry characterizes the whole period. It includes the repetitions indicated above: the recurrence of *kosmos* ("world") at the end of each line and the use of *hina* ("in order to") at the beginning of the last two lines.[21] The period also ends with a *clausula*, a *spondee* that consists of two long syllables (*autou*, "him").

It is no coincidence that the period in 3:17 coincides with an important statement about God's plan for the salvation of the world. Stylistic features are regularly chosen in order to fit and express the content of the passage. The solemn message of 3:17 is thus expressed in a well-formed period characterized by smoothness and approximate rhythm.[22] This period corresponds well with ancient descriptions of the florid (or middle) style with its characteristic smoothness and combinations of rhetorical figures.

Periods occur in varying frequency according to the stylistic level and the content of different parts of the Fourth Gospel. They are found particularly in sections of middle (florid) or grand style, whereas plain style does not leave much room for such elaborate compositions.

In the Fourth Gospel, periods are almost exclusively found in direct address by characters. Accounts by the narrator thus rarely comprise any

---

21. These repetitions constitute the rhetorical figures *epistrophe* and *anaphora* (the period also includes the figure *polyptoton*).

22. The period includes almost no examples of vowel clashes, which is distinct in comparison with the verses that surround it.

periods, although the Prologue constitutes an exception. It contains two periods (in 1:7 and 1:11), in what may be the author's approximation of a grand-style introduction. Outside of the Prologue, characters rather than the narrator speak in periods. Jesus pronounces most of them, especially in the second half of the gospel (chapter 13–21). The disciples rarely speak in periods, however; beside Jesus, it is the discourse of other characters that is combined into this stylistic feature.

The existence of periods in the text signals different things depending upon who comes into contact with them. Lectors (those who read texts aloud in early Christian communities) are informed about which sentences to lift out for special delivery, after which they add a brief pause for emphasis and reflection (and, possibly, interaction from the listeners). To listeners, periods indicate which parts are especially important. They thus focus upon such emphasized sentences, presumably memorize some of them, and use them as interpretative clues to the rest of the gospel.

Levels of Style

All three levels of style can be found in the Fourth Gospel. Sections dominated by narrative or with limited dialogue (for example, John 2) use plain style. These regularly include fewer stylistic features, such as rhetorical figures, distinctive sound quality, and periods. Middle (or florid) style is found in and around many of the passages that are combined into periods, especially in sections dominated by discourse. For example, John 3 comprises several sections of middle style. Approximations of grand style occur sporadically throughout the gospel, such as in parts of the Prologue and in emphatic passages, especially those that contain direct address by Jesus.

An example of a grand-style composition occurs in John 15. Much of Jesus's discourse on the commandment to love (15:12–17) and of the world's hatred (15:18–25) comprises grand style. It begins already in 15:9–10, however, as Jesus concludes his teaching on the true vine and on the importance of abiding in him. The seven clauses of 15:9–10 contain examples of distinctive sound quality, some of which we have studied above, multiple forceful repetitions (for example, five repetitions of agapein/agapē, "love"/"to love"), and a period. Stylistic features such as these raise the stylistic level of the passage. What turns it into grand style, however, is not the amount of stylistic features but rather how they are juxtaposed and combined with the message that the passage contains.

John 15:9-10 includes an emotional appeal, which in turn prepares for the commandment that Jesus gives in 15:11. The content of this appeal is expressed in two parallel exhortations, "abide in my love" (15:9) and "keep my commandments" (15:10). The three clauses in which this appeal is most clearly expressed include the euphonious long vowels that we examined above. This euphony is combined with clashes of vowels, some of which are dissonant, which destroys the smoothness of the passage. Since this combination of forceful stylistic features is intertwined with extensive recurrences that often function as emphatic repetitions, which build up the tension required of grand style, it results in a grand-style passage of emotional appeal.

The identification of a specific level of style would affect the interpretation of singular passages as well as of the gospel as a whole. The effect differed depending upon who came into contact with the text. Those who read the gospel aloud in the community used stylistic features as interpretative clues, which informed their rendering of an appropriate vocal expression of the text. In the case of 15:9-10, the grand level of style guided them to deliver the text with the intensity inherent in the composition as they strove to evoke the emotions of the listeners. The listeners picked up on the mood and comparative emphasis of different passages, among which 15:9-10 would stand out as especially emphasized and significant. Well-educated readers who studied the text privately interpreted the text against the general levels of style (just as Augustine would do several centuries later) and were thus guided in their interpretation of the passage in question as well as of the writing as a whole.

3

TIME

Douglas Estes

Narratives need time to tell their stories. In fact, without time, a narrative is not a narrative. This is because in order to tell a story, the storyteller must relay to the hearer or reader at least one process or event. For example, "Everett" is not a narrative. "Everett walks" is not much of a narrative, though the present tense "walks" in English implies a motion that occurs in time. A better narrative would be, "Everett drove the car to the store, picked up groceries, and came home." This is the beginning of a "real" narrative because it entails multiple events.[1] Philosophers and literary theorists have widely noted that time is the defining characteristic of narrative.[2]

When we consider how John works, we must consider how time works in John as time is the most fundamental aspect of narrative. Yet, the Fourth Gospel's use of time to fulfill its narrative goals is not widely discussed. This is unfortunate, as the narrative dynamic of time in John is both challenging and unfamiliar. It is challenging in that it resists easy delineation or comparison to other gospels. It is unfamiliar because it is

---

1. This fulfills the definition of a "whole" story—one that has a beginning, middle and end—that was first noted by Aristotle (384–322 BCE); see Aristotle, *Poet.* 1450b25–31.

2. Among others, see Paul Ricoeur, "Narrative Time," in *On Narrative*, ed. W. J. T. Mitchell (Chicago: University of Chicago Press, 1981), 165–66; E. M. Forster, *Aspects of the Novel* (New York: Harcourt, 1927), 41–42; Seymour Chatman, *Story and Discourse: Narrative Structure in Fiction and Film* (Ithaca, NY: Cornell University Press, 1978), 21; Tzvetan Todorov, *Introduction to Poetics*, trans. Richard Howard (Sussex: Harvester, 1981), 41–43; Gerald Prince, *Narratology: The Form and Functioning of Narrative* (Berlin: Mouton, 1982), 1; Shlomith Rimmon-Kenan, *Narrative Fiction: Contemporary Poetics*, 2nd ed. (London: Routledge, 2002), 18–19.

constructed with a temporality from antiquity, one that is not accessible to modern readers. To understand how John works, we have to understand how John works in time (and through time). How time works in narrative is what we call its *temporal mechanics*.[3] How the narrator shapes time determines how the narrator assembles the story, and this shaping of time is the precursor to plot.[4]

THE FALLACY OF ASSUMED TIME

One common mistake readers make when thinking about how a gospel like John tells its story is to commit the *fallacy of assumed time*. This fallacy arises whenever we assume we know what time *is* and how it *works*. What is time? How do we define it? There is not a workable explanation of time (without using temporal concepts or modern physics). Time is one of the ineffable qualities of existence, such that it is not possible to offer a definition for time.[5] In fact, thinking about time creates such a quandary that the ancient philosopher Zeno of Elea (ca. 490–454 BCE) used time in his (in)famous paradoxes to reveal this problem and to confound other thinkers (see Aristotle, *Phys.* 6.9, and Simplicius, *Corollary on Time*, 796.33–797.27).[6] This problem becomes more acute when we consider time in narrative. If we were thinking about, say, the narrative dynamics of genre or characterization, we would define genre or characterization, and we would offer theories on what these things mean *before* we applied them to the text. This is rarely, if ever, done with the study of time in narrative. Instead, we readers assume that we know what time *is* based on our cultural understanding of time (really, implicit assumptions). This is akin

---

3. For greater discussion on these subjects, see Douglas Estes, *The Temporal Mechanics of the Fourth Gospel: A Theory of Hermeneutical Relativity in the Gospel of John*, BibInt 92 (Leiden: Brill, 2008).

4. Further, see the essay on "Plot" by Kasper Bro Larsen in this volume.

5. For similar thoughts, see John Earman and Richard M. Gale, "Time," in *The Cambridge Dictionary of Philosophy*, ed. Robert Audi, 2nd ed. (Cambridge: Cambridge University, 1999), 920–22; Ludwig Wittgenstein, *Preliminary Studies for the "Philosophical Investigations": Generally Known as the Blue and Brown Books*, 2nd ed. (Oxford: Basil Blackwell, 1969), 1, 26; and cf. Augustine, *Conf.* 11.14.

6. See also H. D. P. Lee, *Zeno of Elea*, CCS (Cambridge: Cambridge University, 1936), 50–51, 76–78. Though Zeno's paradoxes seem simple, they are still discussed and debated even to this day.

to studying genre by saying genre means what we assume it means from our everyday experiences, without any attempt to define a theory of genre.

When readers read a story, they often make implicit assumptions about that story, for example, that characters look like themselves or would act like themselves or that the narrator is trustworthy and reliable. Readers also implicitly assume that the narrator's view of time is compatible with their own. (This is the reason postmodern novels play with time, just as they play with narratorial reliability, to undermine these ideals.)[7] We may put it another way—every modern reader of the Gospel of John has at least two things in common: they have at least two time-tellers with which to keep track of time—a watch and a calendar. Today, we use these two time-tellers to keep track of big quantities of time and small quantities of time. Yet neither of these two things existed as such in the ancient world. During John's time, clocks were rare and inaccurate by modern standards.[8] Calendars were inaccurate, inconsistent, and (surprising to moderns) existed in several different competitive versions.[9] Therefore, when we moderns read an ancient narrative like John's Gospel, not only do we *not* come armed with a workable definition for time—as we would with genre and character—we also come from a perspective where quantifiable time is the *only* way to look at the world—a view that was not the case in antiquity. This is the defining difficulty of studying time in ancient literature.

For us to understand how time works in John, it will require us to learn not just about time itself and the gospel's use of time, but also to unlearn first many assumptions about time that we implicitly use. While we may not be able to easily define time, we can use metaphors and images to explain how time functions. This will allow us to study time in a narrative such as John in a meaningful way. We will look at John's temporality in two areas: how John structures his narrative (the "calendar") and how John observes time (the "watch").

---

7. Examples include Marcel Proust's *A la recherche du temps perdu*, Peter Ackroyd's *First Light*, Martin Amis's *Time's Arrow*, and James Joyce's *Finnegans Wake*.

8. Examples include the sun clock, or sundial, and the *clepsydra*, or water clock.

9. Modern people struggle with the idea that ancient people could have different, competing calendar systems and understand how to align their lives to multiple systems; see Sacha Stern, *Calendars in Antiquity: Empires, States, and Societies* (Oxford: Oxford University Press, 2012), 425; and competing worldviews in general, see Peter Brown, *Authority and the Sacred: Aspects of the Christianisation of the Roman World* (Cambridge: Cambridge University Press, 1995), 69.

The Calendar: Structures of Time in the Gospel of John

The Gospel of John makes it hard for the reader to ignore time. Before making it past the first couple of words, we read a temporal claim that "in the beginning was the Word" (John 1:1).[10] Here this allusion to Genesis marks out that the starting point for John is at creation and sets up the "when" of the beginning of John's story (cf. Dionysius of Halicarnassus, *Pomp.* 3.8).[11] Unlike many modern novels that begin *in media res*, John does something unusual and begins *ab ovo* (cf. Horace, *Ars* 147–148). So unusual is this type of beginning to modern readers that we pass over it too quickly, without realizing John's epic and dramatic intent. In writing this way, John signals that the temporal scope of his writing will be more extensive than a mere book may allow (John 21:25). We should not expect a simple story.

As the reader continues to read, the narrator introduces John the Baptist and his atemporal role of "witness to the Light" (John 1:7). Soon, the epic opening becomes juxtaposed to an everyday event, which features John the Baptist (John 1:19–28). This zoom in from a narrated, aerial shot to mundane conversation plunges the reader into the story in an intentional way.[12] If this were all we knew about the life of Jesus or if we were reading a novel, we would keep reading until the end (and that would be that). But John tells the reader it is historiography (John 19:35), not a novel; plus readers today are familiar with the other accounts of Jesus from at least the Synoptic Gospels that set up their stories in different ways. This prior knowledge begins to create a tension between how we understand the *fabula* (the raw material that the story is made from) and the *syuzhet* (the story that is recorded in the text).[13] These tensions have

---

10. Unless otherwise stated, all translations of biblical texts are my own.

11. Douglas Estes, "Rhetorical *Peristaseis* (Circumstances) in the Prologue of John," in *The Gospel of John as Genre Mosaic*, ed. Kasper Bro Larsen, SANt 3 (Göttingen: Vandenhoeck & Ruprecht, 2015), 191–207.

12. A similar, modern example of this type of opening is in the movie *Star Wars*. A narrator starts with an epic temporal statement "A long time ago," followed by brief explanation of the circumstances of the story. Then comes an aerial shot, which establishes the setting and quickly zooms in to a seemingly every day (for that narrative universe) event.

13. Viktor Shklovsky, "Art as Technique," in *Russian Formalist Criticism: Four Essays*, trans. Lee T. Lemon and Marion J. Reis (Lincoln: University of Nebraska Press, 1965), 3–24.

led to innumerable, creative (some highly creative) proposals all pur-
porting to explain how the text of John got this way.[14] While the Fourth
Gospel is a rich and complex narrative, the solution to these tensions is
somewhat simple.

The concept of *fabula* and *syuzhet* is a very useful tool for thinking
about how stories work, but the concept originates in the study of fiction,
not historiography. In fiction, the *fabula* exists in the mind of the author;
the reader must discern it from the narrative itself. In historiography, the
fabula is connected to the "real world" and is subject to interpretation by
both the author and later observers. This creates a Pandora's box worth of
problems, as the *fabula* for the Fourth Gospel includes everything from
the moment of creation up until the "present day" of John (late first century CE). What is more, even in the life of Jesus, there are a near infinite
number of events that are a part of, or contribute to, the *fabula* (which
the gospel astutely notes in John 21:25). But this near infinite number of
events is not open to a real, flesh-and-blood author of historiography, as
it is to an author of fiction. The fiction author can create an entire world
with divine, authorial knowledge of everything that can or will happen
in that world, but the historiography author is extremely limited in their
knowledge of the world. While the fiction author sees her *fabula* as a god
sees their creation, the historiography author sees his fabula as a highly
limited, nonneutral observer mired in his place in time. Contrary to the
assumptions of modern readers, John's Gospel and the Synoptic Gospels
do not use the same *fabula*. Instead, each gospel (including each Synoptic)
uses *fabulas* that are related but not identical.

Once John decides to create his gospel, he fashions the *fabula* into the
syuzhet through the writing out of the story. This is standard for telling
stories. What is not standard, to the modern reader, is how John understands the way time frames the story and the events. Our modern way of
looking at time is so quantified that it is hard to understand why ancients
structured some of their stories in the way they did. For example, if a
modern were to write a biography of a famous person, one of the first
things they might do is start collecting details of key events in the person's life (birth, death, marriage, major victories, major defeats, etc.). They
would then organize them and fit them on a time line (intentionally or

---

14. Starting with the *Diatessaron* of Tatian and running all the way to the dis-
placement, redaction, and community theories of our present day.

subconsciously). Even if they started their story at a major victory, then narrated the person's childhood, and ended at the famous person's death—the standard *in media res* approach—the modern biographer would nonetheless be creating a *chronology* of their life. However, when John wrote his gospel, the science of chronology had not yet been invented![15] In fact, this is a major challenge for modern readers of ancient historiography: our chronological view of the world is so fixed by our culture that we cannot help but to try to fit ancient, narrated events onto an absolute axis.[16] Since ancient historiographical writers did not construct the events within their *fabula* using chronology, our attempts to "figure out" the events in their *fabula* using the modern science of chronology will frustrate us and fail.[17]

This is largely because the starting point for the modern science of chronology is the *temporal coordinate*. A temporal coordinate is a time descriptor defined by some greater system of measuring time. A prime example is a date on a calendar, such as July 11, 2011. Knowing what event occurred on July 11, 2011 allows one to fix that event within a chronological time frame. However, the Fourth Gospel does not contain any temporal coordinates for readers to use.[18] This is not because the evangelist did not know temporal coordinates; it is because he chose not to use coordinates (for whatever reason).[19] The lack of any absolute temporal coordinate prevents the creation of an absolute chronology. This is why the temple cleansing event (John 2:12–25) is problematic in the gospels: there is no

---

15. Joseph Scaliger (1540–1609), following the work of Paulus Crusius, was arguably the first scholar to propose an absolute chronology. Though it was not considered revolutionary at the time, Scaliger's work irrevocably changed the way we look at the passage of time; cf. Pascal Richet, *A Natural History of Time*, trans. John Venerella (Chicago: University of Chicago Press, 2007), 46–48; Daniel Rosenberg and Anthony Grafton, *Cartographies of Time: A History of the Timeline* (New York: Princeton Architectural Press, 2010), 65.

16. The modern, Western sense of time is a mashup of quasi-Newtonian and quasi-Kantian ideas about how the world works.

17. Even premodern writers such as Niccolò Machiavelli (1469–1527) and Isaac Newton (1642–1727) did not use absolute chronologies to construct their narratives.

18. See Jörg Frey, *Die johanneische Eschatologie II: Das johanneische Zeitverständnis*, WUNT 110 (Tübingen: Mohr Siebeck, 1998), 154.

19. Numerous ancient examples of temporal coordinates include Gen 7:11; 2 Kgs 25:27; Ezra 7:8–9; Esth 3:13; 8:9; Jer 52:4; Ezek 1:1–2; 24:1; Hag 1:1; 2:1; Zech 1:7; 1 Macc 1:54; Jdt 2:1; Bar 1:2; Add Esth 1:1; Jub 1:1; 14:1; 1QDM I, 1; 4QCommGen A II, 1; 4QCalDoc A I, 6; Josephus, *Ant.* 12.248.

way to establish with certainty whether Jesus cleansed the temple once at the beginning of his ministry, once at the end of his ministry, twice (once at both ends of his ministry), *or* a dozen times throughout his ministry. In this case, we deal with probabilities not certainties. This is not to say that ancient writers such as John did not understand linear temporalities, such as before and after; they just did not understand absolute temporalities. In the Fourth Gospel, the narrator knows when Jesus cleared the temple; but this event is not affixed to a date, as it would for us, but is relative to the other events of the story.[20]

While the Fourth Gospel does not contain temporal coordinates, it does contain *temporal markers*. Temporal markers are relative reckonings of time. Even though we modern readers live in a world where we prefer absolute temporalities, we still use relative temporal markers. For example, if we told friends we went to the store "one day last week," that would be a temporal marker used in a relative way (except that our modern minds might try to figure out exactly which day this was). We use a temporal marker in a relative way when an exact date is unnecessary or unneeded. The importance of the marker is to create a relative frame for which to couch the event we are telling, not to give a way to pinpoint the day on a calendar. In fact, for the point of the story, the exact day probably does not matter. Similarly, the Fourth Gospel uses quite a few temporal markers as a way to organize its narrative (for example, "after these things" or "the next day").[21] These markers serve several narrative purposes: they help to separate events in the story, they help move the narrative along, and they grant a feeling of verisimilitude for later readers. Ancient writers—especially Greek historiographers and narrativists—used these types of temporal markers extensively throughout their works to create a relative time frame for their story.[22]

---

20. This works the same way whether John relies on sources or is an eyewitness as he claims. Either way, John is not privy to know everything of Jesus's life. John knows some events and organizes them as makes the most sense to convey the point of his story.

21. Temporal markers are more than simply references to time; they are a type of linguistic indexical that structures language; see for example, Eros Corazza, "Temporal Indexicals and Temporal Terms," *Synthese* 130 (2002): 441–60.

22. For example, Herodotus's *History*, Xenophon's *Anabasis*, Thucydides's *Histories*, Pompeius Trogus's *Philippic History*, Tacitus's *Histories* and *Annals*, and Procopius's *History of the Wars*. Temporal markers of this kind are less common in ancient

This is where modern readers who study the gospel get sidetracked. With a close reading of the text, modern readers start to notice these temporal markers. They also notice *temporal descriptors* such as "near to the Passover feast" (John 2:13).[23] The occurrences of these markers and descriptors prove too tempting to modern readers, who proceed to pick one (usually a descriptor, like a feast) and try to figure out how to put it on a timeline (the "calendar"). Once accomplished, they then try to cut up the rest of the scenes of the gospel and cut and paste them onto the timeline. When this does not work, they give up in frustration and deem the narrative flawed.[24] Other readers are unhappy that the gospel does not fit into neat categories of exact days and time references (as a modern biography might). To be fair, these feelings extended into the ancient world itself, at least to the time of Tatian (ca. 170 CE). Yet this is the reason John warns his readers that he is not, and cannot be, exhaustive in his story (John 21:25).

Modern historians may use chronology as a starting point to tell the story of a historical person, but modern storytellers often do not. Even modern storytellers are more concerned with what the story means and how it is told than whether every exact date is correct. One reason for this is what it means to define an event. An *event* is a demarcated period of time. However, time has no built-in marks of demarcation—two people who experience the same event will start and stop the retelling of the event at different points in time. Modern historians see an event as quantifiable and use the science of chronology to quantify them. Storytellers, modern or ancient, tend to see an event as relative to the other events of the story they wish to tell.[25] Either way, when a writer of any type goes to tell their story, they must start demarcating their *fabula* in such a way

---

Jewish literature; these texts are often structured with conjunctions that mark the passing of one event to the next.

23. A *temporal descriptor* is a reference to time that does not serve to configure the text and has a lower indexical value than temporal markers. While they are not window-dressing, their primary function is to describe the temporal context of an event.

24. For example, R. Alan Culpepper, *Anatomy of the Fourth Gospel: A Study in Literary Design* (Minneapolis: Fortress, 1983), 231; Urban C. von Wahlde, *The Earliest Version of John's Gospel: Recovering the Gospel of Signs* (Wilmington, DE: Glazier, 1989), 17–25; and Wayne A. Meeks, "The Man from Heaven in Johannine Sectarianism," *JBL* 91 (1972): 48.

25. Sometimes this even led ancient critics to notice; see, e.g., Dionysius of Halicarnassus, *Thuc.* 6–9.

that the events of their *syuzhet* will become distinct and separate. A visual example of this occurs in modern filmmaking, where writers and directors create storyboards for movies. The storyboards contain snapshots of each of the events that will be included in the movie. In order to tell the story, each individual event on each individual board can be shuffled as needed to tell a better story (like a deck of cards). While ancient writers did not have modern cinematic storyboards, they were quite capable of shuffling the events in their mind if it made for a better story.[26] (This is, after all, where the whole idea of *in media res* comes from.) Because modern writers are skilled in the use of chronology, they usually take care to make sure they preserve an underlying chronological system that is accessible to the reader, even if they shuffle the events of the story to make for a better telling. Because John and other ancient writers did not know the science of chronology, they did not know to do this. Instead, they assembled their stories for the good of their stories without making sure their events could be placed on an absolute axis.[27] This is one reason why Thucydides and the other Greek historians produced histories that do not read like histories to us today.[28]

When John created his gospel, his *fabula* was formed from real events in the real world.[29] This required a great deal of interpretation of these events, to demarcate one event from the next and to decide how these events fit together into one coherent story.[30] This makes the historiographer's job far

---

26. Ancient and medieval writers who used relative time frames include, e.g., Herodotus (ca. 484–420 BCE), Thucydides (ca. 460–404 BCE), Polybius (ca. 200–118 BCE), Pompeius Trogus (ca. late first century BCE), Livy (ca. 59 BCE–CE 17), Tacitus (ca. CE 54–120), Procopius (ca. early sixth century CE), Agathius (ca. CE 532–580), Michael Psellus (ca. 1019–1078 CE), Niketas Choniates (ca. mid-twelfth century–1212 CE), and Otto of Freising (ca. 1114/5–1158 CE).

27. Donald J. Wilcox, *The Measure of Times Past: Pre-Newtonian Chronologies and the Rhetoric of Relative Time* (Chicago: University of Chicago Press, 1987), 50; cf. Alex C. Purves, *Space and Time in Ancient Greek Narrative* (Cambridge: Cambridge University Press, 2010), 127.

28. There is some parallel between the increasing standardization of the calendar in late antiquity and the increase in the number of temporal coordinates used in ancient histories along with the experimentation with annals and chronicles starting in this period.

29. A summary for the sake of this essay: the pre*fabula* material cannot exist without interpretation because it only exists in the mind of the observer. Digging further is the concern of epistemology.

30. And what events are left out. As John notes, the vast majority of what could be

more difficult than the novelist's. The novelist can cut events in any way and no one will ever know, but the historiographer should be faithful to (their reading) of the events. To add to the complexity, the historiographer must now create a *syuzhet* that essentially conforms to a *block universe* model of time. In a block universe, past, present, and future are all equally real and accessible. To a historiographer, who may know of or have experienced events simultaneously, there is no way to create simultaneity within the two dimensions of a narrative world. For example, as children, we are fascinated when we learn how to draw a 3D box on a 2D piece of paper. In this drawing, we approximate three dimensions onto two. When a narrator tells his story of events that transpire—each interconnected, without lines of demarcation, and sometimes simultaneously—the narrator tells three dimensions onto a two dimensional text. While the block universe model of narrative is actually pretty close to the way our real world works, it does not feel very close to the reader, since it is not the way humans experience time. People experience the passing of time, not the existence of time itself, which is why the more a text conveys the feeling of the passage of time, the more relatable and interesting we feel the story to be. In order for the Fourth Gospel to convey the feeling of the passage of time, using the events that the narrator wanted to include and without using the science of chronology, the narrator created and used a relative time frame to configure these events within the narrative world of the gospel text.

The Watch: Glimpses of Time in the Gospel of John

Even if John did not configure the events of his gospel in a way modern students of history would wish, John did create a rich temporal tapestry from his *fabula* in order to help readers feel time. For all their lack of understanding of the science of chronology, ancient writers had a more colorful view of the passage of time than moderns do, and at times this makes for better storytelling.[31] In order to tell their stories, ancient writers would

---

included in a life of Jesus cannot be—there is a spatial limitation (John 21:25). John narrates the events of roughly sixteen weeks (and in no chronological order); see Estes, *Temporal Mechanics*, 223. For a similar estimate of Homer, see René Nünlist, "Some Ancient Views on Narrative, Its Structure and Working," in *Defining Greek Narrative*, ed. Douglas Cairns and Ruth Scodel, ELS 7 (Edinburgh: Edinburgh University Press, 2014), 160.

31. At times it makes for more inconsistent storytelling; see David Lowenthal, *The Past Is a Foreign Country* (Cambridge: Cambridge University Press, 1985), 198.

consider the events at hand and group them in the way they felt best to tell their story. Since they were not constrained by modern chronology—and did not feel the need to make sure their events fit into any chronological "order"—ancient writers chose other means to organize their events. Once accomplished, they created their text (*syuzhet*), which is what we read today.

In doing so, ancient writers took events from a near-infinite *fabula*, and in the case of historiography, an infinite number of possible temporal interpretations of those events—and by that I mean when they start, stop, and how they are causally connected—and configured them into a very small number of events that are now locked into place within the block universe of a text. This locking into place of events we call *emplotment*. Rather than experiencing these events as free and open, the emplotment process creates a highly *deterministic* textual world where the reader relies on one event to help explain the next event (even if the relationship between these events in the *fabula* was more complex or nuanced). In the case of John's Gospel, this process of emplotment is without the reader having any access to the original *fabula*. Especially when reading historiography, instead of fiction, this can create a more rigid feel to the passing of events.[32]

With the transition from *fabula* to *syuzhet*, all stories will struggle to some degree with coherence across events. This is because events (most especially real world events) do not have neat points of "beginning" and "end" and because the storyteller must configure these events together into one story. In general, there are two ways storytellers struggle with narrative coherence: the complexity of events comprising the *fabula* and the skillset of the writer to create the *syuzhet*. Any lack of coherence across events can create the appearance of a "seam" in the text. In John, as with other ancient texts, concern over seams and aporias is overblown. This is because when a critic starts with a seam, she can always pull it and prod it and poke it and hope something comes apart. It will because these seams are a natural part of the emplotment process. This is as true of ancient gospels as it is of modern novels, such as Thomas Hardy's *The Return of the Native* or Harper Lee's *To Kill a Mockingbird*.[33] In contrast, what is often ignored in the study of John (and other ancient texts) is how their event

---

32. I would argue this is the primary reason for the whole genre of "historical fiction."

33. See David Leon Higdon, *Time and English Fiction* (Totowa, NJ: Rowman &

structure creates meaningful coherence across a newly emplotted narrative world. Or, to put it another way, for all the seams and aporias and flaws and layers that John is thought to possess, readers have found a way to read a meaningful—and dynamic—narrative from its pages for two millennia.

We can explain this if we look at how a text is temporally determined across its event structure. Texts such as the Fourth Gospel use a variety of textual strategies to accomplish this temporal determination, one of which is *repeating anachronies*.[34] An anachrony is any occurrence in a text of anything "out of time"; a simple example of an anachrony is when a movie or novel starts *in media res* and then has a "flashback" to what went on before the attention-grabbing opening. While there are many types of anachronies, a repeating anachrony is essentially any reference from one event to another event within the same story. The reason these anachronies are so important is that they are traces of the emplotment process; they reveal that, as the narrator tells the story, links between events that do *not* exist in the *fabula* now crop up in the *syuzhet*. Coherent stories use these types of subtle coherence inducers to make meaningful stories. It is no surprise, then, that John's Gospel contains more repeating anachronies than seams.[35]

Because events that come from different places in time and space become configured within the same story, something strange happens when these events are read by later readers. Once they are set in place in the text, they create a new narrative temporality—the temporality of the *syuzhet*. This temporality may or may not reflect the original temporality of the *fabula*, but it does create a movement in time from the beginning to the end of the narrative. It is as though the narrator has taken the events needed to tell the story and strung them on a string. This "string" that connects the events within the narrative (but not the *fabula*) is the narrative's *temporal geodesic*. A geodesic is, for our purpose here, the shortest possible

---

Littlefield, 1977), 31, 37, and Patrick Chura, "Prolepsis and Anachronism: Emmet Till and the Historicity of *To Kill a Mockingbird*," *SLJ* 32 (2000): 1, respectively.

34. Other ways include the interrelationship of diegetic levels, one of several varieties of intratextual diachronics, and many of the other types of anachronies beside repeating anachronies.

35. Examples include John 1:7, 10, 14; 2:19; 3:26; 4:46, (54); 5:16, 33; 6:23, 51, 64, 71; 7:21, 23, 34, 39, 50; 8:21, 28; 9:15; 10:15, 17, 25, 40; 11:2, 4, 8, 11, 57; 12:1, 4, 7, 9, 17, 32–33; 13:1, 2, 11, 19, 21, 33, 34, 38; 14:19; 15:9, 18, 20, 24; 16:16, 20, 28, 32; 17:4; 18:9, 14, 20, 26, 32; 19:39; 20:8, 20, 31; 21:20.

line between two objects. It is the line on which the time of the story flows. However, geodesics do not always look like the shortest possible line to a reader.[36] For example, in the Gospel of John, the event of the miracle at Cana (John 2:1–11) precedes the cleansing of the temple (John 2:12–25). In order to create two edges to these events, the narrator tapers off the Cana story with an aside (John 2:11) and then uses a temporal marker ("after this") to mark off a new event where the reader learns that Jesus went with family to Capernaum to stay there a few days (2:12).[37] Once these events are put on the "string" of the *syuzhet*, the telling of the story draws them "tight" so that the reader will perceive one coherent story. This creates a temporal geodesic because some readers will not perceive this as the shortest distance between these two events; but the narrator does, and this is why he tells his story in this way.

There is a second and more important part that the geodesic plays in creating a beginning-to-end line of time and causality through a written text. Because of the inherently "flat" (nonsimultaneous) nature of written stories, all events in a story are on the geodesic.[38] However, readers are aware that narrated events do not feel flat; some seem to move rapidly and some seem to slow down (the "watch"). The simple truth is that narrators tell the stories they wish to tell, and they tell them how they wish to tell them. As a result, events that take a great deal of time to narrate tend to *warp* the time of the narrative "toward" those events, and events that are quickly narrated tend to *warp* the time of the narrative "away from" those events. For example, take any modern novel with a hero. Those events in which the hero storms castles, rescues heroines, and saves kingdoms are narrated in great detail. However, background events, especially those where the hero is not personally present (such as some battle fought by subordinate commanders for some strategic reason) are quickly summa-

---

36. A classic example of this is the route of an intercontinental airplane. On a two-dimenionsal map, it looks like the airplane is curving way out of its way; in actuality, the airplane is flying in the shortest possible line from airport to airport, as it must take into account the curvature of the earth.

37. After the summary in verse 12, the narrator uses the temporal descriptor "the Passover of the Jews was near" to create a sense of how (and when) the story will progress.

38. There is more complexity to this as weakly-told narratives can have orphaned events and other temporal problems that interfere with the overall coherence of the story.

rized.[39] Why? The reason is that the narrator uses his power over narrative time to warp the events of the story so that certain events pull the rest of the story toward it. This is often more significant with ancient narratives that do not contain any attempt to affix the events to an absolute chronology. Modern histories resist narrative warpage (generally speaking) because they use the science of chronology to keep their event structure in place. In the Fourth Gospel, certain "massive" events such as the crucifixion warp the rest of the other narrative events toward it. This is not just a function of the way time works in narrative. It is also good storytelling.

Narrators warp their narratives in much more subtle ways as well. For example, the temple cleansing event is in John's Gospel a well-demarcated event that uses a temporal marker ("after this," John 2:12) as the event's opening edge. However, in this same clause the narrator explains that Jesus "went down" to Capernaum. What the reader does not know—though critics often assume they know—is what it meant for Jesus to "go down" to Capernaum in the *fabula* of the story. To put it another way, because of the way narrative time works, readers naturally assume that Jesus went quickly and directly (if they think about it at all). Yet "went down" is an example of a *temporal process word*. A temporal process word is a linguistic description of time passing in a story without any clear indication of how long or what exactly occurred.[40] It is a subtle form of summarization. When a narrator uses a temporal process word in this way, the reader does not know (and can usually never discover) what all was involved in the process. Readers of the Fourth Gospel today, steeped as they are in the science of chronology, like to assume that they can calculate the time and distance of this journey (and plot it on a time line). However, they cannot, because there is simply no way to know what the narrator hides in time behind these words.

Another example of the way narrators play with time in narrative is through one of several kinds of *temporal value words*.[41] These words are similar to temporal process words in that, instead of indefinitely summarizing

39. Cf. Paul Ricoeur, *Time and Narrative*, trans. Kathleen McLaughlin and David Pellauer, 3 vols. (Chicago: University of Chicago Press, 1984–1988), 2:121.

40. For example, if I tell a story that includes, "last year I drove around Europe," there is no way to determine if that means I had a few days and saw a few sights or if I (more literally) spent a year hitting all the sights on the continent; in this case, "drove around" is a temporal process word.

41. For related examples and discussion, see Arthur C. Danto, *Narration and*

a movement in time, they indefinitely summarize an event. For example, in the temple cleansing event, the narrator explains that many believed in Jesus "during the feast of the Passover" (John 2:23). Here the word "feast" is a type of temporal value word in that it is one word that describes a whole series of smaller events and actions. While readers may assume they know what a "feast" entails (especially details like its duration), it may or may not be what John thinks it entails.[42] These types of words warp the narrative in the direction that the narrator wants all the while allowing the reader to coherently follow the story without getting lost in time.

Since narratives are finite, the times narrated within narratives are also finite. There are temporal limitations within narratives; thus, narrative is fundamentally *restricted*. A simple example of this is the restriction on narrating two events simultaneously (or perhaps, narrating two simultaneous events simultaneously). This is due to the temporal and spatial restrictions of a narrative world. However, the power of the narrator is so great that there are ways that some of these limitations can be breached or transcended. For example, in a narrative about a hero on a quest to slay an ancient dragon, the hero does not know and cannot know that this same dragon was secretly named "Marvin" by his dragon parents (yes, it is true). Yet, the narrator has the power to breach the restriction on the narrative world of the protagonist to tell the reader directly this information about the name of the dragon. This is not simply a narrator's intrusion; instead, it is an intrusion into the time and space of the hero's world that creates a whole new world of the narrator with its own parameters of space and time. There are now two narrative worlds: the world of the hero and the world of the narrator. This is the case even if this world is almost completely hidden from the reader (or if this world is very apparent, such as occurs in medieval frame narratives such as *Arabian Nights* and *Canterbury Tales*). When a narrative has more than one world, frame, or level of interaction, narratologists often refer to these narratives as having more than one *diegesis*.[43]

Knowledge: Including the Integral Text of Analytical Philosophy of History (New York: Columbia University Press, 1985), 233.

42. Historical critics may argue that they know exactly how long the Passover feast lasted. This is not in dispute. What historical critics cannot know is how long an ancient understood the Passover feast to last and which events it did and did not include.

43. These distinctions are rarely neat and this idea resists a simple definition; see

Turning to John's Gospel, readers can immediately note that there seems to be more than one diegesis at play (the famous Johannine asides are an easy giveaway).[44] In fact, the Fourth Gospel contains two primary diegeses: a *witness world* and an *epic world*. In the witness world, the indexical "now" of the story is set in a time of the events surrounding Jesus's life and death, but in the epic world, the indexical "now" of the story is set in a time after Jesus's life and death. For example, in the witness world, Jesus is misunderstood by his disciples (John 2:22; 8:27; 10:6; 12:16; and 20:9). But in the epic world, the disciples now understand (John 2:22; 12:16; 20:9) and can now grasp the point of Jesus's death and how it relates to the Jewish Scriptures. Each of these diegeses contains a "now" that they use to index what is known and not known in that time frame.[45] As with all great storytellers, the narrator of the Fourth Gospel has no plans to ruin his story by separating these things out (just as the narrator of the hero/dragon story would never tell the reader all of the dragon information and then the hero information or vice versa because it would ruin the story). Whenever a narrator intentionally conflates two or more narrative worlds, *metalepsis* occurs.[46] Reading a narrative with metalepsis is akin to going about the day wearing two watches, one with Pacific Time and one with Greenwich Time and assuming that interactions occur on Greenwich Time only to occasionally discover some occur on Pacific Time. While modern readers may try to separate out the most obvious occurrences of metalepsis in the Fourth Gospel (such as the narratorial asides), the temporal restrictions of each narrative world do not allow for such simple extraction. In order to tell a good story, the narrator fuses these two temporalities into one fixed and determined *syuzhet*. This use of metalepsis is what allows John to tell his story, as it were, while at the same time allowing the reader to feel as if John is recounting the story back to the reader. John weaves its two "nows" to create a more temporally dynamic and meaningful story.

---

for example, William Nelles, *Frameworks: Narrative Levels and Embedded Narrative*, AUS 19/33 (New York: Lang, 1997), 1.

44. See also the essay on "Audience" by Edward W. Klink III in this volume.

45. A narrative's indexical "now" is similar to what theorists call a temporal point of view.

46. See for example, David Herman, "Toward a Formal Description of Narrative Metalepsis," *JLS* 26 (1997): 132.

CONCLUSION

To borrow a spatial metaphor, "under" every story there is a movement in time. This movement in time is what allows a storyteller to create and tell a story. However, this movement is rarely simple or straightforward; often the more interesting the story is, the more twists and turns the story takes. These twists and turns are not just in the plot but are in the very temporal mechanics of the story itself. In our modern era after the discovery of the science of chronology, readers are accustomed to stories that claim to originate with real world events that can be plotted on an absolute time line. Modern readers can accept a biography of Ronald Reagan, which begins with his near assassination (*in media res*) and then goes back to his childhood, through his Hollywood years, and into his years as a United States president and beyond. Modern readers would not readily accept a biography where events in Hollywood were interspersed without exact dates with events in the White House (though possibly this could make for a more powerful story if the storyteller were trying to trace one thread of his life). In comparison, the Gospel of John tells a story of the life of Jesus using a premodern temporal configuration without the benefit (or encumbrance) of an absolute timeline. Without a "calendar" or a "watch" to measure time, the Fourth Gospel does what other premodern narratives do: it tells its story in the way that seems best to convey the truth of the story to its readers. John may seem "out of time" to modern readers, but this is only because John is "in time" with itself.

4

Space

Susanne Luther

Space in the Gospel of John denotes narrative space, which is all the topographical and topological information given in the text that serves to create the setting for the narrative action as well as a narrative world in the reader's mind.[1] Narrative space can be created through reference to geographical spaces like "Jerusalem" or "Galilee"; through the naming of concrete spaces like "synagogue," "praetorium," or "Jacob's well"; or through descriptive ("inside," "outside") or deictic ("here," "there") expressions. However, only fragments of the narrated world are provided through the words of the narrator and the characters of the story. The reader has to complete the gaps, or "empty spaces," in the information given in order to create a comprehensive narrated world.[2] Moreover, narrative space refers not only to spatial dimensions and relationships within the narrative but also to semantics of space, such as the metaphorical creation of space or embedding of "distant, inaccessible, hypothetical, or counterfactual locations"[3] (like utopian or nonlocatable space in dreams, memories, or

---

1. See Bärbel Bosenius, *Der literarische Raum des Markusevangeliums*, WMANT 140 (Neukirchen-Vluyn: Neukirchener Verlag, 2014), 3.

2. See Matias Martínez and Michael Scheffel, *Einführung in die Erzähltheorie*, 9th ed. (Munich: Beck, 2012), 123–24. The world narrated in the text is not necessarily the world in which Jesus lived, but rather the world in which the author lived. See the distinction between fabula-space and story-space: "The fabula-space would be a (theoretically) complete depiction of the location(s) of a narrative, while the story-space is the actual space as the text presents it to us" (Irene J. F. de Jong, "Narratological Theory on Space," in *Space in Ancient Greek Literature: Studies in Ancient Greek Narrative*, ed. Irene J. F. de Jong, MnSup 339 [Leiden: Brill, 2012], 2–3).

3. De Jong, "Narratological Theory on Space," 4.

prophecies) into the narrated world.[4] However, even "logically impossible story spaces" must be compatible in some way with the reader's real-world knowledge; they "cannot be wholly inconsistent, for fear of preventing any kind of mental representation—for fear, in other words, of losing its spatial quality"; even with regard to counterfactual locations,[5] readers must be able to "draw on their normal experience of space in some regions of the narrative world, despite its topological heterogeneity."[6]

Based on this understanding of narrative space, this chapter will present a broad spectrum of approaches to the interpretation of space in the Gospel of John so that readers can gain new perspectives on how space works in the gospel. From the nineteenth century novel forward, critics have noted the importance of space in the creation of narrative. While John is an ancient narrative, it nonetheless demonstrates a wide variety of forms of spatial presentation and spatial functionality that modern theories on space can illuminate.[7]

THE BACKGROUND OF THE NARRATIVE DYNAMIC IN THE GOSPEL OF JOHN

Literary Space in Ancient Narrative and Modern Narrative Theory

Marie-Laure Ryan distinguishes between five categories of narrative space: (1) "spatial frames": the locations where the narrative discourse is situated; applied to the Gospel of John, this would be actual places where the Jesus-narrative is located (village, town, house, synagogue, temple,

4. Cf. Ruth Ronen, "Space in Fiction," *Poetics Today* 7 (1986): 421–38, for the distinction between "setting" and "frames."

5. For the discussion of counterfactual space, see, e.g., Gilles Fauconnier, *Mental Spaces: Aspects of Meaning Construction in Natural Language* (Cambridge, MA: MIT Press, 1985; repr., Cambridge: Cambridge University Press, 1994), 109–27; Barbara Piatti and Lorenz Hurni, "Mapping the Ontologically Unreal: Counterfactual Spaces in Literature and Cartography," *The Cartographic Journal* 46 (2009): 333–42; but cf. Lubomír Doležel, *Possible Worlds of Fiction and History* (Baltimore: John Hopkins University Press, 2010).

6. Quotations from Marie-Laure Ryan, "Space," in *Handbook of Narratology*, ed. Peter Hüh net et al., 2nd ed., 2 vols. (Berlin: de Gruyter, 2014), 2:807.

7. See Alex C. Purves, *Space and Time in Ancient Greek Narrative* (Cambridge: Cambridge University Press, 2010); Irene J. F. de Jong, ed., *Space in Ancient Greek Literature: Studies in Ancient Greek Narrative*, MnSup 339 (Leiden: Brill, 2012).

mountain, etc.); (2) "setting": the social, historical, and geographical aspects of the environment in which the plot is set; for John this would be the eastern Roman Mediterranean world of the early first century CE; (3) "story space": denotes all the locations mentioned or referred to in the plot; in John this would include the house where the official's son lay ill (4:43–54), which is not actually part of the plot; (4) the "narrative (or story) world": consists of "the story space completed by the reader's imagination on the basis of cultural knowledge and real world experience"; in John the reader would have to complete the story space with all those places and buildings not mentioned during Jesus's travels in Galilee and Jerusalem and between those two poles;[8] (5) the "narrative universe": includes "all the counterfactual worlds constructed by characters as belief, wishes, fears, speculations, hypothetical thinking, dreams, and fantasies"; for John this would include not only the places mentioned in Palestine, but also the nonlocatable space of heaven (3:3), preexistence (1:1–2), and the "father's house" (14:2).[9] These different levels are disclosed to the reader successively while reading the text. Ryan terms this "dynamic presentation of spatial information the *textualization* of space.... This textualization becomes a *narrativization* when space is not described for its own sake, as it would be in a tourist guide, but becomes the setting of an action that develops in time."[10]

Space is a basic element of narrative. It may be employed first of all in an ornamental way to create the setting or increase the reality effect of a narrative.[11] However, the use of the category of space in narrative can serve a number of additional functions. Space can attain a thematic function, as in travel narratives, or play a role in mirroring motifs of the

---

8. See Ryan, "Space," 2:804: "A mental map does not have to be nearly as consistent as a graphic map in its representation of spatial relations. While some locations need to be precisely situated with respect to each other because they are the stage of events that involve space in a strategic way, others may occupy free-floating positions in the reader's mind. In many cases, readers will be able to understand stories with only a rudimentary representation of their global geography, because ... space in narrative usually serves as a background for characters and their actions, and not as a focus of interest."

9. For these categories, see ibid., 2:797–99; all quotations from 2:798.

10. Ibid., 2:799.

11. See Roland Barthes, "Introduction à l'analyse structurale du récit," *Communications* 8 (1966): 1–27 ; and Barthes, "L'effet de reel," *Communications* 11 (1968): 84–89.

narrative. It may acquire a symbolic function, as when semantic oppositions are linked with ideological or cultural values or when literary topoi
like the *locus amoenus* in ancient literature are employed.[12] Space may
also be ascribed a characterizing or psychologizing function.[13]

Every narrative text can be analyzed on two levels. Seymour Chatman
called them story ("what") and discourse ("how").[14] According to these
categories, any narrated world can be analyzed by considering its *contents*
as well as the *literary strategies* and *narrative techniques* used to create it.
With a focus on space, the former addresses questions like: Which literary
spaces are created in the narrative? How do they relate to real places? How
do the characters move within these narrative spaces? Which expansion
of narrative space can be detected? The latter focuses on issues like: How
are narrative spaces described and created? Can a development or change
of narrative space be detected? Alongside the text-immanent references to
narrative space, the referentiality to the real world is important, especially
if the gospel is understood in terms of narrative historiography.[15]

The Spatial Turn and Modern Narrative Theory

The category of space has long been neglected in narratology and gained in
importance only in the late twentieth century. The "spatial turn" describes a
turn in humanities and social sciences since the 1980s toward an enhanced
awareness of spatial aspects and a paradigm shift concerning methods and

---

12. The *locus amoenus* is a literary topos that describes an idealized natural setting of safety and comfort; the topos can already be found in Homer and has been
employed in literary landscape descriptions, especially in bucolic literature, ever since;
its counterpart is called *locus terribilis*. In Christian contexts the *locus amoenus* is often
associated with the Garden of Eden; see the motif of the garden in John 18:1, 26; 19:41.
For this motif in Josephus, see Luuk Huitink and Jan W. van Henten, "Josephus," in de
Jong, *Space in Ancient Greek Literature*, 205–6.

13. For these functions in ancient literature, see de Jong, "Narratological Theory
on Space," 13–16, as well as the thematic contributions in de Jong, *Space in Ancient
Greek Literature*.

14. Applied to literary space, Seymour Chatman speaks of "story space" and "discourse space" in analogy to "story time" and "discourse time"; see *Story and Discourse:
Narrative Structure in Fiction and Film* (Ithaca, NY: Cornell University Press, 1978),
96–107.

15. Ryan speaks of "space that serves as context and container of the text" (Ryan,
"Space," 2:800).

the leading questions of spatial concepts.[16] With a view to theoretical conceptualizations of the cultural, social, and medial establishment of space, two different paradigms can be distinguished: the *topographical turn*, with an emphasis on technical and cultural forms of representation of space, and the *topological turn*, with a specific interest in the phenomenological perspective, that is, in the description of spatial relations concerning cultural and medial aspects.[17] Hence, modern literary theory emphasizes the category of space, especially literary space, that is, of social and constructed space in literature. Two classical theories will be presented here concerning the space-time paradigm and the semantic topological approach.

From the perspective of structuralism and cultural semiotics, Juri M. Lotman developed a model that perceives topology as a metalanguage to describe cultural, ethical, or political relations.[18] He observes that narrative spatial oppositions infer nonspatial meaning. For example, "top versus bottom" may be interpreted to mean "good versus evil." These connotations are culturally and historically determined signs, which charge space with metaphorical meaning: "The most general social, religious, political, and ethical models of the world, with whose help man comprehends the world around him at various stages in his spiritual development, are invariably invested with spatial characteristics—sometimes in the form of oppositions such as 'heaven vs. earth' or 'earth vs. the nether regions.'"[19] Lotman analyzes fixed spaces as well as movement in space and stresses

---

16. See Edward W. Soja, *Postmodern Geographies: The Reassertion of Space in Critical Social Theory* (New York: Verso, 1989); Jörg Döring and Tristan Thielmann, "Einleitung: Was lesen wir im Raume? Der Spatial Turn und das geheime Wissen der Geographen," in *Spatial Turn: Das Raumparadigma in den Kultur- und Sozialwissenschaften*, ed. Jörg Döring and Tristan Thielmann (Bielefeld: transcript, 2008), 7–45; Stephan Günzel, "Spatial Turn—Topographical Turn—Topological Turn: Über die Unterschiede zwischen Raumparadigmen," in Döring and Thielmann, *Spatial Turn*, 220–37; John Corrigan, "Spatiality and Religion," in *The Spatial Turn: Interdisciplinary Perspectives*, ed. Barney Warf and Santa Arias (London: Routledge, 2009), 157–72, who names among religious categories of space: invisible worlds, pilgrimage, ritual, body, religious practice, time, and memory.

17. See Katrin Dennerlein, *Narratologie des Raumes*, Narratologia 22 (Berlin: de Gruyter, 2009), 6–7.

18. Juri M. Lotman, "O semiosfere," *Sign Systems Studies* 17 (1984): 5–23.

19. Juri M. Lotman, *The Structure of the Artistic Text*, Michigan Slavic Contributions 7 (Ann Arbor: University of Michigan Press, 1977), 218. See also Sylvia Sasse, "Poetischer Raum: Chronotopos und Geopoetik," in *Raum: Ein interdisziplinäres Handbuch*, ed. Stephan Günzel (Stuttgart: Metzler, 2010), 301–4.

the semantics of spatial expressions, the implied meaning within the narrative structure. Within this semantic framework boundaries are also important, since "boundary divides the entire space of the text into two mutually non-intersecting subspaces. Its basic property is impenetrability. The way in which the boundary divides the text is one of its essential characteristics. This division can be between insiders and outsiders, between the living and the dead, between rich and poor."[20] Lotman proposes that a narrative event occurs when a character in a narrative crosses such an impenetrable boundary between symbolically charged spaces, which results in an infringement and transformation of the rules and thus of the structure of the literary space.

Going back to the thought of Gotthold Ephraim Lessing and Ernst Cassirer on space in literature,[21] Mikhail Bakhtin's model of the *chronotope* provides a helpful way to understand the close link between space and time in narrative. He defines chronotope as

> the intrinsic connectedness of temporal and spatial relationships that are artistically expressed in literature.... In the literary artistic chronotope, spatial and temporal indicators are fused into one carefully thought-out, concrete whole. Time, as it were, thickens, takes on flesh, becomes artistically visible; likewise, space becomes charged and responsive to the movements of time, plot and history. This intersection of axes and fusion of indicators characterizes the artistic chronotope.[22]

Bakhtin employs the chronotope in order to analyze the interplay and emphasis of plot-components or motifs, space, and adventure-time in the ancient novelistic narrative. Hence through the materialization of time in space, the chronotope constitutes the precondition for a scenic development

20. Lotman, *Structure of the Artistic Text*, 229–30.

21. See Gotthold Ephraim Lessing, "Laokoon oder Über die Grenzen der Malerei und Poesie [1766]," in *Werke* (Munich: Hanser, 1974), 6:7–187; Ernst Cassirer, "Mythischer, ästhetischer und theoretischer Raum [1931]," in *Symbol, Technik, Sprache: Aufsätze aus den Jahren 1927–1933*, ed. Ernst Wolfgang Orth and John Michael Krois (Hamburg: Meiner, 1985), 93–119.

22. Mikhail M. Bakhtin, "Forms of Time and of the Chronotope in the Novel: Notes towards a Historical Poetics," in *The Dialogic Imagination: Four Essays*, ed. Michael Holquist, trans. Caryl Emerson and Michael Holquist (Austin: University of Texas Press, 1981), 84. For an application to John, see Zbynek Garský, *Das Wirken Jesu in Galiläa bei Johannes: Eine strukturale Analyse der Intertextualität des vierten Evangeliums mit den Synoptikern*, WUNT 2/325 (Tübingen: Mohr Siebeck, 2012), 152–54.

of the plot; at the same time empty, formless space is ascribed meaning and dimension through the chronotopic relation with time.[23] Bakhtin distinguishes between the real chronotope—the spatial-chronological structure of the human worldview—and the literary chronotope, which is the artistic reflection and representation of the real chronotope in literature. He goes so far as to claim that "every entry into the sphere of meaning is accomplished only through the gates of the chronotope."[24]

Bakhtin and Lotman take into account the fact that, on the one hand, the reader is confronted with a cultural construction of reality through narrative space; and, on the other hand, both authors increase the reader's awareness of the different levels to read and interpret space in narrative.[25] Modern theory of space may be applied to ancient texts, as antiquity narrative spaces and places were also employed as "dynamic and multi-layered social constructs whose possible meanings [were] created and negotiated in a variety of ways."[26] These constructs have to be analyzed in order to conceive the cultural values and forms of discourse and power encoded in ancient texts through textual strategies. In what follows, I will demonstrate how the Fourth Gospel makes use of a variety of different aspects concerning literary space and highlight how these interact in the narrative text to influence our reading and our creation of meaning in the text.

ASPECTS OF NARRATIVE SPACE AND THE NARRATIVE DYNAMIC IN THE FOURTH GOSPEL

Scenic Space: The Horizontal Expansion of Space in the Narrated World

Description is the technique most often employed to present space. Description can visualize the narrative world through "object or character movement…; characters' perceptions…; narrativized descriptions…; and

---

23. See Michael C. Frank and Kirsten Mahlke, "Nachwort," to Mikhail M. Bakhtin, *Chronotopos*, trans. Michael Dewey (Frankfurt am Main: Suhrkamp, 2011), 206.

24. Bakhtin, "Forms of Time," 258.

25. For a chart of chronological and topographical information in John, see Garský, *Wirken Jesu*, 309–11.

26. See Kate Gilhuly and Nancy Worman, "Introduction," in *Space, Place, and Landscape in Ancient Greek Literature and Culture*, ed. Kate Gilhuly and Nancy Worman (Cambridge: Cambridge University Press, 2014), 1–2; for the ancient Greek terminology on space, see p. 4.

implications from reports of events."[27] The Gospel of John provides many concrete topographical references, but detailed descriptions (*ekphrasis*) of these places, as we often find them with ancient historians, are in most cases withheld.[28] A precise knowledge of places where historical events took place was required when writing ancient historiography.[29] Studies on the places mentioned in John have concluded that John's geographical references are accurate and reliable and that he must have been familiar with the places where the episodes of his narrative are located.[30] Although John includes roughly the same number of topographical references as the Synoptics, he provides several unique references to specific places.[31] More-over, John frequently uses exact measurements to specify the dimensions of space (e.g., John 6:17–19; 11:18; 21:8–9).[32]

Richard Bauckham reads the precise topographical information of John's Gospel as "largely independent of Synoptic tradition" and as a characteristic indicator for John's claim to write historiography, as "all events in John's Gospel are located, and most are located quite precisely—in a named town, village, or even more specifically. They are placed not just in Galilee, but in Cana or Capernaum; not just in Jerusalem but at the pool of Bethesda near the Sheep Gate; not just in the temple but even in Solomon's

27. Ryan, "Space," 2:803.

28. For detailed descriptions of places (versus a scarce use of spatial detail) in historiographical accounts, see Tim Rood, "Herodotus," in de Jong, *Space in Ancient Greek Literature*, 121–40; Rood, "Polybius," in de Jong, *Space in Ancient Greek Literature*, 179–97; Rood, "Thucydides," in de Jong, *Space in Ancient Greek Literature*, 141–59; and Rood, "Xenophon," in de Jong, *Space in Ancient Greek Literature*, 161–78.

29. See Richard Bauckham, "Historiographical Characteristics of the Gospel of John," in *The Testimony of the Beloved Disciple: Narrative, History, and Theology in the Gospel of John* (Grand Rapids: Baker, 2007), 95–96.

30. See Craig R. Koester, "Topography and Theology in the Gospel of John," in *Fortunate the Eyes That See: Essays in Honor of David Noel Freedman in Celebration of His Seventieth Birthday*, ed. Astrid B. Beck et al. (Grand Rapids: Eerdmans, 1995), 436; Ingo Broer, "Knowledge of Palestine in the Fourth Gospel?" in *Jesus in Johannine Tradition*, ed. Robert T. Fortna and Tom Thatcher (Louisville: Westminster John Knox, 2011), 83–90.

31. Places mentioned in the total: Matt: 35, Mark: 30, Luke: 30, John: 31. Places unique to this gospel: Matt: 8, Mark: 2, Luke: 5, John: 17. See further Bauckham, "Historiographical Characteristics," 98.

32. See Paul N. Anderson, "Aspects of Historicity in the Gospel of John: Implications for Investigations of Jesus and Archaeology," in *Jesus and Archaeology*, ed. James H. Charlesworth (Grand Rapids: Eerdmans, 2006), 604.

Portico."[33] Although there are exceptions to this rule (see 6:1–3; 21:1), the narrative locates Jesus very precisely in specific places, in contrast to the Synoptics in which references like "a certain village"[34] (Luke 10:38) or to an unspecified house (Mark 2:1–12) or synagogue (Matt 12:9–14) are common.[35]

John's narrative account of the history of Jesus advances a claim to be perceived as factual with a decided claim to historical referentiality. Through historical referentiality, that is, through topographic and chronological references, personal names, and other references to the historical past, the narrative is directly linked with ancient history. Especially extratextual spatial references serve to root John's accounts firmly within ancient history and geography. Yet the narrator also introduces spatial references and spatial information, which do not play any direct role within the plot but primarily serve to create a "reality effect" that is intended to authenticate the narrative and to root it in historical reality (see the description of the soldiers in John 18:3).[36] Hence, even references to historical places in John's Gospel may exist in order to serve a special purpose within the narrative dynamics: to create meaning and construct a text-internal geography.

If we take the claim to historical reference in John's account seriously, it leads to the conclusion that the Fourth Gospel should be read as a historiographical account. This in turn has consequences for the perception of John's narrative as a historical source. In order to stress the adequacy of including John amongst the sources used for historical Jesus research,[37] scholars have, over the last decade, increasingly stressed the accuracy and reliability of the Johannine topographical information and have attempted to identify the places mentioned in the literary context with the help of archaeological excavations.[38] There are, however, refer-

---

33. Bauckham, "Historiographical Characteristics," 99.
34. Unless otherwise stated, all translations of biblical texts are my own.
35. Bauckham, "Historiographical Characteristics," 99.
36. See also the essay on "Point of View" by James L. Resseguie in this volume.
37. See Anderson, "Aspects of Historicity," 614–18; Paul N. Anderson, Felix Just, and Tom Thatcher, eds., *John, Jesus, and History, Volume 1: Critical Appraisals of Critical Views*, SymS 44 (Atlanta: Society of Biblical Literature, 2007); Anderson, Just, Thatcher, eds., *John, Jesus, and History, Volume 2: Aspects of Historicity in the Fourth Gospel*, ECL 2 (Atlanta: Society of Biblical Literature, 2009).
38. The places taken into archaeological focus are Bethany beyond Jordan (1:28; 10:40), Bethsaida (1:44), Cana in Galilee (2:1, 11; 4:46–54; 21:2), Capernaum (2:12;

ences that are not precisely located, like the house where the wedding of
Cana took place or the house where Mary, Martha, and Lazarus lived, as
well as places that some argue are fictive.[39] Though the historicity of the
topographical references is assumed within the context of the Johannine
narrative account, they also invite an interpretation from the perspective
of theological symbolism.[40]

Movement in Space: The Horizontal and the Vertical Axis

Jesus's movement in space can first and foremost be localized in his travels around Palestine and up to Jerusalem. John reports three visits to the
holy city, for Passover (2:13), for "a feast of the Jews" (5:1), and for the
feast of Succoth (7:2), followed by a fourth, and final, journey to the city
(12:12–19). In addition to detailed reference of place names in connection with Jesus's travels, John uses spatial aspects of verbs that indicate
the direction of movement, such as *anabainō*, to "go up" to Jerusalem
(2:13; 5:1; 7:8, 10; 11:55; 12:20) or to the temple (7:14), or *katabainō*, to
"descend" to Capernaum (2:12; 4:47, 49). These highlight the geographical situation and elevation of Israel.[41] For Jesus's final journey to Jerusalem, the Evangelist replaces his regular use of *anabainō*, "go up," with
erchomai, "come" (11:56; 12:12), thus indicating a new perspective from
which the movement is perceived.[42] Besides this horizontal movement in

4:46; 6:17, 24), the harbour (6:24–25) and the synagogue (6:59), the area of the cleansing of the temple (2:13–16), Aenon near Salim (3:23), Sychar (4:5), Jacob's Well (4:4–6),
Mount Gerizim (4:20), the Sheep Pool/Gate (5:2), the Pool of Bethesda (5:2), Tiberias
(6:1, 23; 21:1), the Pool of Siloam (9:1–9), Bethany near Jerusalem (11:1–17; 12:1–11),
Ephraim (11:54), the Kidron (18:1), the praetorium (18:28, 33; 19:9), the Lithostrotos
(19:13), Golgotha (19:17–18, 20, 41), and a tomb in the garden (19:41–42). See Urban
C. von Wahlde, "Archaeology and John's Gospel," in *Jesus and Archaeology*, ed. James
H. Charlesworth (Grand Rapids: Eerdmans, 2006), 526–27 and passim.

39. See further Norbert Krieger, "Fiktive Orte der Johannes-Taufe," *ZNW* 45
(1954): 121–23.

40. See below. See similarly Bauckham, "Historiographical Characteristics," 97;
Craig R. Koester, *Symbolism in the Fourth Gospel: Meaning, Mystery, Community*, 2nd
ed. (Minneapolis: Fortress, 2003), 309–11. For a symbolic interpretation of space in
ancient literature, particularly in epic, historiography and ancient novel, see the contributions in de Jong, *Space in Ancient Greek Literature*.

41. See Anderson, "Aspects of Historicity," 604–05.

42. See Thomas L. Brodie, *The Gospel according to John: A Literary and Theological
Commentary* (Oxford: Oxford University Press, 1993), 27.

space, the vertical axis is prevalent in the gospel. Jesus's being sent into the world (1:14) and ascending to the Father (16:28) or the opposition of "from above" and "from below" (8:23) constitute part of the inherent structure of the text. The Farewell Discourse focuses on the translocation of Jesus from one sphere to another (see 13:33, 36; 14:4, 5, 28).[43]

A symbolic interpretation of movement in space has focused on the ways in which advances in understanding and faith are mirrored through spatial metaphors.[44] In John 20:1–18, the spatial movement of Mary Magdalene and the Beloved Disciple within the vicinity of the empty tomb can be interpreted as echoing their thought processes; hence, the movement in space as described in the scene seems to reflect the characters' inner movement and processes of theological cognition. At the same time, the discourses embedded within the narrative address the destination of Jesus's path of life in spatial metaphors (20:17). The story opens with Mary Magdalene going to the tomb in search for the dead (20:1–2). The prevailing darkness symbolizes the absence of Jesus as well as ignorance and misunderstanding apart from the insight brought about by the Easter experience.[45] The following movement initiated by Peter and the Beloved Disciple approaching the tomb (20:3–10) parallels their growing understanding of the Easter event. Then the focus of the narrative turns back to Mary Magdalene (20:11–18), describing her movement into the grave to look for the dead (20:11) and then gradually outwards (20:14, 16) to meet and recognize the risen Jesus. When she finally turns away from the tomb (20:18) in order to bear witness to Jesus's resurrection, the nature of her movement is different from her first flight from the tomb (20:2), just as the first glance into the empty tomb is different from Mary's final recognition of its meaning. The narrative recognition and movement are mutually dependent and maintain a focus, which turns from the locus of Jesus's tomb to the resurrected Christ. The pace of the narrated movement in space dictates both the pace of the narrative and of the disciples' as well

---

43. See Fernando F. Segovia, "The Journey(s) of the Word of God: A Reading of the Plot of the Fourth Gospel," *Semeia* 53 (1991): 23–54; Kristina Dronsch, "Der Raum des Geistes: Die topographische Struktur der Rede vom Geist im Johannesevangelium," *ZNT* 13 (2010): 39.

44. For this approach, see Andrea Taschl-Erber, "Erkenntnisschritte und Glaubenswege in Joh 20,1–11: Die narrative Metaphorik des Raumes," *Protokolle zur Bibel* 15 (2006): 93–117.

45. See ibid., 95.

as the reader's understanding. Whereas the disciples are characterized by a searching movement to and from the tomb, Jesus and the angels are pictured as static. The center around which the narrative evolves is the question of the location of Jesus: Mary searches for the body (20:2, 13, 15); the positions of the angels symbolize the empty space where the body is not to be found (20:12); even when Mary recognizes him, he insists on a spatial distance (20:17); only her dialogue with Jesus indicates his destination and provenance (20:17).[46]

Distanced Space: Extrascenic, Nonlocatable and Empty Space

Extrascenic and Nonlocatable space: While the Fourth Gospel frequently makes reference to extrascenic space, such as in the story of the healing at a distance (John 4:46–54), the locations mentioned in the Johannine parabolic passages present nonlocatable space (10:1–10; 12:24). In the context of the Farewell Discourses, nonlocatable space refers to Jesus's provenance and destination: "In my Father's house there are many dwelling-places" (14:2–4).[47] This space is located beyond the narrative space of the gospel and is withdrawn from the direct access of the characters (13:33). Yet it belongs to the gospel's narrative universe as it is part of the theological and eschatological implications of the text.[48] Through semantization John transforms a real-world location, the temple, into an other-worldly space, the Father's house (cf. John 2:16).[49] This is apparent in Thomas's question and Jesus's reply: "'Lord, we do not know where you are going. How can we know the way?' Jesus answered, 'I am the way, and the truth, and the life. No one comes to the Father except through me'" (14:4–6). Jesus's

---

46. See ibid., 113–17.

47. See John 1:1–2, 14. For the interpretation of this space as temple, see James M. McCaffrey, *The House with Many Rooms: The Temple Theme in Jn. 14,2–3*, AnBib 114 (Rome: Pontifical Institute, 1988), 67–70. Robert H. Gundry, "In My Father's House Are Many Μοναί (John 14,2)," *ZNW* 58 (1967): 70, reads this space in as spiritual. Jerome H. Neyrey, "Spaces and Places, Whence and Whither, Homes and Rooms: 'Territoriality' in the Fourth Gospel," *BTB* 32 (2002): 60–74, associates "ample residence, and insider status," but also indicates that "it is a social, but not necessarily a spatial metaphor" (66).

48. See the categories of Marie-Laure Ryan above.

49. See Martin Pöttner, "'Im Haus meines Vaters gibt es viele Aufenthaltsorte...': Erwägungen zur räumlichen Symbolik des johanneischen Sprechens in Joh 13,33–14,7," *MARG* 14 (1999): 145.

self-designation in this context is a spatial reference: his being sent into the world from a withdrawn space and his ascending into this very same space (16:28) allows him to overcome the void in space, to bridge the gap between the disciples and the father, between the world and the other-worldly space.[50]

Empty Space: In connection with the main character, Jesus, the gospel emphasizes empty space, particularly in the image of the empty tomb with the missing body of Jesus and the description of the two angels guarding the tomb; by sitting where his head and his feet had been, the angels mark the place where Jesus's body had been laid.[51] While Jesus's ascension to the Father leaves an empty space in a metaphorical way, his resurrection leaves an empty space where his dead body previously had been lying. The narrative employs two angels to mark this empty space in the sepulchre, which can possibly be read as a reference to the aniconic worship in the Jerusalem temple.[52] Just as the most sacred Jewish space, the holy of holies, marked an "empty space" for the absence of an image of God because of the prohibition on making graven images, so may the empty space in the tomb symbolize sacred space with regard to its testimony to the resurrection and divinity of Jesus.

Crossing Borders: Outside-Inside Oppositions in the Passion Narrative

The author's play with spatial oppositions can be observed in the scene of Jesus before Pilate. The following structure has been suggested:[53]

---

50. Another, closely related aspect is the "in-dwelling" of the Spirit in the Son (John 1:33), of the Father in the Son (John 14:10), and of the Spirit or Jesus in the disciples (John 14:17; 15:7). These are spatial metaphors that imply an immanence and relationship (cf. 14:20). Cf. Raymond E. Brown, *The Gospel according to John*, 2 vols., AB 29–29A (Garden City, NY: Doubleday, 1966–1970), 1:510–12; Neyrey, "Spaces and Places," 76–78; Mary L. Coloe, *God Dwells in Us: Temple Symbolism in the Fourth Gospel* (Collegeville, MN: Liturgical Press, 2001).

51. See Taschl-Erber, "Erkenntnisschritte und Glaubenswege," 102.

52. Andrew T. Lincoln, *The Gospel according to Saint John*, BNTC (Peabody, MA: Hendrickson, 2005), 492, refers to the "two cherubim positioned to face each other at the two ends of the mercy seat on the ark of the covenant."

53. For this approach, see Ruben Zimmermann, "'Deuten' heißt erzählen und übertragen: Narrativität und Metaphorik als zentrale Sprachformen historischer Sinnbildung zum Tod Jesu," in *Deutungen des Todes Jesu im Neuen Testament*, ed. Jörg Frey and Jens Schröter, 2nd ed., WUNT 181 (Tübingen: Mohr Siebeck, 2012), 341;

Scene	Topic	Space	Interlocutors
Introduction, part 1: 18:28	Jesus is taken to Pilate	(outside)	
Scene 1: 18:29–32	Opening of the trial against Jesus	outside	Pilate–Jews (–Jesus)
Scene 2: 18:33–38a	First conversation	inside	Pilate–Jesus
Scene 3: 18:38b–40	First statement of innocence	outside	Pilate–Jews
Introduction, part 2: 19:1–3	Proclamation as "king"/ flagellation	(inside?)	(soldiers)
Scene 4: 19:4–8	Second statement of innocence	outside	Pilate–Jews (–Jesus)
Scene 5: 19:9–11	Second conversation	inside	Pilate–Jesus
Scene 6: 19:12	Verdict	outside?	Pilate–Jews
Final Scene: 19:13–15	Pilate delivers Jesus to the Jews	Gabbatha	Pilate–Jews–Jesus

The "drama" of the trial before Pilate is characterized by movement between two stages,[54] inside the praetorium and outside (18:29, 33, 38b; 19:4, 9, 13). John 18:28–19:15 is structured in two parallel parts,[55] each starting with a short introduction (18:28; 19:1–3) followed by three short scenes. In the first and fourth, all protagonists are assembled in front of the praetorium (18:29–32; 19:4–8). Though the spatial dimension is not explicitly mentioned in 19:1–3, the action on the inner stage can be derived from 19:4.

---

see also Ludger Schenke, *Johannes: Kommentar* (Düsseldorf: Patmos, 1998), 345–56, and Uta Poplutz, "Das Drama der Passion: Eine Analyse der Prozesserzählung Joh 18,28–19,16a unter Berücksichtigung dramentheorethischer Gesichtspunkte," in *The Death of Jesus in the Fourth Gospel*, ed. Gilbert Van Belle, BETL 200 (Leuven: Leuven University Press, 2007), 772.

54. Or "Zwei-Bühnen-Technik" according to Ernst Haenchen, *Das Johannesevangelium: Ein Kommentar* (Tübingen: Mohr Siebeck, 1980), 544.

55. For the structure, see Zimmermann, "Deuten," 341–42; see also Schenke, *Johannes*, 349–50; Dirk F. Gniesmer, *In den Prozeß verwickelt: Erzähltextanalytische und textpragmatische Erwägungen zur Erzählung vom Prozeß Jesu vor Pilatus (Joh 18,28–19,16a.b.)*, EHS 23/688 (Frankfurt am Main: Lang, 2000), 433–36.

In John 19:8, reference is made to verse 7, which indicates that verse 8 is probably to be situated outside the praetorium. The next scene in each of the two parts is located inside the praetorium (scene 2: 18:33–38a; scene 5: 19:9–11) and presents a conversation between Pilate and Jesus. The third pair of scenes shows Pilate once again exiting the official residence in order to offer Jesus's release (scene 3: 18:38b–40; scene 6: 19:12). John 19:12 is problematic, as there is no detailed information concerning the location; Pilate is pictured inside the building in verses 9–11 but hears the shouts of the Jews in verse 12. The Jews' reply presupposes Pilate's attempt to release Jesus and his contact with the Jews, who refused to enter the praetorium for purity reasons (18:28). However, he might also have heard their voices from inside and be prompted to take Jesus outside (19:13).[56] The drama concludes with a final scene with very detailed spatial information (John 19:13). From the perspective of ancient drama theory,[57] the alternating between the two stages suggests that parts of the conversation were not public, and yet the central aspects of Pilate's conversation with Jesus are reported to the Jews. The plot is not primarily moved forward by the narrator but rather by the characters' speech acts. This can be seen, for example, in Pilate's words: "I am bringing him out to you to let you know that I find no basis for a charge against him" (John 19:4). By uttering those words, Pilate moves the action forward and initiates a change in the characters' location on the stage.[58]

Applying Lotman's theory, semantics of space in the Johannine account of Jesus's trial before Pilate are charged with meaning. The spatial categories of "inside" and "outside" (of Pilate's official residence) connote the opposition of "unclean" and "clean." Similar meaning is expressed with dichotomies like "Jewish" and "Roman," "king (of the Jews)" and "(Roman) emperor," "Jewish law" and "Roman law," "man" and "Son of

---

56. See Poplutz, "Drama," 770–71.

57. See Jo-Ann A. Brant, *Dialogue and Drama: Elements of Greek Tragedy in the Fourth Gospel* (Peabody, MA: Hendrickson, 2004). For the use of space in ancient tragedy, see R. Rehm, "Aeschylus," in de Jong, *Space in Ancient Greek Literature*, 307–24; Rehm, "Sophocles," in de Jong, *Space in Ancient Greek Literature*, 325–40; M. Lloyd, "Euripides," in de Jong, *Space in Ancient Greek Literature*, 341–58; and A. M. Bowie, "Aristophanes," in de Jong, *Space in Ancient Greek Literature*, 359–73.

58. See Poplutz, "Drama," 775. See also Gilhuly and Worman, "Introduction," 8, for a differentiation between "representational space" in texts and "performative space" in theater plays.

God," et cetera.[59] The characters—"Jews" and "Romans"—are allocated to the two spheres. The drama's narrative dynamic unfolds through Jesus's crossing the border and his breach of the given order. Jesus, who is the accused on the outside stage, is considered innocent on the inside stage; though he enters the praetorium, he maintains his cultic purity.[60] Hence, the spatial aspects of the dramatic narrative illustrate central aspects of the meaning conveyed and encourage the readers to interact, to take their own stand, and to reconsider set categories.[61]

Narrative Transformation of Space: Political, Sacred, and Memory Space

Political Space: Throughout the Johannine narrative, Jerusalem and the temple are presented as the epic center of God's self-revelation.[62] Each of Jesus's visits to the temple is associated with a discourse of self-revelation. Although in John 2 he speaks of the temple as his Father's house, his rights in the Jerusalem temple dwindle with the progression of the plot, the enmity of the Jews grows continually, and the intention to kill Jesus becomes more and more prevalent (5:18; 7:32, 44; 8:40, 59; 10:31, 39).[63] This tension associated with political space is transformed into theological space as the reference to the historical location of the Second Temple shifts to an allusion to Jesus's body, the new temple (2:21).[64] In contrast to the accounts in the Synoptics, the temple in John's Gospel is generally

---

59. See Zimmermann, "Deuten," 343–44.

60. See ibid., 344.

61. For the use of semantically charged space and the use of space in characterization and mirroring in ancient literature, see Irene J. F. de Jong, "Homer," in de Jong, *Space in Ancient Greek* Literature, 21–38; Mark Beck, "Plutarch," in de Jong, *Space in Ancient Greek* Literature, 441–62; and Koen de Temmerman "Chariton" in de Jong, *Space in Ancient Greek Literature*, 483–502.

62. See also the discussion on the use of public and private space in ancient literature in Temmerman, "Chariton."

63. Though the positioning of the pericope of the temple cleansing in John as opposed to its positioning in the Synoptics constitutes a creative intervention into the narrative space and a text-internal construction of space, limitations of space preclude it being covered in this article.

64. See further Johanna Rahner, *"Er aber sprach vom Tempel seines Leibes": Jesus von Nazareth als Ort der Offenbarung Gottes im vierten Evangelium*, BBB 117 (Bodenheim: Philo, 1998). Rahner stresses the christological and soteriological implications of the Temple metaphor in John.

given a positive connotation due to its key role as the space where salvation history is located. Through this construction of a text-internal geography, Jerusalem is constructed as a public space for Jesus's preaching and
self-revelation.[65] At first the Second Temple is the center of this revelation.
As the plot progresses, Jesus's teaching and residing in this space becomes
life-threatening for political reasons. Hence, the temple is transformed
into a temple-substitute, the body of Jesus.

Sacred Space: The Fourth Gospel describes Jesus's presence in the
world with metaphors adhering to sacred space (1:14, 51; 4:23), especially to the Jerusalem temple (2:19, 21).[66] In John 5–12, Israel's festival
calendar is linked with Jesus's visits to Jerusalem, such as the context of
the pilgrimage festival of Succoth (7:2) or with Hanukkah and the festival
of the renewal and rededication of the temple (10:22).[67] Throughout the
gospel these allusions to Israel's sacred space imply that "cultic space is
superfluous,"[68] as "Jesus is in some sense a new temple, a new place where
God dwells,"[69] a space that cannot be linked with a "fixed geographical
place."[70] Hence, the close correlation between time and space becomes relevant to the message of the text, "as the sacred space has changed, the time
that stands in correlation with it changes. The divisions that had marked
time in the past have collapsed. If the old temple stood in correlation with
the sequence of festivals, with change and renewal, the new temple stands
in relationship with eternity, an a-temporal eternity that is present in Jesus
and in the community of his disciples."[71]

Memory Space: Through the semantization of places, objects, and
events, John emphasizes the significance of space for historical consciousness and cultural memory. Since memories of historical events are used to

65. See Neyrey, "Spaces and Places," 67–70.
66. Taking up Rahner's approach, see Harold W. Attridge, "Temple, Tabernacle,
Time, and Space in John and Hebrews," *Early Christianity* 1 (2010): 262–69.
67. See also Konrad Huber, "Theologie als Topologie: Bemerkungen zum Raumkonzept von Joh 1,43–51," *ZKT* 121 (1999): 300–310, who argues that the space of
divine presence and divine revelation is not linked with a geographically locatable
place, but rather with the characterization of the Son of Man (1:51).
68. Attridge, "Temple," 264.
69. Ibid., 265.
70. Neyrey, "Spaces and Places," 71. Neyrey emphasizes the "rejection of fixed
sacred space" in John (83) and the transformation of the category into "fluid sacred
space," constituted by the gathering community of believers as the "new temple" (82).
71. Attridge, "Temple," 267.

construct and interpret history, narrative serves a productive function for collective and cultural memory, for identity construction, and for the generation of conceptions of history for the contemporary society. Memory space has often been considered within the thought framework of a "community-historical reading." This is not without controversy, since it aims for an interpretation of John's use of topographical references as a reflection of the history of the Johannine community: "Here the main starting point has been an attempt to correlate the major regions of Palestine in the gospel with stereotypical responses to Jesus: rejection in Jerusalem and Judea, acceptance in Samaria and Galilee. These are then thought to reflect the experience of groups of Johannine Christians in Palestine."[72] The current debate about memory theory in historical Jesus research, however, has suggested new avenues:[73] the focus on the media and mechanism through which Jesus's memory was shaped promises new insights into the generation of memory space, such as through literary models.[74] Moreover,

---

72. Bauckham, "Historiographical Characteristics," 97–98. See also Wayne A. Meeks, "Galilee and Judea in the Fourth Gospel," *JBL* 85 (1966): 159–69; Neyrey, "Spaces and Places," 65–67; Karl Kundsin, *Topologische Überlieferungsstoffe im Johannes-Evangelium*, FRLANT 22 (Göttingen: Vandenhoeck & Ruprecht, 1925). Charles H. Scobie, "Johannine Geography," *SR* 11 (1982): 80–82, is critical of this approach.

73. See, e.g., James D. G. Dunn, *Jesus Remembered*, vol. 1 of *Christianity in the Making* (Grand Rapids: Eerdmans, 2003); Alan Kirk and Tom Thatcher, eds., *Memory, Tradition, and Text: Uses of the Past in Early Christianity*, SemeiaSt 52 (Atlanta: Society of Biblical Literature, 2005).

74. On the way narration of space was shaped through the influence of literary tradition, see, e.g., Christiane Koch, "'Es war aber an dem Ort ein Garten' (Joh 19,41): Der Garten als bedeutsames Erzählmotiv in den johanneischen Passions- und Auferstehungstexten," in *Im Geist und in der Wahrheit: Studien zum Johannesevangelium und zur Offenbarung des Johannes sowie andere Beiträge; Festschrift für Martin Hasitschka zum 65. Geburtstag*, ed. Konrad Huber and Boris Repschinski (Münster: Aschendorff, 2008), 229–38; Christos Karakolis, "'Across the Kidron Brook, There Was a Garden' (John 18:1): Two Old Testament Allusions and the Theme of the Heavenly King in the Johannine Passion Narrative," in Van Belle, *The Death of Jesus in the Fourth Gospel*, 751–60; Christian Grappe, "Du sanctuaire au jardin: Jésus, nouveau et véritable Temple dans le quatrième évangile," in *Studien zu Matthäus und Johannes/ Études sur Mattheu et Jean: Mélanges offerts à Jean Zumstein pour son 65e anniversaire*, ed. Andreas Dettwiler and Uta Poplutz, ATANT 97 (Zürich: Theologischer, 2009), 285–94.

the influence and reception of ancient genre conventions is of vital interest
for any historiographical reading of narrative space in John.

We have seen how a variety of very different narrative strategies concerning "space" are used in the Gospel of John with a view to constructing a
specific text-internal geography as well as to create meaning on a deeper
textual level through processes of construction, production, and empty-
ing of space. A spatial approach also promises new insights into the contemporary cultural practices received in these processes, the spatializa-
tion of social relations, and the spatial construction of order, identity, and
memory in groups. Moreover, spatial analysis may grant an understanding
of this ancient author's perception of the historical and social geography
and the narrative dynamics set forth to encode theological, ethical, and
political messages in the depiction of or reference to space. Reading John
from the perspective of spatial theory thus offers the chance to open up
new ways of interpreting individual passages as well as the narrative of the
gospel as a whole.

5

POINT OF VIEW

James L. Resseguie

Point of view "signifies the way a story gets told."[1] It elaborates the relationship between the storyteller and the story and the reception of the story by developing the way the author or narrator presents the reader with the characters, dialogue, actions, setting, and events of the story.[2] It is a multifaceted concept that biblical critics avoid—perhaps because it seems confusing or even irrelevant to the text's meaning—yet nothing could be more important to the study of a biblical narrative text than the way the story gets told and the mode or modes by which the reader receives that story.

One aspect of point of view refers to the angle of vision or technique of narration that the narrator, the voice of the implied author, uses to tell the story.[3] The narrator can tell the story as an observer outside the story

---

1. Meyer H. Abrams and Geoffrey Galt Harpham, *A Glossary of Literary Terms*, 10th ed. (Boston: Wadsworth, 2012), s.v. "Point of View." Although point of view is a modern concept, aspects of point of view are discussed in ancient literature. Lucian speaks of a narrator taking a "bird's-eye view" of his material that is omnipresent and omniscient (*Hist. conscr.* 49). This is similar to the spatial point of view discussed by Boris Uspensky, *A Poetics of Composition: The Structure of the Artistic Text and Typology of a Compositional Form*, trans. Valentina Zavarin and Susan Wittig (Berkeley: University of California Press, 1973), 57–80. On Lucian and the narrator's spatial stance in an historical narrative, see Alicia D. Myers, *Characterizing Jesus: A Rhetorical Analysis on the Fourth Gospel's Use of Scripture in its Presentation of Jesus*, LNTS 458 (New York: T&T Clark, 2012), 29.

2. Abrams and Harpham, *Glossary of Literary Terms*, s.v. "Point of View."

3. The implied author is the persona the real author creates to write the story. Some literary critics separate point of view into two activities: Who sees? and Who speaks? The one who speaks is the narrator; the one who sees is the focalizer. I have

proper or as an actual character. The character-as-narrator may be objective or subjective. The objective narrator observes actions and events and reports only what he or she can see or know; the subjective narrator comments on and evaluates characters and events. Narrators outside the text refer to characters by name or by "he," "she," or "they" and know all that takes place or will take place. Additionally, outside narrators, which are also known as third-person omniscient narrators, have privileged access to characters' thoughts, motivations, and feelings. Similar to a moving camera and montage, third-person narrators roam from character to character, provide close-ups of some characters, glances at others, and move at will from one event to another. A variation of the third-person omniscient narrator is the intrusive narrator who not only reports but also adds commentary, evaluates characters and actions, and even shares his or her worldview.[4]

In her work on point of view in prose fiction, Susan Lanser calls angle of vision or the technique of narration an "objective" point of view.[5] Another

---

not followed this distinction because, in many instances, the one who sees and the one who speaks are the same in John. See James L. Resseguie, *Narrative Criticism: An Introduction* (Grand Rapids: Baker, 2005), 170 n. 12 for a fuller explanation. For the development of the concept of focalization, see Shlomith Rimmon-Kenan, *Narrative Fiction: Contemporary Poetics*, 2nd ed. (London: Routledge, 2002), 72–86; Gérard Genette, *Narrative Discourse: An Essay in Method*, trans. Jane E. Lewin (Ithaca, NY: Cornell University Press, 1980), 185–211; Mieke Bal, *Narratology: Introduction to the Theory of Narrative*, 3rd ed., trans. Christine van Boheemen (Toronto: University of Toronto Press, 2009), 145–63.

4. All the gospel writers are intrusive narrators that comment on and evaluate characters while sharing the worldview of the protagonist, Jesus. On intrusive narration in ancient Greco-Roman and Jewish historiographies and biographies, see Myers, *Characterizing Jesus*, 31–35. Intrusive narration is also a common practice among the "greatest novelist," such as Henry Fielding, Jane Austen, Charles Dickens, William Makepeace Thackeray, George Eliot, Thomas Hardy, Fyodor Dostoevsky, and Leo Tolstoy. See Abrams and Harpham, *A Glossary*, s.v. "Point of View."

5. Susan Sniader Lanser, *The Narrative Act: Point of View in Prose Fiction* (Princeton: Princeton University Press, 1981), 16. Some literary critics further develop the concept of objective point of view into a more refined study using such terms as "extradiegetic," "intradiegetic," "heterodiegetic," and "homodiegetic." The terms are Gérard Genette's in *Narrative Discourse*. Jeffrey Lloyd Staley, *The Print's First Kiss: A Rhetorical Investigation of the Implied Reader in the Fourth Gospel*, SBLDS 82 (Atlanta: Scholars Press, 1988), 38–39, uses Genette to describe the relation of narrator to narratee; see also D. Francois Tolmie, *Jesus' Farewell to the Disciples: John 13:1–17:26 in Narratological Perspective*, BibInt 12 (Leiden: Brill, 1995), 145–65.

aspect, "subjective" point of view, focuses on the narrator's evaluation of or attitude towards characters, dialogue, actions, setting, and events. The subjective point of view is known by several names: (1) evaluative point of view,[6] (2) conceptual point of view,[7] (3) ideological point of view,[8] and (4) standards of judgment.[9] Critics sometimes separate objective and subjective points of view, distinguishing between technique and ideology or method of narration and evaluative point of view. As a result, they fail to develop the full potential of point of view. However, both aspects of point of view—"objective" and "subjective"—are intertwined and should not be separated, for the method of narration or the technical angle of vision adopted by the narrator inevitably implies an ideology.

How does the reader—or more precisely, the implied reader—determine the narrative point of view?[10] Russian literary critic Boris Uspensky identifies five planes on which point of view is expressed in a narrative text: spatial, temporal, psychological, phraseological, and ideological.[11]

---

6. Mark Allan Powell, *What Is Narrative Criticism?* GBS (Minneapolis: Fortress, 1990), 24; Cornelis Bennema, *A Theory of Character in New Testament Narrative* (Minneapolis: Fortress, 2014), 48.

7. Seymour Chatman, *Story and Discourse: Narrative Structure in Fiction and Film* (Ithaca, NY: Cornell University Press, 1978), 152.

8. Uspensky, *Poetics*, 8–16.

9. David Rhoads, Joanna Dewey, and Donald Michie, *Mark as Story: An Introduction to the Narrative of a Gospel*, 3rd ed. (Minneapolis: Fortress, 2012), 45–46.

10. The implied reader is not an actual flesh-and-blood reader but the reader that the implied author has in mind when he or she writes a narrative. The implied reader knows the full repertoire of linguistic, cultural, social, and literary assumptions of the original authorial audience and can read the text as the implied author intended. On the implied reader in the Fourth Gospel, see James L. Resseguie, *The Strange Gospel: Narrative Design and Point of View in John*, BibInt 56 (Leiden: Brill, 2001), 23–26. The real flesh-and-blood reader, of course, may "resist" the text's ideology. On the "resisting reader" in the Fourth Gospel, see Adele Reinhartz, *Befriending the Beloved Disciple: A Jewish Reading of the Gospel of John* (New York: Continuum, 2001), 81–98.

11. Uspensky, *Poetics*. Other important discussions of point of view by literary critics may be found in Bal, *Narratology*, 145–63; Rimmon-Kenan, *Narrative Fiction*, 72–86; Chatman, *Story and Discourse*, 151–58; Lanser, *Narrative Act*; Wayne C. Booth, *The Rhetoric of Fiction*, 2nd ed. (Chicago: University of Chicago Press, 1983); Robert Scholes, James Phelan, and Robert Kellogg, *The Nature of Narrative, Fortieth Anniversary Edition*, rev. and expanded ed. (New York: Oxford University Press, 2006), 240–82; Wallace Martin, *Recent Theories of Narrative* (Ithaca, NY: Cornell University Press, 1986), 130–51; Juri M. Lotman, "Point of View in a Text," *NLH* 6 (1975): 339–52;

Each plane represents a particular stance the implied author or narrator takes in relationship to his or her textual world.[12]

The spatial plane describes the narrator's stance in space in relationship to the textual world. From where does the narrator tell the story: from outside the narrative or within the narrative? What effect does the narrator's chosen stance have on the reader? Does the narrator provide close-ups of a character that create affinity with a character's point of view, or does the narrator create distance from the character's perspective?

The temporal plane describes the temporal distance between the moment of writing and when the events of the narrative take place. Do the events take place before, after, or during the narration, and what effect does the temporal stance have on point of view? Does the temporal point of view create an immediacy that highlights the importance of events? Temporal point of view also looks at the pace of the narration in relation to the time lapse of the actual events of the story. The slowing down of narrative pace foregrounds events and suggests what is important and to be noticed by the reader. But the speeding up of narrative pace places events in the background and diminishes their importance.

Psychological point of view focuses on characters' thoughts and motivations and the effect they have in creating distance or affinity to a character's point of view. Negative comments increase the distance between the character's point of view and the reader while positive comments create affinity with the character's point of view.

Phraseological point of view focuses on the speech characteristics of characters and the narrator that may foreground the point of view of a character or narrator. Names, titles, and epithets are especially important on the phraseological plane.

Perhaps the most important plane of point of view for biblical literary critics is the ideological plane that develops and elaborates the norms,

Norman Friedman, "Point of View in Fiction: The Development of a Critical Concept," *PMLA* 70 (1955): 1160–84.

12. In the Fourth Gospel the implied author and narrator share the same point of view; see R. Alan Culpepper, *Anatomy of the Fourth Gospel: A Study in Literary Design* (Minneapolis: Fortress, 1983), 16–17, 43; Myers, *Characterizing Jesus*, 23. The Fourth Gospel narrator is also a "reliable" narrator, which Booth defines as follows: "I call a narrator *reliable* when he speaks or acts in accordance with the norms of the work (which is to say, the implied author's norms), *unreliable* when he does not" (*The Rhetoric of Fiction*, 2nd ed. [Chicago: University of Chicago Press, 1983], 158–59). On reliable and unreliable narrators in the ancient world, see Myers, *Characterizing Jesus*, 26–39.

values, beliefs, and general worldview of the implied author/narrator. Where possible, the technique or method of narration will be used to explore the text's ideology or to convey how the narrator uses his or her technique of narration to communicate an ideological perspective.

SPATIAL POINT OF VIEW

A narrator may adopt the spatial stance of a character within a story and move with that character throughout the narration.[13] "If the character enters a room, the narrator describes the room; if the character goes out into the street, the narrator describes the street."[14] The character-as-narrator stance is generally limited to what the character observes and knows. The narrator, however, may adopt a more flexible stance either within or outside a narrated scene. For instance, the narrator may offer a "bird's-eye" perspective that looks at the entire scene from a stance far above the action, creating a perspective that distances the reader from individual characters and actions. This perspective provides an overview and avoids identification with any one character's point of view. Or the narrator may be within a scene but avoid adopting the perspective of an individual character.[15] In this instance, the narrator sequentially surveys characters from a particular spatial stance, but the perspective is not of any one character. It is the point of view of the narrator. In a banquet scene, for example, the narrator describes the guests at the table by moving from one character to the next as if the narrator were a guest sitting at the table. Or the narrator may simply be an invisible, roving presence similar to a moving camera and montage, which moves freely from one character to another, pausing long enough to focus on certain details and then moving on.

The narrator of the Fourth Gospel is a third-person omniscient and intrusive narrator who roams freely from character to character, delves into the thoughts and motivations of some characters, comments on others, and evaluates characters' motives and worldview.[16] The roving nar-

---

13. Uspensky (*Poetics*, 58–59) calls this the concurrence of the spatial position of the narrator and a character.

14. Ibid., 58.

15. Uspensky (ibid., 59–65) calls this the nonconcurrence of the spatial position of the author and a character.

16. On occasion the narrator adopts a first person point of view as in 1:14, 16 and 21:24, 25. This shift from third-person to first-person may be due to the narrator's

rator presents the characters' conflicting points of view with ease, aiding the reader in identifying with or becoming estranged from an individual character's point of view. If, on the one hand, the narrator gives a positive evaluation of a character's actions, thoughts, and motivations, then the reader is more likely to identify or have empathy with that character's point of view. If, on the other hand, the narrator provides a negative evaluation, then the reader is distanced from that character's point of view and may reject his or her perspective as inadequate, misguided, or simply wrong.

In John 2:13–22, third-person, omniscient, and intrusive narration clarifies the significance of the cleansing of the temple. After Jesus says "destroy this temple, and in three days I will raise it up" (2:19),[17] the hearers naturally assume he is referring to the temple complex that had been under construction for forty-six years. But the narrator clarifies this misunderstanding with an aside to the reader: "But he was speaking of the temple of his body" (2:21). Yet his intrusiveness does not stop with this aside; he goes on to explain the disciples' postresurrection response: "After he was raised from the dead, his disciples remembered that he had said this; and they believed the scripture and the word that Jesus had spoken" (2:22). In this example, the spatial stance of the narrator influences the implied reader's response. First, it lays bare the assumption of the hearers, allowing the reader to understand the original audience's misunderstanding. Second, it undermines the audience's assumption that Jesus is talking about the physical structure with an explanatory comment on the deeper meaning of the "temple." Third, the spatial/temporal stance allows the narrator to record the disciples' correct understanding of this misunderstanding—but only after they reflect upon it from a postresurrection perspective. If the narrator were strictly within the narrative and recording events as an objective observer within the narrative, the complexity of this saying would disappear. The narrator's omniscience—and especially his intrusive commentary—allows Jesus's saying to dissemble opposing points of view and to establish Jesus's view as the correct one.

The Fourth Gospel narrator, however, adopts a complex point of view in the telling of his story. He is not only a third-person omniscient and intrusive narrator. He is a character in the story; in fact, he is one of the inner disciples who is always present but self-effacing, remaining in the

---

desire to assure the reader that he is an eyewitness to the events or it may be due to a different narrator speaking.

17. Unless otherwise stated, all translations of biblical texts are from the NRSV.

background during significant events and happenings of the gospel but always present. The character-as-narrator role is not easily discerned for the narrator does a masterful job of remaining elusive and keeping his identity hidden as a character from the reader. The character-as-narrator of John is the Beloved Disciple who is unnamed in the gospel and referred to as "the one whom Jesus loved" (*hon ēgapa ho Iēsous* or *hon ephilei ho Iēsous*) at 13:23–26; 19:26–27; 20:2–10; 21:7, 20–23. In two passages, he is anonymous (1:35–40; 18:15–16), and twice he is the subject of narrative asides (19:35; 21:24).[18]

The advantages of the character-as-narrator taking on a third-person omniscient and intrusive voice are twofold. First, the narrator is able to remain elusive and invisible throughout the story until an opportune time to reveal his presence. Elusiveness allows him to speak as an eyewitness to the events and happenings of the gospel without tipping his hand to the reader that he is a character in the narrative. This allows him to report and comment without drawing attention to himself as a character in the story. Not until the end is it clear that the narrator has all along been a character in the story. Second, he is an omniscient and intrusive narrator who comments freely on characters and actions. He knows all that is happening or will happen, even what characters are thinking and feeling. He is not limited by the usual constraints of a character within a story who lacks omniscience or takes an objective stance of reporting without evaluation. The spatial stance expresses an ideology: he knows all that happens or will happen in the story, and he is present as a follower of Jesus during his lifetime, but he remains invisible to the reader, drawing attention not to himself but to the protagonist, Jesus.[19]

Temporal Point of View

Temporal point of view "encompasses two aspects of the narrator's relation to the story world: the pace of the narration, and the temporal distance between the moment of telling and when the narrated events take place."[20] The narration can take place *before* the events happen as in the

---

18. On the Beloved Disciple as narrator, see James L. Resseguie, "The Beloved Disciple: The Ideal Point of View," in *Character Studies in the Fourth Gospel: Narrative Approaches to Seventy Figures in John*, ed. Steven A. Hunt, D. Francois Tolmie, and Ruben Zimmermann, WUNT 314 (Tübingen: Mohr Siebeck, 2013), esp. 544, 547–49.

19. See also the essay on "Space" by Susanne Luther in this volume.

20. Lanser, *Narrative Act*, 198. See also Douglas Estes, *The Temporal Mechanics of*

case of prophecy, or it can take place *after* the events have happened, called *posterior* narration.[21] Two other temporal stances are *simultaneous* and *interspersed*.[22] In simultaneous narration, the narration takes place as the story unfolds, and the present tense is used. In interspersed narration, the actions happen between and during the moments of narration, which is the mode of the journal or epistolary narrative.

The Johannine narrator uses posterior narration to recount events that are viewed entirely from a postresurrection perspective.[23] Posterior narration clarifies the significance of Jesus's proclamation when he says on the last day of the Festival of Booths, "Let anyone who is thirsty come to me, and let the one who believes in me drink. As the scripture has said, 'Out of his belly[24] shall flow rivers of living water'" (7:37b–38; cf. 19:34). By adopting a postresurrection perspective, the narrator is able to explain the real meaning of this saying: "Now he said this about the Spirit, which believers in him were to receive; for as yet there was no Spirit, because Jesus was not yet glorified" (7:39).[25] The advantage of posterior narration is that the significance of events that are misunderstood or puzzling to the characters—the disciples, the religious authorities, or the general population—is transparent, even obvious, when viewed from a postresurrection perspective. By adopting a posterior stance, the narrator can delve into the deeper significance of events and happenings and point out the missteps and missed meanings of the characters. The many double entendres and ironies of the gospel, for instance, are enhanced by a posterior point of view that sharpens the disparity between what appears to be the meaning at the surface and what is actually meant.[26]

---

the *Fourth Gospel: A Theory of Hermeneutical Relativity in the Gospel of John*, BibInt 92 (Leiden: Brill, 2008), esp. 239–41.

21. Lanser, *Narrative Act*, 198–99, who relies on Genette, *Narrative Discourse*, for the relationships between the time of the story and the time of narration. See further the essay on "Time" by Douglas Estes in this volume.

22. See Lanser, *Narrative Act*, 198–99.

23. Culpepper, *Anatomy*, 27, uses the term "retrospective."

24. Literally in Greek. The NRSV has "out of the believer's heart," which obscures the christological significance of this verse, although in a footnote the New Oxford Annotated Bible gives the literal interpretation.

25. Other examples of posterior narration from a postresurrection perspective occur in 2:22; 12:16; 20:9.

26. See, for example, John 11:49–52.

The second aspect of temporal point of view is the pace of the narration. The narrator may speed up the narrative pace to summarize events or slow down the narrative pace to foreground events.[27] With a slower, more deliberate pace, events and happenings are foregrounded, drawing the reader's attention to what is important and to what is to be noticed. The opposite effect occurs when events are summarized: they are placed in the background and are less noticeable since narrative time is speeded up in comparison with story time. A striking example of narrative retardation—that is, the slowing down of the pace of narration to make events and happenings stand out—occurs in the second half of the gospel. Whereas John 1–12 covers the material in a period of two and a half years, the narrative pace in John 13–19 covers the material in a mere twenty-four hours. Consequently, the snail-pace crawl elongates and heightens the details of the story from the table (John 13) to the cross (John 19), focusing on the significance and importance of Jesus's passion and death. As Jesus is "lifted up" in his passion and death in the second-half of the gospel (see 3:14; 8:28; 12:32), the narrator "lifts up," so to speak, the accompanying events with a slow, deliberate detailed pace of narration.

The advantage of narrative retardation is that it forces the reader to pay close attention to what is happening and to events that appear familiar but need to be seen in a new way. The retardation of the reading process is what the Russian Formalist, Viktor Shklovsky, calls defamiliarization, the technique of making what is well-known and overly-familiar seem unfamiliar.[28] Shklovsky uses the metaphor of the *stony* stone to illustrate

---

27. Genette, *Narrative Discourse*, 93–95, uses the terms "summary" and "scene" to describe narrative speeds. In "summary," narrative time is shorter than story time; in "scene," narrative time is approximately equivalent to story time; see also Martin Löschnigg, "Scene and Summary," in *Routledge Encyclopedia of Narrative Theory*, ed. David Herman, Manfred Jahn, and Marie-Laure Ryan (New York: Routledge, 2005), 576–77. For the significance of "summary" and "scene" material for biblical point of view analysis, see Gary Yamasaki, *Watching a Biblical Narrative: Point of View in Biblical Exegesis* (New York: T&T Clark, 2007), 36, 165–66.

28. Viktor Shklovsky, "Art as Technique," in *Russian Formalist Criticism: Four Essays*, trans. Lee T. Lemon and Marion J. Reis (Lincoln: University of Nebraska Press, 1965), 3–24. On defamiliarization in the gospels, see James L. Resseguie, "Defamiliarization and the Gospels," *BTB* 20 (1990): 147–53; and Resseguie, "The Woman Who Crashed Simon's Party: A Reader-Response Approach to Luke 7:36-50," in *Characters and Characterization in Luke-Acts*, ed. Frank E. Dicken and Julia A. Snyder, LNTS 548 (New York: Bloomsbury T&T Clark, 2016), 7–22.

the effect that art has as a defamiliarizing device. "Habitualization devours works, clothes, furniture, one's wife, and the fear of war.... Art exists that one may recover a sensation of life; it exists to make one feel things, to make the stone *stony*."[29] This is an apt metaphor to describe the effect of slowing down the narrative pace. When the narrative pace is retarded, the implied reader pays attention. He or she sees the *stony* stone—that is, the character and even small details of the stone—and sees what cannot be seen when the routine of a rapid pace blurs the narrative details. The narrator of the Fourth Gospel stretches out the events of Jesus's last days, forcing the implied reader to pay attention to the disciples' missteps, the antagonists' plot to destroy Jesus, the bumbling miscues of Pilate, and the surprising discoveries at the tomb.

Psychological Point of View

Psychological point of view develops and elaborates the point of view that is expressed through behaviors. It is "an extremely complex aspect of point of view, for it encompasses the broad question of the narrator's distance or affinity to each character and event ... represented in the text."[30] Uspensky and Lanser describe two ways human behavior may be observed by the narrator.[31] If the narrator takes the point of view of an outside observer, then he or she is restricted to what can be observed objectively. This stance is similar to a camera that records the behavior of a person without access to the person's internal consciousness, such as thoughts, feelings, and emotions. If the narrator abandons the objective observer perspective, then he or she may look inside the consciousness of a character and describe the feelings, thoughts, and motivations of the character. Or the point of view may even be described from the perspective of the character.[32] An interior monologue in which the narrator records what a character is thinking in his or her own words is an inward plunge that lays naked the perspective

---

29. Shklovsky, "Art as Technique," 12.

30. Lanser, *Narrative Act*, 201–2.

31. Uspensky, *Poetics*, 83; Lanser, *Narrative Act*, 207.

32. Lanser, *Narrative Act*, 201–15, develops a complex analysis of point of view that describes the narrator's distance or affinity to each character and event, the quantity of information, subjectivity or objectivity of information, internal or external vision, and depth of vision.

of the character.[33] In the Third Gospel, for example, the narrator lets the reader overhear Simon the Pharisee's interior monologue, what he thinks but only says beneath his breath. "If this man [Jesus] were a prophet, he would have known who and what kind of woman this is who is touching him—that she is a sinner" (Luke 7:39).

The narrator of the Fourth Gospel employs on occasion an internal stance to highlight characters' feelings, thoughts, and motivations. These inside views, as they are often called, let the reader evaluate characters' points of view. A negative evaluation creates distance from the character's perspective while a positive evaluation encourages affinity with his or her point of view. Inside views in the Fourth Gospel are used, for instance, to inform the reader of impending trouble within the ranks of the disciples. Jesus "knew from the first who were the ones that did not believe, and who was the one that would betray him" (6:64b). At the washing of the disciples' feet in John 13, Jesus announces that "not all of you are clean" (13:11b). The narrator delves into Jesus's reasoning: "for he knew who was to betray him" (13:11a). Other inside views may highlight a character's disappointment. "Peter felt hurt because he [Jesus] said to him the third time, 'Do you love me?'" (21:17b). Still other inside views expose a character's devious motivations, such as the narrator's comment on Judas Iscariot's objection to the wasting of a costly ointment for the anointing of Jesus's feet. Judas's po-faced deceit is laid bare in harsh terms. "He said this not because he cared about the poor but because he was a thief; he kept the common purse and used to steal what was put into it" (12:6).[34]

Inside views, which is the most common manner in which psychological point of view is expressed in the Fourth Gospel, penetrate a character's inner life and shape the reader's response to a character's point of view.[35] Probing the inner life allows the implied reader to identify the

---

33. On interior monologues see Philip Sellew, "Interior Monologue as a Narrative Device in the Parables of Luke," *JBL* 111 (1992): 239–53; Dorrit Cohn, *Transparent Minds: Narrative Modes for Presenting Consciousness in Fiction* (Princeton: Princeton University Press, 1978).

34. This bold comment causes William Klassen, *Judas: Betrayer or Friend of Jesus?* (Minneapolis: Fortress, 1996), 146, to accuse the narrator of "bearing false witness, slander, and calumny" and of sullying Judas's reputation!

35. Inside views are not the only way psychological point of view is expressed. The quantity of information presented about any character or event also creates distance or affinity with a character's point of view. See Lanser, *Narrative Act*, 202–5, and the essay "Characterization" by Christopher W. Skinner in this volume.

conflicts between characters, to evaluate points of view that are at odds with the protagonist Jesus, and to identify with or be estranged from an individual character's point of view. The implied reader relies upon the narrator to express the norms and values of the narrative and how the reader should respond to the points of views expressed by characters. A character that voices the narrative norms and values often receives approval while a character at odds with the narrative worldview is cast in a strong negative light by the narrator.[36]

PHRASEOLOGICAL POINT OF VIEW

Phraseological point of view focuses on the narrator's discourse and a character's speech.[37] The narrator may speak in his or her own voice, expressing a distinct point of view, or the narrator may use the discourse of a character to express an ideological point of view. A third possibility, noted by both Uspensky and Lanser,[38] occurs when a character's speech infiltrates the narrator's speech or the narrator's speech merges with a character's discourse. In 3:31–36, for example, it is unclear whether John (the Baptist) is speaking or the narrator. In this instance, John's speech and point of view has infiltrated the narrator's discourse and point of view or vice versa. In another example, it is unclear whether Jesus is speaking or the narrator: the speaking voice in 3:13–21 is ambiguous, suggesting that the narrator has adopted the point of view of the central character, Jesus, which R. Alan Culpepper calls "a classic instance of the blending of the narrator with Jesus' voice."[39]

The changes in names, titles, and epithets, which are often saturated with meaning, are not to be ignored as a marker of point of view. To illus-

---

36. An example of the narrator's comment that places "the Jews" in a negative light is found in 9:22: The blind man's parents "said this because they were afraid of the Jews; for the Jews had already agreed that anyone who confessed Jesus to be the Messiah would be put out of the synagogue." And again in 6:41: "Then the Jews began to complain about him because he said, 'I am the bread that came down from heaven.'" The negative comment concerning Judas's motives in 12:6 is another example.

37. For an application of phraseological point of view in Matthew, see Mark Allan Powell, "Characterization on the Phraseological Plane in the Gospel of Matthew," in *Treasures New and Old: Recent Contributions to Matthean Studies*, ed. David R. Bauer and Mark A. Powell (Atlanta: Scholars Press, 1996), 161–77.

38. Uspensky, *Poetics*, 32–50; Lanser, *Narrative Act*, 185–86.

39. Culpepper, *Anatomy*, 42.

trate, three characters in John 20—Simon Peter, the Beloved Disciple, and Mary Magdalene—undergo changes in names or descriptions that draw attention to their newfound points of view or underscore their surprising discoveries. At the beginning of the chapter, the narrator gives Peter his full name, Simon Peter (20:2), and then follows with his shortened name, Peter (20:3, 4). This is the narrator's general pattern throughout the gospel: he introduces Peter into a narrative with his expanded name and then follows with his shortened name.[40] But when the narrator deviates from this established pattern, the reader needs to pay close attention. At the moment Peter discovers the grave clothes in the tomb, the general pattern is abrogated, and he expands his name from the abbreviated form, Peter, to the full name, Simon Peter. "Then Simon Peter came … and went into the tomb. He saw the linen wrappings lying there, and the cloth that had been on Jesus' head, not lying with the linen wrappings but rolled up in a place by itself" (20:6–7). At the precise moment of his surprising discovery, Peter's name swells, heightening his prominence as the one who enters the tomb first and underlining his important discovery.

The Beloved Disciple, however, is not outdone in terms of naming and description. He is introduced into the narrative as "the other disciple, the one whom Jesus loved" (20:2), and he is subsequently called "the other disciple" (20:3, 4). But at the moment he believes, the narrator expands his epithet from the abbreviated form of "the other disciple" to the expanded form, "the other disciple, who reached the tomb first" (20:8). Similar to the swelling of Peter's name at the climactic moment in the story, the elongation of the Beloved Disciple's narrative description draws attention to his priority in two ways: he is the first to reach the tomb and the first to believe in the resurrection. The expanded name at an unexpected point underscores Peter's expanded discovery in the tomb, while the overfull description of the Beloved Disciple corresponds to a new, more expansive point of view that now includes belief in Jesus's resurrection. On the phraseological plane, the changes in names, title, and epithets is the narrator's way of telling the reader to pay close attention.

Mary Magdalene also undergoes changes in names and epithets that call a reader's attention to a change in her point of view. The following

<hr>

40. J. K. Elliott, "Κηφᾶς: Σίμων Πέτρος: ὁ Πέτρος: An Examination of New Testament Usage," *NovT* 14 (1972): 243: "The rule is that Πέτρος is written only after the name Σίμων Πέτρος has occurred: the latter always appears first in the context by way of reintroducing the disciple."

list demonstrates the intentional changes in Mary's names and epithets in
John 20.

> Narrator: Mary Magdalene (20:1)
> Narrator: Mary (20:11)
> Angels: Woman (20:13)
> Jesus: Woman (20:15)
> Jesus: Mary (20:16)
> Narrator: Mary Magdalene (20:18)

At the beginning and the end, the narrator calls her Mary Magdalene, an
inclusio that says that Mary is the central character. Then, at 20:11, the
narrator drops the more formal name and uses the shortened form, Mary.
The characters, on the other hand, use an epithet to address Mary. Both
the angels and Jesus avoid her personal or formal name and simply address
her as "woman" (20:13, 15). Yet this stark and naked epithet gives way
to a personal address when Jesus calls her by her given name at 20:16.
The naming startles her into recognition of her Lord and recalls (for the
implied reader) an earlier narrative in which the shepherd calls his own
sheep by name (10:3). Yet the personal name not only identifies her as one
of the Lord's own; it marks a new ideological point of view. Mary is no
longer the "woman" who weeps and mourns for her dead and buried Lord.
That epithet is inappropriate now, for she is "Mary"—no longer a gener-
alized subject ("woman") but an individual who is not only recognized
by her Lord but recognizes her Lord. The sudden switch from "woman"
to "Mary" draws attention on the phraseological plane to a new point of
view: Jesus is not at all dead, nor is he missing; he is alive and present to
her in a new way (20:18).

Phraseological point of view of a narrative relies on a close reading of
the speech characteristics of both the characters and the narrator. When
the narrator deviates from established patterns of discourse or expands
descriptions or alters names, titles, and epithets, then the reader should
pay close attention to the development of a new point of view or an important discovery.

IDEOLOGICAL POINT OF VIEW

Ideological point of view is not only "the most basic aspect of point of
view" but also "least accessible to formalization, for its analysis relies, to

a degree, on intuitive understanding."[41] This plane focuses on the norms, values, beliefs, and general worldview of the author or narrator or the point of view of a character. The ideological perspective may be stated outright, laying on the surface which Lanser labels "explicit ideology," or it may be embedded at "deep-structural" levels of the text and not easily identified.[42]

The ideological point of view of the Fourth Gospel is an example of explicit ideology. Mary Coloe,[43] Cornelis Bennema, [44] and others[45] claim the ideological perspective is stated outright at John 20:31: "But these are written so that you may come to believe that Jesus is the Messiah, the Son of God, and that through believing you may have life in his name." This is an important summary of the ideological point of view of the gospel, but it is not the only statement of the text's ideology. Another, more nuanced point of view lies at the surface in the Prologue: "The Word became flesh [sarx] and lived among us, and we have seen his glory [doxa], the glory as of a father's only son, full of grace and truth" (1:14). As 1:14 suggests, some of John's characters see only flesh and stumble over Jesus's words and actions; others see the glory in the flesh, the otherworldly in the ordinary. In general, the characters within the gospel see either the glory in the flesh and come to believe that "Jesus is the Messiah, the Son of God" (20:31), or they fall victim to appearances and are blinded to the glory in the flesh.[46]

---

41. Uspensky, *Poetics*, 8.

42. Lanser, *Narrative Act*, 216–17. Lanser cites Virginia Woolf's *The Waves* as an example of embedded ideology.

43. Mary L. Coloe, "The Mother of Jesus: A Woman Possessed," in Hunt, Tolmie, and Zimmermann, *Character Studies in the Fourth Gospel*, 203. See also Mary L. Coloe, "The Woman of Samaria: Her Characterization, Narrative, and Theological Significance," in Skinner, *Characters and Characterization in the Gospel of John*, 182.

44. Cornelis Bennema, "Judas (the Betrayer): The Black Sheep of the Family," in Hunt, Tolmie, and Zimmermann, *Character Studies in the Fourth Gospel*, 363. See also Bennema, "A Comprehensive Approach to Understanding Character in the Gospel of John," in Skinner, *Characters and Characterization in the Gospel of John*, 93.

45. E.g., Mark W. G. Stibbe, *John as Storyteller: Narrative Criticism and the Fourth Gospel*, SNTSMS 73 (Cambridge: Cambridge University Press, 1992), 28.

46. This is a development of Bultmann's observation: "The δόξα is not to be seen *alongside* the σάρξ, nor *through* the σάρξ as through a window; it is to be seen in the σάρξ and nowhere else. If man wishes to see the δόξα, then it is on the σάρξ that he must concentrate his attention without allowing himself to fall victim to appearances." See Rudolf Bultmann, *The Gospel of John: A Commentary*, trans. G. R. Beasley-Murray (Philadelphia: Westminster, 1971), 63.

The glory-in-the-flesh point of view is seen more clearly when its counterpart is laid alongside it. The counter view sees only flesh—Jesus's humanness—and is blinded by appearances or self-confident in its point of view that triumphs in appearances as reality. In Jesus's confrontation with the crowd and the Pharisees, for example, he reveals the misguided nature of an appearance-oriented point of view. He warns the crowd not to judge "by appearances, but judge with right judgment" (7:24). This is the problem with a point of view that relies on appearances: it judges at a superficial level and misses the deeper meaning of Jesus's words and actions. Later, in a discussion with the Pharisees, Jesus accuses the leaders of judging "by human standards" or, literally, "according to the flesh" (8:15). This once again highlights the problem with an appearance-oriented point of view. The crowd, some Jewish authorities, and others in the gospel evaluate characters, events, and happenings according to the flesh or by human standards. An appearance-oriented point of view is also self-serving, for it seeks human glory rather than glory from God (5:44; 7:18; 12:43).

Jesus voices the correct ideological point of view that is marked by "right judgment" that sees beyond mere appearances (7:24). This perspective evaluates characters and happenings correctly, not according to the flesh or by the human standards that are often set by the religious elite. It is not self-serving but seeks glory from God (5:44; 7:18; 8:15; 12:43). In sum, it exegetes at a deeper level than the surface level appearances and thus judges rightly. John 9 is a fine example of a glory-in-the-flesh point of view that clashes with an appearance-oriented perspective. The religious authorities of John 9, who claim to know more than they do,[47] judge at the level of appearances and conclude that Jesus must be a sinner because he violates the Sabbath laws when he heals the man born blind (9:24). Their judgment is according to the flesh or by the human standards accepted by the culture. The man born blind, on the other hand, is not a victim of appearances. He knows more than he appears to know, refuses to judge by the human standards upheld by the religious authorities, and evaluates rightly. He exegetes at a level deeper than an appearance-oriented point of view and correctly concludes that Jesus must be "from God" (9:33). Not blinded by appearances, he sees the glory in the flesh.

---

47. The Pharisees play the role of the corporate *alazōn*, self-deceived and self-confident braggarts, while the blind man plays the role of the *eirōn*, the dissimulator who knows more than he is perceived to know and brings to light the *alazony* of the authorities. See Resseguie, *Narrative Criticism*, 151.

The Beloved Disciple is also a character who sees what others do not see and speaks what others do not say. He is the first in many ways. He is the only male disciple to witness Jesus's death on the cross and the first of a new spiritual family (19:26–27). He is the first to reach the tomb and the first to believe Jesus has risen from the dead (20:4, 8). He is the first to recognize the risen Lord on the shore at the Sea of Tiberias (21:7). He is a perceptive witness who does not fall victim to appearances but sees what the other disciples do not at the outset see: the glory in the flesh. He recognizes the significance of Jesus's death on the cross and, as narrator, gives an aside to inform the reader that he has judged rightly (19:35).[48] He sees the significance of a tomb with its grave clothes and believes in the resurrection (20:7, 8). He sees the meaning behind the miraculous catch of fish and recognizes that it is the Lord on the shore (21:7). He sees the glory in the flesh, and as the authoritative voice of the narrative, he writes to persuade the reader to see beyond appearances, to recognize the glory in the flesh, and believe that Jesus is "the Messiah, the Son of God" (20:31).

CONCLUSION

Point of view is simply the way a story is told. The characters, the actions and dialogue, the settings and events are told through the voice and eyes of the narrator who shapes his story with an ideological point of view. The narrator of John adopts the spatial perspective of a third-person omniscient narrator that sees all and knows all that happens or will happen. He is also an intrusive commentator who evaluates events, characters, and actions. This subjective posture provides invaluable guidance to the implied reader in the discernment of the narrative point of view.

The narrator is also a character within the gospel, the Beloved Disciple, who disguises his role as narrator until an opportune time to reveal who he is (21:24; cf. 19:35). The narrator-as-character lends authority to the story he tells, for he is an eyewitness to the events, while his elusiveness allows him to tell the story from the advantageous perspective of omniscience.

The narrator adopts a retrospective point of view (posterior narration on the temporal plane), which looks back at the events that have already taken place through the lens of the resurrection event. By looking back, he can accentuate the characters' misunderstandings of events, highlight

---

48. See Resseguie, "Beloved Disciple," esp. 543–44.

the conflicts between characters, and sharpen the differences between
the point of view of the antagonists and protagonist. A retrospective perspective allows the reader to see the deficiency and wrongheadedness of
a character's point of view. Irony, for instance, is strengthened by posterior
narration and allows the implied reader to see a character's point of view as
undesirable, deficient, and mistaken.[49] The narrator also highlights events
and happenings of the story by slowing down the narrative pace. The
retardation of narrative pace forces the reader to look at events that took
place long ago—events that are perhaps overly familiar—and see them in
a new, fresh way.

The narrator's inside views (psychological plane) penetrate a character's inner life and reveal his or her behaviors, motivations, and thinking.
By providing a negative evaluation of a character's motives and actions, the
narrator manipulates the reader's response, and in terms of point of view,
creates distance between the reader and that character's perspective. A
positive evaluation creates affinity with the character and places the character's point of view in a favorable light.

Names, titles, and epithets (phraseological plane) are saturated with
meaning and draw attention to a character's perspective. Especially important are the occasions the narrator deviates from an established pattern
and alters, however slightly, the names, titles, or epithets of a character. Or
the narrator may expand the narrative description of the character, which
is one way of alerting the reader to pay close attention. The narrator may
also express a distinctive tone—either approving or disparaging—that
manipulates the reader's response. While a disparaging tone elongates the
distance from a character's point of view, an approving tone establishes
affinity with the character's perspective.

Ideological point of view is the most important aspect of point of view
for it illumines the norms, values, beliefs, and worldview of the narrative.
This perspective is found at the surface in the Prologue: the glory is seen
in the flesh (1:14). Jesus's other-worldliness can only be seen in his flesh,
his humanness. That is the paradox of the gospel. While some characters
stumble over appearances and see only flesh, others see the glory in the
flesh and believe.

49. On the use of irony to establish point of view, see Resseguie, *Strange Gospel*,
28–41.

6

PLOT

Kasper Bro Larsen

The Gospel of John is a narrative with a plot: "For God so loved the world that he gave his only Son" (John 3:16).[1] According to Peter Brooks, scholar of comparative literature, human beings "read for the plot" in order to satisfy their desire for meaning.[2] Human existence is a series of disparate episodes; but narratives, with a beginning, a plot, and an ending, project a sense of direction and meaning onto our lives, be it on a small scale in autobiographical posts on Facebook and shared family tales at the dinner table or on a larger scale in artistic literature, in national histories, and in religious stories like John's Gospel. Human beings are storytelling animals.[3]

The purpose of the present chapter is to discuss the nature of the plot in the Fourth Gospel. First, we must define what we mean by plot in the context of narrative theory. Second, we need to consider in what manner it makes sense to subject a gospel such as John's to literary plot analysis. Third, the plot of John's story must be analyzed—which is not as straightforward as it may seem. We shall look at John's plot with analytical tools fabricated by the French-Lithuanian semiotician and narratologist Algirdas Julien Greimas. This is not new theory. It was developed in the heyday of French structuralism in 1960s and 1970s, and it owes a lot to the *Poetics* of Aristotle (384–322 BCE). But Greimas has much to offer. In Johannine Studies, particularly in the Anglo-American realm, Greimas is often

---

1. Unless otherwise stated, all translations of biblical texts are from the NRSV.

2. Peter Brooks, *Reading for the Plot: Design and Intention in Narrative* (Cambridge: Harvard University Press, 1984).

3. Jonathan Gotschall, *The Storytelling Animal: How Stories Make Us Human* (Boston: Houghton Mifflin Harcourt, 2012).

overlooked. This is probably due to the fact that alternative narratologies (such as those of Seymour Chatman and Gérard Genette) were applied in R. Alan Culpepper's otherwise brilliant and highly influential pioneering work on John as narrative, *Anatomy of the Fourth Gospel* (1983).[4] But Greimas is important because he not only discusses how narratives work but also offers a set of analytical tools that can be fruitfully applied to John's plot.

What Is a Plot? Aristotelian and Modern Answers

In modern English, the word *plot* carries different meanings. One common meaning in everyday language concerns a secret plan, a complot, or a conspiracy (as in, for example, the title of Philip Roth's 2004 novel *The Plot against America*). In John, there is certainly a plot against Jesus by the authorities of Jerusalem, but this meaning of the word is not the most relevant in literary plot analysis. Another meaning is more apt: if one looks up any novel or movie in Wikipedia, one finds a section describing the "plot" of the work. Here, plot is understood as a summary or paraphrase of the story, chapter-by-chapter or scene-by-scene.

In narrative criticism, however, the understanding of plot is often even narrower. Plot is not simply an outline of the events in the story but pertains to the underlying *causality* of the story. As the English novelist E. M. Forster famously phrased it: "'The king died, and then the queen died' is a story. 'The king died, and then the queen died of grief' is a plot."[5] Forster's first sentence indicates that in order to have a story, a series of events is required. "The king died, and then the queen died" is a story. "The king slept," however, is not a story since it describes a state, not an event. In Forster's second sentence, plot is described as the element that creates a sense of causality (and thus purpose and meaning) in the story. Readers are not only reading a series of events (as in the case of a story), but rather engage in a kind of detective work or emplotment activity where the reader investigates the causality and direction of the events (plot).[6]

---

4. R. Alan Culpepper, *Anatomy of the Fourth Gospel: A Study in Literary Design* (Minneapolis: Fortress, 1983).

5. E. M. Forster, *Aspects of the Novel* (New York: Harcourt, 1927), 82.

6. In different narratologies, the plot and its causality is regarded either as the author's tool to create narrative coherence or as inherent in the text or as something produced by the reader in the reading process. See Karin Kukkonen, "Plot," in *The*

Aristotle, author of a classic in the history of narrative theory, was also the progenitor of such an understanding of plot. In his *Poetics*, which theorizes about ancient tragedy and epic, *mythos* is the equivalent to what we designate as plot. Aristotle understood *mythos* as "the construction of events [*tēn synthesin tōn pragmatōn*]" (*Poet.* 1450a3–4). Being the very soul and backbone of any good tragedy, it is more essential than, for example, character. *Mythos* creates a "whole [*holon*] … which has a beginning, middle, and end [*archēn kai meson kai teleuthēn*]" (1450b25–26; see also *Poet.* 1459a18–19). According to Aristotle, the plot serves to establish an inherently necessary and probable chain of events so that the beginning sets the scene for adequate action in the middle, which, again, points toward a corresponding end (1451a36–39;1452a18–22). A haphazard *deus ex machina* to finish the story is, in other words, not Aristotle's cup of tea. On the contrary, if the sense of a whole is lacking so that the beginning, middle, and end of the story do not correspond, the story becomes arbitrary and episodic (1451b33–1452a10). Aristotle divides plots or *mythoi* into simple and complex ones (1452a11–22). We shall return to that distinction in relation to John's plot, but now that we have an understanding of plot as the causal backbone of narrative, it is time to move toward John's Gospel.

PLOT ANALYSIS AND GOSPEL LITERATURE: OBJECTIONS AND APOLOGIES

Is it at all legitimate to subject a gospel like John's to plot analysis? Scholarship has presented several objections to such an endeavor, but I do not find them quite convincing. Let me mention the most important ones before we proceed.

First, there is the generic objection. One may claim that John's Gospel resists plot analysis since it is not pure fiction but a kind of writing with historiographical ambition. In response to this objection, it is important to notice that plot is not dependent on how the story-world may possibly relate to the world behind the text. Even historiographical writings are plotted narratives.[7]

The second objection is source critical. Scholarship often claims that the Gospel of John as we know it is a composite text consisting of mate-

---

Living Handbook of Narratology, ed. Peter Hühn et al. (Hamburg: Hamburg University), http://tinyurl.com/SBL0392a.

7. Hayden White, *The Content of the Form: Narrative Discourse and Historical Representation* (Baltimore: Johns Hopkins University Press, 1987).

rial from different sources of different provenance (among the commonly suggested ones are a pre-Johannine prologue, a signs source, and secondary redactions). Due to these circumstances, one might not expect the text to appear to be an Aristotelian whole. In answer to this, I do agree that there are residues in John from different narratives in the early tradition of Christ-belief; however, redaction criticism has also taught us that in spite of the use of tradition in the gospels, there are clear traces of authorial redaction toward unified, literary wholes in all New Testament gospels. Even if this were not the case, the Gospel of John still stands as one narrative to the reader, whatever sources it may contain.

A third objection can be raised from a performance critical point of view. The gospel may appear to be a unified narrative to readers in a post-Gutenberg era, but the ancient audiences were not readers, first and foremost, but listeners. In oral/aural performances of the gospel (even today), listeners seldom have the chance to monitor the whole text but often relate to particular scenes or pericopes in isolation.[8] A reading of the gospel's plot thus appears to be an academic exercise with little relevance to real text reception. Whatever truth there may be in this, however, I do not think that it should prevent us from trying to understand how the Gospel of John functions as a narrative whole, not least because individual scenes in the gospel appear to be microcosms that reflect the entire narrative. In John, the plot of individual pericopes is often parallel to the plot of the whole narrative (which may, by the way, contribute to a sense of redundancy in the reading process).

Finally, a reader-response critical objection ought to be mentioned. This objection does not target plot analysis as such but claims that the plot is not an inherent and fixed phenomenon in the text. A text does not *have* a plot in itself, but readers perform emplotment in a process of progressive structuration in response to the signals of the text.[9] Moreover, real readers always negotiate with the text from their historical and intersectional location in terms of class, race, age, gender, sexual orientation, and so on. This objection certainly discloses that the kind of narratological plot analysis

---

8. For a discussion of the extent of the reading/hearing sessions in an early Christian context, see Dan Nässelqvist, *Public Reading in Early Christianity: Lectors, Manuscripts, and Sound in the Oral Delivery of John 1–4*, NovTSup 163 (Leiden: Brill, 2016), 108–10.

9. James Phelan, *Experiencing Fiction: Judgments, Progressions, and the Rhetorical Theory of Narrative* (Columbus: Ohio State University Press, 2007).

(Aristotelian and Greimasian), which we shall perform in the following has a blind spot in terms of the contextual dimension of reading. But no reading strategy is omnipotent. Narratological plot analysis provides a common platform from which real readers can discuss their various culturally embedded readings. After all, no one claims that the backbone of narrative is the whole body.

John's Plot: The Constellation of Actantial Roles

As mentioned in the introduction, the present chapter's approach to John's plot is Greimasian. Greimas's best-known tool for plot analysis is his actantial model. The actantial model depicts a map of relations between the main forces (*dramatis personae*) in a narrative by defining six basic and abstract roles (actants) that narratival story-worlds contain or presuppose. The actantial model is often illustrated in a diagram like the following:[10]

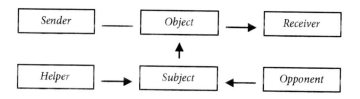

Let me explain: The *Subject*, often identified as the main character, seeks to obtain an *Object*. This is illustrated with a vertical arrow depicting the "axis of desire." The *Sender* on the upper left side is the force that prompts the *Subject* to obtain the *Object*. The *Object* is bound for the *Receiver* as illustrated on the upper horizontal "axis of communication." The lower horizontal "axis of conflict" shows that the *Subject* is challenged in his or her enterprise by the *Opponent* but has the support of the *Helper*.

The model is abstract and calls for illustration by example. In a short, well-known nursery rhyme like the "Itsy Bitsy Spider," it is relatively easy to identify the concrete characters that hold the actantial roles, even though not all of the roles are explicitly mentioned in the rhyme.[11] The spider

---

10. See A. J. Greimas, *Structural Semantics: An Attempt at a Method* (Lincoln: University of Nebraska Press, 1983), 197–213.

11. For the sake of the forgetful, let me cite the whole rhyme: "The itsy bitsy spider climbed up the waterspout. / Down came the rain and washed the spider out. / Out

(*Subject*) is on a mission to climb the waterspout, probably to reach the roof of the house (*Object*). (Is the spider climbing to attain something or to flee from something? We do not know.) The force (*Sender*) prompting the spider to embark on the quest for the object is not mentioned, but we may speculate: instinct, Mother Nature, or God? The spider itself is the one who benefits (*Receiver*) from the mission. Finally, the rain (*Opponent*) prevents the spider from reaching the roof, whereas the sun (*Helper*) dries the rain away so that the spider is given another chance:

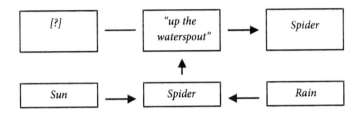

In much longer and multifaceted narrative like John's Gospel, the analysis is not as simple as this. A point of departure is required, and I suggest John 3:16 for that purpose: "For God so loved the world that he gave his only Son, so that everyone who believes in him may not perish but may have eternal life." This brief narrative is very much the Gospel of John in a nutshell, as it consists of elements that resonate in the whole gospel. It is not only a story with a series of events, but it is also a teleological plot in Forster's sense. (Let me try to rephrase Forster in relation to the Fourth Gospel: "God gave his only Son" is a story. "For God so loved the world that he gave his only Son, so that everyone ..." is a plot. There is causality and purpose in the story.)

In John 3:16, God acts as the *Sender* who "gives" his Son (Jesus, the *Subject*) in order to prevent mortal humanity ("the world," the *Receiver*) from perishing. As in the rest of John's Gospel, nothing is explicitly stated about whether death was always in the world or if it came to humans as a punishment for primordial sin by Adam or fallen angels. God created everything by his Word (*logos*), says John's Prologue (1:3), but in spite of this there was also darkness in the cosmos (1:5). This dualism is presupposed but never

---

came the sun and dried up all the rain, / and the itsy bitsy spider climbed up the spout again" (origin unknown).

explained. It is simply a matter of fact that the world is in a state of deficiency, and deficiencies are often what trigger narrative plots. Likewise in John 3:16: the Father intervenes in the human condition by giving his only son so that "eternal life" (the *Object*) becomes available. Eternal life in John, by the way, is another name for divine/human coexistence, be it in the present or in the eschatological future (5:24; 17:3). The *Receiver* is, as already mentioned, "the world," but only in a potential sense. Reception of eternal life is dependent upon human reaction to the Son. In other words, the believers and not the whole world are the actual receivers ("so that everyone who *believes* in him may not perish").

In the Son's communication of eternal life to the world, "belief" thus becomes the *Helper*—together with those who testify to that belief, for example, Moses, John the Baptist, and the Beloved Disciple. Finally, John 3:16 does not mention the *Opponent*; in light of the following verses (3:17–18) and the whole gospel as such, however, we may suspect that it is "unbelief" and its representatives, such as the worldly authorities like the devil, the Romans, and the *Ioudaioi* (the Jews, the Judeans, or the Jewish priests). Verse 18 describes the *Opponent* as unbelief in the world: "those who do not believe are condemned already, because they have not believed" (3:18). Unbelief is what hinders acquisition of eternal life, so that humans remain condemned and perishable.

This analysis establishes the following actantial constellation in John's plot:[12]

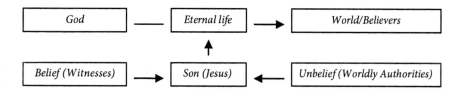

---

12. For other attempts at applying Greimas's actantial model to John, see Mark W. G. Stibbe, "'Return to Sender': A Structuralist Approach to John's Gospel," *BibInt* 1 (1993): 189–206; Stibbe, *John's Gospel*, New Testament Readings (London: Routledge, 1994), 32–53; and Andrew T. Lincoln, "Trials, Plots and the Narrative of the Fourth Gospel," *JSNT* 17 (1995): 3–29. It is an interesting exercise to insert other characters than Jesus in the actantial role of *Subject* and identify the other actants from that perspective. With the worldly authorities as *Subject*, for example, an impression of the story's "counter-plot" materializes.

The upper horizontal axis of communication illustrates one dimension of John's plot: that God by his loving initiative offers eternal life to believers in the world. In this communication, the Son acts as the courier on a journey. This is hinted at in the phrase "he gave his only Son" in John 3:16 and often articulated in other passages in the gospel describing the hero's journey and homecoming (called a universal *monomyth* by some narratologists). One example arises from Jesus's words in 16:28: "I came from the Father and have come into the world; again, I am leaving the world and am going to the Father." This journey is fundamental to the plot since it facilitates the communication of eternal life, but its significance is easily overestimated.[13]

As we can see from the actantial model's lower horizontal axis of conflict, the actual dynamics of the plot are not about the journey as such, for instance whether or not Jesus will come to the world, will submit to the Father's commission, or will be able to return to his heavenly home. Rather, as Culpepper has phrased it, the "plot of the gospel is propelled by conflict between belief and unbelief as responses to Jesus."[14] This is what individual scenes dramatize, from Jesus's encounter with the first disciples, through Jesus's ministry and the confrontations with the *Ioudaioi* and the trials before the high priest and Pilate, to the ultimate exclamation of belief by Thomas after the resurrection: "My Lord and my God!" (20:28). In other words, the dynamic conflict of John's plot is to be found in the cognitive dimension of the story-world.

THE PRAGMIC AND COGNITIVE DIMENSIONS OF THE PLOT

In the analysis above, two different but interrelated perspectives on John's plot become apparent: the journey, on the one hand, and the conflict between belief and unbelief, on the other. For a clearer view of these two perspectives, Greimas once again can be of assistance with his analytical

13. Fernando F. Segovia, "The Journey(s) of the Word of God: A Reading of the Plot of the Fourth Gospel," *Semeia* 53 (1991): 23–54; Stibbe, "Return to Sender"; and Adele Reinhartz, *The Word in the World: The Cosmological Tale in the Fourth Gospel*, SBLMS 45 (Atlanta: Scholars Press, 1992), 16–28.

14. Culpepper, *Anatomy*, 97. See also Culpepper, "The Plot of John's Story of Jesus," *Int* 49 (1995): 352; Culpepper, *The Gospel and Letters of John*, Interpreting Biblical Texts (Nashville: Abingdon, 1998), 68; and Jan A. du Rand, "Plot and Point of View in the Gospel of John," in *A South African Perspective on the New Testament: Essays by South African New Testament Scholars Presented to Bruce Manning Metzger during His Visit to South Africa in 1985*, ed. J. H. Petzer and P. J. Hartin (Leiden: Brill, 1986), 162.

distinction between the pragmic (or material) and the cognitive (or mental) dimension of narrated plots.[15]

The distinction is based on the already mentioned Aristotelian differentiation between simple and complex plots. According to Aristotle, simple plots lack cognitive elements such as *anagnōrisis* (recognition) and *peripeteia* (mental reversal), which, in contrast, are characteristic of complex plots (*Poet.* 1452a11–17). Let us, for the sake of clarity, evoke "Itsy Bitsy Spider" once again. This is a one-dimensional narrative with a simple, pragmic plot. The spider is on a quest for a pragmic object and encounters pragmic obstruction and pragmic assistance. The cognitive or epistemological value (true/false/secret) of these pragmic existents is never questioned in the story-world. Is the waterspout really a toilet drain pipe or an exhaust pipe on a truck? If so, would the rain then in fact be the helper and the sun the opponent? Such questions do not appear in "Itsy Bitsy Spider," but when they are thematized by characters in a given story-world, a cognitive dimension rises above the pragmic dimension, and the simple plot becomes complex.

As can be seen in "Itsy Bitsy Spider," plots do not necessarily contain a cognitive dimension, but plots without a pragmic dimension are hardly imaginable. The cognitive dimension needs a content, and that content is the pragmic dimension. This is, for example, the case in Hans Christian Andersen's fairy-tale *The Princess on the Pea*. In a sense, it is a simple boy-meets-girl plot about a prince who finds his princess after having given up his own search (pragmic dimension), but the queen's peculiar test of her future daughter-in-law (a pea under forty mattresses) makes the plot complex by turning focus to a cognitive question: is she a real princess? The cognitive dimension, in other words, raises questions concerning the epistemological status of pragmic phenomena in the story-world. In some narratives such as courtroom dramas or detective novels (for example a

---

15. The theory appears in its most elaborate form in A. J. Greimas and J. Courtés, "The Cognitive Dimension of Narrative Discourse," *NLH* 8 (1976): 433–47. Greimas and Courtés's terminology is "pragmatic vs. cognitive," not "pragmic vs. cognitive." I prefer "pragmic," however, since the term is intended to describe the material actions and events within the story-world (e.g., journeys, battles, and object exchanges), not the pragmatic use of the text in different social contexts. See also Ole Davidsen, "The Lord, the Lamb, and the Lover: The Gospel of John as a Mixture of Spiritualized Narrative Genres," in *The Gospel of John as Genre Mosaic*, ed. Kasper Bro Larsen, SANt 3 (Göttingen: Vandenhoeck & Ruprecht, 2015), 131.

whodunit), the cognitive dimension of the plot becomes the most important place for real drama to take place.

The Gospel of John is such a narrative—even to a greater extent than
the Synoptic Gospels.[16] Think of how the miracle stories in the Synoptics
become sign narratives in John, where focus is not on the actual miracle
(pragmic event) but on its interpretation and reception (cognitive event).
As Jesus says before the raising of Lazarus: "This illness does not lead to
death; rather it is for God's glory, so that the Son of God may be glorified through it" (11:4). Lazarus's death and revivification (pragmic event)
serves a revelatory purpose in relation to the bystanders (cognitive event).
Through John's story, the main cognitive question resounds: is Jesus
really the one he claims to be? It is raised from the very beginning in the
Prologue (1:12, 14, 18); and it is thematized in the story-world in various ways, like in forensic debates where Jesus defends his identity claims
(the trial motif; see John 5; 7–8) and in the gospel's glorification language
where "glory" (*doxa*; see 1:14; 2:11; 12:41) designates Jesus's true divine
identity and where "glorifying" refers to the act of honoring that identity
(see *doxazō* in the quotation above from John 11:4). Not least, the question
of Jesus's true identity is central to the gospel's many encounters between
Jesus and human actors who are confronted by the challenge of recognizing the divine stranger (the so-called recognition scenes/*anagnōriseis* in
John 1:35–51; 4:4–42; 9; 20–21).[17]

As mentioned, the cognitive dimension relates to events and existents
in the pragmic dimension as can be seen in John 3:16, where the plot is
woven together by means of both pragmic and cognitive elements: the
Father gives his only Son to the world (a pragmic event), and to those
who believe in the Son (a cognitive event), eternal life is given (a pragmic
event). This can be illustrated in the following manner:

---

16. See Kasper Bro Larsen, "Narrative Docetism: Christology and Storytelling in
the Gospel of John," in *The Gospel of John and Christian Theology*, ed. Richard Bauckham and Carl Mosser (Grand Rapids: Eerdmans, 2008), 346–55.

17. Culpepper, *Gospel and Letters of John*, 72–86; Kasper Bro Larsen, *Recognizing
the Stranger: Recognition Scenes in the Gospel of John*, BibInt 93 (Leiden: Brill, 2008).

John 3:16

Pragmic Dimension	Cognitive Dimension
For God so loved the world that he gave his only Son,...	
	... so that everyone who believes in him ...
... may not perish but may have eternal life.	

The pragmic events in the left column constitute the initial prerequisite and the eventual result, respectively, of the plot. The cognitive event on the right side, however, is where the gospel's focus and dynamics are concentrated as shown in the actantial model (belief versus unbelief). The same pragmic and cognitive events appear in the Prologue:

John 1:12, 14

Pragmic Dimension	Cognitive Dimension
	But to all who received him, who believed in his name ...
...he gave power to become children of God. And the Word became flesh and lived among us, ...	
	... and we have seen his glory, the glory as of a father's only son, full of grace and truth.

By the end of the gospel, the narrator's purpose statement in 20:31 once again interweaves the two dimensions of the plot and puts emphasis on the cognitive dimension. Not only the plot in the story-world but also the gospel as such in relation to its audience aims to promote or confirm belief that leads to eternal life:

John 20:31

Pragmic Dimension	Cognitive Dimension
	... so that you may come to believe that Jesus is the Messiah, the Son of God, and that through believing ...
... you may have life in his name.	

THE PHASES OF JOHN'S PLOT

The actantial model and the distinction between the pragmic and the cognitive dimension are maps of role relations and forces in the plot, but they are not dynamic models. They do not describe, for example, how the plot progresses so that the value object can finally be obtained. In order to analyze how the plot develops in the course of the narrative, one will of course have to read the gospel from beginning to end. But Greimas also offers a theory of plot development that helps us see how John's plot develops both parallel to and different from other narratives.

According to Greimas, plotted narratives contain or presuppose four phases that the subject (main character) undergoes.[18] We may understand these phases as Greimas's way of refining Aristotle's idea of the beginning, middle, and end of the plot. First, there is a *Phase of Manipulation*.[19] In this phase, the *Subject* receives her or his task from the *Sender* (see the actantial model). The task concerns the acquisition of the value *Object*, and suspense relates to whether or not the *Subject* is willing to do the task. Some narratives concentrate extensively on this phase. Think, for example, of Homer's *Iliad*, which to a great extent is a narrative about whether or not Achilles is willing to let go of his wrath and join the battle of Troy. The actual outcome of the battle, however, is not even part of the epic.

In the Gospel of Mark, the baptism of Jesus serves as his appointment by God ("You are my Son, the Beloved" [Mark 1:11]), but John's Gospel does not dramatize the phase of manipulation in a particular scene or

---

18. See also the essay on "Protagonist" by Mark Stibbe in this volume.

19. Manipulation has no derogatory meaning here, but describes employment or appointment. For the different phases, see the relevant entries in A. J. Greimas and Joseph Courtés, *Semiotics and Language: An Analytical Dictionary*, Advances in Semiotics (Bloomington: Indiana University Press, 1982).

series of scenes. There is no explicit mention of the appointing baptism in John's version of the first encounter between Jesus and John the Baptist (John 1:29–34). Instead, the appointment or manipulation of Jesus is thematized in Jesus's discourses, for example, in his final prayer as he looks back: "I glorified you on earth by finishing the work that you gave me to do" and "you loved me before the foundation of the world" (17:4, 24b). Jesus had apparently already received his commission in heaven from God before appearing in human form.

As mentioned, suspense during the phase of manipulation relates to the subject's willingness to undertake the task. Here is another difference between John and Mark. In Mark, Jesus is tempted for forty days in the wilderness immediately after his baptism. In John, however, Jesus does not struggle to align his will with God's, neither in the wilderness (1:12–13) nor in Gethsemane (Mark 14:32–42; cf. John 18:1–11) nor on the cross (Mark 15:29–30, 34; cf. John 19:30). The Son performs the will of the Father without hesitation, as stated by Jesus in 12:27, possibly as a criticism of the Markan Jesus: "Now my soul is troubled. And what should I say—'Father, save me from this hour'? No, it is for this reason that I have come to this hour." In John, we have the lost temptation of Christ. The phase of manipulation is already fixed and preexistent.

After the phase of manipulation comes the *Phase of Competence* in Greimas's scheme. In order for the subject to be able to perform the task, it is important that he or she prepare by acquiring necessary knowledge and skill. Again, some narratives will concentrate heavily on this phase. The first *Karate Kid* movie (1984), to mention an example from my personal canon, remains in the phase of competence for quite some time as Mr. Miyagi gradually reveals the mental secrets of martial art to his novice ("Wax on, wax off"). In contrast, the actual final fight occupies only a small final fraction of the movie.

In Mark's Gospel, knowledge and skill is conferred upon Jesus in the baptism, where he receives God's Spirit that enables him to demonstrate the proximity of the kingdom of God in word and deed. The baptism in Mark, in other words, represents both the abovementioned phase of manipulation and the phase of competence. In John, however, the encounter between Jesus and John the Baptist does not establish a new Spirit-possessed status for Jesus (an event in the pragmic dimension). The heavenly voice and the Spirit rather serve to *inform* the Baptist (an event in the cognitive dimension) about Jesus's true and already established identity: "He on whom you see the Spirit descend … is the one …" (1:33). Jesus, the

Logos, already possesses the necessary divine status and equipment when he first appears on stage, and the meeting between the Baptist and Jesus thus becomes a cognitive event, hardly a pragmic event. Like the phase of manipulation, the phase of competence is not dramatized but only hinted at in statements where Jesus in retrospect refers to his preexistent acquisition of divine powers: "The Son can do nothing, but only what he sees the Father doing…. The Father … shows him all that he himself is doing" (5:19–20).

If the subject in a narrative acquires his or her necessary competence, the plot can move into the *Phase of Performance*. This is where the subject carries out the actual task. Hollywood action thrillers where the story is one long battle between the hero and the villain are notorious for focusing on this particular phase of the plot. In John, Jesus's whole ministry with its constant battles between belief and unbelief (especially in chapters 5–19) functions as the phase of performance. According to Greimas, the phase of performance culminates in *the decisive test* where the subject succeeds or fails in the mission. In fairy tales, it is the famous moment where, for example, the dragon is (hopefully) beheaded.[20]

Now, what is that exact decisive test or, as it were, soteriological moment in John? Many debates in Johannine scholarship have revolved around that specific question—without actually calling it the decisive test. The Father "gave" his only Son (3:16), but what is the precise deed (*ergon*; see 6:29; 17:4) that generates eternal life? Is it, for example, the incarnation (1:14a; 3:16; 6:33), Jesus's revelation of God (1:18; 2:11), his death on the cross (3:14–16; 12:23; 19:30), the resurrection (12:24), the sending of the Spirit-Paraclete (7:37–39), or the genesis of belief in human individuals (1:14b; 17:3; 20:31)? Or, as is more likely, do these moments interrelate in some sophisticated sense? Space does not allow an actual discussion of this complicated topic, but it seems obvious to me, in spite of what was famously claimed by Ernst Käsemann, that the death of Jesus (with its multiple meanings) is an indispensable event in this respect. After all, it is on the cross that Jesus exclaims that his quest is accomplished: "It is finished [*tetelestai*]!" (19:30).[21]

The fourth and final phase is the *Phase of Sanction*. The subject receives punishment or reward according to his or her performance of the task

---

20. Greimas and Courtés, *Semiotics and Language*, 68.

21. Ernst Käsemann, *The Testament of Jesus: A Study of the Gospel of John in Light of Chapter 17*, NTL (London: SCM, 1968), 7.

assigned in the initial phase of manipulation. In the early Christ movement, Jesus's resurrection was understood as the reward bestowed upon him by God, as the Philippians hymn clearly explains: "Therefore God also highly exalted him ..." (Phil 2:9; see also Rom 1:4 and Acts 2:32–36). A similar understanding of the resurrection appears in the New Testament gospels.

John has a distinctive language for this sanction: Jesus is "glorified." In anticipation of his death and resurrection, Jesus says: "So now, Father, glorify me in your own presence with the glory that I had in your presence before the world existed" (17:5; see also 10:17). But John's point is not that Jesus receives a price that was already available to him before his mission. Jesus's mission was not only to obey the Father and be glorified for his own benefit but first and foremost, as we have seen in John 3:16, to generate belief and eternal life for the benefit of human beings. In other words, two different sanctions take place in the phase of sanction in John's gospel narrative: God restores Jesus to his glory in the resurrection (pragmic sanction), and believers obtain eternal life by recognizing Jesus's true identity (cognitive sanction).[22]

Greimas calls this kind of sanction *the glorifying test*, that is, the confirmation of the hero's true identity.[23] In the *Odyssey*, for example, Odysseus after twenty years returns to Ithaca in disguise. He has conquered Troy and thus passed the decisive test in the phase of performance. Now he is on his way home to receive his reward in the phase of sanction. However, it is not until he is recognized by his dear wife Penelope in the glorifying test (which he passes by disclosing his knowledge of the secret features of their wedding bed) that they can live happily ever after. In John, the postresurrection appearances to Mary Magdalene, the Disciples, and Thomas dramatize the glorifying test. This is where Jesus is ultimately recognized: "My Lord and my God!" (20:28). Doubting Thomas becomes the true confessor and belief defeats unbelief.

CONCLUSION

As a narrative with a plot, the Gospel of John is a text that offers an interpretation of human existence as purposeful and meaningful. Above, we

---

22. The interrelation between these two sanctions is a delicate question. For more elaborate analysis, see Jesper Tang Nielsen, "The Narrative Structures of Glory and Glorification in the Fourth Gospel," *NTS* 56 (2010): 343–66.

23. Greimas and Courtés, *Semiotics and Language*, 137.

have conducted a basic analysis of the plot in the Gospel of John by means of Greimasian narratology (with some recourse to Aristotle's *Poetics*). As we have seen, John 3:16 epitomizes the actantial forces interacting in the plot. The Father sends the Son on a mission to give eternal life to the world, but the plot of the gospel is more complex since it contains not only a pragmic but also a cognitive dimension. The latter sets the stage for the plot's dynamic struggle between belief and unbelief. In terms of the progressive phases of the narrative, the Gospel of John differs from the Gospel of Mark by locating the phases of manipulation and competence in Jesus's preexistence. Jesus's public ministry is the phase of performance with a decisive moment in his death, and regarding the phase of sanction in the resurrection, the glorifying test plays a crucial role when Jesus is finally recognized—a recognition that the gospel's audience is supposed to confirm or emulate (20:31).

A general plot analysis of this kind is basic for an understanding of John's Gospel as narrative, but it may also serve as a point of departure for more specific understandings of John's plot from various perspectives. Some scholars have tried to classify the gospel's plot in relation to universal types of plot in world literature.[24] Others have sought to understand the plot in its historical context by comparing it with plot conventions in ancient literature. Within the ancient literary landscape, different plot types come to mind. With its story about the origin, public life, and death of its main character, the gospel contains elements from the "biographical plot" known from ancient *bioi/vitae*.[25] But like in the *Odyssey* and the ancient Greek romances, there is also a "*nostos* (homecoming) plot" in Jesus's journey from heaven to earth and back.[26] John's emphasis on the recognition of Jesus's hidden identity bears resemblance to the "dramatic plot" of Greco-Roman drama.[27] Finally, a "romantic plot" reminiscent of the ancient novels may be identified in the fact that the plot is set in

---

24. See Stibbe, *John's Gospel*, 62–70 (applying Northrop Frye's theory of literary archetypes) and Davidsen, "Lord, the Lamb, and the Lover" (using Patrick Colm Hogan's cognitive-anthropological theory).

25. Culpepper, "Plot"; Warren Carter, *John and Empire: Initial Explorations* (London: T&T Clark, 2008), 144–75.

26. Jo-Ann A. Brant, "Divine Birth and Apparent Parents: The Plot of the Fourth Gospel," in *Ancient Fiction and Early Christian Narrative*, ed. Ronald F. Hock, J. Bradley Chance, and Judith Perkins, SymS 6 (Atlanta: Scholars Press, 1998), 199–217.

27. Jo-Ann A. Brant, *Dialogue and Drama: Elements of Greek Tragedy in the Fourth Gospel* (Peabody, MA: Hendrickson, 2004), 26–63.

motion by God's love (3:16) and ultimately aims toward the consummation of a divine/human love relationship called eternal life (see 15:9–10; 17:3).[28] There are, as we have seen in the this chapter, basic narrative structures in John's plot, but we must keep in mind that the plot always functions in relation to a historical, literary context. When comparing John's Gospel with other ancient narratives, one sees how John plays into different ancient plot types at the same time, thus seeking to convey meaning upon diverse aspects of human experience. As we read for the plot, the plot reads us.

---

28. Sjef van Tilborg, *Imaginative Love in John*, BibInt 2 (Leiden: Brill, 1993).

7

CHARACTERIZATION

Christopher W. Skinner

Understanding John's characters and the ways the Fourth Gospel employs characterization is crucial to appreciating both its story and Christology.[1] Studies of Johannine characterization have proliferated in recent years, and the result is that much helpful light has been shed on a previously overlooked topic.[2] This chapter is devoted to helping the reader come to terms with the function and significance of Johannine characters other than Jesus. Since Jesus is the protagonist of the story, we are given access to a tremendous amount of information about his background and identity (1:1–18), and we are occasionally told what he thinks, how he feels, and what his intentions are for a given action. By contrast, we learn about most other characters in the Fourth Gospel by observing what they say and do. While it is true that Jesus is the only character to be substantially developed

---

1. Several paragraphs in this chapter have been adapted from Christopher W. Skinner, "Misunderstanding, Christology, and Johannine Characterization: Reading John's Characters through the Lens of the Prologue," in *Characters and Characterization in the Gospel of John*, ed. Christopher W. Skinner, LNTS 461 (London: T&T Clark, 2013), 111–27; Skinner, *John and Thomas: Gospels in Conflict? Johannine Characterization and the Thomas Question*, PTMS 115 (Eugene, OR: Pickwick, 2009), 19–41.

2. See, most recently, Cornelis Bennema, *Encountering Jesus: Character Studies in the Gospel of John*, 2nd ed. (Minneapolis: Fortress, 2014); Steven A. Hunt, D. Francois Tolmie, and Ruben Zimmerman, eds., *Character Studies in the Fourth Gospel: Narrative Approaches to Seventy Figures in John*, WUNT 314 (Tübingen: Mohr Siebeck, 2013); Susan E. Hylen, *Imperfect Believers: Ambiguous Characters in the Gospel of John* (Louisville: Westminster John Knox, 2009). For a detailed overview of the recent history of this discussion, see my chapter, "Characters and Characterization in the Gospel of John: Reflections on the *Status Quaestionis*," in Skinner, *Characters and Characterization in the Gospel of John*, xvii–xxxii.

in the narrative, there is much to be gained from an analysis of the other figures in the story world of the Fourth Gospel. It is also worth noting that even though Jesus is the dominant figure in the narrative, John's Gospel is the only one of the four canonical accounts to give extended space to single characters, such as Peter, Nicodemus, the Samaritan woman, Thomas, and the Beloved Disciple.

Few elements of a story can capture our imagination and help us see the world around us like characters can. Anyone who has done much reading knows that character development—especially as it relates to a character's inner life—is an important element in much contemporary writing. The construction of personal identity is of paramount importance to modern individuals and therefore plays a prominent role both in the modern novel and the short story, the standards by which we judge contemporary literature in the Western world. When we encounter characters in contemporary literature, we are often treated to psychological profiles as figures move toward and, in some cases, away from moments of redemption. As familiar as this scenario is to readers of modern literature, this is not how characters typically functioned in ancient literature. Therefore, when approaching the New Testament narratives, we must be careful to situate characters within the thought worlds that gave rise to them. Against that backdrop, the remainder of this chapter will unfold along three lines: first, we will examine how characters functioned in ancient literature; second, we will look at the categories of characterization that have developed within contemporary literary studies; and finally, we will turn to a discussion of how the previous two models help us understand the specific characters and patterns of characterization in the Fourth Gospel.

Characterization in Ancient Literature

In the narrative literature of the Greco-Roman world, action was generally considered to be the most important element in any dramatic presentation. Aristotle (385–322 BCE), in particular, understood the function of characters in tragedy in this way, noting that while it was possible to have a tragedy without a character it was not possible to have a tragedy without an action.[3] At least two practical implications arise from this approach

---

3. Aristotle's description of how action and character function is spelled out explicitly in *Poet.* 1449b21–1450b20. See also Seymour Chatman's helpful treatment of Aristotle's approach vis-à-vis contemporary Western storytelling in *Story and Dis-*

to character construction. First, the figure performing a given action is necessarily secondary to the action being performed. Second, when the interests of character are subjugated to the action(s) of a story, characters tend to become nearly invisible and seemingly superfluous. Consequently, characters in ancient writing were often reduced to the role of faceless, formless vehicles that existed primarily to advance the action of the story. By and large, the narrative was less concerned about the inner machinations of a character's thought life and more focused on the character's spatial and situational settings and ultimate purpose. However, this only tells part of the story. There is undoubtedly a greater degree of development within ancient Greek (and Greco-Roman) literature than Aristotle's categories allow for, and while we should not paint centuries of narrative literature with such a broad brush, it is probably safe to say that many characters in the New Testament narratives function in a manner similar to that envisioned by Aristotle.[4]

When we shine a light upon characters in the Fourth Gospel, we see that, while some are developed in greater detail than others, in general most figures exist to serve the narrator's characterization agenda, which is to have John's characters clarify the gospel's exalted Christology. These characters appear briefly in the story, allowing little room for substantial formation or development; their raison d'etre is to confirm, deny, or question something about Jesus that will allow the literary audience to advance in its understanding of Jesus's message, mission, and identity. We see this trend even from the outset of the story, where selected characters appear primarily to confess something about Jesus in a way that is either consistent with or different from what has been revealed in the Prologue.[5] These figures appear and disappear just as quickly as part of

---

course: *Narrative Structure in Fiction and Film* (Ithaca, NY: Cornell University Press, 1978), 108–27.

4. Cornelis Bennema has provided a lengthy discussion of the ways in which Greco-Roman characters differed from the simplistic formulation offered by Aristotle. See "A Theory of Character in the Fourth Gospel with Reference to Ancient and Modern Literature," *BibInt* 17 (2009): 375–421. It is important also to recognize that we must separate narrative and its characters from other ancient literature specifically focusing on characters (e.g., Plutarch's *Lives*).

5. E.g., John the Baptist (1:26–36), Andrew (1:41), Philip (1:45), and Nathanael (1:49). For more on my own approach to reading the entire gospel, including characters, through the lens of the Prologue, see my chapter, "Misunderstanding, Christology, and Johannine Characterization," 111–27.

the progressive unfolding of the narrative. Though the narrator reports what these characters say and what they appear to know, they ultimately have little importance beyond their initial appearance. In what follows, we will discuss the significance of this understanding of characterization in greater detail.

DISCUSSIONS OF CHARACTER IN MODERN LITERARY STUDIES

Unlike the conclusions arising from Aristotle's treatment of character, modern literary studies assume a stronger and more intricate relationship between action and character.[6] This gap is one of the obstacles we face when attempting to apply modern literary theory to an ancient text like the Gospel of John. We must be careful to treat the gospel as a first-century text with its own form and genre expectations without importing too many modern assumptions about how narratives are supposed to work. As always, there is need for a delicate balance between the demands of an ancient text and the assumptions of modern critical methods applied to that text.

While important work was being done on the interpretation of Johannine characters prior to the publication of R. Alan Culpepper's groundbreaking work, *Anatomy of the Fourth Gospel*, there is little doubt that contemporary character studies within Fourth Gospel research are an outgrowth of narrative criticism as it was originally articulated in *Anatomy*.[7] The book advanced the idea that, despite questions about sources and redactional layers, the Gospel of John was a complete and autonomous narrative that was worthy of being studied in its final form and on its own terms.[8] While today this insight seems rather banal and possibly even

---

6. For a detailed discussion of issues covered cursorily by this section, see Steven A. Hunt, D. Francois Tolmie, and Ruben Zimmerman, "An Introduction to Character and Characterization in John and Related New Testament Literature," in Hunt, Tolmie, and Zimmerman, *Character Studies in the Fourth Gospel*, 1–33.

7. R. Alan Culpepper, *Anatomy of the Fourth Gospel: A Study in Literary Design* (Minneapolis: Fortress, 1983).

8. Thatcher states it well when he writes that "the most enduring contribution of *Anatomy of the Fourth Gospel* rose from its point where the book diverged most sharply from the mainstream of its day: the thesis that John's story is inherently meaningful, regardless of its sources, composition history, or historical value. At a time when scholars were deeply absorbed in speculations about literary sources, the Johannine community, and the number of revisions leading up to the present text, Culpepper

self-evident, at the time it was a radical departure from the *status quo*. The chapter on characters in *Anatomy* was the second longest in the book, and Culpepper's analysis remained fairly close to the predominant discussions that were taking place in literary circles at that time. Of particular importance to his treatment of Johannine characters were categories set forth in Raymond Collins's two foundational articles on "representative figures" in John,[9] along with insights from the works of Seymour Chatman, E. M. Forster, and W. J. Harvey—literary critics who were concerned with the intricacies of Western, secular, and predominantly modern, literature.[10] Using the work of these three scholars, Culpepper raised questions about (1) how, if at all, characters in literature, including biblical narrative, correspond to reality; (2) how characters should be classified; and (3) how different types of characters function in different types of literature.

Seymour Chatman

Chatman's work raised the larger question of whether or not characters correspond to reality in any meaningful sense. On one side of this debate is the assertion that characters "acquire an independence from the plot in which they occur ... and can be discussed apart from their literary contexts."[11] This has been variously known as the realist or mimetic position. On the other side of the spectrum is the purist or functional position, which rejects the idea that characters can be extracted from their literary contexts or viewed in hypothetical, nonliterary situations.

---

boldly declared that a close reading of the Gospel of John as a unified narrative could produce striking new insights" (Tom Thatcher, "Anatomies of the Fourth Gospel: Past, Present, and Future Probes," in *Anatomies of Narrative Criticism: The Past Present, and Futures of the Fourth Gospel as Literature*, ed. Tom Thatcher and Stephen D. Moore, RBS 55 [Atlanta: Society of Biblical Literature, 2008], 1).

9. The articles first appeared as Raymond F. Collins, "The Representative Figures of the Fourth Gospel, Part I," *DRev* 94 (1976): 26–46; Collins, "The Representative Figures of the Fourth Gospel, Part II," *DRev* 94 (1976): 118–32 (reprinted together as "Representative Figures," in *These Things Have Been Written: Studies on the Fourth Gospel* [Leuven: Peeters; Grand Rapids: Eerdmans, 1990], 1–45).

10. For Chatman's work, see n. 3 above; E. M. Forster, *Aspects of the Novel* (New York: Harcourt, 1927), 43–84; W. J. Harvey, *Character and the Novel* (Ithaca, NY: Cornell University Press, 1965), 52–73.

11. Fred W. Burnett, "Characterization and Reader Construction of Characters in the Gospels," *Semeia* 63 (1993): 4.

The debate over realist and purist approaches to defining character has been an important area of discussion among literary critics over the past few decades. Using the realist approach, scholars extract characters from their narrative worlds and treat them as real people in hypothetical situations in the real world. This approach is primarily associated with the Romantic writers of the nineteenth century and finds fewer advocates today, especially among those working with the New Testament narratives. As an example, the realist approach might take Shakespeare's character Hamlet, extract him from his literary setting, and place him hypothetically into a modern setting, all with the intent of asking, "How might Hamlet respond in such-and-such a situation?" Hamlet's psychological profile as revealed in the Shakespearean tragedy would be used to treat him as an autonomous individual in the twenty-first century. This approach would thus seek to analyze the character in question on the basis of what has been revealed in his or her original literary setting.

On the other end of the debate is the purist approach, which rejects the idea that characters can be taken out of their literary contexts or viewed in hypothetical, nonliterary situations as autonomous individuals. Advocates of this view would argue that Hamlet is necessarily defined by literary parameters associated with his own story like events, time period, characters, and so forth. Thus, to remove him from his literary setting would be to create an entirely new character.

The purist view is, at its most basic level, derived from Aristotle's view of character discussed above. If Aristotle's categories raise the question of the character's importance, the modern purist approach builds on that foundation by raising the question of the character's autonomy apart from the narrative in which that character originally appears. Here, Culpepper contributes a helpful point to this discussion:

> We must face the question of the legitimacy of treating the people described in a historical writing as characters.... Even if one is disposed to see real, historical persons behind every character in John and actual events in every episode, the question of how the author chose to portray the person still arises.[12]

In that same vein, Robert Scholes provides a necessary safeguard to overemphasizing the historicity of a given character in any narrative: "The

---

12. Culpepper, *Anatomy of the Fourth Gospel*, 105.

greatest mistake we can make in dealing with characters in fiction is to insist on their 'reality.' No character in a book is a real person. Not even if he is in a history book and his name is Ulysses S. Grant."[13] So, as these views are articulated, we are presently at an impasse. How shall we proceed? Do we abandon both approaches? For our purposes here, I propose that the answer is not to reject both views but rather to take the best of both and create a *via media*. This middle ground should see a given character's correspondence to reality and balance that with an understanding that each character is unique to, and ultimately a product of, his or her literary environment.[14] This means that no character can be understood as a "real" individual apart from his or her narrative framework but that (1) each is understood to possess a certain level of autonomy within the context of the narrative; and (2) every character reflects some correspondence to reality, even if he or she is not understood to be real. If we approach characterization in this way, we will see that the characters of the Fourth Gospel create sympathy among the readers as they are continually pushed toward a decision about the identity of Jesus.

E. M. Forster

Forster is perhaps best known, at least in the conversations between those working with New Testament narratives, for his hard-and-fast distinction between so-called round characters—those characters who display a host of potentially conflicting traits—and flat characters, who are predictable and largely one-dimensional. In his classic work *Aspects of the Novel*, Forster asks and then attempts to answer whether characters should be viewed as human beings, historical persons, or something else altogether.[15] Prefiguring the positions of the purist camp, Forster concludes that

---

13. Robert Scholes, *Elements of Fiction* (New York: Oxford University Press, 1968), 117.

14. Numerous recent studies of characterization have tackled the realist/purist debate only to arrive at a *via media* in recognition of the gospels' distinctive genre and other cultural considerations; see, for example, the fine discussion of these issues in Kelly R. Iverson, *Gentiles in the Gospel of Mark: "Even the Dogs Under the Table Eat the Children's Crumbs,"* LNTS 339 (London: T&T Clark, 2007), 3–19; see also Skinner, *John and Thomas*, 19–41.

15. "What is the difference between people in a novel and people like the novelist or like you, or like me, or Queen Victoria? There is bound to be a difference. If a character in a novel is exactly like Queen Victoria—not rather like but exactly like—

characters should not be extracted from the narrative and given uncondi-tional autonomy.[16] However, his deeper concern in posing the question is to understand how characters function with respect to the other elements of the narrative. This is the context in which he sets forth his well-known distinction between round and flat characters.[17]

While Forster's categories have proven helpful, many literary critics have found his dichotomy between round and flat characters problem-atic in that it too rigidly compartmentalizes characters that seem to exist on a larger literary spectrum. For instance, seemingly flat characters can express genuine insights and momentarily be transformed into characters with multiple rounded edges.[18] In the Fourth Gospel, this is particularly true of a character like Nicodemus, who early in the narrative displays an inability to comprehend Jesus's message and mission (3:1–15), then moves to a position of veiled sympathy with Jesus (7:48–52), and in his final appearance seems to be a follower of the crucified Jesus (19:38–42). His seemingly flat characteristic of misperception is rounded by the narrator to indicate not just a new trait (belief), but rather a genuine, thoroughly Johannine transformation. In this case and others, strict adherence to the categories of round and flat fail to recognize the complexity in many of the minor characters found in New Testament narratives.[19]

---

then it actually is Queen Victoria, and the novel, or all of it that the character touches, becomes a memoir" (Forster, *Aspects of the Novel*, 71).

16. Ibid., 100.

17. Ibid., 103–25.

18. Shlomith Rimmon-Kenan comments: "A trait may be implied both by one-time (or non-routine) actions.... One-time actions tend to evoke the dynamic aspect of character, often playing a part in a turning point in the narrative. By contrast, habit-ual actions tend to reveal the character's unchanging or static aspect, often having a comic or ironic effect, as when a character clings to old habits in a situation which ren-ders them inadequate" (*Narrative Fiction: Contemporary Poetics*, 2nd ed. [New York: Routledge, 2002], 61).

19. In recent years, a number of helpful publications have appeared that focus on the role of minor characters in the canonical gospels. See, for instance, Joel F. Wil-liams, *Other Followers of Jesus: Minor Characters as Major Figures in Mark's Gospel*, JSNTSup 102 (Sheffield: Sheffield Academic, 1994); Elizabeth Struthers Malbon, "The Major Importance of Minor Characters in Mark," in *The New Literary Criticism and the New Testament*, ed. Elizabeth Struthers Malbon and Edgar V. McKnight, JSNTSup 109 (Sheffield: Sheffield Academic, 1994), 58–86; and Colleen M. Conway, "Speak-ing through Ambiguity: Minor Characters in the Fourth Gospel," *BibInt* 10 (2002): 324–41.

W. J. Harvey

Harvey classified characters into numerous groups, including protagonists, intermediate characters (for example, cards and *ficelles*), and background characters. Harvey's categories—particularly protagonist and
ficelle—fit nicely with Culpepper's classification of Johannine characters.
Using Harvey's categories, Culpepper argued that Jesus is the clear protagonist of the story, while most of the other characters in the narrative
function as *ficelles*—characters that are easily recognizable and often carry
symbolic value. In an oft-cited article in which he draws upon the work of
Adele Berlin, Fred Burnett writes that it "seems best to speak of *degrees of
characterization* in biblical texts, and to plot textual indicators on a continuum for any particular text, from words at one pole to 'persons' at the
other pole."[20] This continuum must include at least three categories: (1)
agents, which have little or no development and function essentially to
advance the plot; (2) *types*, which have differing levels of character development and typically reveal a prominent, mainly static trait; and (3) *full-
blown characters* with differing levels of direct and indirect characterization. Each of these individual categories must also be understood to exist
on a continuum.[21]

CHARACTERIZATION IN THE GOSPEL OF JOHN

While the reading experience of each real reader will invariably be different, the hypothetical implied reader (or implied audience) consistently
perceives the message of the implied author correctly. In a manner of
speaking, the implied reader "gets it right" every time.[22] A necessary first

---

20. Burnett, "Characterization and Reader Construction," 19 (emphasis added).
See also Adele Berlin, *Poetics and Interpretation of Biblical Narrative* (Winona Lake,
IN: Eisenbrauns, 1994), 23–42.

21. Burnett's continuum is a construct upon which Cornelis Bennema relies
heavily in his work on this subject; see Bennema, "Theory of Character in the Fourth
Gospel," and Bennema, "A Comprehensive Approach to Understanding Character in
the Gospel of John," in Skinner, *Characters and Characterization in the Gospel of John*,
36–58.

22. Terminology such as *implied audience, implied author, narrator,* and *real
reader* is well known among those working with narrative-critical research. Within
secular literary criticism, see the pioneering work of Wayne C. Booth, *The Rhetoric of
Fiction*, 2nd ed. (Chicago: University of Chicago Press, 1983), and Wolfgang Iser, *The*

step in understanding how John uses characterization is the observation that the implied audience and the narrator form an "inside group" that has privileged knowledge about Jesus. By contrast, the characters in the story are part of an "outside group" that is constantly struggling to come to terms with Jesus's identity and mission. This insider/outsider dichotomy comes to the fore at the very beginning of the narrative through the Prologue (John 1:1–18). The Prologue describes the Word (*logos*) as existing with God with a uniquely divine status before time began (vv. 1–2). He is the agent of all creation (v. 3), the light of humanity that enlightens those in the world (vv. 4, 9), and the one with authority to both appoint God's children (v. 12) and display God's glory (v. 14). He exists in intimate union with the Father (v. 18b) and reveals the Father to humanity (v. 18c). This detailed description of Jesus lays an important foundation for our understanding of how John uses characterization; it provides the implied audience with information necessary first, to identify Jesus and second, to evaluate every character's response to him. The Prologue is thus the interpretive grid through which the implied audience can understand the gospel's main purpose, which is to engender belief in those who hear the story (see 20:31).[23] John quite often provides a dualistic presentation of the cosmos. There are the things above and the things below, light and dark, truth and falsehood. Within that dualistic framework there are also those who accept Jesus and those who reject him; there is no in-between. Thus this dualistic dynamic is also reflected in how John uses characterization.

The narrator is omniscient, knowing whom Jesus loves (11:5; 13:1–3, 23; 19:26; 20:2), what Jesus perceives (6:6, 15, 61, 64; 13:1; 19:28), and

---

Implied Reader: Patterns of Communication in Prose Fiction from Bunyan to Beckett (Baltimore: Johns Hopkins University Press, 1978). For a primer on the use of these and other important terms as applied to the New Testament narratives, see Elizabeth Struthers Malbon, "Narrative Criticism: How Does the Story Mean?" in Malbon, *In the Company of Jesus: Characters in Mark's Gospel* (Louisville: Westminster John Knox, 2000), 1–40.

23. In my recent book, *Reading John* (Cascade Companions [Eugene, OR: Cascade, 2015], 8–31), I liken the reader's experience with the Prologue to a viewer's experience with the TV show *Columbo*. Unlike most detective shows, in which the viewing audience has the same information as the characters in the TV drama, the viewer of *Columbo* has access to privileged information in the very first scene of each episode that others in the show do not know about. Thus, the Johannine Prologue and the first scene of each episode of *Columbo* serve as "audience-elevating devices" that allow for a more informed interpretation of the events that unfold as the story moves forward.

when Jesus is troubled (11:33, 38; 13:1).[24] The narrator also provides information about the beliefs (2:11, 22; 20:8), suppositions (13:19; 20:15), and memories of the disciples (2:22; 12:16; 13:28; 19:35), guiding the reader skillfully through a maze of reported activities, interactions, and conversations. Unlike the narrator, the reader is informed but not omniscient; the reader has access to much of this privileged information but continues to learn throughout the story. By contrast, the characters of the gospel do not have access to this inside view. This literary feature places readers in a position to evaluate every character's response to and interaction with Jesus. Now that we have examined the dynamics that exist between John's narrator and implied audience, it remains to look at specific characters and character dynamics within the gospel.

John's Presentation of Named and Anonymous Characters

In his analysis of anonymity in the Gospel of John, William Watty notes the remarkable precision displayed by the narrator in identifying characters by name, birthplace, and parentage.[25] He also recognizes the way in which the evangelist meticulously identifies places, defines Semitic terms, and possesses knowledge of events beyond the scope of any character in the narrative. Against that backdrop, it is compelling to note those places where concern for detail is conspicuous by its absence, particularly when it comes to the anonymous but literarily significant characters in the narrative.

Very often in narrative literature anonymous characters serve as simple agents who help guide the action of the story. We often see this phenomenon in the Synoptic Gospels where the absence of a name is often an indicator of unimportance. Noting this general trend, David Beck comments that, "some Fourth Gospel anonymous characters invert this tendency [in the Synoptics], occupy more textual space, and demonstrate narrative significance by their faith response to Jesus's word, a response

---

24. It is common for narrative critics—specifically those working with biblical literature—to affirm the narrator's omniscience. For a discussion that attempts to nuance this common assertion, see Jonathan Culler, "Omniscience," *Narrative* 12 (2004): 22–34.

25. William Watty, "The Significance of Anonymity in the Fourth Gospel," *ExpTim* 90 (1979): 209–12.

of witness to the efficacy of his word."[26] Those who might otherwise be regarded as unimportant seemingly become models of Johannine faith that is greater than those who are named directly. The mother of Jesus is a poignant example of this. Though she is called Mary in the Synoptic Gospels, she is never directly named in John. Few would argue, however, that her role is an insignificant one. In fact, some have identified the mother of Jesus as the first true example of Johannine faith within the story.[27] Though anonymous, she ultimately becomes paradigmatic for belief. Further, her simple identification as "woman" (2:4; 19:26) indicates a great deal about how John intends to present her to the literary audience.[28] Much discussion has been generated over this issue in the recent commentary tradition. While some modern readers may consider "woman" a strange and potentially disrespectful appellation, this is probably an example of how anonymity works within the specific approach to characterization that is operative in John. From an analysis of John's nameless figures, we see that the use of anonymity is an important part of the Fourth Gospel's approach to characterization.

Those interested in exploring this narrative dynamic in greater detail need only look more closely at the Samaritan woman (4:4–42) who becomes the first evangelist within the story; the royal official (4:46–54) who believes on the basis of Jesus's word rather than his works—a key theme in the gospel; the sick man at the pool of Bethesda (5:15); the young man born blind (9:1–34); and the Beloved Disciple (13:21–30; 18:15–18; 19:26–27; 21:7, 20), the one character who (I will argue) serves as the paradigmatic example of what it means to follow Jesus.

A quite common opinion expressed by literary critics is that in ancient literature a name is important for a character to have any real value within a given story. In other words, characters must necessarily have a *proper name* in order to avoid being a nameless, faceless, agent.[29] This is an

---

26. David R. Beck, *The Discipleship Paradigm: Readers and Anonymous Characters in the Fourth Gospel*, BibInt 27 (Leiden: Brill, 1997), 2.

27. See Francis J. Moloney, *Belief in the Word: Reading John 1–4* (Minneapolis: Fortress, 1993), 80–92; Collins, "Representative Figures," 30–33.

28. On this, see Raymond E. Brown, *The Gospel according to John*, 2 vols., AB 29–29A (Garden City, NY: Doubleday, 1966–1970), 1:99, 107–9.

29. On this assertion as it relates to characters in biblical narratives, see Meir Sternberg, *The Poetics of Biblical Narrative: Ideological Literature and the Drama of Reading* (Bloomington: Indiana University Press, 1985), 331. For a more robust consideration of anonymity in biblical narrative, see Adele Reinhartz, *"Why Ask My*

important claim to consider when approaching the characters of John vis-à-vis the Synoptic Gospels. On one hand, this assertion proves to be true almost without exception in the Synoptic Gospels and Acts: characters with names are examples of greater significance in the story, while anonymous characters act as agents, serving primarily, or almost solely, to advance the action of the plot. However, this is not at all the case in the Fourth Gospel, where anonymous characters represent some of the most significant figures and actions in the story. By contrast, the Fourth Gospel also introduces us to named characters who, far from becoming key figures in the narrative, serve as faceless agents who exist to guide the plot; this is particularly true of a figure like Malchus, the servant of the high priest (19:10). Within John's story-world, named characters often, if not characteristically, represent misunderstanding of or opposition to Jesus.[30] Readers interested in how John uses characterization must pay close attention to the presence or absence of a proper name and the various character contrasts that emerge.

JOHN'S PRESENTATION OF MISUNDERSTANDING CHARACTERS

Misunderstanding is a major motif in the Fourth Gospel, though little has been written on the connection between misunderstanding and character development.[31] Many characters are unable to understand Jesus, and thus incomprehension is one of the most important things we should pay attention to when it comes to John's characters. Apart from the Beloved

---

Name?": Anonymity and Identity in Biblical Narrative (New York: Oxford University Press, 1998).

30. Another interesting contrast within John's approach to characterization is the elevation of women over men as positive models with more praiseworthy characteristics and responses to Jesus. There is not space here for a full exegetical consideration of each figure, but there can be little doubt that the mother of Jesus (2:1–12), the Samaritan woman (4:4–42), Mary of Bethany (11:1–2, 28–32; 12:1–11), her sister Martha (11:20–27), and Mary Magdalene (19:25; 20:11–18) each hold special significance in the wider story. By and large, female characters—especially in their lack of association with official societal structures—appear in a more positive light throughout the gospel. On this, see Colleen M. Conway, *Men and Women in the Fourth Gospel: Gender and Johannine Characterization*, SBLDS 167 (Atlanta: Scholars Press, 1999).

31. This has been a major concern in my own writing on this subject; see Skinner, *John and Thomas*, 227–31; "Misunderstanding, Christology, and Johannine Characterization," 111–27; *Reading John*, 96–121.

Disciple (and possibly John the Baptist),[32] no character fully grasps what the audience has learned from the Prologue. Armed with this information, the audience is able to evaluate the different character responses to Jesus—all of which fail in one way or another—and further grants the Johannine Jesus narrative space to clarify elements of his message, mission, and identity.[33] In a very real sense, the Prologue fashions the implied audience by raising expectations and explaining things heretofore unknown. The narrator shapes the implied audience both by providing claims about Jesus that must be tested and by drawing the audience more deeply into the unfolding story of Jesus. One major way in which the audience tests the truthfulness of this information is by observing character interactions, specifically interactions between Jesus and uncomprehending characters.

As the story moves forward, characters appear to understand or misunderstand Jesus to the degree that they grasp ideas earlier unveiled in the Prologue. Since no character other than the Beloved Disciple (see the discussion below) fully grasps this information, each expresses some degree of misunderstanding. The narrator then uses Jesus's words to clarify the fuller meaning of these themes. Readers soon discover that numerous character interactions in the gospel follow a predictable pattern:

(1) Jesus speaks or acts in the presence of another character. This activity usually addresses some element of Jesus's mission.

(2) The character in question misperceives some element of Jesus's words or actions. This misunderstanding requires either correction or further instruction.

---

32. It is commonplace within the commentary tradition to regard John the Baptist as a reliable witness to Jesus. In John 1:6, the narrator describes him as "sent from God," a description that only applies to John and Jesus in the Fourth Gospel. However, even though John is reliable, his knowledge of Jesus is incomplete, unlike the Beloved Disciple. For more on this, see my article "'Son of God' or 'God's Chosen One'? (John 1:34): A Narrative-Critical Solution to a Text-Critical Problem," *BBR* 25 (2015): 341–58.

33. There are levels of misunderstanding in the gospel. Clearly, a character like Nicodemus represents a much greater degree of incomprehension than the Samaritan woman, who subsequently goes on to evangelize her entire village. Nevertheless, the Samaritan woman and other characters that are ultimately characterized in a favorable way display elements of misunderstanding that allow Jesus to clarify something about his message, mission, identity, origins, etc.

(3) Jesus speaks again, this time in a way that is intended to clarify what has been misunderstood.

(4) In each instance, one or more themes from the Prologue are raised, revealing the character's misunderstanding, exposing the reader's knowledge once again, and ultimately clarifying the truth about Jesus.

It is not a problem for the implied audience that characters have not been exposed to the information revealed in the Prologue. This is part of the narrator's rhetorical strategy. These misunderstandings heighten the audience's awareness and understanding of Jesus's origins, mission, and identity. The narrator then uses the discourses of Jesus to shed light on the fuller meaning of these misunderstood themes and accomplishes this in contexts where Jesus is instructing or correcting a given character.

Throughout the story, the audience is forced to return to the insider information provided by the Prologue, which allows them to evaluate character responses to Jesus along with other elements of the narrative. These misunderstanding characters advance the plot by causing the audience to look back at what has been revealed, which in turn points forward to the cumulative effect of the story to that point. In these instances of incomprehension, the audience is reminded of the information already given about Jesus and also how each character in the story has responded to Jesus thus far. This constant back-and-forth movement helps contribute to the narrator's desired effect by keeping the audience aware of what has transpired and building anticipation for what will take place as the story moves toward its climax. Keeping this narrative feature in mind, the audience sees how John's uncomprehending characters advance the action of the story also while emphasizing the gospel's Christology.

Some Examples of Character Misunderstanding in the Gospel of John

2:19–22: Jesus tells the crowds, "Destroy this temple and I will raise it again in three days." They take him literally, but he is referring to the "temple of his body."

3:3–4: Nicodemus mistakenly thinks that Jesus is talking about a literal second birth, but he is actually speaking about being born "from above."

4:10–15: Jesus speaks to the Samaritan woman about "living water" but he is figuratively referring to "water that imparts life."

She mistakenly believes he is talking about "running water" and asks her to provide this for her.

4:31–38: Jesus tells his disciples, "I have food that you do not know about." He is speaking figuratively of fulfilling the Father's will, but they believe he is talking about food.

6:43–56: Jesus tells the crowds that they must eat his flesh and drink his blood, which they mistakenly take as a reference to cannibalism. However, he is referring, figuratively, to the practice John's original audience had come to know as the Eucharist.

11:4–16: When discussing Jesus's upcoming trip into Judea, Thomas tells the other disciples, "Let us go also that we may die with him," but he fails to realize that Jesus's trip to Judea is about life rather than death. Jesus intends to raise Lazarus from the dead.

JOHN'S PRESENTATION OF THE BELOVED DISCIPLE

The figure known as "the disciple whom Jesus loved" appears in five scenes in the Gospel of John (John 13:21–30; 18:15–18; 19:26–27; 20:2–10; 21:7 with 21:20), though some also regard the unnamed disciple in John 1:35–39 as the Beloved Disciple. In these scenes the Beloved Disciple often stands in contrast to Simon Peter, who is characterized less positively. In each instance the Beloved Disciple responds to Jesus in a way that the narrator considers praiseworthy, while Peter expresses confusion, doubt, and misunderstanding before he denies that he knows Jesus. As a player in the Johannine drama, the Beloved Disciple gets everything right: twice he is found in a location that indicates his loyalty to Jesus (John 18:15–18; 19:26–27); he responds appropriately by believing at the empty tomb, even when he does not understand (John 20:3–8); he also recognizes the risen Jesus from afar while the other disciples do not (John 21:7). In what is probably the most important comment about the Beloved Disciple, the narrator depicts him as "leaning back on the chest of Jesus" (*en tō kolpō tou Iēsou*, John 13:23 [my translation])—an English rendering of the nearly identical Greek phrase used to describe the relationship between Jesus and the Father, "close to the Father's heart" (*eis ton kolpon tou patrou*, John 1:18 [my translation]). Each of these depictions reinforces the idea that the Beloved Disciple should be seen as an ideal follower of Jesus—one with whom any faithful reader can and should identify.

In his first four appearances, the Beloved Disciple is presented in a substantially positive way. He is superior in his displays of love and insight and in his proper responses to both the living and the resurrected Jesus. Out of all the disciples, he stands alone in a number of respects. He alone is privileged to lie at Jesus's side (13:23). He alone is able to ask Jesus directly about the betrayer at dinner (13:25). He alone appears at the foot of the cross (19:25–27). He alone is said to believe in the resurrected Jesus (20:8–9).

In each of these scenes, the Beloved Disciple contrasts with Peter who has failed to understand Jesus's message and mission (13:6–11, 24, 36–38), resisted Jesus's return to the Father (18:10–11), and denied Jesus three times (18:17, 25–27). However, the scene in 20:2–10 provides a truly compelling moment in the presentation of Peter and the Beloved Disciple. Both disciples have run to the tomb (vv. 3–4). Both have witnessed the same reality—Jesus's linens are there but he is no longer in the tomb (vv. 5–8). Neither disciple understands the Scripture that Jesus must rise from the dead (v. 9).[34] But, without either the benefit of sight or understanding, the Beloved Disciple alone is said to believe (v. 8).

Thus, it is clear that the story is meant to evoke in the implied audience, if not the real audience, sympathy for the Beloved Disciple while using Peter as a foil. Within the story the Beloved Disciple functions as the disciple *par excellence*. The various characters in the gospel approach Jesus with different levels of understanding, but no one—outside of the Beloved Disciple—approaches him with a complete understanding of the truths that have been revealed to the audience. In light of his overall depiction in the narrative, we can discern a specific reason for the anonymity of the Beloved Disciple. Any reader who wishes to follow Jesus as prescribed by the Fourth Gospel can become a "beloved disciple" by following his lead. The Beloved Disciple beckons the reader: "Follow Jesus as I have followed him, and you too can become a disciple whom Jesus loves."

CONCLUSION

In order to understand how John uses characterization, we must begin with the exposition of Jesus's identity and mission as it appears in the Pro-

---

34. For further reflections on this important verse, see Francis J. Moloney, "'For as Yet They Did Not Know the Scripture' (John 20:9): A Study in Narrative Time," *ITQ* 79 (2014): 97–111, and, in response, Brendan Byrne, "A Step Too Far: A Critique of Francis Moloney's Understanding of 'the Scripture' in John 20:9," *ITQ* 80 (2015): 149–56.

logue and continues to be developed throughout the story. This information provides the audience access to everything it needs to enter into the story world in a meaningful way. The audience must also remain aware that the characters in the story do not have access to the same privileged information that has been revealed to them. The intentional connection between the narrator and the audience, who together form an "inside group," thus stands in contrast to the various characters, who constitute an "outside group" shrouded in darkness, ambiguity, and misunderstanding.

John's characters also help to clarify the presentation of several interwoven theological themes in the gospel. The identity of Jesus is laid out in the Prologue and a proper or improper understanding of Jesus's identity has implications for the audience's view of belief, Christology, and the Johannine theology of the cross. These related themes emerge every time a character fails to understand Jesus. The implied audience (which already knows the story of Jesus but is being exposed to the Johannine version for the first time) understands that Jesus is "from above" and that he is the revealer of the Father. An understanding of Jesus's identity informs the gospel's christological presentation. An understanding of John's Christology further clarifies Jesus's mission toward the cross, which in turn clarifies the nature of authentic Johannine belief. Whether under the surface or at the forefront, these themes are present in every encounter the audience has with a character in the Fourth Gospel. The narrative provides the audience with the knowledge that Jesus is the Christ, the Son of God, and the revealer of the Father who has come from above, to be glorified on the cross and at the tomb. For one to believe in Jesus, an understanding of these truths must be present. By using the Prologue in concert with various characters, the narrator consistently illustrates improper belief in Jesus and beckons the audience to respond in belief (see 20:31) from a perspective informed by knowledge of Jesus's origins and identity.

8

PROTAGONIST

Mark W. G. Stibbe

John's portrayal of Jesus is notable for many reasons, but one of the most intriguing is the fact that Jesus knows what is going on in other characters' minds and hearts, while these same characters have no grasp of what is going on in his. This means that the Johannine Jesus appears elusive throughout the story John tells, just as he has done throughout history.

In my earlier years writing about John's narrative art, I emphasized the elusiveness of John's Jesus.[1] I pointed out that John portrays Jesus as evasive both in his speech and his actions. At both levels—words and deeds—he is presented as difficult to apprehend.

This elusiveness goes back to the strategy of deliberate evasion employed by the historical Jesus. This strategy, reconstructed by the author of Mark's Gospel as the messianic secret, is enlisted by John to reinforce his portrayal of Jesus as the stranger from heaven, the outsider on earth, whose actions and discourses require considerable revelatory insight if we are to penetrate their otherworldly significations. In John's Gospel, Jesus's actions are windows into his divinity, a divinity radiant with transcendent glory. His words, similarly, have more to them than meets the eye or the ear. They carry the life of the age to come within their deceptively accessible vocabulary. If a character is going to be able to experience this divine life, then a special kind of attentiveness—one not offended by "hard words"—is required (John 6:60).[2] The same, in both the context of Jesus's

---

1. See, for example, Mark W. G. Stibbe, "Hero," in *John's Gospel*, New Testament Readings (London: Routledge, 1994), 5–31; also Stibbe, "The Elusive Christ: A New Reading of the Fourth Gospel," *JSNT* 44 (1991): 20–38.

2. Unless otherwise stated, all translations of biblical texts are my own.

actions and his words, goes for the reader. Readers external to the story, like characters within John's narrative world, have to respond to Jesus "from above" if they are to comprehend him.

All this talk of the elusiveness of Jesus's words and works has proven helpful because it enables us to see within the content of the story some of the dynamics that make Jesus so consistently mysterious.[3] At the same time, these narrative probes, focused almost exclusively on content, have never addressed how this capacity for multiple responses is created in the form of the story. What I want to ask is this: what is it about John's mode of characterization that makes space for such a diversity of readings?

In this chapter, my aim is to contribute to our understanding of how John works. I want to explain what it is about John's characterization of Jesus that creates a dynamic field of so many interpretative possibilities. To that end, I am going to begin with storytelling in the twenty first century and specifically with the ways in which contemporary novelists tend to create characters. This may seem like a case of anachronistic interpretation—of imposing the standards and expectations of today's world on an ancient text. We will find, however, that John's way of revealing character, especially in the case of his protagonist, anticipates in a quite remarkable way the requirements and tactics of contemporary storytelling.

From Telling to Showing

In a chapter entitled "Welcome to the Twentieth Century," Sol Stein, a contemporary novelist, editor, and fiction-writing coach, highlights three ways in which characterization in storytelling has undergone a seismic change since the days of Jane Austen and Charles Dickens.[4]

The first is in the area of *description*. Fiction writers today spend far less time having their narrator describe characters directly. In the nineteenth century novel, a great deal of time was spent on detailed depictions of a person's appearance, personality, backstory, and habits. All this was usually done directly by the narrator. In other words, the narrator told

---

3. See Steven A. Hunt, D. Francois Tolmie, and Ruben Zimmermann, eds., *Character Studies in the Fourth Gospel: Narrative Approaches to Seventy Figures in John*, WUNT 314 (Tübingen: Mohr Siebeck, 2013), xii. "The one whom Mark Stibbe has aptly described as 'the elusive Christ.'"

4. Sol Stein, *Solutions for Writers: Practical Craft Techniques for Fiction and Nonfiction* (London: Souvenir, 1998), 42–48.

the reader everything she or he needed to know about a character's inner world and past experiences. This mode of storytelling was therefore full of references to what a character felt or experienced. Today such leisurely excursions by the narrator are regarded as intrusive. They draw too much attention to the narrator's voice; they leave far less work for the reader to do (especially in the area of inferring character); and they also slow the pace of the story down. Direct descriptions of the history and psychology of characters are therefore largely discouraged.

The second way in which fiction writing has changed since the Victorian novel pertains to *narrative summaries*. The descriptions to which I have just referred can be very brief—sometimes as brief as "Darcy felt aggrieved." Narrative summaries are far more extensive, and in today's storytelling they are deemed unwelcome. Gone are the lengthy ruminations of the nineteenth century narrator, providing expansive summaries of a character's backstory and characteristics. Readers today are used to the large and the small screen where such information has to be provided in a visual and indirect way. Narrative summaries therefore tend to be rejected in favor of "immediate" and "visible scenes." These are not connected by detailed and neat narrative segues. Today's stories move "from one scene into the next with no transition for time to pass or locales to change."[5]

The third area of difference relates to *immediate scenes*. Readers of modern fiction want scenes in which everything, including a character's thoughts and feelings, are rendered visually or audibly through action and speech. If the scene being described is not filmable, then the scene concerned is not visible. Fiction writers today are more likely to portray the inner workings of a character through indirect means, such as mannerisms, behavior, dialogue, and action. In such scenes, the narrator becomes invisible and inaudible. The storyteller now gives clues to what a character is thinking or feeling through visible or audible means. This is why we very rarely hear the voice of a narrator in movies and TV shows.

Characterization has therefore undergone a shift from direct to indirect depiction. Stories today tend to be a sequence of scenes in which there is much less direct description and far fewer narrative summaries. This minimalist style is tailor-made for movie-making and indeed to theatre, which Stein calls "a truly durable art."[6]

---

5. Ibid., 44.
6. Ibid., 43.

In my capacity as a storyteller, editor, and writing coach, I find myself having to communicate these changes all the time, especially to first time novelists who have been brought up on the nineteenth century novel. I find myself reiterating Stein's point that "imitating nineteenth century writing impedes the chances of publication."[7] We have moved from stories told to stories shown. Until the emerging author has come to terms with this tectonic shift from telling to showing, she or he is likely to continue writing in a style that will be ignored by readers and rejected by publishers. As Stein puts it, "Every form of pleasurable writing benefits from conveying as much as possible before the eye, onstage rather than offstage."[8]

Mistakes in Characterization

Stein points out that there are at least two main areas in which authors today are especially vulnerable to telling rather than showing. The first is when an author uses a narrator to provide a character's backstory. This often consists of a narrator telling readers what they want the reader to know, leaving us without any work to do inferring what a character is feeling or what they have experienced in the past. Today's fiction writers must prevent their narrators from intruding like this. This information needs to be revealed, especially through subtly crafted dialogue. This dialogue needs to be selective and largely staccato. The author must avoid what is known as *info dumping*—a tactic in which background information is dumped into a character's speech. "Henry, your son the doctor, is at the door" is an example of such a contrivance. As Stein says, "one character should never tell another character what the second character already knows."[9]

The alternative to info dumping is what is known as *including*.[10] Stein does not write about this, but it is the antithesis of info dumping and therefore has to be included in any discussion of contemporary storytelling. What, then, is *including*? Instead of a narrator describing a character's history and personality, able storytellers insert visible clues throughout

---

7. Ibid., 46.

8. Ibid., 43.

9. Ibid., 123.

10. The word is generally attributed to science fiction writer Jo Walton, who described *including* as "the process of scattering information seamlessly through the text, as opposed to stopping the story to impart the information." See Adam Roberts, *Get Started In: Writing Science Fiction and Fantasy* (London: Teach Yourself, 2014).

their story. They do not provide a complete narrative profile up front.
They distribute hints concerning a character's background and personality
through showing, giving the reader the task of building a picture from the
dispersed and gradual dissemination of information in what a character
says and does. Thus the reader of a contemporary novel is challenged to
respond in the same way as the viewer of a movie by inferring a general
portrait from particular hints.

The second way in which inexperienced authors are liable to tell rather
than show is in their description of what a character senses—what characters are thinking, feeling, tasting, hearing, seeing, smelling, and touching.
In these instances, the narrator's voice can become especially intrusive.
Stein provides some examples:

> He was nervous—telling.
> He tapped his finger on the tabletop—showing.[11]

In the first example, the narrator's voice is audible. He or she has told the
reader what the character is feeling and experiencing. This is intrusive,
leaving no work for the reader to do. In the second example, the narrator is
completely inaudible, invisible, and unobtrusive. He or she has shown the
character performing an action that functions as a prompt to encourage
the reader to infer an emotion. The tapping of the finger is therefore an act
of *incluing*. It is a visible insinuation of an invisible emotion.

When it comes to characterization, modern storytellers use different
tactics from their predecessors. The primary organ of receptivity today is
the eye. Since the advent of cinema and television, we have become used to
seeing stories rather than being *told* them. This is why Stein urges storytellers to ask the following useful questions:

> Are you allowing the reader to *see* the character?
> Can you silence the narrator by using an action to help the reader
> see what a character feels?
> Are you naming emotions instead of conveying them by actions?[12]

---

11. Stein, *Solutions for Writers*, 124.
12. Ibid., 128.

Ernest Hemingway's Iceberg

Although Stein does not mention this, Ernest Hemingway developed a strategy of characterization that is relevant here. Like Mark Twain and Stephen Crane, Hemingway was a journalist before he became a novelist. Working as a young man for the *Kansas City Star*, Hemingway learned that the truth of a story often lurks beneath the surface. Later, when covering the Greco-Turkish War for the *Toronto Star*, he developed a style of writing in which he focused intensely on surface events in such a way that the reader could infer their deeper meaning by what Hemingway had skillfully omitted. By 1923, Hemingway had started writing short stories. From his experience of journalism, Hemingway understood that a skillful writer can deliberately omit material and that these omissions could actually strengthen the story. This artful pruning of language enabled Hemingway to suggest far more by saying far less. This led him to develop what he called "the iceberg theory," also known as "the theory of omission."

In *Death in the Afternoon*, Hemingway explained how characterization benefits from the iceberg theory: "If a writer of prose knows enough of what he is writing about he may omit things that he knows and the reader, if the writer is writing truly enough, will have a feeling of those things as strongly as though the writer had stated them. The dignity of movement of an iceberg is due to only one-eighth of it being above water."[13] In other words, the author's job is to show only one-eighth of a person's character and to do that through the careful selection of details that the author wants the reader to see. If that selection is judicious enough, then the reader will infer the seven-eighths of that character that remains unseen—the bulk that never made it into the story.

Hemingway had learned from the short stories of Rudyard Kipling how to strip stories down. What he brought to the table was an understanding of the artful use of omission. Focus intensely on the right details, and you *show* only that which will entice the reader to sense the greater story that this suggests. As Hemingway said in "The Art of the Short Story," you could omit anything if the omitted part strengthened the story by making the reader feel more than they understood.[14]

---

13. Quoted in Charles M. Oliver, *Ernest Hemingway A to Z: The Essential Reference to the Life and Work* (New York: Checkmark, 1999), 322.

14. Oddvar Holmesland, "Structuralism and Interpretation: Ernest Hemingway's

Hemingway's iceberg theory signaled the shift from telling to show-ing, from narrators telling readers about a character to authors *including* information throughout a story in details that are shown not told. The small amount of revealed data becomes the raw material with which the reader imagines the much greater amount of concealed data. His or her task is to fill in the gaps that the author has deliberately omitted and then form a portrait of a character from these gaps and clues.

Hemingway's stories are collections of snapshots whose visible details and intricate juxtapositions provoke a wide range of readings. In his story-telling, physical actions and audible speeches become the apex of a more symbolic, even spiritual reality in which the significance of a character's life are accessed by indirect means. In all of this, the aim is to elicit an *expe-rience*. Storytellers do not write to convey data or facts. They write to evoke an experience that is greater than what readers encounter in everyday life. Characters are crucial in creating such an experience and—as Hemingway understood so well—this is done through artful and selective showing not through undisciplined and rambling acts of telling. As one critic of *Across the River and into the Trees* remarked, "Hemingway walks the reader to the bridge which he alone must cross without the narrator's help."[15]

John's Gospel and the Novel

How does all this relate to John's Gospel? The first thing to say is that it is not anachronistic to compare John's storytelling with twenty-first cen-tury fiction. Ever since narrative criticism of John's Gospel began, scholars have referred to the novel.[16] These allusions do not mean that John's story is itself a novel but that John's story enlists some of the tactics we see in

---

'Cat in the Rain,'" in *New Critical Approaches to the Short Stories of Ernest Hemingway,* ed. Jackson J. Benson (Durham, NC: Duke University Press, 1990), 59.

15. Ben Stoltzfus, "The Stones of Venice, Time and Remembrance: Calculus and Proust in *Across the River and into the Trees," The Hemingway Review* 22 (2003): 19–29.

16. So, for example, R. Alan Culpepper in *Anatomy of the Fourth Gospel: A Study in Literary Design* (Minneapolis: Fortress, 1983). For Culpepper's comments on John's characterization of Jesus, see 106–12. See also Robert C. Tannehill, "The Disciples in Mark: The Function of a Narrative Role," *JR* 57 (1977): 387. He defends the legitimacy of comparing John's storytelling with the modern novel: "There are qualities which all narratives share and further qualities which various narratives may share, even when some make use of historical fact."

contemporary fiction. Indeed, I would contend that John's minimalistic characterization of Jesus has a very contemporary feel.

The second thing to say is that this comparison includes discussion of John's characters. Studies of characterization in John are a relatively recent addition. Cornelis Bennema stated that character in general has been the neglected child of literary theory, and in gospel studies he describes character study as in its infancy.[17] However, Bennema's work, along with that of Christopher W. Skinner's (see his chapter in this book), has certainly advanced the discussion.

Bennema distinguishes between characterization and character. Characterization is the means by which an author constructs a character. Character refers to the way in which readers reconstruct characters from indicators in a story. In the matter of characterization, Bennema proposes that John is primarily influenced by the way characters are drawn in the Hebrew Bible.[18] Relying on Robert Alter's groundbreaking *Art of Biblical Narrative*, Bennema shows how biblical authors convey information about a character indirectly, through speech and action.[19] This artful restraint demands that readers infer a character's motivation and feelings from fragmentary data. It also results in multiple and even wavering perspectives about characters from readers both ancient and modern.

Bennema argues that readers infer what John's characters are like in the same way they infer what characters are like in Hebrew storytelling.

---

17. Cornelis Bennema, "A Theory of Character in the Fourth Gospel with Reference to Ancient and Modern Literature," *BibInt* 17 (2009): 375–76. The scene has fast been changing, however. There are now more and more studies of characterization in John. See Cornelis Bennema, *Encountering Jesus: Character Studies in the Gospel of John*, 2nd ed. (Minneapolis: Fortress, 2014). For a useful overview of recent research on characterization in John, see Steven A. Hunt, D. Francois Tolmie, and Ruben Zimmerman, "An Introduction to Character and Characterization in John and Related New Testament Literature," in Hunt, Tolmie, and Zimmermann, *Character Studies*, 1–33.

18. Robert Alter, *The Art of Biblical Narrative* (London: George Allen & Unwin, 1981). See also Adele Berlin, *Poetics and Interpretation of Biblical Narrative* (Winona Lake, IN: Eisenbrauns, 1994); Meir Sternberg, *The Poetics of Biblical Narrative: Ideological Literature and the Drama of Reading* (Bloomington: Indiana University Press, 1985); and Shimon Bar-Efrat, *Narrative Art in the Bible* (Sheffield: Almond, 1989). These ground-breaking studies all emphasized the point that Hebrew narrative reveals character primarily through a character's words and actions, not through the narrative summaries and descriptions of the biblical narrator.

19. Bennema, "Theory of Character," 378.

He also allows that John may have been influenced by Greco-Roman biographies, but here again characters are inferred from their speeches and actions, not from the psychological reflections of narrators. So even if John drew on other genres, his method is consistent.

These observations lead Bennema to conclude that John's characters are like the characters in ancient Hebraic and Hellenistic storytelling. They are unlike what we find in modern novels. He proposes that "since characterization in ancient literature was primarily indirect, the reader is often left with the device of inference or gap-filling to reconstruct character."[20] In Bennema's mind, this is where John's characters depart from those in modern novels. He writes that "the ancients did not portray character individually and psychologically *as much as* the moderns do in the Western world."[21]

Here Bennema may be over-emphasizing the differences between characterization in John and characterization in contemporary novelistic fiction. Part of the problem here has to do with what we mean by "contemporary." Bennema based his views on the conclusions of scholars whose picture of the novel may well have been more of the telling rather than the showing variety. But we live in the twenty-first century and the novel (if we can even speak of it in such a monolithic way) has morphed dramatically since even the beginning of the millennium. Whilst I agree with many of Bennema's insights about John's characters, I also want to suggest that John's method of characterization, dependent as it is on showing more than telling, has a surprisingly contemporary resonance to it.

JOHN'S METHOD OF SHOWING

I am not the first to point out the similarities between the "show, don't tell" approach in contemporary novels and in gospel narratives. Mark Alan Powell touches on this in *What Is Narrative Criticism?* James Resseguie followed suit in *Narrative Criticism of the New Testament*.[22] To my knowledge, I am the first to apply it to John's Gospel.

---

20. Ibid., 419.
21. Ibid.
22. Mark Alan Powell, *What Is Narrative Criticism?* GBS (Minneapolis: Fortress, 1990), 51–61; James L. Resseguie, *Narrative Criticism of the New Testament: An Introduction* (Grand Rapids: Baker, 2005), 126–30. See also David Rhoads, Joanna Dewey,

As we look at John's portrayal of Jesus, we can see that his instincts are strikingly minimalist and contemporary. Earlier I pointed out that twenty-first century fiction differs radically from its predecessors by engaging in far less direct description of characters, employing fewer narrative summaries, and choosing instead to present stories in a sequence of immediate scenes, using show not tell.

When we study how John chooses to portray his protagonist, we can observe that there is almost no detailed description whatsoever of Jesus. Notice how Jesus is introduced in the first episode after the Prologue, in John 1:19–28 (NRSV):

> Now this was John's testimony when the Jewish leaders in Jerusalem sent priests and Levites to ask him who he was. He did not fail to confess, but confessed freely, "I am not the Messiah."
> They asked him, "Then who are you? Are you Elijah?"
> He said, "I am not."
> "Are you the Prophet?"
> He answered, "No."
> Finally they said, "Who are you? Give us an answer to take back to those who sent us. What do you say about yourself?"
> John replied in the words of Isaiah the prophet, "I am the voice of one calling in the wilderness, 'Make straight the way for the Lord.'"
> Now the Pharisees who had been sent questioned him, "Why then do you baptize if you are not the Messiah, nor Elijah, nor the Prophet?"
> "I baptize with water," John replied, "but among you stands one you do not know. He is the one who comes after me, the straps of whose sandals I am not worthy to untie."
> This all happened at Bethany on the other side of the Jordan, where John was baptizing.

I have quoted this passage in full because it is a useful example of John's method of characterization.

Observe how the whole episode is presented as one single scene. There is virtually no telling. The narrator does not tell us what John the Baptist is thinking or feeling, only that his answer to his interrogators is a citation from Isaiah. This is minimalist storytelling; there is no narrative summary about John the Baptist's backstory, appearance, or personality,

---

and Donald Michie, *Mark as Story: An Introduction to the Narrative of a Gospel*, 3rd ed. (Minneapolis: Fortress, 2012), 99–136.

no narrative summary describing the setting in which this took place, other than it happened at Bethany, on the other side of the River Jordan. Everything is presented in an immediate scene, and anything we know about John the Baptist has to be inferred from stripped-back dialogue in which metaphors such as voice are inserted as clues. In fact, this gospel text is almost as sparse as the text of a screenplay.

Now notice how Jesus is introduced. The narrator does not intrude in the story and tell us, "While John was testifying, a man called Jesus of Nazareth was standing among the Levites. He had long black hair and deep black eyes and was watching with a deep concern for his cousin." There is no mention of Jesus at all and no mention of his thoughts or feelings about the forensic examination of the Baptist. We simply hear John the Baptist declaring to his inquisitors that "among you stands one you do not know" (John 1:26). This is a reference to Jesus. But his name is not mentioned at all.

The verb "know" here is a tactical term, as we will see soon. In this instance, it could be translated "recognize." Jesus is standing among the religious interviewers who have travelled from Jerusalem, but they do not recognize who he is. John the Baptist is talking to them about one who would come after him (one who presently follows him, that is). He is the Lord for whom John is preparing the way.

See how much the storyteller omits. All we see is the tip of the iceberg. The rest is submerged underneath John's restrained and economic showing. This establishes the ground rules right at the outset. The storyteller issues the reader with a challenge: "I will present Jesus to you in immediate scenes with no long and intrusive explanations. Jesus will stand among you as you walk through the landscape of my narrative. Will you recognize him? Will you know who he is, where he's come from, what he's here for? Will you infer from the little I reveal the much that I conceal? Will you take up the challenge to piece together the clues and fill in the gaps so that you can acknowledge him for who he really is?"

No wonder readers of all backgrounds keep coming back to John's Gospel. This story is truly cut back, like the branches of a fruitful vine no less.[23]

---

23. Further, see the essay on "Persuasion" by Ruth Sheridan in this volume.

Elevating the Reader

None of this is to say that the art of telling is entirely dead in today's storytelling. One of the ways in which fiction writers and moviemakers depart from the normal preoccupation with showing is through the use of prologues. These allow for a momentary engagement in telling and provide readers with enough vital backstory to give them some lights by which to navigate for the rest of the plot. Even some of the finest films use this strategy. The opening crawl of the first three *Star Wars* movies is a classic example.[24]

John's story of Jesus uses this tactic but restricts this kind of telling to the opening eighteen verses (just as in the *Star Wars* movies, this tactic is confined to the opening shots). For the rest of the gospel story, characters are indirectly portrayed through their words and actions, in immediate and visible scenes. Even in the Prologue—where the narration takes us further back in time and further beyond in space than *Star Wars* does— the telling is not simple and literalistic (the reason, incidentally, why the *Star Wars* prologues have been parodied so often and so mercilessly).[25] John's Prologue is full of richly metaphorical language. With its figures of the Logos and Light, it resists spoof readings and speedy comprehension. Indeed, Jesus is not mentioned by name until the penultimate verse (v. 17). So even here, in this rare foray into telling, the narrator portrays his protagonist indirectly, setting in motion a process of *including* that continues to the final paragraphs of the story.

All this is to say that the Johannine narrator does, from time to time, indulge in telling, but it is the exception not the rule. His normal method is to show Jesus's character through words and actions. The exceptions to this rule tend for the most part to serve the theme of knowing in the gospel. So,

---

24. The original text from *Star Wars Episode IV: A New Hope*: "A long time ago, in a galaxy far, / far away.... / It is a period of civil war. / Rebel spaceships, striking / from a hidden base, have won / their first victory against / the evil Galactic Empire. / During the battle, rebel / spies managed to steal secret / plans to the Empire's / ultimate weapon, the DEATH / STAR, an armored space / station with enough power to / destroy an entire planet. / Pursued by the Empire's / sinister agents, Princess / Leia races home aboard her / starship, custodian of the / stolen plans that can save / her people and restore / freedom to the galaxy...."

25. The parodies of the opening crawl of the first *Star Wars* movie (*A New Hope*) have been many. The standout example is probably the opening Mel Brooks's *Spaceballs* (MGM: 1987).

for example, the narrator informs the reader that there are things that Jesus knows that no one else knows. One notable example occurs at the end of John 2 where the narrator informs us that, while Jesus was in Jerusalem during the Passover festival, he kept his distance from others because he knew what was in their hearts. He did not need anyone else to give him witness statements about those whom he met. As the Johannine narrator observes, "he knew all people," and "he knew what was in each person" (2:24–25).

This example of the narrator telling us what Jesus knows is revealing because it not only tells us something about the character of Jesus (that he has supernatural knowledge about the inner thoughts and feelings of others). It also tells us something about the character of the narrator. In the very act of revealing Jesus's inner world, the narrator also reveals his own inner world. He shows us that he operates just like Jesus, with a superior and higher knowledge of all those within the narrative world of the gospel. Just as Jesus knows from above, so the narrator knows what occurs on earth from a heavenly perspective. In fact, this is one of the primary purposes of the Prologue, which not only hints at Jesus's transcendent backstory, but also introduces us to a storyteller whose point of view is just like the protagonist's—a fact which may go some way to explaining why it is occasionally hard to discern whether it is the narrator or the protagonist who is speaking (e.g., in John 3:16–21).

In this way the narrator artfully elevates the reader from the restricted knowledge of characters within the narrative world, so often marked by misunderstanding, to a level of knowledge that he enjoys "from above" and which Jesus maintains even while he is below. The narrator's rare acts of telling therefore serve a vital function. They open the door to a field of vision that allows the reader to experience the higher knowledge that the hero and the narrator possess. This in turn serves the rhetorical function of the gospel, which is to persuade the reader to have faith in the messianic and divine status of Jesus of Nazareth. These acts of telling are therefore not careless violations of a "show don't tell" method. They are careful and deliberate infringements designed to create a specific reader response.

JOHN'S TELLING AND SHOWING

The normal method John employs to portray Jesus's inner thoughts and feelings relies on showing rather than telling, which is why the Prologue of the gospel stands out. There are of course occasional exceptions to this preference for showing. I have already alluded to the narrator's comments at the end of John chapter 2 about Jesus knowing what was in every person, what other characters were thinking and feeling. At the start of the story of Jesus's meeting with the Samaritan woman (4:4–5), we see other instances of telling:

> Now he had to go through Samaria. So he came to a town in Samaria called Sychar, near the plot of ground Jacob had given to his son Joseph. Jacob's well was there, and Jesus, tired as he was from the journey, sat down by the well. It was about noon.

While the majority of John 4:4–42 consists of showing, there are several moments where the narrator breaks into telling. Firstly, we are told that Jesus "had to" go through Samaria. This is direct information about Jesus's inner thoughts (although the exact reason why Jesus had to take this route is not explained). Secondly, the narrator tells us that Jesus was tired, a clear insight into Jesus's feelings. What is interesting about these references, especially the tiredness of Jesus, is how they are often plundered by commentators keen to prop up theories of the humanity of Jesus in the Fourth Gospel. Scholars with a humanizing christological agenda tend to seize upon these telling moments because they are such rare indicators that Jesus thought and felt as we do.[26] However, this very tendency to maximize these minimal references only serves to highlight what I am proposing in this chapter, which is that the narrator very rarely breaks from the normal praxis of showing to tell us about Jesus's inner thoughts and feelings. Most often he chooses to display Jesus's thoughts and feelings through dialogue and action. These indirect indicators serve as clues about his character. They then function as the building blocks with which the reader can construct a portrait of Jesus's character—a portrait created almost entirely by inference.

There are occasions when the storyteller uses both telling and showing to underscore a particular emotion in Jesus's story. The best example of this is in John 12–13, as the hour of Jesus becomes imminent. In John 12:27, Jesus says, "Now my soul is troubled." This is showing. Jesus's inner feelings are conveyed to the reader through what Jesus says. But then in

---

26. See for example, Stephen Voorwinde, *Jesus' Emotions in the Fourth Gospel: Human or Divine?* LNTS 284 (London: T&T Clark, 2005).

John 13:21, the narrator reports that, "Jesus was troubled in spirit." This is telling.

Indirect Characterization

Most of the time, Jesus's thoughts and feelings have to be inferred from his words and actions, which is why at times scholars have given such diverse interpretations of his motivation. Take John 11 as an example, the climactic miracle Jesus performs in the gospel: the raising of Lazarus. His feelings towards Lazarus are established through an act of showing right at the beginning. Lazarus's sisters send a message to him saying "the one you love is sick" (v. 3). Through dialogue we are shown that Jesus has a special affection for Lazarus—that Lazarus is indeed a beloved disciple. But then the next act of showing seems to contradict this. Jesus stays where he is for two further days (v. 6). Here Jesus delays before going to help his beloved friend.

What are we to make of these two acts of showing? In the first, conveyed through words, we are shown Jesus's love for his sick friend. In the second, through actions (or more specifically, through inaction), we are shown something that looks very different—a deliberate delay in going to his aid. See how we are presented with only the tip of an iceberg here. Is Jesus being cold in this instance? Is he being callous allowing the sisters to grieve so intensely, knowing full well that he is going to raise Lazarus four days after receiving their message? Or is this an example of some higher form of humanity, in which it is possible to suffer with the afflicted here below while reigning in resurrection life from above?

See how John's very restraint makes room for wavering and wildly different views of his protagonist's character—from cold and aloof to compassionate and creative.

All this is because John's narrator most of the time refuses to indulge in acts of simplistic telling. He is not writing a didactic treatise about Jesus, in which he tells us about Jesus's motivation. He is writing a story and stories at their best show rather than tell.

The Artistry of John

Before I conclude, I want to look briefly at one passage that, more than any other, showcases John's brilliance as a storyteller of the show rather than tell variety. I am referring to John 17, the High Priestly Prayer of Jesus.

One of the greatest challenges faced by any storyteller trained in the art of showing is how to maintain the praxis of showing when your lead character is a loner. If a novelist chooses to write a story about an outsider or someone with a particularly isolated life (such as a spy), it is extremely difficult not to fall back into acts of telling when attempting to describe what they are thinking and feeling. Novelist William Boyd fell for this when he was invited to write the most recent James Bond novel entitled *Solo*.[27] The very title of the book highlights the lone wolf lifestyle of the secret agent. While Boyd tells a strong story, with all the traditional clichés, his narrator also has the annoying habit of frequently telling the reader Bond's thoughts and feelings.[28] But then how does a storyteller get round this? Does she or he have to create a character to accompany their hero so that thoughts and feelings can be conveyed through dialogue? Do writers have to construct a Robin for every Batman to get round this?

Jesus, in a sense, is the ultimate outsider. He is the loner from heaven, the Father's emissary on earth. For much of the time, John can show the character of Jesus through his interactions with those travelling with him. But there is at least one moment in the story where he is seemingly alone, longing to pour out his heart and to give voice to his secret thoughts and plans. This occurs in John 17, a chapter devoid of any narrative summary about time or location, let alone any other characters within earshot.

In John 17, John gets round the obstacles created by having a solitary protagonist by having him say everything that is on his heart and in his mind through Jesus looking up to heaven and praying to the Father:

> Father, the hour has come. Glorify your Son, that your Son may glorify you. For you granted him authority over all people that he might give eternal life to all those you have given him. Now this is eternal life: that they know you, the only true God, and Jesus Christ, whom you have sent. I have brought you glory on earth by finishing the work you gave

---

27. William Boyd, *Solo: A James Bond Novel* (London: Vintage, 2014).

28. See the two following examples of *telling* in Boyd, *Solo*: "The air smelt of booze, sweat and cheap perfume—redolent of sex and danger. There was a kind of frontier recklessness about the atmosphere, Bond thought, and recognised its allure" (79). "Bond went back to room 325 and poured himself two fingers of bourbon from his bottle and switched on the television while he waited for Delmont. He watched a game of baseball uncomprehendingly—the Senators versus the Royals—thinking that it made cricket seem exciting" (182).

me to do. And now, Father, glorify me in your presence with the glory I had with you before the world began. (John 17:1–5)

See here how the storyteller reveals the inner world of the Son by having his thoughts and feelings conveyed through dialogue—no ordinary dialogue either but intimate prayer to the Father in heaven, overheard by the elevated and privileged reader of the story. In such a way, John manages to resist departing from his normal method of showing. What so many would have communicated through artless telling, or through contrived internal monologue, John transmits through an artful and innovative act of showing.

Conclusion

The seismic change in storytelling over the last one hundred years has caused authors and readers to place a very high value on showing over telling. This showing is conveyed primarily through a character's words and works. In this way, storytelling has undergone a kind of *inclusio*, returning in the twenty-first century to the *modus operandi* of Hebrew and Greco-Roman storytellers in the first century. The preference for showing in the earlier era had a lot to do with stories being written for dramatic, oral performances. The preference today almost certainly has a lot to do with the impact of visual media such as TV and cinema. *Readers today want stories to be shown more than told.*

It is worth mentioning by way of conclusion that this may well be one of the reasons why John's stories and indeed his entire gospel lend themselves so readily to cinematic representations. In a volume celebrating the twenty-fifth anniversary of Alan Culpepper's groundbreaking book, *Anatomy of the Fourth Gospel* (a volume to which I was also invited to contribute), Jeff Staley wrote a typically insightful chapter on one hundred years of cinematic reconstructions of the raising of Lazarus.[29] He states, "The story of Jesus raising Lazarus from the dead has offered film directors one of their most dramatic visual scenes for telling the story of Jesus."[30] He

---

29. Tom Thatcher and Stephen D. Moore, eds., *Anatomies of Narrative Criticism: The Past, Present and Futures of the Fourth Gospel as Literature*, RBS 55 (Atlanta: Society of Biblical Literature, 2008). My contribution was a chapter entitled "Magnificent but Flawed: The Breaking of Form in the Fourth Gospel," 149–66.

30. Jeffrey L. Staley, "Resurrection Dysfunction, or One Hundred Years of Cin-

goes on to examine nine cinematic versions, dating from 1905 to 2003. He demonstrates that no other miracle has received as much attention from movie directors as this one. Having dissected the nine reconstructions, Staley ends up celebrating the narrative artistry of the original text, stating that "paper and parchment trump celluloid at every turn."[31]

I enjoyed Staley's chapter very much; it is beautifully written and a fine example of interdisciplinary criticism. However, I was left asking one question that Staley did not address. Why is it that John's storytelling is so particularly conducive to cinematic reconstructions? Maybe this chapter on the protagonist of John's Gospel goes some way towards answering this. One reason why John's story is so adaptable to the small and large screen is because the original script anticipates with such startling prescience the predilection for showing over telling in modern screenplays and stories. The way John shows Jesus, through immediate scenes, lends itself to cinematic representations. John's scenes are visible, and because they are visible, they are filmable.

Any discussion of how John works must therefore include discussion of John's lead character, Jesus of Nazareth. He is indeed an elusive hero, but this abiding and mesmerizing sense of elusiveness is not just communicated in and through the gospel's content. It is also brilliantly conveyed through the form in which the story is told. John gives us only the tip of the iceberg in his portrait of his protagonist. He employs a subtle strategy of omission and creates wide open spaces for seemingly endless exploration by refusing to have a narrator who tells us everything and opting instead for one who courteously shows Jesus's character primarily through what he says and does, thereby letting the reader assemble the clues and build their own picture—one seen from above, not below.

---

ematic Attempts at Raising a Stiff (John 11:1–46)," in Thatcher and Moore, *Anatomies of Narrative Criticism*, 197.

31. Ibid., 220.

9
IMAGERY

Dorothy A. Lee

Images in literary works are words that appeal to the senses to conjure up a corresponding picture in the mind of the reader. By definition, such images appeal to the reader's imagination, which has the capacity both to visualize and to interpret. The Gospel of John uses a remarkable number of sensory images to tell its story and express its unique perspective on faith. Many of these images, through the course of the Johannine narrative, take on the character of religious symbols: vehicles of the divine world. Appealing to the imagination, image and symbol make it possible for the implied reader, not only to envisage the message of the gospel in concrete terms, but also to be transformed by the life it evokes. So foundational is the imagery to the world of the Fourth Evangelist that it is impossible to read the narrative or comprehend its theology without paying heed to it.

JOHN'S IMAGES

The focus on Johannine imagery is a relatively recent phenomenon in New Testament studies. Only in the 1970's was it studied at depth or seen as little more than background for the evangelist's message.[1] The study of Johannine imagery began as part of a wider movement to take seriously the mode and means, as well as the message, of the gospel and, in

---

1. For a comprehensive outline of recent scholarship on imagery in the Gospel of John, see Ruben Zimmermann, "Imagery in John: Opening Up Paths into the Tangled Thicket of John's Figurative World," in *Imagery in the Gospel of John: Terms, Forms, Themes, and Theology of Johannine Figurative Language*, ed. Jörg Frey, Jan G. van der Watt, and Ruben Zimmermann, WUNT 200 (Tübingen: Mohr Siebeck, 2006), 1–43.

particular, its fundamental character as narrative.[2] Since then, not only has the imagery been more clearly defined, but individual images have also emerged from the shadows, along with other literary devices, to be given center stage in the gospel's storytelling.

The imagery of the Fourth Gospel is drawn from a variety of sources. Many of the images arise from common human experience (such as food, water, light, blood, paths, gates, birth); others arise out of religious experience and ritual, particularly that of the Old Testament and Judaism (the temple and the feasts associated with it, pastoral imagery, viticulture). Still others are unexpected, hardly seeming to qualify as imagery at all and possessing a uniquely overturning quality (images like the cross). Images often function in pairs, expressing varying degrees of opposition and conveying the characteristic dualism of John's Gospel (as in light-darkness, sight-blindness).[3] Even images that clearly have an Old Testament background or are located in universal experience may demonstrate a wider cultural appeal. This is true equally of imagery that has resonance in the Greco-Roman world of which the gospel is so integrally a part.[4]

The Johannine images are interwoven like a multicolored tapestry. Their narrative movement and interrelationships are intuitive rather than logical, and they weave in and out of the Johannine story in a spiral manner that defies linear logic: with repetitions, ambiguity, prefiguring, echoes, and synonymous references.[5] Ruben Zimmermann speaks of John's imagery as a "tangled thicket," a metaphor that suggests something

---

2. The classic text in this movement was R. Alan Culpepper, *Anatomy of the Fourth Gospel: A Study in Literary Design* (Philadelphia: Fortress, 1983).

3. See John Ashton, *Understanding the Fourth Gospel*, 2nd ed. (Oxford: Oxford University Press, 2007), 387–417.

4. See, e.g., Harold W. Attridge on the similar role of imagery in Philo and Plutarch ("The Cubist Principle in Johannine Imagery: John and the Reading of Images in Contemporary Platonism," in Frey, van der Watt, and Zimmermann, *Imagery in the Gospel of John*, 54–60); Silke Petersen on common images of light ("Ich-bin-Worte als Metaphern," in Frey, van der Watt, and Zimmermann, *Imagery in the Gospel of John*, 121–38); and Warren Carter on Johannine christological titles in common with Roman imperial titles (*John and Empire: Initial Explorations* [London: T&T Clark, 2008], 185–97).

5. Karoline M. Lewis defines these as features that challenge a linear reading of the Fourth Gospel; see *Rereading the "Shepherd Discourse": Restoring the Integrity of John 9:39–10:21*, StBibLit 113 (New York: Lang: 2008), 81–127. In addition, see the essay on "Time" by Douglas Estes in this volume.

of the complexity and, at times, density and even confusion of the images within the Johannine story.[6] Through linkage and enlargement, an image can become a network, shifting in unexpected ways. Water, for example, can be used variously in different contexts of the gospel for drinking (4:13–14; 7:37–38), cleansing rites (2:6), washing away dirt (13:5–10), pruning (15:2–3), and the turbulence of the sea (6:18); in turn, these portray, variously, the satisfying of the desire for authentic life, the need for a sense of purification and release from sin, the increase of love, and authority over the forces of chaos and futility.

Not all images have equal weight in John's narrative. R. Alan Culpepper makes a distinction between different types of imagery, whether personal or impersonal. Some images have core status within the gospel while others have only peripheral significance. Culpepper identifies the three core impersonal images of the gospel as light, bread, and water, which expand throughout the narrative and take on additional meaning.[7] Craig Koester likewise speaks of "core" and "supporting" images. Thus the water which becomes wine at the wedding at Cana is a core image because it recurs throughout the narrative in significant contexts, as we have noted, whereas the stone water jars, found only in the one narrative context, have only a supporting function.[8]

To the core impersonal images of light, bread, and water we can add the two main personal images of the gospel that function as narrative pairs: flesh-glory and Father-Son. Both are christological, depicting Jesus's complex identity in the gospel, the unique relationship he shares with God, and his self-revelation to believers.[9] A further image that wends its way through the gospel story, from beginning to end, is that of the courtroom, on which other imagery and concepts such as witness, testimony, truth and trial hang (see, for example, 1:7–8, 19–27; 3:11; 4:39; 5:31–47;

6. Zimmermann, "Imagery in John," 1, quoting A. Jülicher.

7. Culpepper, *Anatomy of the Fourth Gospel*, 189–97, 189–90. See Jan G. van der Watt, *Family of the King: Dynamics of Metaphor in the Gospel according to John*, BibInt 47 (Leiden: Brill, 2000), 101.

8. Craig R. Koester, *Symbolism in the Fourth Gospel: Meaning, Mystery, Community*, 2nd ed. (Minneapolis: Fortress, 2003), 3–15.

9. On "flesh" and "glory" in the Fourth Gospel, see Dorothy A. Lee, *Flesh and Glory: Symbol, Gender, and Theology in the Gospel of John* (New York: Crossroad, 2002), 29–64; on the Father-Son figurative network throughout the gospel, see Adesola Joan Akala, *The Son-Father Relationship and Christological Symbolism in the Gospel of John*, LNTS 505 (London: Bloomsbury, 2014), 127–213.

11:47–53; 15:28–29; 16:8–11; 18:28–19:16a; 19:35; 21:24).[10] The most significant animal image (and there are several) is that of the lamb (1:29, 36). These all play a core function within the wider panoply of imagery within the gospel, forming the pillars of the Johannine gospel around which the storytelling turns.

There is no actual term for "image" in the Gospel of John. The nearest is the word *paroimia*, which John uses in two narrative contexts (10:6; 16:25) and which is usually translated "figure of speech" or "parable." One proposal is that "image" could translate *paroimia*, which seems at first to make sense in the gospel—though the lack of explicit terminology need not deny the centrality of imagery within the narrative.[11] However, the point of the *paroimiai* is that they are inaccessible to the disciples until Jesus enlightens them; their significance lies, not in their sensuous quality, but rather in their incomprehensibility.[12] From the viewpoint of the disciples, they are indeed "riddles," requiring a new vision to grasp their meaning.[13]

The term "image," moreover, has another implicit parallel in the Fourth Gospel. In Gen 1, on the sixth day human beings are created in the "image and likeness" of God; they are made *kat' eikona hēmeteran/ theou* ("according to our/God's image," LXX Gen 1:26–27).[14] With its background in the creation narratives, the Johannine Prologue echoes this language in the synonymous imagery of believers becoming *tekna theou* ("children of God," 1:12).[15] Here the "image of God," once given but by implication lost in creation, is restored in the new "birth" through the regenerative work of the Spirit (1:13; 3:3–9).

---

10. For a summary of the trial imagery and its symbolic import, see Dorothy A. Lee, "Witness in the Fourth Gospel: John the Baptist and the Beloved Disciple as Counterparts," *ABR* 61 (2013): 2–9.

11. Zimmermann, "Imagery in John," 9–14.

12. So Lewis, "Shepherd Discourse," 2–7, 82–84.

13. Further on this, see Paul N. Anderson, *The Riddles of the Fourth Gospel: An Introduction to John* (Minneapolis: Fortress, 2011), esp. 67–90.

14. Unless otherwise stated, all translations of biblical texts are my own.

15. Further on creation language and the Prologue, see Mary E. Coloe, "Theological Reflections on Creation in the Gospel of John," *Pacifica* 24 (2011): 1–12.

IMAGES AND THE SENSES

The way the senses operate in John's storytelling is definitive for under-standing his use of imagery.[16] Images appeal to the senses by definition, through sight, hearing, taste, touch, and smell, but John explicitly features all five senses within his narrative. All the senses are overt in the imagery of the Fourth Gospel, and all engage the reader at a physical level. The most important senses, for this Evangelist, are those of seeing and hearing, which are common Johannine metaphors for believing and the life of faith.

Visual imagery is present from the beginning of the Johannine story. "Come and see!" say the characters in the opening narrative (1:39, 46). Similarly, towards the end of the public ministry, Greeks (gentiles) come and ask to "see Jesus," now a metaphor of incipient faith (12:21)—as is clear from Jesus's response to their request, with its discipleship imagery (12:25-26).[17] While there is a mundane meaning, there is also a meta-phorical sense for those verbs connected to sight in the gospel. Characters may see Jesus with physical eyes, but only those who believe truly see him, since to see Jesus is to see the glory of God (12:45; 14:7-9; 17:24). Jesus also has the ability to see into the human heart (1:48-49; 2:23-25; 4:18; 8:38). Sight imagery is closely allied to the core image of light (1:9; 8:12; 9:5-7, 37), with its opposing pairs, blindness and darkness, signifying unbelief. For John, human beings gain sight, not by their own nature or capacities (1:12-13), but through the revivifying work of the Spirit (3:3-8). In the resurrection narratives, the various images—the folded linen cloths, the presence of the two angels, the wounds of Jesus, the miraculous catch of fish, and the charcoal fire on the beach with fish and bread—all point to the new life embodied in the resurrected Jesus and his ongoing presence in the community beyond Easter (John 20-21).[18]

---

16. See Dorothy A. Lee, "The Gospel of John and the Five Senses," *JBL* 129 (2010): 115-27.

17. So, e.g., Francis J. Moloney, *The Gospel of John*, SP 4 (Collegeville, MN: Litur-gical Press, 1998), 359; Craig S. Keener, *The Gospel of John: A Commentary*, 2 vols. (Peabody, MA: Hendrickson, 2003), 2:871-72. Jean Zumstein sees the coming of the Greeks as pointing to the effects of Jesus's death on the pagan world; see *L'Évangile selon Saint Jean (1-12)* (Genève: Labor et Fides, 2014), 398-99.

18. Assuming that John 21, whatever its prehistory, is to be read as integral to the narrative of the Fourth Gospel; see R. Alan Culpepper, "Designs for the Church in the Imagery of John 21:1-14," in Frey, van der Watt, and Zimmermann, *Imagery in*

Disciples are exhorted not only to see but also to hear the words of Jesus and heed them. Hearing is the second most frequent and important of the senses in John's Gospel, and it has a mundane as well as metaphorical meaning (3:32). To hear means, for John, to follow Jesus and so attain eternal life, and authentic hearing is the sign that final judgment has taken place in the life of the believer (5:24). The first two disciples hear the witness of John the Baptist and follow Jesus (1:37, 40), and the Baptist hears the voice of the Bridegroom (3:29).[19] The mother of Jesus tells the servants at the wedding to heed the commands of her son (2:5). The sheep hear the voice of the Good Shepherd who names them (10:3, 27), and Mary Magdalene hears and recognizes the same voice on Easter Day (20:16). Above all, Lazarus hears the word of life summoning him to life through the cold, stone walls of death, in that place of silence where no voice speaks (5:25, 28; 11:43–44).

The capacity for "hearing," moreover, originates in the divine realm. Jesus uniquely hears the Father's voice and speaks it (8:26, 40), so that to hear his words is to hear the words of God (14:24). God only speaks once in the gospel, and those standing around do not hear it aright, in contrast to Jesus himself (12:29). This capacity marks Jesus out from others, since only he hears the Father's voice, while the Father, in turn, hears the voice of the Son (11:41). The Spirit-Paraclete shares in the same divine hearing, voicing only what has first been heard (16:13).

Taste is a further sensual image that helps to define relationship with Jesus for the Evangelist. The imagery is present mainly in the language of eating and drinking, where food and drink signify participation in the revelation. Jesus offers the Samaritan woman the "living water" (*hydōr zōn*, 4:10–14) of Wisdom and the Spirit (7:37–39). Even Jesus himself hungers and thirsts (4:6–7) and participates in meals (12:1–8; 13:1–30). At the second Passover in the gospel, Jesus feeds the multitude, revealing himself to be the manna, the bread of heaven: he is the hospitable host and also the food itself.[20] In the passion narrative, Jesus makes clear his intention

---

the Gospel of John, 369–72. See also the essay on "Closure" by Francis J. Moloney in this volume.

19. On the bridegroom imagery, see Mary L. Coloe, "Witness and Friend: Symbolism Associated with John the Baptiser," in Frey, van der Watt, and Zimmermann, *Imagery in the Gospel of John*, 319–32.

20. For more on the pattern of feeding throughout John's Gospel, see Adam C. English, "Feeding Imagery in the Gospel of John: Uniting the Physical and the Spiri-

to drink the Father's cup (18:11) and, on the cross, his thirst for God's will is fulfilled in his last words: "I thirst ... it is accomplished" (*Dipsō ... tetelestai*, 19:28, 30). The raging thirst immediately before Jesus's death indicates the zeal that takes him to the cross. After death, Jesus becomes the source of living water and sacramental blood for all believers, quenching the desire for life in the search for God (19:37). The imagery portrays access to eternal life: the deathless life that the Johannine Jesus donates through his own hunger and thirst, his own self-giving.[21]

Images of touch are less frequent in John but nonetheless present. Jesus's touch expresses the intimacy of love and healing, as in the healing of the man born blind. The spittle, the dust, the physical touch, and the waters of Siloam operate as primary images to give the man a sight he has never possessed (9:6–7; cf. Gen 2:7). The sensuous anointing of Jesus's feet as well as his washing of the disciples' feet are further examples of the imagery of touch. Mary's action corresponds to the costliness of Jesus's act in raising her brother to life (11:45–57), while his washing of the feet articulates what it means to be in union with him and cleansed in his sacrificial death (13:8). The resurrection narratives also use images of touch, though more ambiguously. Mary Magdalene's touch suggests misunderstanding, since Jesus's glorification is incomplete (20:17), while Thomas seems rather to choose confession of faith in the risen Christ (20:27–28).

John also uses the striking metaphor of the Father giving all things into the Son's hands (3:35, 13:3), a metaphor that encapsulates the agency of the Johannine Jesus and the unique role he plays in bridging the gulf between Creator and creation. As a consequence, believers can never be taken from the Son's—and therefore the Father's—hands (10:28–29). The handing over of all things to the Son includes the community of the faithful, who are protected even in the midst of persecution because they are secure in the hands of the Shepherd, a hold that is stronger than death.

---

tual," *PRSt* 28 (2001): 203–14; see also Petrus Maritz and Gilbert Van Belle, "Imagery of Eating and Drinking in John 6:35," in Frey, van der Watt, and Zimmermann, *Imagery in the Gospel of John*, 333–52.

21. On hunger and thirst as expressions of Johannine anthropology, see Craig R. Koester, "What Does It Mean to Be Human? Imagery and the Human Condition in John's Gospel," in Frey, van der Watt, and Zimmermann, *Imagery in the Gospel of John*, 409–14.

Here the imagery of touch reveals the tangible nature of Jesus's ongoing presence with believers.

Even the sense of smell, though rare, is palpable in the narrative: in the stench of death (11:39), the odor of nard (12:3b), and the overpowering smell of a hundredweight of spices (19:39). The home of Martha, Mary, and Lazarus is flooded with the scent of life in Mary's anointing: "a pound of costly oil, made from pure nard" (*litran myrou nardou pistikēs polytimou*, 12:3a).[22] The Johannine Jesus explicitly connects the fragrance to his own death and burial (12:7) and, by implication, his resurrection, to which the raising of Lazarus points.[23] Similarly, in the burial, Jesus's body is embalmed in myrrh and aloes, prepared by Joseph of Arimathea and Nicodemus (19:38–42).[24] The body does not decompose, as does that of Lazarus: its short sojourn in the tomb, and the fragrant spices which embalm it, ensure no decay is possible. Odor itself prefigures the garden (*kēpos*, 18:1, 26; 19:41), with the fragrance of spring and blossoming flowers and herbs. In this aromatic place, Mary Magdalene finds new life in the presence of the "gardener" (*kēpouros*, 20:15). Thus, in two narrative contexts, the imagery of touch and smell signify both life and death: the tangible reality of human mortality but also, at a deeper level, the presence of eternal life.

There are other senses beyond the traditional five. The sense of movement, for example, is evoked in verbs that outline an active and committed discipleship—paradoxically, in the abiding language (1:38–39; 6:56; 15:4–10), which evokes images of rest and relationship, and more dynamically (and more familiarly from the Synoptic tradition) in the imagery of following (1:43; 12:26; 13:36–37; 21:19–22). It is present in corresponding nouns that evoke a sense of place, geographical destiny, and home: rooms, the path, the way, the door, as well vertical imagery of "above" and "below." Images of growth also belong within this kinesthetic sense, as in the fields

---

22. On the contrast between the two odors, see Dorothy A. Lee, *The Symbolic Narratives of the Fourth Gospel: The Interplay of Form and Meaning*, JSNTSup 95 (Sheffield: JSOT Press, 1994), 222 n. 2; and Lee, *Flesh and Glory*, 205–6; see also Gail R. O'Day, "John," in *The Women's Bible Commentary*, ed. Carol A. Newsom and Sharon H. Ringe, expanded ed. (Louisville: Westminster John Knox, 1998), 387.

23. Brendan Byrne, *Life Abounding: A Reading of John's Gospel* (Collegeville, MN: Liturgical Press, 2014), 198–99.

24. On the link between the two odors, see Dominika A. Kurek-Chomycz, "The Fragrance of Her Perfume: The Significance of Sense Imagery in John's Account of the Anointing in Bethany," *NovT* 52 (2010): 334–54.

ripe for harvest (4:35–38), the buried seed that will suddenly shoot into fecundity and life (12:24), and the burgeoning clusters of grapes on the vine (15:5).

A further set of imagery founded on sensual human experience is present in the subjective arena of human relationships: in the birth of children (1:12–13; 3:3–8), in the relationship between siblings (20:17), and above all in the foundational intimacy of parent and child (1:14–18; 5:18–23; 14:8–13; 17:1–5, 25–26; 19:25–27). These images have a core place in the gospel's Christology and in its understanding of the community of faith. Here traditional kinship imagery becomes the means of depicting the significance of Jesus and his disciples. Similarly, other, more public kinds of relationship are employed as images in the Fourth Gospel, often in a deconstructive way that reshapes the basic power relationship: the affinity and interdependence between a ruling king and his subjects or citizens (1:49; 6:1–15; 10:11–15; 12:13–15; 18:37; 19:19–20), a lord or master and his servants (15:12–17, 20; 20:16), a teacher and his band of students (1:38–39; 13:12–16).

Image and Metaphor

Johannine imagery, apprehended through the senses, displays itself most commonly through metaphor, which locates a distinct image within the structure of a sentence. Metaphor can be defined as "that figure of speech whereby we speak about one thing in terms which are seen to be suggestive of another."[25] Real metaphors possess cognitive content as well as intuitive power, engaging and enlarging the reader's understanding. For that reason, they are not decorations to sweeten the plain meaning of the story, nor are they pedagogical aids to illustrate the message. They are constitutive of meaning, giving rise to a sense of delight, surprise, or shock, taking the conventional and transforming it into something fresh and vital, so that "the power of the familiar is altered and a new potency infused."[26] They have the capacity to carry the reader "into the figurative or spiritual world" and

25. Janet Martin Soskice, *Metaphor and Religious Language* (Oxford: Oxford University Press, 1987), 15.

26. Robert Kysar, "The Making of Metaphor: Another Reading of John 3:1–15," in *"What Is John?" Volume 1: Readers and Readings of the Fourth Gospel*, ed. Fernando F. Segovia, SymS 3 (Atlanta: Scholars Press, 1996), 37.

to "transform realities."[27] Indeed a series of different but related metaphors can combine to create a "metaphorical field." Jan van der Watt, for example, sees the metaphor of believers belonging to "the family of the King" as one such example, where, through the familial metaphor, "John creates what can be called a metaphorical network based on the social reality of family life."[28]

Metaphor is created by bringing together two separate elements to create something new: the object of the image ("tenor"), sometimes implied rather than explicit, and the image itself ("vehicle").[29] The reader must move from the literal sense to the metaphorical, which is the spiritual meaning the gospel intends. Thus the metaphor contains an "is" and an "is not" dimension. In the metaphor "Jesus is the light of the world" (*to phōs tou kosmou*, 8:12; 9:5), "Jesus" is the object or tenor while "light" is the image itself, the vehicle. It is true that this particular metaphor is already present in the Old Testament, in depictions of God or the torah as light (see, for example, Pss 27:1; 36:9; 43:3; 119:105; Prov 6:23; Isa 60:1, 19–20), and in the Feast of Tabernacles. Nonetheless, the Fourth Evangelist gives this Old Testament metaphor a new tenor or object in relation to the Johannine Jesus. The movement from the literal to the metaphorical thus begins when the reader realizes the inadequacy of the literal level to convey the meaning, since Jesus is not literally the sun, and is compelled to search out a further meaning to make sense of the metaphor, leaping beyond the "is not" of the first level to the metaphorical "is." In order to grasp the metaphorical meaning, however, the reader needs to retain a firm grasp on the literal meaning. This process has been called the capacity for "stereoscopic vision," the ability of the reader to find figurative meaning without abandoning the original image.[30] The literal is thus never abandoned, so that a literary critic such as Northrop Frye can speak of a paradoxical reversal where, in the deepest sense, the "literal meaning" is the poetic meaning.[31]

---

27. Van der Watt, *Family of the King*, 151.

28. Ibid., 162.

29. See I. A. Richards, *The Philosophy of Rhetoric* (New York: Oxford University Press, 1936); Paul Ricoeur, *The Rule of Metaphor: Multi-disciplinary Studies of the Creation of Meaning in Language*, trans. Robert Czerny with Kathleen McLaughlin and John Costello, S. J. (London: Routledge & Kegan Paul, 1977), 80–81.

30. Ricoeur, *Rule of Metaphor*, 247–56.

31. Northrop Frye, *The Great Code: The Bible and Literature* (London: Routledge & Kegan Paul, 1981), 61.

This intricate yet intuitive process in which the reader is involved (mostly unconsciously) demonstrates that metaphors and the images on which they are centered have the function of creating meaning. The metaphors of the gospel are neither arbitrary nor decorative—as if the image were to be discarded once the kernel of meaning had been located.[32] Rather image and metaphor are fundamental to the meaning of the gospel and foundational to its structure. John's metaphors convey what is, for the Evangelist, the very heart of truth, as he understands it. They are not present to decorate the meaning or to make it palatable to the reader. They are substantial and meaningful, possessing cognitive content; content that can be both analyzed and paraphrased but never replaced. The medium, in this sense, is the message; the outer form communicates and conveys the inner meaning.[33]

Many similes share the same structure as metaphor. Janet Soskice has argued that intense and vivid similes have the same incremental nature as metaphor—that is, they contain meaning and are not merely decorative or illustrative—and function in a similar way.[34] The "like" or "as" contained in the simile does not significantly alter the metaphorical character. There is one such simile in John's Gospel that clearly possesses metaphorical force. The divine glory revealed in the flesh of the Logos is described as being "as of an only child from a father" (*hōs monogenous para patros*, 1:14). This familial simile operates as a metaphor, with an "is" and "is not" dimension. The Logos is not biologically the Son of God; indeed, no mention of Jesus's literal parentage occurs until the wedding at Cana, in the appearance of "the mother of Jesus" (2:1). Yet the simile creates meaning by enlarging the reader's metaphorical understanding. The abstract and confusing language of the opening verses, in which *logos* ("word") and *theos* ("God") exist in a complex interrelationship of identity and difference ("with God," "was God," 1:1–2), now becomes comprehensible in the core simile of a son disclosing the identity of his father, without the two being one and the same. The imagery may be unpacked and even paraphrased, but in the Johannine worldview it cannot be exchanged; it does not decorate or illustrate Johannine truth but both possesses and discloses it.

---

32. See Lee, *Flesh and Glory*, 9–28.
33. See Ashton, *Understanding the Fourth Gospel*, 491–529.
34. Soskice, *Metaphor*, 58–60.

Image and Narrative

The images and metaphors of the gospel are inextricably linked to the Johannine story, each supporting and depending on the other. The narrative is created by the images, which give the narrative its unique shape and form in turn. This process of unveiling the imagery occurs mostly in dialogue with Jesus, through misunderstanding of the image and subsequent elucidation by Jesus. Indeed, much of the characteristic misunderstanding of the dialogues in the Fourth Gospel arises from the struggle of the characters to find the metaphorical meaning in and through the literal meaning. In some cases, the figurative meaning is grasped, and the main character reaches faith and understanding, at least in good part (water and thirst in the dialogue with the Samaritan woman, 4:1–42).[35] In other cases, the metaphor remains stubbornly opaque and the character remains frozen, unable to choose between belief and unbelief ("birth" in the story of Nicodemus, 3:1–21). In still other narratives, the metaphorical meaning is rejected by the main character or character group, which leads to the deepening of misunderstanding and final rejection of the Johannine Jesus (bread and manna in the feeding story, 6:35–65). In most cases, this movement to and from faith takes place in conversation with Jesus. In the story of the man born blind, however, Jesus is mostly absent. The same process takes place this time through interrogation and persecution, so that the imagery of light and darkness, blindness and sight, reveals itself paradoxically in the experience of the man and his judges (9:1–41).[36]

Within this framework, image, metaphor, and narrative work together to disclose the symbols of the narrative.[37] Metaphor is itself the linguistic side of symbol drawing together, as we have seen, two unlike elements in a phrase or sentence to create a new, semantic identity. The emergent symbolic meaning pushes us into and beyond the literal level. In this sense, metaphor sometimes works closely alongside irony in the narrative, both

---

35. See the essay "Characterization" by Christopher W. Skinner in this volume.

36. For a summary of the steps in the narratives, see Lee, *Symbolic Narratives*, 228–30.

37. As Koester points out, not all images become symbols (*Symbolism*, 7–8), a point that raises the question of how far we can go in interpreting images as Johannine symbols; on this, see especially Paul N. Anderson, "Gradations of Symbolization in the Johannine Passion Narrative: Control Measures for Theologizing Speculation Gone Awry," in Frey, van der Watt, and Zimmermann, *Imagery in the Gospel of John*, 157–94.

of them drawing out the symbolism in the contrast between the literal level and the metaphorical.[38] The two levels may be in opposition—as in irony—or there may be an extension of the literal level. Usually, however, the literal level collapses or gives way before the metaphorical and symbolic level. At the same time, the literal is necessary for the symbol to emerge and cannot be discarded without damage to John's message.

One of the best examples of this use of imagery in John's storytelling is that of the cross (*stauros*). This image, though it constitutes the heart of the passion narrative, also wends its way throughout the gospel so that, by the time we reach the crucifixion story, the reader's mind has been formed and stretched through supporting images in the earlier narratives of the gospel. The reader does not approach the crucifixion, therefore, as a despairing narrative of shame and degradation, but rather as the climactic high point of the incarnation: the full and radiant revelation of God's being. The cross itself, while an image in its own right—and a countercultural image at that—now becomes infused with other images to direct and shape the reader's imagination.

There are three types of images, in particular, that bring about this metaphorical shift and display John's unique understanding of the cross.[39] In the first place, John reshapes the cross through pastoral imagery. The imagery of the lamb is already a complex image of life in the Old Testament. John uses it in a specific sense, drawing out the implicit, paschal symbolism, as well as other Old Testament imagery of cult and atonement, to depict Jesus on the cross as the Passover lamb, the means of liberation for the community of faith. The core paschal meaning is overlaid also with the definitive overcoming and removal of sin: "Behold, God's Lamb who takes away the world's sin!" (*ho amnos tou theou ho airōn tēn hamartian tou kosmou*, 1:29).[40]

This image is connected, within its own metaphorical field, to other pastoral images, and particularly that of the Good Shepherd (*ho poimēn ho kalos*, 10:1–18). Much of this text and its imagery is concerned with the meaning of eternal life, drawing on Old Testament images of Israel as the

---

38. On irony in the Johannine narrative, see, e.g., Paul D. Duke, *Irony in the Fourth Gospel* (Atlanta: John Knox, 1985).

39. For a comprehensive outline of John's theology of the cross, see John Morgan-Wynne, *The Cross in the Johannine Writings* (Eugene, OR: Pickwick, 2011), 132–85.

40. For more on this image, see Dorothy A. Lee, "Paschal Imagery in the Gospel of John: A Narrative and Symbolic Reading," *Pacifica* 24 (2011): 13–28.

flock with God as their true Shepherd-King. Once again, John reshapes Old Testament imagery to give it a radically new meaning. The Johannine Shepherd is good, not just because he knows the sheep by name or because he makes provision for their safety and nourishment (which he does), but ultimately because he gives up his life for theirs. Here the imagery becomes stretched to breaking point: no shepherd is expected to give that degree of service! What stretches the imagery, however, is not just the degree of love shown by the Good Shepherd, but also the authority which he possesses: the uniquely divine authority over life and death. He has authority not only to give away his life but also to take it back on the other side of the grave (10:17–18). When we come to the passion narrative, we read in it the paschal lamb whose death drives out sin, but we also perceive the Good Shepherd, the Lord of life, giving up his own life (which is not, despite appearances, taken from him) and therefore capable of, and intent on, taking back that life. We read in it, not just the incomparable divine love of the Shepherd for the flock, but also his authority (*exousia*) over all the forces of destruction and harm.

Second, the cross as symbol is restructured through the Old Testament image of the bronze serpent in the wilderness, a serpent erected to give healing to those rebellious Israelites who were poisoned by snake-bite (Num 21:8–9). John sees the image of the snake as a type of Christ and the pole as a type of the cross (3:13–17). Jesus, too, is lifted up on a "pole"; Jesus too will give "healing" to those who gaze upon him as he hangs from the cross (see 19:37). This language of exaltation, which has parallels in wider traditions of ascent including in the Roman *imperium*, is exploited theologically for the crucifixion.[41] The cross, for John, now depicts the glorious ascent of the one who first descended from heaven to earth in the incarnation in order to reveal God, overpower evil, and restore creation: "and I, when I am lifted up from the earth, will draw all people to myself" (12:32).[42]

41. See, e.g., Carter, *John and Empire*, 315–34. On the context for the descent-ascent of heavenly figures, see Catherine A. Playhoust, "Lifted Up from the Earth: The Ascent of Jesus and the Heavenly Ascent of Christians" (PhD diss., Harvard University, 2006), 7–37; on the schema in John's Gospel, see Wayne A. Meeks, "The Man from Heaven in Johannine Sectarianism," *JBL* 91 (1972): 50–66.

42. A venerable alternative reading has "all things" (*panta*) rather than "all people" (*pantas*); see Bruce M. Metzger, *A Textual Commentary on the Greek New Testament: A Companion Volume to the United Bible Societies' Greek New Testament*, 3rd ed. (London: United Bible Societies, 1971), 238; and George R. Beasley-Murray, *John*, WBC 36 (Waco, TX: Word, 1987), 205.

The one who is lifted high above the earth on the cross to be displayed to the contemptuous gaze of all as an image of ignominy and shame—the "scripted index of Roman imperial power"[43]—now becomes an image of cosmic honor and victory.[44] The elevation of the cross displays to the full the life-giving glory of God (13:31–32), the divine love for the world (3:16–17), and the godly triumph over all the powers of darkness (12:31; 16:11).

Third, the cross is linked to two distinctive images of change and growth: the agricultural image of the grain seed that "dies" by being planted in the soil before sprouting and producing "fruit" (*karpos*, 12:24) and the imagery of giving birth (16:21). The seed implies the sower or farmer who metaphorically "buries" the seed in the earth and awaits its emergence: from a minute seedling to a grain-bearing plant, rising from the earth into a new shape and form. The imagery is the geographical opposite of the ascent language, with its metaphorical emphasis on exaltation in death. Now the seed descends into the earth, prefiguring Jesus's dying and burial, and the new growth signifies his rising from the tomb. As the plant emerges from the soil, so too does the Johannine Jesus, with his unique authority over life and death.

The image of the woman in labor occurs in the context of Jesus's departure. The imagery of birth is, at first glance, relevant only to the disciples and their progress through grief to joy; but the same movement accompanies also Jesus's death and resurrection, his departure and return, which parallels that of the mother's labor-pains as she gives birth.[45] As she first suffers pain and anguish before experiencing joy, so too will Jesus in his dying and rising. Both the seed and the birth are images of overturning, where the joy of harvest and the joy of birth are preceded by either death or unmitigated pain and distress. These images display the opposition of the cross, serving to reshape the pain, desolation, ignominy, and death into the very means of life and joy. The two images, drawn from nature, point to a transformation that goes beyond the natural world at its deepest level: life rising triumphant in the face of death.

---

43. Tom Thatcher, *Greater Than Caesar: Christology and Empire in the Fourth Gospel* (Minneapolis: Fortress, 2009), 88.

44. See Judith L. Kovacs, "'Now Shall the Ruler of This World Be Driven Out': Jesus' Death as Cosmic Battle in John 12:30–36," *JBL* 114 (1995): 227–47.

45. See Kathleen P. Rushton, *The Parable of the Woman in Childbirth of John 16:21: A Metaphor for the Death and Glorification of Jesus* (Lewiston, NY: Mellen, 2010), 247–72.

Theology and Imagination

Because they are content-laden, the Johannine images, metaphors, and symbols are replete with theological meaning. At the core of John's theology lies the incarnation, representing God's advent into the world, not as an external (albeit celestial) visitor, but rather as intrinsic to the world itself—in the same shape and form, made of the same substance, sharing the same ingredients. God enters flesh, becomes flesh and redeems flesh by flesh (*sarx*). On this theological point, the imagery of the gospel hangs: God can be perceived only through images and that implies, for John, the incarnation.[46] As a consequence of the incarnation, creation itself, already the work of God, is now able to image God within its own terms and framework: "earthly things" have the capacity to reveal "heavenly things" (3:12). This is the theological foundation of the gospel, explicit in its articulation and implicit in its grounding of the core images and symbols. John uses images because of the incarnation, because flesh now has the capability of imaging and imagining God. In John's Gospel, Jesus is the image of God. The one who is, for John, the ultimate, divine image makes possible the images (cf. 2 Cor 4:4; Col 1:15) and what they have to reveal.[47] That is the meaning, in part, of the Father-Son imagery and other aspects of the familial metaphorical field through the Fourth Gospel.[48] The Johannine Son is the only means by which human beings can be re-made and restored as sons and daughters of God (20:17): "It is through the images that Jesus is placed onto the domain of God, becomes transparent for God, and becomes an image or likeness of God ... for John the images finally enable perception of God himself."[49]

Towards the end of the Farewell Discourse, Jesus promises to speak to the disciples no more *en paroimiais* ("enigmatic figures") but *parrēsia*

---

46. Rainer Hirsch-Luipold, "Klartext in Bildern," in Frey, van der Watt, and Zimmermann, *Imagery in the Gospel of John*, 65–66.

47. Ibid., 98–99. Sandra M. Schneiders speaks of Jesus as the foundational symbol of God in the Fourth Gospel; see *Written That You May Believe: Encountering Jesus in the Fourth Gospel* (New York: Crossroad, 1999), 69–74.

48. Note Marianne Meye Thompson's important point that, despite common imagery for God and Jesus, some Johannine images apply only to God—e.g., sender, vinedresser, giver of law, Father—while other images relate only to Jesus—e.g., lamb, bread, Son; "'Every Picture Tells a Story': Imagery for God in the Gospel of John," in Frey, van der Watt, and Zimmermann, *Imagery in the Gospel of John*, 259–65.

49. Zimmermann, "Imagery in John," 37.

("openly," 16:25), and the disciples exclaim that they at last understand him (16:29–30).[50] The evangelist does not suggest that there is an accessible form of speech more basic or quintessential than image or metaphor. The point is that the language Jesus uses is incomprehensible to the disciples; this is also the case with the first occurrence of *paroimia* at 10:6, as we have seen, which the disciples at first fail to understand and which is "fundamentally enigmatic."[51] For John, with the advent of the Spirit-Paraclete, the disciples will finally understand the purpose of Jesus's coming and therefore the images he uses (16:28); they will no longer appear as enigmas. The images will be able to function, by faith, as authentic symbols that invite and give access, not as opaque barriers that bar the way and exclude. The flesh will no longer be a closed door but an open path to lead believers to apprehend the glory (*doxa*) of the divine love, as it is unveiled in the Johannine Jesus, the true image of God.[52]

According to Paul Ricoeur, there are two different yet interrelated types of imagination: the productive and the reproductive.[53] These are not easy to separate and exist more as a spectrum than strict alternatives. The productive imagination is concerned at a more limited level to copy or emulate something that already exists. Thus a business company might borrow ideas and images from another company and reframe them, or a photographer might endeavor to capture accurately a family event in photographs. The reproductive, on the other hand, is creative, envisaging a new reality, a new way of being. For Ricoeur, both are needed for true imagination to flourish. John's Gospel is about the transformation of the imagination that brings into being a new reality: "eternal life." This reality, far from being disconnected to fleshly existence, is formed from it and through it. In other words, eternal life is both productive and reproductive. The images enable this emulative and transformative dynamic to operate within the framework of the gospel.

---

50. Uta Poplutz sees the death of Jesus as enabling the movement from *paroimia* to *parrēsia*, since only the cross provides the horizon to make sense of Jesus's message ("Paroimia und Parabolē," in Frey, van der Watt, and Zimmermann, *Imagery in the Gospel of John*, 103–20).

51. Lewis, *Shepherd Discourse*, 103.

52. On the theme of love throughout John's Gospel, see Francis J. Moloney, *Love in the Gospel of John: An Exegetical, Theological, and Literary Study* (Grand Rapids: Baker Academic, 2013).

53. See George H. Taylor, "Ricoeur's Philosophy of Imagination," *Journal of French Philosophy* 16 (2006): 93–104. Taylor's essay is based on notes from Ricoeur's lectures.

The potential for a God-donated, symbolic meaning already exists intrinsically in created things, since "all things came into being through him" (1:3), or, in the words of Rowan Williams, "every finite phenomenon is at some level a carrier of divine significance."[54] The incarnation does not give "flesh" its symbolic meaning; rather, it draws out a meaning that is always, implicitly, present. What then of "flesh" that "profits nothing" (*ouk ōphelei ouden*, 6:63)?[55] This description is simply another way of depicting the one thing "lost" to humankind, as implied in the Prologue: the imaginative capacity to recognize the Creator in all things (1:10). This capacity is what the Word comes to restore: the ability to connect, to perceive, to communicate, to know, to recognize—in a word, to imagine. Imagination is the creative ability to envisage what is not through images of what is.

The reader thus requires a renewed imagination to enter the Johannine story, to grasp symbolically its imagery, and to be transformed, thereby gaining eternal life through faith (20:30–31). Authentic reading needs the insight of imagination as well as faith, the capacity to envisage the world as larger, more comprehensive, more hopeful, and more divinely-filled than it appears at face value. To know Jesus and to know God, in John's terms, means to enter into the "imaginary" world of the text, apprehending its imagery in lived encounter. It means apprehending the world as created by God, as re-created by God and as profoundly turned towards God by virtue of both creation and incarnation. For this gospel, imagination lies at the heart of believing.

CONCLUSION

Images belong at the center of the Johannine narrative. Within it, the narrator employs a variety of images from different sources, and particularly the Old Testament, that operate in counterpoint to create a rich harmony of sound. The images are often framed as metaphors or similes, a number of which become key symbols of life for the evangelist and enable what has been rightly called a "theo-symbolic reading" of the Fourth Gospel.[56] Behind the imagery lies the implicit, theological foundation of the Word who is the Son and the image of God in creation and redemption.

---

54. Rowan Williams, *The Edge of Words: God and the Habit of Language* (London: Bloomsbury, 2014), 120.

55. See further Lee, *Symbolic Narratives*, 155–57.

56. Akala, *Son-Father Relationship*, 215–17.

By exploring sensuous imagery in its narrative framework, the implied reader of the gospel is able to enter imaginatively into the Johannine world, not only at a cognitive but also at an affective level. Through the union of the productive and reproductive imagination, conversion takes place in John's storytelling, as the true purpose and goal of the narrative: the conversion of imagination, faith, and life.

10

Scripture

Rekha M. Chennattu

This chapter illustrates how the Fourth Evangelist uses and interprets Scripture to develop the Johannine narrative of Jesus in a unique manner in order to make John's Gospel truly credible and normative. In what follows, we shall first examine the use of Old Testament theological motifs, metaphors, imageries, allusions, festivals, and structural frameworks in John's Gospel. We shall then explore the use and interpretation of direct and indirect Old Testament citations as well as references to the law in the gospel. An investigation of the understanding of the words as well as commandments of Jesus in the gospel will follow. The chapter will conclude with a discussion of the understanding of John's Gospel as Scripture that promises eternal life to all those who believe in Jesus as the Messiah.

The Old Testament Theological Motifs and Structural Frameworks

It is generally accepted that the Judaism of the first century CE in general, and the Old Testament theological traditions in particular, constitute the central background against which the Fourth Evangelist wrote his narrative presentation of Jesus Christ.[1] The evangelist has interwoven many of the Old Testament themes into the Jesus materials, forming both theological and structural frameworks for the gospel. For example, at the very outset of the gospel, the Prologue (1:1–18) makes allusions to the cre-

---

1. Raymond E. Brown, *The Gospel according to John*, 2 vols., AB 29–29A (Garden City, NY: Doubleday, 1966–1970), 1:lix–lxiv; C. K. Barrett, "The Old Testament in the Fourth Gospel," *JTS* 48 (1947): 155–69.

ation story of Gen 1. The first words of the gospel—*en archē*, "in beginning" (John 1:1a)—echo the first words of the book of Genesis—*barē'šît*, "in beginning" (Gen 1:1a).[2] John the Evangelist does not talk about the birth or earthily origins of Jesus but goes back to the beginning of creation and begins his gospel by introducing the existence of the Word with God in eternity (John 1:1–2) and the participation of the Word in the creation work of God—that all things came into existence through the Word (John 1:3). The eternal Word (*logos*) becomes a human being in Jesus and makes the cosmos its dwelling place: "The Word became flesh and lived [pitched its tent (*skēnoō*)] among us" (John 1:14a). The expression "to pitch a tent" reminds the readers of the ark of the covenant and the indwelling of the divine glory in the midst of the Israelites during their wilderness journey (Exod 25:8, 10–22; 37:1–9). In the Old Testament tradition, the word of God refers to both the torah as well as the transforming presence of God's power that was active in God's creative work, in the lives of the patriarchs, in the experiences of the exodus journey of the Israelites, and in the lives of the prophets.[3] Therefore, many traditions— the torah, the patriarchs, the exodus journey, the indwelling presence of God, the prophetic and wisdom traditions—lie behind or within John's logos theology and Christology.

There are also numerous other metaphors, motifs, and imagery evoking the rich religious and cultural background of the Old Testament. For example, the references to glory (1:14; 2:11; 5:41, 44; 7:18; 8:50, 54; 9:24; 11:4, 40; 12:41; 17:5, 22, 24); grace and truth (1:14, 17); Lamb of God (1:29, 36); the messianic banquet (2:1–11); the hour (2:4; 4:21, 23; 5:25, 28; 7:30; 8:20; 12:23, 27; 13:1; 16:2, 25, 32; 17:1); and temple (2:14, 15, 19, 20, 21; 5:14; 7:14, 28; 8:2, 20, 59; 10:23; 11:56; 18:20). There is an allusion to Jacob's ladder (1:51) as well as allusions to the events of Exodus—the use of "signs" for Jesus's miracles just as Moses's miracles are referred to as signs (2:11, 18, 23; 3:2; 4:48, 54; 6:2, 14, 26, 30; 7:31; 9:16; 11:47; 12:18, 37; 20:30), the serpent in the wilderness (3:14), the manna (6:31), the water from the rock (see similarly 7:38); the pillar of fire (light) (see similarly 8:12). The readers are also overwhelmed by the references to Moses (1:17, 45; 3:14; 5:45,

---

2. Unless otherwise stated, all translations of biblical texts are from the NRSV.

3. Rekha M. Chennattu, "The Word Became Flesh (John 1:1–18): A Cross-Cultural/Religious Expression of the Divine," in *Cross-Cultural Encounter: Experience and Expression of the Divine*, ed. Mohan Doss and Andreas Vonach (Innsbruck: Innsbruck University Press, 2009), 43–51.

46; 6:32; 7:19, 22, 23; 8:5; 9:28, 29), Abraham (8:39, 40, 52, 53, 56, 57, 58), and Jacob (4:6, 12). Other Old Testament theological motifs include the "I am" sayings in the gospel (4:26; 6:35, 41, 51; 8:12; 10:9, 11; 15:1, 5), the discourse of the Good Shepherd and flock (10:1–21; 21:14–19), the farewell meal (13:1–11), the allegory of the vine and the branches (15:1–11), and the commandment motif (10:18; 12:49, 50; 13:34; 14:15, 21, 31; 15:10, 12). Moreover, there are many references to the Jewish festivals and celebrations: Sabbath (5:9, 10, 16, 18; 7:22, 23; 9:14, 16; 19:31), Passover (2:13, 23; 6:4; 11:55; 12:1; 13:1; 18:28, 39; 19:14), the Feast of Tabernacles (7:2), the Feast of Dedication (10:22), and the Day of Preparation (19:14, 31, 42).

The theological and structural framework of some of the chapters in the gospel is shaped by the celebrations of Jewish feasts or covenant renewal ceremonies. For instance, the evangelist has used the four important Jewish feasts (Sabbath, Passover, Tabernacles, and Dedication) for the gospel's narrative structure in chapters 5–10.[4] John situates the ministry of Jesus within the literary context of the celebrations of these feasts and develops a unique Christology in each section in relationship to the rituals associated with the respective Jewish festival. The setting, formation, and theology of John 13:31–16:33 have been influenced by the book of Deuteronomy.[5] One can also identify a covenant renewal ceremony in John 13–17, which is very similar to that of Josh 24.[6] The ongoing revelation of Jesus's identity as the embodiment of God's presence and the repeated call to decision in chapters 2–12 serve as a hortatory preparation for the covenant renewal in chapters 13–17. Moreover, the covenant themes—election, intimate abiding relationship, indwelling presence, keeping God's commandments, and mutual knowledge—run through the discourses in these chapters. In sum, the Old Testament as a whole formed the background, both structural and theological, for the development of the narratives of the new revelation of God in the Jesus of John's Gospel.

---

4. For a detailed analysis of John 5–10 from the perspective of Jewish feasts, see Francis J. Moloney, *Signs and Shadows: Reading John 5–12* (Minneapolis: Fortress, 1996), 1–153.

5. See A. Lacomara, "Deuteronomy and the Farewell Discourse (John 13:31–16:33)," *CBQ* 36 (1974): 65–84.

6. For a detailed study of John 13–17 from the perspective of a covenant renewal, see Rekha M. Chennattu, *Johannine Discipleship as a Covenant Relationship* (Peabody, MA: Hendrickson, 2006), 50–139.

The Old Testament Citations and References to Scripture

When we compare John's Gospel with the Synoptic Gospels, John has fewer direct Old Testament citations than the Synoptic Gospels have.[7] Although there are fifteen explicit Old Testament quotations indicated most of the time by one or other introductory formula in John's Gospel,[8] John shares only three Old Testament texts in common with the Synoptic Gospels (Isa 40:3 in John 1:23; Zech 9:9 in John 12:14–15; and Isa 6:10 in John 12:40). These texts are dealing with (1) the identity of John the Baptist and the announcement of the messianic or eschatological era: "I am the voice of one crying out in the wilderness, 'Make straight the way of the Lord,' as the prophet Isaiah said" (John 1:23); (2) the identity of Jesus as the king riding on a donkey: "Look, your king is coming, sitting on a donkey's colt!" (John 12:15); and (3) the rationale for the rejection of Jesus by God's people: "He has blinded their eyes and hardened their heart, so that they might not look with their eyes, and understand with their heart and turn—and I would heal them" (John 12:40). The rest of the twelve quotations are unique to John's Gospel. It seems therefore reasonable to say that the Fourth Evangelist has his own unique way of choosing and interpreting Old Testament texts to develop his unique story of Jesus Christ.

Scholars have different opinions regarding the source that the Fourth Evangelist used when quoting Old Testament texts. Some argue in favor of the LXX;[9] others opt for the Hebrew text[10] or the Palestinian targums (the local Aramaic translations of Scripture);[11] and yet others are of the opinion

---

7. For a lists of Old Testament citations in all four gospels, see Robert. G. Bratcher, ed., *Old Testament Quotations in the New Testament* (London: United Bible Societies, 1967), 1–25.

8. See John 1:23; 2:17; 6:31, 45; 7:38, 42; 10:34; 12:14–15, 38, 39–40; 13:18; 15:25; 19:24, 36, 37. One can also find the introductory formula "the Scripture might be fulfilled" in 17:12 and 19:28, but there are no explicit Old Testament citations there. I have not included 12:13 in the list as it is not preceded by an introductory formula.

9. For example, Bruce G. Schuchard, *Scripture within Scripture: The Interrelationship of Form and Function in the Explicit Old Testament Citations in the Gospel of John*, SBLDS 133 (Atlanta: Scholars Press, 1992).

10. For example, Maarten J. J. Menken, *Old Testament Quotations in the Fourth Gospel: Studies in Textual Form*, CBET 15 (Kampen: Kok Pharos, 1996).

11. See Brown, *Gospel according to John*, 1:lxi.

that the Fourth Evangelist is quoting from memory.[12] In fact, Johannine Old Testament quotations do not agree fully either with the Greek (LXX) or the Hebrew (MT) texts. This does not matter much as the evangelist points to the fact that the whole of Scripture—not merely the details contained in one or the other particular textual tradition of Old Testament—bears witness to Jesus Christ.

When we examine these direct citations, sometimes we have clear and explicit quotations from a single Old Testament text (for example, the reference to Ps 82:6 in John 10:34 or to Isa 53:1 in John 12:38). On other occasions, texts are a conflation of two or more Old Testament passages and can have links and connections with more than one Old Testament text, which naturally leads to different interpretations of the given text. For example, the source of the citation in John 19:36 ("For these things came to pass, that the Scripture might be fulfilled, 'Not a bone of Him shall be broken'") can be either Exod 12:46 ("It shall be eaten in one house; you shall not take any of the animal outside the house, and you shall not break any of its bones") or Ps 34:20 ("He keeps all their bones; not one of them will be broken"). If the evangelist had Exod 12:46 in mind, then Jesus in his death is being depicted as God's Passover lamb, who achieved the definitive redemption of the second exodus. On the other hand, if John had Ps 34:20 in mind, Jesus is presented as the one who fulfills the mission of the righteous one of the Psalms who brings about salvation by his death.

Sometimes it is difficult to discern which Old Testament texts John has in mind since no single Old Testament passage conforms fully to the citation in John. For example, for the citation in 7:38 ("As the scripture has said, 'Out of the believer's heart shall flow rivers of living water'") commentators suggest a number of possible Old Testament sources: Prov 18:4 ("The words of the mouth are deep waters; the fountain of wisdom is a gushing stream"), Zech 14:8 ("On that day living waters shall flow out from Jerusalem, half of them to the eastern sea and half of them to the western sea; it shall continue in summer as in winter"), Isa 55:1 ("Everyone who thirsts, come to the waters; and you that have no money, come, buy and eat!"), and Isa 58:11 ("You shall be like a watered garden, like a

---

12. See Paul J. Achtemeier, "*Omne verbum sonat*: The New Testament and the Oral Environment of Late Western Antiquity," *JBL* 109 (1990): 3–27.

spring of water, whose waters never fail").[13] Similarly, the source for the idea expressed in 12:34 ("We have heard from the law that the Messiah remains forever") can be gleaned through many Old Testament texts, such as Isa 9:7 ("His authority shall grow continually, and there shall be endless peace for the throne of David and his kingdom. He will establish and uphold it with justice and with righteousness from this time onward and forevermore"), Ezek 37:25 ("my servant David shall be their prince forever"), Dan 7:14 ("His dominion is an everlasting dominion that shall not pass away, and his kingship is one that shall never be destroyed"), or Ps 89:4 ("I will establish your descendant [your seed] forever, and build your throne for all generations").[14]

We also find a direct citation from the Old Testament without any introductory formula indicating it as such. The proclamation of the identity of Jesus as the eschatological messiah in 12:13 ("Blessed is the one who comes in the name of the Lord—the King of Israel!") seems to be a direct quotation of Ps 118:26 ("Blessed is the one who comes in the name of the Lord"). The evangelist also weaves the Old Testament themes into the discourses of the gospel without any reference to the Old Testament. For example, although John does not cite Isa 29:13, the idea, namely, that the Israelites honor God only with their lips and their hearts are far from God, is developed well all throughout Jesus's arguments with the Jews in chapters 5–12.[15]

To present his arguments in a convincing manner or to persuade his readers to believe in Jesus as the one who fulfills Old Testament expectations and prophesies, John's Gospel sometimes has recourse to Scripture (graphē) (7:38; 13:18) and at other times talks about either the words of the prophet Isaiah (1:23; 12:38) or the words written in the law (nomos) (10:34; 15:25). However, the Scripture, the writings of the prophets, and the law are not one and the same. The writings of the prophets and

13. For a discussion on John 7:38, see Edwin D. Freed, Old Testament Quotations in the Gospel of John, NovTSup 11 (Leiden: Brill, 1965), 21–38.

14. Following the tradition of the rabbinic exegesis that interprets "his seed" as a reference to "the Anointed One (the Messiah)," some exegetes suggest Ps 89:4 ("I will establish your descendant [your seed] forever, and build your throne for all generations") as the most reasonable source for John 12:34, "We have heard from the law that the Messiah remains forever." For example, see W. C. van Unnik, "The Quotation from the Old Testament in John 12:34," NovT 3 (1959): 174–79.

15. See also Raymond E. Brown, An Introduction to the Gospel of John, ed. Francis J. Moloney (New York: Doubleday, 2003), 132–38.

the law, in their conventional usage, are integral parts of the Scripture. Indeed, Scripture includes and transcends both the words of the prophets and the law.

The law in John's Gospel is used both in its strictly juridical sense as a reference to a particular Mosaic law and in its wider sense as Scripture in general. Sometimes the law refers to the Mosaic law proper; for example, during the controversies connected to the Sabbath laws, Jesus refers to the law of Moses to justify his actions (7:19, 23). At other times, the law refers to Scripture as a whole or part of it, for instance in 10:34, where the law refers to Ps 82:6 and is used as a substitute for the term Scripture. Such interplay between the law and Scripture is evident from the fact that Jesus himself referred to it as Scripture in 10:35 ("Scripture cannot be broken").

In both cases, the law is predominantly used in the context of christological controversies to legitimize the users' arguments based on Scripture. Jesus, his mission, and death stand at the center of these controversies. The law is used by Jesus (7:19, 23; 8:17; 10:34; 15:25), the chief priests and Pharisees (7:49), Nicodemus (7:51), and the Jewish crowd (12:34; 19:7). In 18:31, Pilate also speaks of the law ("take him yourself and judge him according to your law"). Almost always, the characters or the narrator speak of the law with the definite article (*ho nomos*), with the exception of 19:7 ("we have a law"). The law in John's Gospel is therefore a comprehensive term which refers not only to the Mosaic law or the Pentateuch but at times also to Scripture in general.

A close look at the use of these Old Testament citations exposes two details. First, the more general references to the writings of Moses and Scripture as a whole are made mostly by Jesus in the great christological controversies (chs. 5–10) as well as in his Farewell Discourses (chs. 13–17). Second, most of the references to the specific texts of the Scripture are made by the narrator in the Passion narrative as Old Testament authentications or fulfillments in the story of Jesus (John 19:24 [Ps 22:18]; John 19:36 [Exod 12:46; Num 9:12]).[16] While the narrator uses specific texts to show that all the details of the passion and death of Jesus are in accordance with the Scripture ("These things occurred so that the scripture might be fulfilled" [19:36]), the Johannine Jesus elsewhere insists that the whole of Scripture bears witness to his life and ministry (5:39; 10:31–38).

---

16. For a detailed analysis, see Johannes Beutler, *Judaism and the Jews in the Gospel of John*, SubBi 30 (Rome: Pontifical Biblical Institute, 2006), 36–37.

Whether by characters in the story, Jesus, or the narrator, the use of the Scripture, both explicit citations as well as allusions to the Scriptures, is very closely associated with the revelation of the identity, mission, and destiny of Jesus. Jesus makes an allusion to Jacob's dream (Gen 28:11–13) in 1:51 to reveal his identity as the "Son of Man," a title used by Jesus of himself, who is "the locus of divine glory, the point of contact between heaven and earth."[17] Jesus, the perfect version of Moses, provides the authoritative interpretation of the Mosaic law in chapter 5, and he is presented as being in conflict with others in their interpretation of the law, especially in the Sabbath controversy stories. During the christological debate, Jesus challenged his opponents by saying: "You search the scriptures because you think that in them you have eternal life; and it is they that testify on my behalf" (5:39). Jesus himself used Scripture to establish his Sonship (10:34 [Ps 82:6]). The Scripture bears witness to Jesus (5:39); Jesus himself bears witness to himself; and the Father bears witness to Jesus ("I testify on my own behalf, and the Father who sent me testifies on my behalf" [8:18]). Philip, one of the characters in the story, introduces Jesus to Nathanael as the one who is mentioned in the Law and the Prophets: "We have found him about whom Moses in the law and also the prophets wrote, Jesus son of Joseph from Nazareth" (1:45). In other places, characters in the story use citations to debate and confirm the identity of Jesus. For example, the messiah comes from Bethlehem (7:42 [Mic 5:2]), comes "in the name of the Lord" (12:13 [Ps 118:26]), and is a king who is humble and sits on a donkey's colt (12:15 [Zech 9:9]). Most of the titles given to Jesus also have a rich religious background in the Old Testament. Jesus's self-understandings as "the Son of God," "the Son of Man" (Dan 7), the one who is from above, the one who comes from heaven, and the Good Shepherd (Zech 13) deeply resonate with Old Testament expectations. The Fourth Evangelist aims at convincing his readers that in Jesus Christ one can find the definitive fulfillment of the christological prophecy of the entire Scripture.[18]

Of the fifteen explicit Old Testament citations announced by an introductory formula, eight are in the first part of the gospel and use verbs such as "to say" and "to write": "as Isaiah the prophet said" (1:23), "it is written" (2:17), "as it is written" (6:31), "does not the Scripture say" (7:42), and "is it

---

17. Brown, *Gospel according to John*, 91.
18. For a discussion in detail, see Martin Hengel, "The Old Testament in the Fourth Gospel," in *The Gospels and the Scriptures of Israel*, ed. Craig A. Evans and W. Richard Stegner, JSNTSup 104, SSEJC 3 (Sheffield: Sheffield Academic, 1994), 380–95.

not written in your law" (10:34). In the second half of the gospel, with few exceptions, fulfillment formulae generally have the verb "to fulfill" (*plēroō*) (12:38; 13:18; 15:25; 19:24, 36). One can observe three recurring formulae: "that the word of Isaiah the prophet might be fulfilled" (12:38); "that the Scripture might be fulfilled" (13:18); "It was to fulfill the word that is written in their law" (15:25).[19] Whether in the first part or in the second part, the Fourth Evangelist is using "words of the prophet Isaiah," "words written in Scriptures," and "the words written in the law" interchangeably as a reference to Scripture, the authoritative words spoken on behalf of God (or by God) to prepare God's people to welcome the eschatological era and receive messianic blessings and eternal life through Jesus Christ.

The references to the fulfillment of the Scripture made in the context of the death of Jesus follow a chiastic structure in 19:24–36. In order to express the idea of fulfillment, the evangelist uses three verbs: "to fulfill" (*plēroō*), "to bring to its perfection" (*teleioō*), and "to bring to its end or completion" (*teleō*). The fulfillment formula in 19:28b with the use of the verb *teleioō* is sandwiched between two identical fulfillment formulae of *plēroō* in verse 24 (the narrator's announcement of fulfillment) and in verse 36 (narrator's announcement of fulfillment) as well as the two identical fulfillment formulae of *teleō* in verse 28a (narrator's comment on Jesus's awareness) and in verse 30 (Jesus's announcement of the fulfillment).

A: Narrator's announcement of the fulfillment—So they said to one another, "Let us not tear it, but cast lots for it to see who will get it." This was *to fulfill* [*plēroō*] what the scripture says, "They divided my clothes among themselves, and for my clothing they cast lots." (19:24)

   B: Narrator's comment on Jesus's awareness—After this, when Jesus knew that all *was now finished/fulfilled* [*teleō*]" (19:28a)

      C: Narrator's announcement of the fulfillment—He said [*in order to fulfill* [*teleioō*] the scripture], "I am thirsty" (19:28b)

---

19. Andreas Obermann argues that the form of the citations ("it is written" in chapters 1–12 and "might be fulfilled" in chapters 13–20) has a correlative rhetorical function in the gospel narrative, pointing to Jesus as the christological fulfillment of Scripture (*Die christologische Erfüllung der Schrift im Johannesevangelium: Eine Untersuchung zur johanneischen Hermeneutik anhand der Schriftzitate*, WUNT 2/83 [Tübingen: Mohr Siebeck, 1996], 409–22).

B¹: Jesus's announcement of the fulfillment—When Jesus had received the wine, he said, "It *is finished/fulfilled* [*teleō*]" (19:30)

A¹: Narrator's announcement of the fulfillment—These things occurred so *that the scripture might be fulfilled* [*plēroō*], "None of his bones shall be broken" (19:36)

As the above illustration shows, we have the following sequence of verbs: "fulfill" (*plēroō*) (v. 24), "complete/bring to perfection" (*teleō*) (v. 28a), "complete/bring to perfection" (*teleioō*) (v. 28b), "complete/bring to perfection" (*teleō*) (v. 30), and "to fulfill" (*plēroō*) (v. 36). This sequence places the verb "to complete/bring to perfection" (*teleioō*) at the center of the chiastic structure (ABCB¹A¹), highlighting the fact that every minute detail of Jesus's death is performed in order to fulfill or bring to perfection (*teleioō*) what is foretold about the messiah in the Scripture (19:24–36).

Jesus's proclamation of the final fulfillment expressed by the verb *teleō*—namely, that Jesus has brought the Scripture to its ultimate completion or fulfillment by his death (19:30)—is very significant. Echoing the words of God when God completed (*synteleō*) the work of creation on the seventh day in the book of Genesis (LXX Gen 2:1–2), Jesus's mission is brought to completion or perfection as he announced, "It is finished/fulfilled [*teleō*]" (19:30).[20] Moreover, Jesus's mission is to complete or to make perfect (*teleioō*) God's work (4:34), and Jesus's actions are placed on a par with God's works among his people as Jesus does nothing of his own ("Very truly, I tell you, the Son can do nothing on his own, but only what he sees the Father doing; for whatever the Father does, the Son does likewise" [5:19]). At the final farewell prayer, Jesus also claims that he has finished or completed (*teleioō*) the work that God gave him to do (17:4). The life, mission, and death of Jesus brings God's work among his people to its climax, to its end, and to its perfection.[21] Moreover, the references to Scripture in general in 2:22 and 20:9 legitimize the point that Jesus is risen on the third day as preannounced by Jesus as well as foretold by the Scriptures. Everything that is written about the messiah in the law of Moses, books of the prophets, and in the entire Scripture has been fulfilled, per-

---

20. The Johannine Jesus also used the word of God elsewhere to interpret what was going on in his own life as a fulfillment of the Scripture (see, e.g., 15:25).

21. See also Obermann, *Christologische Erfüllung*, 350–64.

fected, and brought to its culmination in the person, life, ministry, death, and resurrection of Jesus Christ.

It seems reasonable therefore to conclude that the Old Testament citations have a revelatory function with a distinct christological focus and the evangelist uses them—the words written in the law, the words of the prophet Isaiah, and Scripture as a whole—to interpret the life, mission, death, and resurrection of Jesus as the climax of God's work among human beings.

THE WORDS OF JESUS AS SCRIPTURE

As we have seen above, the Fourth Evangelist uses both the law and Scripture almost interchangeably (10:34–35). He understands both as God's authoritative and normative word addressed to people. The words of Jesus, "the Scripture cannot be broken" (10:35), endorse the same concern. More significantly, the evangelist makes special efforts to present the words of Jesus as part of Scripture. First, there is a close link made between the commandments of God and those of Jesus in the gospel. Second, a close association is made between remembering and believing in God's words as well as remembering and believing in the words of Jesus. Third, John refers to the fulfillment of the words of Jesus in the gospel.

There is a gradual progression in the development of the commandment motif in the gospel.[22] Both the noun *entolē* ["commandment"] and the corresponding verb *entellomai* ["command"] refer to the law (*nomos*) to a large extent. The Johannine Jesus gives three different meanings to the concept of commandment: (1) the commandment that Jesus has received from the Father or the will of the Father for the Son to which Jesus has direct access (10:18; 12:49; 14:31); (2) the love commandment of the Old Testament interpreted or paraphrased in the gospel as mutual love of the disciples by Jesus or the will of God written down in the Old Testament for the people of God (13:34; 15:12, 17); and (3) the commandments of Jesus for his disciples or Jesus's articulation of the will of God for his own disciples (14:15, 21; 15:10). Just as Jesus keeps the commandments of the Father, so also the disciples are called to keep the commandments of Jesus (15:10). Jesus exhorts his disciples to love him and to keep his commandments so that Jesus and the Father can come and make their dwelling among and

---

22. For a detailed discussion, see Beutler, *Judaism and the Jews*, 42–46.

within them (14:15–24). Loving God and keeping God's commandments were an integral part of the covenant theology in the Old Testament (see Deut 7:9).[23] What is foretold by the prophets concerning the new covenant ("My dwelling place shall be with them; and I will be their God, and they shall be my people" [Ezek 37:27]) is fulfilled in Jesus's promises in 14:23: "Jesus answered him, 'Those who love me will keep my word, and my Father will love them, and we will come to them and make our home with them.'" Jesus's commandments are placed on a par with, and are even considered superior to, the Old Testament commandments of God. Jesus's own words gradually become part of the normative Scripture for his disciples.

Two important activities and corresponding verbs used in the Old Testament in connection with God's word are to "remember" and to "believe." The Lord asked Moses to remind the people of Israel to remember the commandments of the Lord: "You have the fringe so that, when you see it, you will remember all the commandments of the Lord and do them, and not follow the lust of your own heart and your own eyes" (Num 15:39). Likewise, Joshua reminded the people of Israel to "Remember the word that Moses the servant of the Lord commanded you" (Josh 1:13). The Psalmist reminded Israel to believe in God's commandments ("Teach me good judgment and knowledge, for I believe in your commandments" [Ps 119:66]) or talks about their failure in believing in God's word ("In spite of all this they still sinned; they did not believe in his wonders" [78:32]; "Then they despised the pleasant land, having no faith in his promise [literally, both in LXX and MT, 'they did not believe in his word']" [106:24]). Just as in the Old Testament, remembering God's and Jesus's commandments and believing in the Scripture are also two expected or required activities of the disciples in John's Gospel.

After Jesus's death and resurrection, the disciples remember what had been written in the Scripture about Jesus as well as what they had heard from Jesus about his death and destiny (2:15–22).[24] In 2:14–17, the ministry (words and deeds) of Jesus stirred the disciples to remember what was written in Scripture: "Zeal for your house will consume me" (v. 17). The disciples are here remembering what had been written of Jesus in Scripture as Jesus drove the merchants out of the temple asking them to stop making his Father's house a marketplace. In verses 18–21, Jesus is talking about the

---

23. For a reflection on loving God and keeping God's commandments in John's Gospel, see Chennattu, *Johannine Discipleship*, 110–18, esp. 111.

24. See also 12:16; 15:20; 16:4.

destruction of the temple in a metaphorical way referring to his own body. In verse 22, the narrator places both Scripture and Jesus's words on a par with one another by drawing to the attention of his readers that the disciples believed in the Scripture as well as in the words of Jesus ("they believed the Scripture and the word that Jesus had spoken" [2:22]). In John 2:22, the expressions "the Scripture" and "the word which Jesus had spoken" are juxtaposed by an explanatory *kai* ("that is to say").[25] The disciples believed in the Scripture; that is to say, they believed in the word spoken by Jesus. There are also other occasions in which Jesus exhorted the disciples to remember his words: "remember the word that I said to you" (15:20); "I have said these things to you so that when their hour comes you may remember that I told you about them" (16:4). The act of remembering is applied to both the Scripture (2:17, 22; 12:16) and to the words of Jesus (15:20; 16:4). A parallel connection with the verb "to believe" worth mentioning is that of Jesus and Moses: "If you believed Moses, you would believe me, for he wrote about me" (5:46). The Johannine Jesus also makes a link between abiding in God's word and believing in Jesus: "You do not have his word abiding in you, because you do not believe him whom he has sent" (5:38). Although Jesus has presented witnesses, the Jews refused to believe in Jesus and the claims he made on a Sabbath day (5:1–47). Jesus concludes his argument with the question, by placing his words on a par with the writings of Moses: "But if you do not believe what he wrote, how will you believe what I say?" (5:47). In sum, the acts of believing and remembering are applied to the Scripture in general, to the words of Moses in particular, and to the words of Jesus. John gives to the words of Jesus a divine authority similar to that of the Old Testament Scripture in general (2:22) and the writings of Moses in particular (5:47).

The Fourth Evangelist also draws a close association between the fulfillment of the words of Scripture and those of Jesus.[26] Just as in the case of the words of the prophets in the Old Testament or the words of the law, so also the words of Jesus are fulfilled (*plēroō*) in the gospel in and through the life and death of Jesus. The idea expressed in the words of Jesus in 6:39—"This is the will of him who sent me, that I should lose nothing of all that he has given me, but raise it up on the last day"—is repeated again by Jesus in 17:12—"while I was with them, I protected them in your

---

25. For the use of the explanatory *kai*, see BDF §442.9. See also Francis J. Moloney, *The Gospel of John: Text and Context*, BibInt 72 (Leiden: Brill, 2005), 343.

26. Ibid., 340.

name that you have given me. I guarded them, and not one of them was lost except the one destined to be lost, so that the scripture might be fulfilled." This idea is fulfilled in 18:9—"This was to fulfill the word that he had spoken, 'I did not lose a single one of those whom you gave me.'" Similarly, the narrator reminds the readers of the fulfillment of Jesus's own words in 12:32–33, namely, that the kind of death Jesus had announced earlier is fulfilled in the passion narratives in 18:32 ("This was to fulfill what Jesus had said when he indicated the kind of death he was to die").

Even though the Fourth Evangelist does not explicitly identify the word of Jesus with that of Scripture, John has made deliberate and conscious efforts to make the close link between the two or to put them on a par with each other (see especially 2:22; 5:47).[27] What human beings have received from the Word is life and light (1:4). The Word thus enlightens every human being, and it is the guiding light of their life's journey. It empowers human beings to discern what is good, right, and true. Moreover, Jesus's commandments are placed parallel to the Old Testament commandments of God. The Word incarnated in the person of Jesus Christ, in and through his words and deeds, gives to the disciples what God gave to the Israelites, namely, "right ordinances and true laws, good statutes and commandments" (Neh 9:13). John presents Jesus as the divine word incarnated in human form (1:14), the one who is in the bosom of the Father (1:18) and has come "from above" (anōthen) (3:31; 8:23). The words of Jesus are the continuation of God's words to his people since Jesus speaks what he hears from the Father (8:26) or Jesus speaks as the Father has taught him. The Johannine Jesus repeats that he does nothing on his own, but he speaks what he is taught by his Father (8:28b). Jesus therefore proclaimed, "When you have lifted up the Son of Man, then you will realize that I am he, and that I do nothing on my own, but I speak these things as the Father instructed me" (8:28). During the Farewell Discourses, Jesus again challenges his disciples by saying: "Do you not believe that I am in the Father and the Father is in me? The words that I say to you I do not speak on my own; but the Father who dwells in me does his works" (14:10). Moreover, the Johannine Jesus is the personification of the divine Word (logos) (1:14). In the light of the above discussion, we have good reasons to uphold the view that in John's Gospel the Word of Jesus is indeed the

---

27. See also ibid., 341. But Beutler rejects this proposal by saying that "the words of Jesus have an authority comparable to that of Moses' writings, without actually becoming 'Scripture'" (Judaism and Jews, 36).

Word of God (*hē graphē*). The messianic era is inaugurated in and through the life and ministry of Jesus who also reclaimed, created, and constituted a new covenant community and through whom God's faithfulness to his covenant promises continued to be revealed and fulfilled.

JOHN'S GOSPEL AS SCRIPTURE

The Fourth Evangelist gradually understood his story of Jesus as the authoritative Scripture and presented it as such to his readers.[28] As the narrator reminds the readers in 19:35, "He who saw this has testified so that you also may believe. His testimony is true, and he knows that he tells the truth," the evangelist presents his gospel as the Scripture, the most authoritative and reliable testimony of the life of Jesus. The same conviction is highlighted again in the epilogue in 21:24 by the narrator—"This is the disciple who is testifying to these things and has written them, and we know that his testimony is true." The Johannine community believed in his gospel and some Jews rejected John's testimony. Although the evangelist gives pastoral reasons based on the experiences of his community for the rejection of his message ("Nevertheless many, even of the authorities, believed in him. But because of the Pharisees they did not confess it, for fear that they would be put out of the synagogue" [12:42]), John also supports it through the Old Testament prophetic lenses: "He has blinded their eyes and hardened their heart, so that they might not look with their eyes, and understand with their heart and turn—and I would heal them" (12:40 [Isa 6:10]). As we have seen above, John understands and presents his story of Jesus as a Scripture, which is not merely a continuation of the Old Testament Scriptures but its completion and fulfillment (19:28–30). Moreover, the concluding statement of the narrator in 20:31 ("these are written so that you may come to believe that Jesus is the Messiah, the Son of God, and that through believing you may have life in his name") further signals the community's understanding of John's Gospel as Scripture.[29] In other words, John's Gospel is presented as a Scripture for the new covenant/eschatological community, as a normative and authoritative revelation of God in Jesus Christ for the redemption of humanity.

---

28. The focus here is not on the formation of the Christian canon but John's own understanding of his story of Jesus as Scripture.

29. See also the discussion in Obermann, *Christologische Erfüllung*, 418–22.

Conclusion

At the end of this brief review, it seems reasonable to make the follow-ing persuasive, if not conclusive, observations. The Fourth Evangelist used Old Testament theological motifs and the Jesus materials at hand in order to drive home what he wanted to share with his readers about his unique understanding of the new revelation of God in Jesus. The Old Testament citations in John's Gospel have a distinct christological focus. Since the Fourth Evangelist does not focus on one tradition or one book alone from the Old Testament but uses texts and theological motifs from across the Old Testament to pursue his arguments, John seems to be more interested in presenting Jesus—his life, words, deeds/signs, passion, death, and resurrec-tion—as the fulfillment of Scripture in general rather than the fulfillment of the individual passages from the Old Testament. John takes special care to underline that the whole of Old Testament Scripture points to Jesus Christ: his identity, mission, and destiny. In other words, the Johannine Jesus lived, taught, performed signs, died, and was raised in accordance with the Scrip-tures. John reinterprets Scripture and illustrates that what was implicit in the Old Testament becomes explicit and is fulfilled in the life and person of Jesus Christ. Both Old Testament quotations and Old Testament motifs in John's Gospel illustrate that the mighty work of God begun in the Old Testament has its climax in the death and resurrection of Jesus.

Although John's Gospel sometimes refers to Scripture in general and at other times to the Mosaic law or the writings of the prophets in par-ticular, it is God's word that is articulated and preserved in the Scriptures (including the Mosaic law and the writings of the prophets), and the life of the Johannine Jesus is presented as the continuation and fulfillment of the Scriptures. The words of Jesus are understood as part of the ongo-ing revelation of God's interventions in human history and are placed on a par with Scripture or God's Word. A faithful presentation of Jesus is assured in John's Gospel and the evangelist understands his story of Jesus as an authoritative testimony, which is not merely a continuation of the Scripture but the fulfillment and completion of the salvation history begun in the Old Testament. In other words, Jesus brought to completion or perfection the entire Scripture for a covenant people that transcends the boundaries of Jewish religious traditions and history, and John's account of Jesus's story is a theological culmination of the Scripture that guarantees eternal life to all those who believe in Jesus as the Messiah, the Son of God (20:31).

11

Rhetoric

Alicia D. Myers

That the Gospel of John is rhetorical is not debated among recent narrative and literary-minded interpreters. Pointing to the gospel's thesis statement at 20:30–31, these readers often argue that the gospel's rhetorical goal is to affirm that Jesus is the Christ and the Son of God.[1] Beginning with the acknowledgement of the gospel's rhetorical nature enables us to ask more questions about the types of rhetoric the gospel uses as well as their potential impact on the gospel audience. The present chapter will focus primarily on John's relationship to classical rhetoric, meaning the tools of rhetoric used by speakers and authors in Greece and early Imperial Rome (ca. 400 BCE–200 CE).[2] The rhetorical techniques employed by orators and authors are outlined in a number of preliminary exercise books (*progymnasmata*) and rhetorical handbooks used for instructing intermediate and advanced-level students.[3] These works describe features common to ancient oratory and literature, providing a compendium of possible techniques and models for ancient authors and speakers alike to

---

1. For an overview of the debate concerning the purposes of John, see Charles H. Talbert, *Reading John: A Literary and Theological Commentary on the Fourth Gospel and the Johannine Epistles*, rev. ed. (Macon, GA: Smyth & Helwys, 2005), 267–68.

2. For contemporary understandings of rhetoric, especially as they pertain to ideological and literary methods of persuasion in John's Gospel, see Ruth Sheridan's chapter "Persuasion" later in this volume.

3. The present chapter will focus especially on several works by the Greek philosopher, Aristotle (384–322 BCE); a famous orator of the Roman Republic, Cicero (106 BCE–43 CE); Quintilian (35–ca. 96 CE), who wrote during the Roman imperial era of the first century; and Aelius Theon, who composed the *Progymnasmata*, which is the earliest and most complete of surviving collections (first century CE; see n. 13 below).

imitate and adapt for their own purposes.[4] While the explicit use of these resources is most clear among other Greek and Roman authors, their general description of communication styles makes them useful for analyzing Second Temple era Jewish writings and the New Testament as well. The Gospel of John's employment of common rhetorical techniques should not, therefore, be understood as an implicit argument against its Jewish roots. Instead, awareness of classical rhetorical practices offers another way to understand *how* John's Gospel communicates its Jewishness in a context saturated by Greco-Roman models of speech and writing.[5]

The study of *progymnasmata* and rhetorical handbooks was limited largely to the most elite Roman citizens. The ideas, culture, and morality communicated by them, however, were prevalent throughout the empire, even in the works of marginalized groups whose authors never experienced the full spectrum of Roman education. Rhetorical training, and the rhetoric it produced, was not simple pedantry; it was meant to shape the ethics of its highly trained practitioners, the audiences who heard them, and the empire that they sought to lead. The potential power of rhetoric also made it useful for marginalized groups, such as early Jesus-followers who offered a vision of salvation through a crucified Messiah instead of a conquering Caesar.[6] Thus, rather than suggesting the author(s) of John's Gospel used these handbooks, the present chapter will examine how this

---

4. Ruth Webb, "The *Progymnasmata* in Practice," in *Education in Greek and Roman Antiquity*, ed. Yun Lee Too (Leiden: Brill, 2001), 289–316.

5. This approach does not suggest that John simply replicates Greek and Roman practices without any connection to Jewish counterparts. Instead, it builds on the work of a number of earlier scholars who have noted the overlap between Jewish interpretive practices and Greco-Roman rhetoric. David Daube ("Rabbinic Methods of Interpretation and Hellenistic Rhetoric" *HUCA* 22 [1949]: 239–64) and Saul Lieberman (*Hellenism in Jewish Palestine: Studies in the Literary Transmission, Beliefs and Manners of Palestine in the I Century B.C.E.–IV Century C.E.*, TS 18 [New York: Jewish Theological Seminary of America, 1962], 59–61) demonstrate the similarities between *synkrisis* and the Jewish practices of *gezera-shewa* and *qal-walhomer*. More recently, Dennis Stamps suggested it is "arguable that rhetoric was a 'universal' influence upon communication conventions in the Greco-Roman world, including Palestine" ("Use of the Old Testament in the New Testament as a Rhetorical Device: A Methodological Proposal," in *Hearing the Old Testament in the New Testament*, ed. Stanley E. Porter [Grand Rapids: Eerdmans, 2006], 25).

6. On the employment and subversion of Greco-Roman categories in Jewish and early Christian writings, including the New Testament, see Mikeal C. Parsons, *Body and Character in Luke and Acts: The Subversion of Physiognomy in Early Christianity,*

gospel demonstrates awareness of classical rhetorical practices in general and how it uses them to achieve its goals. This approach opens contemporary audiences to hearing this gospel attuned to ancient expectations, highlighting the literary and rhetorical artistry that has served to make it such an enduring work.

The World of Classical Rhetoric

Before delving into the rhetorical components of John's Gospel, we must first get a bit of a handle on classical rhetoric itself: what are its contexts, sources, and purposes in the first-century Mediterranean world from which the gospel emerges? These questions lead us into the tricky territory of investigating Roman educational practices, which are themselves an amalgamation of classical and Hellenistic Greek elements shaped to fit Roman sensibilities of "ideal" citizenship. As Anthony Corbeill explains, "the Romans selectively fashioned Greek educational principles into a uniquely Roman form of citizen training," which "served to create and validate those characteristics that constituted a proper Roman male of the urban elite."[7] In this way, the Roman educational regimens imitated their more organized Greek predecessors by establishing the means (and limits) of access and the evaluative lenses for the ethical and social ideals of the empire. Corbeill continues, "In this context 'knowledge' [including rhetorical knowledge] becomes something more than the collection of facts and the development of an expertise. It also provides the means for preserving elite privilege" by defining what it means to *be* an ideal citizen.[8]

The path of education in the Roman world is commonly considered less formalized than in the Greek city-states (especially Athens). Raffaella Criboire, however, argues that there is a discernable four-step process that the most advanced students would complete.[9] Since the process

---

2nd ed. (Waco, TX: Baylor University Press, 2011); Brittany E. Wilson, *Unmanly Men: Refigurations of Masculinity in Luke-Acts* (Oxford: Oxford University Press, 2015).

7. Anthony Corbeill, "Education in the Roman Republic: Creating Traditions," in Too, *Education in Greek and Roman Antiquity*, 261–62.

8. Ibid., 283.

9. Raffaella Criboire (*Gymnastics of the Mind: Greek Education in Hellenistic and Roman Egypt* [Princeton: Princeton University Press, 2001], 160–244) argues for four stages of education in contrast to three. These include informal education at home from birth as the first stage, followed by what more classic educational theorists

of education required serious investment by a household for the duration of many years, only elite boys and very few elite girls could reach
advanced stages of education.[10] The initial enculturation of values ideally began at birth, with fathers and mothers working alongside hired or
enslaved nurses and pedagogues forming the young child with positive
examples of language and behavior.[11] For this reason, ancient authors
include comments on the choice of wet-nurses and the role of parents,
alongside their discussions of pedagogues, in their writings on education.[12] Even Quintilian (35–ca. 96 CE), whose *Institutes on Oratory* is
written for those instructing the most advanced students, comments on
the need to educate a child from birth if he is to be a good orator; it is not
enough for him to learn under a tutor or professional rhetorician when
he comes of age to learn. He explains:

> We naturally retain most tenaciously what we learned when our minds
> were fresh: a flavor lasts a long time when the jar that absorbs it is new,
> and the dyes that change wool's pristine whiteness cannot be washed out.
> Indeed, the worse these impressions are, the more persistent they are.
> Good is easily changed to worse: can you ever hope to change bad to
> good? (*Inst.* 1.1.5 [Russell, LCL])

---

describe as primary (elementary skills), secondary (grammar school), and tertiary
(specialized training).

10. Emily A. Hemelrijk (*Matrona Docta: Educated Women in the Roman Élite
from Cornelia to Julia Domna* [London: Routledge, 1999]) demonstrates that the education of elite women was more common and, to some extent, even expected in the
Roman world (republic and empire) than in classical era Greece. Nevertheless, even
elite women were not generally given a complete education but stopped after the secondary level. The few women who demonstrate more specialized knowledge seem
to have been educated privately by male family members. Such is the case with the
exceptional Hortensia, who eloquently argues in the Forum against the *Lex Oppia*.

11. A "pedagogue" was literally a "child leader." Often a male slave from within
the household, a pedagogue was responsible for watching over children, guiding them
to and from school, and demonstrating proper moral conduct. On the role of nurses
and pedagogues in the elite Roman household, see Keith R. Bradley, *Discovering the
Roman Family: Studies in Roman History* (Oxford: Oxford University Press, 1991),
13–36.

12. Pseudo-Plutarch, *Lib. ed.* 5 [3e]; Quintilian, *Inst.* 1.1; Alicia D. Myers, "'In
the Father's Bosom': Breastfeeding and Identity Formation in John's Gospel," *CBQ* 76
(2014), 483–92.

According to Quintilian, education *must* begin at birth, continue throughout childhood, and last into adulthood so that it can be demonstrated in a socially proper, or virtuous, life.[13] Without the privilege of well-educated parents with the time and means to devote attention to their children's education, therefore, later effort is largely wasted. It may produce sufficient copyists or scribes, and certainly corrupt speakers, but never a true orator.

At the age of seven, what we would recognize as formal education began. At the primary level, students learned the alphabet and writing skills, with an emphasis on speed and quality of writing rather than comprehension of that which was written. It should be noted that both boys and girls of various social standings participated in this level of education, depending on the training needed either to communicate social class or for their employment.[14] Secondary education required the attention of an instructor, called a *grammatikos*, who guided a student through nuances of grammar and syntax. It was only at the tertiary level that students learned the techniques of classical rhetoric described in surviving *progymnasmata* ("preliminary exercises") and in handbooks such as Aristotle's *Rhetoric* and *Poetics*; Cicero's *On the Orator, On Invention*, and *Topics*; and Quintilian's *Institutes on Oratory* cited above, to mention only a few. In addition to works devoted to the description of rhetoric, students had plenty

---

13. It should be noted that gender constructions are embedded in rhetorical theory and practice in the ancient Mediterranean world. Thus, Quintilian, just like Cicero before him, links a well-trained orator with the idea of a good or virtuous "man" (*vir*; Quintilian, *Inst.* 12.1.3; Cicero, *Nat. d.* 1.8.34). There are profound theological implications concerning the gender assumptions that John's Gospel both incorporates and subverts, but space prevents their articulation in this essay. For more information, see Maud W. Gleason, *Making Men: Sophists and Self-Presentation in Ancient Rome* (Princeton: Princeton University Press, 1995); Michael L. Satlow, "'Try to Be a Man': The Rabbinic Construction of Masculinity," *HTR* 89 (1996): 19–40; Colleen M. Conway, *Behold the Man: Jesus and Greco-Roman Masculinity* (Oxford: Oxford University Press, 2008).

14. Facile literacy such as this, however, was *not* widespread, nor did aristocratic children learn alongside their poorer or enslaved peers. While archaeological evidence supports the view that boys and girls studied together, a general distinction between social classes was maintained. See W. Martin Bloomer, "The Ancient Child in School," in *The Oxford Handbook on Childhood and Education in the Classical World*, ed. Judith Evans Grubbs and Tim Parkin (Oxford: Oxford University Press, 2013), 447–56; Ronald F. Hock, "Homer in Greco-Roman Education," in *Mimesis and Intertextuality in Antiquity and Christianity*, ed. Dennis R. MacDonald, SAC (Harrisburg, PA: Trinity Press International, 2001), 57–58.

of examples both to read aloud and hear performed that demonstrated styles to imitate and avoid. Indeed, the classic examples of Homer, Plato, Thucydides, Euripides, Cicero, and others provided the reservoir from which rhetorical instructors pulled when teaching their students. The goal of such exposure, according to the *progymnasmatist* Aelius Theon (first century CE),[15] was the production of good orators as well as historians and poets, since these examples are "the foundation of every kind of discourse" (*Prog.* 61).[16] Theon writes that imitating "beautiful examples (*kalōn paradeigmatōn*)," "stamped" or "molded" (*typōthentes*) students' minds, so that they would create similarly beautiful compositions (*Prog.* 61, 71). With the mastery of rhetorical techniques, along with details of gesture and general comportment (dress and hair styles, facial expressions, voice, and movement), fully educated orators were expected to embody and enact the ideals of Roman citizenship.

Classical rhetoric, then, is more than simply a collection of commonly regarded techniques and pedantic flourishes for communication in the Roman Empire. It is a key component of identity for the ruling elite and, therefore, a component that needed constant care, attention, and demonstration so that other members of society could recognize *this* ideal.[17] In this way, education and rhetorical performances were a crucial part of the "cultural capital" of the Roman hierarchical system just as study of the torah and wisdom was in Jewish and later rabbinic circles.[18] Rhetorical performances were a key means of demonstrating the superiority of the elite class by educating both aristocratic children and even illiterate subjects what it meant to be *elite*. In other words, everyone needed to be

---

15. The precise date of Aelius Theon and his *progymnasmata* is debated. The consensus position, however, dates his writing to somewhere in the first century CE. For a review of viewpoints, see Malcom Heath, "Theon and the History of the Progymnasmata," *GRBS* 43 (2002): 129–60; Heather M. Gorman, *Interweaving Innocence: A Rhetorical Analysis of Luke's Passion Narrative (Luke 22:66–23:49)* (Eugene, OR: Pickwick, 2015), 32–37.

16. Translations of Theon's *Progymnasmata* are from George A. Kennedy, trans., *Progymnasmata: Greek Textbooks of Prose Composition and Rhetoric*, WGRW 10 (Atlanta: Society of Biblical Literature, 2003).

17. Indeed, in this context, the recognition of superior rhetorical ability is part of the narrative used to proclaim nearness to perfection, orderliness and virtue, the right to rule, and even potential nearness to divinity. On the connections between divine honors and Roman education, see Conway, *Behold the Man*, 36–39.

18. Gleason, *Making Men*, xxi–xxvi; Satlow, "Try to Be a Man," 22–35.

culturally instructed, whether formally or not, to recognize which elite individual they were expected to follow.[19] Rhetoric, performed well and by someone who looked the part, was a key part of such recognition.

John's Rhetorical World

As a literary piece written in the late first century, the Gospel of John exists in the midst of this complicated web of rhetoric and power. Certainly the gospel's message is different than that of a tragic hero, a Roman general on the battlefield, or an orator before the Roman Senate. Its hero is Jewish and crucified, after all. But the Gospel of John also communicates in and to a world that associates persuasive rhetorical performances with virtue and the ability to lead. Jesus repeatedly participates in rhetorical exchanges in John, engaging in private dialogues and more formal discourses with crowds, Jewish religious leaders, and the Roman procurator, Pontius Pilate. Although Jesus's speeches often fail to win unambiguous faith from other narrative characters, they work alongside the rest of the gospel to convince its hearers of Jesus's superior identity. Even outside speech performances, the gospel employs classical rhetorical components and regular appeals to the Old Testament to present Jesus as perfectly aligned with God's will, even when he does and describes shocking things. In this way, the gospel uses and subverts cultural narratives of power and privilege in its proclamation of Jesus as God's Son, the very Word (*logos*) through whom God initiated all life now made flesh (John 1:1–14; Gen 1:1–2:3).[20] Space prevents a comprehensive investigation of all the rhetorical features of this gospel. The following section will instead focus on two of the most prominent—genre and characterization—as a means to discuss a number of more specific rhetorical elements of John's Gospel.[21]

---

19. Gleason, *Making Men*, xxiii, 159–62.

20. For more on the associations between Genesis and John, see Rekha Chennattu's chapter in this volume, "Scripture"; Mary Coloe, "The Structure of the Johannine Prologue and Genesis 1," *ABR* 45 (1997): 40–55; John Painter, "The Earth Made Whole: John's Rereading of Genesis," in *Word, Theology, and Community in John*, ed. John Painter, R. Alan Culpepper, and Fernando F. Segovia (St. Louis: Chalice, 2002), 65–84; Alicia D. Myers, *Characterizing Jesus: A Rhetorical Analysis on the Fourth Gospel's Use of Scripture in its Presentation of Jesus*, LNTS 458 (London: T&T Clark, 2012), 39–75.

21. See also the chapters by Harold Attridge ("Genre") and Christopher Skin-

Genre

We begin our discussion with genre since it is the most macrolevel of our categories to analyze. Knowing what type of writing the Gospel of John is sets the foundation for our more microanalyses as we investigate its various features. Nevertheless, as Harold Attridge notes, the question of genre in the Fourth Gospel is fraught with complexity because it delights in bending genres and, therefore, the expectations of audiences both ancient and contemporary.[22] As he so eloquently explains, in John's Gospel "the Word is honored by the manifold variety of words used to express it, words that charm, words that challenge, words that evoke, and words that provoke" since no one genre is "adequate to speak of the Word incarnate."[23] Instead, it is by means of such "manifold variety" that the gospel tries to "force its audience away from words to an encounter with the Word himself."[24] It is not surprising, then, to peruse various commentaries and find discussions of the gospel's genre in relationship to ancient biography, drama, juridical speech, historical testimony, encomiastic (praise) literature, along with revelatory, consolatory, and philosophical discourse, and more.[25] Instead of choosing only one of these elements, however, Attridge is right to guide us toward a more pluralistic understanding of genres within the gospel. The lenses of classical rhetoric, however, can also help us refine our view further, even in the midst of, and indeed as a result of, such variety.

---

ner ("Characterization"). Instead of investigating each feature in full, I will only be addressing them in light of classical rhetoric.

22. Harold W. Attridge, "Genre Bending in the Fourth Gospel," *JBL* 121 (2002): 3–21; Ruth Sheridan, "The Gospel of John and Modern Genre Theory: The Farewell Discourse (John 13–17) as a Test Case," *ITQ* 75 (2010): 287–99; Kasper Bro Larsen, ed., *Gospel of John as Genre Mosaic*, SANt 3 (Göttingen: Vandenhoeck & Ruprecht, 2015).

23. Attridge, "Genre Bending," 11 and 21, respectively.

24. Ibid., 21.

25. Ibid., esp. 3–10. More recent contributions of note include Jo-Ann A. Brant, *Dialogue and Drama: Elements of Greek Tragedy in the Fourth Gospel* (Peabody, MA: Hendrickson, 2004); Brant, *John*, PCNT (Grand Rapids: Baker Academic, 2011); Richard Bauckham, "Historiographical Characteristics of the Gospel of John," *NTS* 53 (2007): 17–36; Kasper Bro Larsen, *Recognizing the Stranger: Recognition Scenes in the Gospel of John*, BibInt 93 (Leiden: Brill, 2008); George L. Parsenios, *Rhetoric and Drama in the Johannine Lawsuit Motif*, WUNT 258 (Tübingen: Mohr Siebeck, 2010).

Classical rhetorical writings, such as Theon's *Progymnasmata*, provide a clearer understanding of genre in the Greco-Roman world. For Theon, there are distinct differences and overlaps between what he describes as "species of hypothesis" (*hypotheseōs eidē*) and "exercises" (*gymnasia*). Species, the broadest headings for classical rhetoric, include (1) encomiastic or epideictic (praise and blame[26]) rhetoric; (2) juridical or legal rhetoric; and (3) deliberative rhetoric, which advises.[27] Within each of these species, however, there are a number of "exercises" (*gymnasia*) that are used to make one's case, whether oral or written (*Prog.* 60, 70). These exercises include *chreia* (anecdote), maxim, fable (*mythos*), narration (*diēgēsis*),[28] topos (common-place), *ekphrasis* (vivid description), *prosōpopoiia* (speech-in-character), *encomion* and invective, *synkrisis* (comparison), thesis, and *nomos* (law). Within each exercise, however, there are additional types and variations in style, arrangement, and purpose. Narration (*diēgēsis*), for example, can vary widely being either "mythical" (*mythika*) or "factual" (*pragmatika*), or even a combination of the two, if it serves the purpose of the overall work (*Prog.* 66). Indeed, Theon recommends collecting "good examples of each exercise from ancient prose works (*palaia syngrammata*)" because they combine, elaborate, refute, and rearrange any number of exercises for their rhetorical ends (*Prog.* 65–66, see also 61–72). Thus by stringing together narrations to describe "things that have happened or as though they had happened," an author creates a "historical writing" (*historion*) (*Prog.* 78, 60). *Historia* are defined further in Theon's list of genealogical history, political history, mythical history (legends), "memories of fine sayings," biographical writings, "general" histories that

---

26. Although defined as "praise" rhetoric, epideictic rhetoric has also a correlated opposite: blame or invective. As Theon writes at the conclusion of his instructions for *encomia*, "these are the sources of praise, and we shall derive blame (*psexomen*) from the opposites" (*Prog.* 112). See also Jerome H. Neyrey, *The Gospel of John in Cultural and Rhetorical Perspective* (Grand Rapids: Eerdmans, 2009), 3–28; Myers, *Characterizing Jesus*, 42–47.

27. Theon, *Prog.* 61; Aristotle, *Rhet.* 1.3; Rhet. Her. 1.2.2. One quickly sees that there is significant overlap in these "species" as well—juridical discourse *uses* epideictic speech to either praise or blame in order to persuade a judge, and epideictic speech may recall a subject's greatness by means of juridical causes, etc. That ancients were also aware of these overlaps is clear in Quintilian, *Inst.* 3.4.12–16.

28. Theon collapses the headings of a "narration" (*diēgēsis*) with "narrative" (*diēgēma*), although other handbooks can reserve *diēgēsis* for the "statement-of-the-facts" at the outset of a forensic speech (Aristotle, *Rhet.* 3.14).

describe "countries, towns, rivers, situations, nature, etc.," as well as "more highly developed history, practiced by Herodotus and many other historians, *which combines features of all the genres just described*" (*Prog.* 104P, emphasis added).

The Gospel of John, then, is an example of a "historical writing," since it is a combination of narrations that describe something and someone who lived and the effects of his deeds. More precisely, John's Gospel corresponds most closely to "biographical writings," by devoting significant attention to the portrayal of its subject, Jesus. Nevertheless, being a biographical work does *not* limit our gospel from describing actions and events or employing any number of exercises to do so, as though a biography could describe a person without describing that person's context or activities. In this way, the gospel still overlaps with other genres of historical writings and uses any number of styles found in other types of literature. The gospel bends and blends exercises as its narrator sees fit, but it remains a historical writing.[29] The influence of the Old Testament, which contains material similar to Greco-Roman historical writings, in addition to poetry, is also felt in the ways in which this gospel bends and blends its styles.[30]

Theon instructs his readers that in order to be "complete" (or "perfect," *teleia*), narrations need to exhibit clarity, conciseness, and credibility in their descriptions of the following elements: person, action, place, time, manner of action, and cause (*Prog.* 28).[31] The selection and

---

29. This description still holds even with poetic elements found in the gospel, most notably in the Prologue. Aristotle argues that prologues or *prooimia* are useful for "all branches of rhetoric" (*Rhet.* 3.14.7 [Freese, LCL]) and are, indeed, common in historical narratives (Plutarch's *Lives*; Suetonius's *Lives of the Twelve Caesars*; Lucian of Samosata, *A True Story, Alexander the False Prophet*, etc.) as well as dramas. Also encouraging for our gospel is its allusion to the Greek version of Gen 1:1 ("In the beginning God made the heaven and the earth"), which situates John's Gospel in the context of the Old Testament story of God's creation and covenant commitments to the Jewish people. See further the essay on "Genre" by Attridge in this volume.

30. On the ways in which portions of the Old Testament resemble Greco-Roman historiographies, see R. N. Whybray, *The Making of the Pentateuch: A Methodological Study*, JSOTSup 53 (Sheffield: Sheffield Academic, 1987); John Van Seters, *The Life of Moses: The Yahwist as Historian in Exodus-Numbers* (Louisville: Westminster John Knox, 1994); James W. Watts, *Ritual and Rhetoric in Leviticus: From Sacrifice to Scripture* (Cambridge: Cambridge University Press, 2007). These similarities indicate cross-cultural influences in Mediterranean antiquity, particularly in the wake of Greek and Persian conflicts.

31. Theon's description of these virtues (clarity, conciseness, and credibility) is

implementation of various exercises within a narration add to the overall persuasive effect, or credibility, which Theon calls narration's "most special feature" (*Prog.* 28). In other words, it is not at all surprising to find a number of exercises, which contemporary scholars often call "genres" or "forms," within a larger narration. Instead, this type of imitation, combination, and adaptation is exactly what ancient rhetorical instructors taught their students. The effective bending of exercises for rhetorical ends was a mark of an accomplished orator and writer. Knowing "beautiful examples" from a variety of more ancient authors and orators, such as Old Testament scripture, an author molds and weaves styles to create something new from that which is well known.[32] Painting a scene before the audience's eyes helps to convince them to honor or shame, to declare innocent or guilty, and ultimately to follow the author's will as that which seems the best (Quintilian, *Inst.* 8.3.61–82). Perhaps, then, it is not so much that the Fourth Gospel is bending a lot of genres, but rather is bending a lot of exercises *as a part of* the larger category of narration and "historical writing," which the gospel represents. Like a yoga instructor, the gospel narrative bends into new shapes, some that astound and surprise, in an attempt to call students to do likewise. Bending and molding along with the teacher, the gospel promises not just good health but "eternal life" (*zōē aiōnia*) to those persuaded by this message (John 3:15–16; 6:47; 17:3).

Characterization

Space prevents a full discussion of *all* the exercises described by Theon, though it is quite clear that examples of most, even if "bent," can be found in John's Gospel. Moreover, discussion could be extended to cover various figures, or techniques, used within each exercise to increase its effectiveness.[33] While we will touch on a few of these, fuller explanation and

---

consistent with other rhetoricians including Aristotle, Cicero, and Quintilian. See Myers, *Characterizing Jesus*, 27–39.

32. John's employment of Old Testament examples for comparison and context emphasizes the gospel's Jewish roots. Gentile orators would not be especially compelled by Old Testament examples, although they might show deference toward their antiquity.

33. Examination of rhetorical figures in John's Gospel is a strength of Brant's commentary, *John*.

exploration must be relegated to another place. Recall above that "person" (*prosōpon*) is one of the elements that Theon says must be described in a narrative for it to be complete. Further, the biographical focus on Jesus encourages centering attention on the construction of this person, whose identity is the heart of its persuasive purpose. John's Gospel, however, also gives significant attention to a large cast of subordinate characters, both individuals and groups. These subordinate characters contribute to the primary characterization of Jesus, as they react and struggle to recognize rightly the strange Logos-man before them. They also challenge the gospel audience, who likewise encounters Jesus through this story, by constantly prompting them to reflect on their own understandings of Jesus.

Providing further instructions on *how* to construct a "person" within a narrative, Theon includes a broad list of topics or topoi, which function as "places" (topoi) from which to begin an argument.[34] This list includes "origin, nature, training, disposition, age, fortune, morality [or, moral choices], action, speech, manner of death, and what followed death" (*Prog.* 78). Theon repeats much of this list in his instructions concerning how to praise a person in an *encomion* but divides them into groups of "goods" (*agathoi*): those that are external, of the body, and of the mind.[35] It is significant to note that for Theon, as for other rhetoricians and philosophers, the most praiseworthy "goods" are those of the "mind" (*psychē*) or "character" (*ēthos*), which correspond to virtues such as prudence, self-control, justice, piety, generosity, and magnanimity (*Prog.* 109–110).[36] These qualities might be predisposed by one's ancestry and foreshadowed by signs surrounding birth, but they are only realized in one's deeds, including speech, which are done by choice, on behalf of others, and with lasting, positive results (*Prog.* 110–113).[37] These priorities for praise and characterization again bring to the fore the overlap between rhetoric and virtue

---

34. Topoi or "common-places" are quite flexible in the rhetorical tradition; see James R. McConnell Jr., *The Topos of Divine Testimony in Luke-Acts* (Eugene, OR: Pickwick, 2014), 23–47.

35. Aristotle, Quintilian, and Cicero offer similar topic lists, and a perusal of ancient literature demonstrates their use by actual authors and orators (see Myers, *Characterizing Jesus*, 43–61).

36. See also Quintilian, *Inst.* 3.7.14–15; Aristotle, *Eth. nic.* 2.6.

37. On the topos of deeds, see Myers, *Characterizing Jesus*, 90–92. On the connection between speech and deeds, see Brant, *Dialogue and Drama*, 74–149, and descriptions of speech as "an index of character" in Plutarch, *Alex.* 1.2; Quintilian, *Inst.* 11.1.30; Matt 12:34; Luke 6:45.

described above. More than simply a list for academic construction, the lists and value of topoi reflect and reinforce social mores. They provide models for students to imitate not only as they mature as orators and writers but also as they mature as ideal citizens.

The topoi of person also correspond to how characters are presented in the Gospel of John. Again indicative of the gospel's biographical focus, Jesus's person receives the most attention, as the most thoroughly developed topoi concern him. We learn of Jesus's origins from "the beginning" and his "becoming flesh" (John 1:1–14). He is identified as the Logos—the Word, Will, Reason, Logic, Order—by and through whom creation was initiated and sustained in Genesis who has been made flesh.[38] Jesus's nature and disposition throughout the gospel reinforce this presentation since he is entirely dependent on the Father, who supplies his words and motivation (5:30; 8:25–26; 10:25–30). Jesus's deeds are called "signs" and "works," which simultaneously encourages a comparison (*synkrisis*) between himself and Moses as worker of "signs" in Israel's past and demonstrates his life-giving ability described in the Prologue (2:11; 5:36; 10:25).[39] John's Gospel also emphasizes Jesus's free choice in doing these deeds, including "laying down" his life so that he can "take it up" again (10:17–18). While dependent on the Father, therefore, Jesus is not without agency. Instead, his disposition and morality align so completely with the Father that his free choices *always* coincide with those of the Father; these two are united as "one" (10:30). Jesus *acts like God's Word* by manifesting his will as the Logos made flesh.

As the Will of God come down, Jesus desires "abundant" life and shows astounding "love" to the world (3:14–16; 10:10; 13:1). Further, Jesus emphasizes that such a relationship between himself and the Father is not new. Instead, the gospel uses a variety of comparisons and descriptive settings (*ekphrastic* language) to argue that Jesus's behavior continues God's actions from the Old Testament.[40] Jesus's words and actions not only remind his audiences of scriptural events, but they are meant to effect

---

38. For a review of the meanings of Logos in John's milieu, see Daniel Boyarin, "The Gospel of the Memra: Jewish Binitarianism and the Prologue to John," *HTR* 94 (2001): 243–84.

39. On *synkrisis*, see Aristotle, *Rhet.* 1.9.39–41; 2.23; Theon, *Prog.* 112; Quintilian, *Inst.* 5.10.86–93; Cicero, *Top.* 3.23; Rhet. Her. 1.6.10; 4.45.59–4.48.61. See also Myers, *Characterizing Jesus*, 47–49.

40. On *ekphrasis*, see Theon, *Prog.* 118, and the importance of vivid description in

greater results than what the gospel presents as temporary remedies from
Scripture (3:14; 4:13–14; 6:49–50; 8:51). Although such claims are impossible for other people to satisfy, the gospel justifies Jesus's behavior by identifying him as the Logos whose now enfleshed existence continues to effect
God's will just as he did at the moment of creation and throughout the Old
Testament. Thus, Jesus and the gospel narrator interpret Scripture with
Jesus at its center: he is the one on whom the angels ascend and descend
(1:51); he gives life like the snake in the wilderness (3:14); he offers water
like the rock Moses struck (4:7–15; 7:37–39); he acts as "true" food and
drink as the bread from heaven (6:1–58); and he is the "glory" that Isaiah
beheld in the temple (1:16–18; 2:12; 12:40–41). In other words, Jesus is
"the one about whom Moses and the prophets wrote" (1:45, 5:47).[41]

One of Jesus's deeds, his speech, has attracted the most attention for
rhetorical interpreters of John's Gospel due to the clear use of oratorical
elements. The speeches crafted for Jesus by the narrator are examples of
prosōpopoiia, which aim to create speech that is both appropriate to Jesus's
character and to the situations in which he finds himself (Theon, *Prog.*
115–118).[42] John's Jesus uses many recognizable rhetorical techniques and
figures in his speeches.[43] In Jesus's speeches and dialogues, for example, he
uses components of juridical rhetoric, demonstrating an awareness of different types of causes rather than simply denying the charges against him.

Thus in John 5, Jesus does not deny his equality with God but rather
moves to demonstrate the validity and, therefore, nonblasphemous nature
of his claim. In terms of forensic rhetoric, this is an "absolute cause" or an
"issue of quality," and it seems to be one of Jesus's favorite types of arguments to debate.[44] He uses a variety of recognizable rhetorical proofs to

---

Quintilian, *Inst.* 5.11.82; 8.3.61–72; 9.2.40–44; Cicero, *De or.* 3.53.202–205; Rhet. Her.
2.30.49; 4.39.51. See also Myers, *Characterizing Jesus*, 49–51, 86–93.

41. For a detailed overview of these features, see Myers, *Characterizing Jesus*,
78–179.

42. Ibid., 51–54.

43. Harold W. Attridge, "Argumentation in John 5," in *Rhetorical Argumenta-
tion in Biblical Texts: Essays from the Lund Conference*, ed. Anders Eriksson, Thomas
Olbricht, and Walter Überlacker, ESEC 8 (Harrisburg, PA: Trinity Press International,
2002), 188–99; Alicia D. Myers, "'Jesus Said to Them': The Adaptation of Juridical
Rhetoric in John 5:19–47," *JBL* 132 (2013): 415–30; Neyrey, *Gospel of John*, 191–251;
Parsenios, *Rhetoric and Drama*.

44. Rhet. Her. 2.13.19; Quintilian, *Inst.* 3.6.66–82; 3.11.1–8. See also Myers, "Jesus
Said," 419–20.

show that he is innocent of wrongdoing because of his unique identity. He urges "right judgment" (*dikaia krisis*, 7:24) from his interlocutors by encouraging them to pay attention to his words and deeds rather than to his appearance. Common proofs in John include descriptions of Jesus's manner of life (5:19–30; 10:1–18; 13:1–20; 15:13–17), analogies and precedents that function as examples and comparisons (3:14; 4:7–15; 6:26–58), and testimonies. These testimonies include the verbal confessions of John (the Baptist) as an extraordinary man whose words Jesus's opponents seem to respect, but they also extend to "greater testimony" (*martyria meizō*, 5:36) from the Father: Jesus's works, words, and relationship to the Old Testament (5:36–47; 8:12–20; 10:25–30). The written testimony of the Old Testament, in particular, stretches the categories of testimony as an acknowledged authority for Jesus's (and the gospel's) first-century audiences. As a collection of acknowledged truths both ancient and divine in origin, this form of written testimony was considered less biased and particularly persuasive.[45] Based on these sacred witnesses, Jesus makes the provocative statement not only that Moses wrote about him (5:46) but also that Abraham "rejoiced that he might see my [Jesus's] day" (8:56); and, somehow, he intentionally fulfills Scripture even as he hangs upon the cross (19:23–37). Again, the rhetorical weaving of Scripture throughout the gospel reinforces the narrator's initial claim that Jesus is the Logos.[46]

Yet, many of the subordinate characters in the gospel repeatedly *misrecognize* Jesus because they have not heard the entire presentation of his character. Especially significant is their lack of access to the Prologue, which articulates the foundational topoi of Jesus's origins, his nature and relationship with the Father, as well as his life-giving abilities and purpose (1:1–18). Without knowing the topoi that set Jesus apart as God's uniquely superior revelation, much of Jesus's behavior in the remaining narrative

---

45. Quintilian, *Inst.* 5.11.36–42; Aristotle, *Rhet.* 1.15.13–17; Cicero, *Top.* 20.76–78; Pseudo-Aristotle, *Probl.* 18.3.32–34; Rhet. Her. 4.1.2.

46. Again, the identification of classical rhetorical categories in Jesus's style of argumentation does not displace his use of Jewish interpretive practices (*middoth*). See n. 5 as well as Peder Borgen, *Bread from Heaven: An Exegetical Study of the Concept of Manna in the Gospel of John and the Writings of Philo*, NovTSup 10 (Leiden: Brill, 1965); A. T. Hanson, "John's Use of Scripture," in *The Gospels and the Scriptures of Israel*, ed. Craig A. Evans and W. Richard Stegner, JSNTSup 104, SSEJC 3 (Sheffield: Sheffield Academic, 1994), 358–79; Ruth Sheridan, "The Testimony of Two Witnesses: John 8:17," in *Abiding Words: The Use of Scripture in the Gospel of John*, ed. Alicia D. Myers and Bruce G. Schuchard, RBS 81 (Atlanta: SBL Press, 2015), 161–84.

seems inappropriate and, therefore, unpersuasive to the narrative characters. Recalling the association between rhetorical performance and identity in the first century described above, we can see how Jesus's physical appearance contrasts his actual identity. As a result, Jesus's rhetoric is undermined for many narrative characters who only have short episodes with a Galilean Jewish man who is not even fifty years old and lacks any formal education but who still makes superlative claims (1:45; 6:42; 7:15, 45–52; 8:57). In an environment where Rome was quick to silence potential rabble-rousers, Caiaphas's decision to sacrifice Jesus for the sake of the nation makes sense to him and his allies (11:47–52). Without the entire story provided by John's Gospel, many of the narrative characters simply cannot recognize Jesus. Although *they* may not be able to come to a "right judgment" (7:24), the gospel audience listening can.

Scholars have long noticed this irony in John: the privileging of the audience listening to the entire narrative in contrast to the narrative characters who only catch glimpses of Jesus.[47] In many ways, such rhetoric seems unfair. But in elevating its audience, even at the expense of its narrative characters, the gospel again reflects its rhetorical milieu, which encourages authors and speakers to complement their audiences with insider-information, thereby making them predisposed to respond positively to the message offered.[48] Since the goal is to convince the audience listening to the gospel as a whole, the rhetoric is tailored for *their* perspective. John's Gospel embraces, and even heightens, the tension caused by the coming of the Logos into the world. In stressing Jesus's rejection by "his own" (1:10), the gospel encourages its audience to remain faithful in spite of any rejection they may also face (15:18–19).

---

47. R. Alan Culpepper, *Anatomy of the Fourth Gospel: A Study in Literary Design* (Minneapolis: Fortress, 1983); Paul Duke, *Irony in the Fourth Gospel* (Atlanta: John Knox Press, 1985); Gail O'Day, *Revelation in the Fourth Gospel: Narrative Mode and Theological Claim* (Philadelphia: Fortress, 1986); Jeffrey Lloyd Staley, *The Print's First Kiss: A Rhetorical Investigation of the Implied Reader in the Fourth Gospel*, SBLDS 82 (Atlanta: Scholars Press, 1988); Christopher W. Skinner, *John and Thomas: Gospels in Conflict? Johannine Characterization and the Thomas Question*, PTMS 115 (Eugene, OR: Wipf & Stock, 2009); Myers, *Characterizing Jesus*. Also see the discussions of irony in Quintilian, *Inst.* 8.6.54–59; 9.2.44–45.

48. Quintilian describes currying audience favor in *Inst.* 3.7.23–35; 3.8.1–48; 6.2.1–24; 11.1.43–44. For additional references, see Myers, *Characterizing Jesus*, 113–14, esp. 114 n. 95.

Conclusions: John's Use of Rhetoric

In this chapter, we have explored John's use of techniques and forms common to classical rhetoric in the first-century Mediterranean world. Rather than arguing that John's author(s) must have had a formal, Roman education, this chapter suggests that the gospel's familiarity with common rhetorical forms demonstrates the pervasiveness of classical rhetoric as a means of communication in this context. John's Gospel, therefore, never loses its deep-rootedness in Jewish traditions or outlook. Instead, the gospel uses rhetoric common to its context to communicate a version of Jesus's life that emphasizes his continuity with God's revelation in the Old Testament. The brief analysis of classical rhetorical elements provided here underscores the care with which John's Gospel was composed as well as its connection to first-century communication practices. Influenced by its ancient context, the gospel proclaims a message meant to convince its audience both of Jesus's unique identity and the type of discipleship required to follow him.[49]

Indeed, the gospel's concern for its external audience not only shapes its use of rhetoric but also contributes to its enduring quality for contemporary readers. Like other ancient authors, the gospel draws audiences into its story-world by privileging them with a more complete story. Unlike the narrative characters, John's audiences receive a presentation of Jesus that explains the potentially unsavory aspects of his life: his rejection by Jewish religious leaders, crowds, and Roman authorities that results in his humiliating death upon the cross. Rather than failure, however, John argues that Jesus's rejection and death are more evidence of his alignment with God's salvific will. As a result, the gospel's message of encouragement to all believers remains; contemporary readers join with their ancient counterparts in receiving John's word that those who believe without needing to see Jesus are truly "blessed" (*markarioi*, 20:29).

---

49. Plutarch makes the ethical implications of biographical writing explicit in his preface to the *Life of Aemilius Paulus*, writing, "I began writing my 'Lives' for the sake of others, but I find that I am continuing the work and delighting in it now for my own sake also, using history as a mirror and endeavoring in a manner to fashion and adorn my life in conformity to the virtues therein depicted" (1.1 [Perrin, LCL]).

12

PERSUASION

Ruth Sheridan

John's Gospel is an inherently persuasive narrative text. Toward the end of the gospel story, the narrator famously explains his purpose in writing his account of Jesus's life: "Now Jesus did many other signs in the presence of his disciples, which are not written in this book. But these are written so that you [pl.] may come to believe that Jesus is the Messiah, the Son of God, and that through believing you may have life in his name" (John 20:30–31).[1] To assist its readers in believing, the gospel narrative employs a variety of literary and rhetorical techniques. For example, the symbolic world of John's story is governed by rich imagery that is frequently structured in binary categories, such as "light" (1:5, 8–9; 3:19; 5:35; 8:12; 9:5; 11:9, 25–26; 12:35, 46) and "darkness" (1:5; 3:19; 8:12; 12:46); "life" (1:3; 3:15, 36; 4:10, 13; 5:21, 24–25, 29, 40; 6:33, 35, 40, 47, 58; 10:28; 14:19) and "death" (8:51; 11:25–26); or of realms "above" (3:3, 7, 31; 8:23) and "below" (8:23).[2] This structured symbolism reflects the possibility of a stark choice with corresponding consequences: "Those who believe in [Jesus] are not condemned; but those who do not believe are condemned already because they have not believed in the name of the only Son of God" (3:18; see also 3:34–36; 12:48–49). The gospel's presentation of definitive divine revelation in Jesus accounts for the urgency of its binary rhetoric, as characters in the story are said to reveal their "origins" and fate by virtue of their choice for Jesus.[3]

---

1. All biblical citations are from the NRSV.
2. See "Imagery" by Dorothy A. Lee in this volume.
3. See Adele Reinhartz, *Befriending the Beloved Disciple: A Jewish Reading of the Gospel of John* (New York: Continuum, 2001), 25.

John's narrative "works" to persuade its readers, in part, by establishing such "high stakes" with little to no middle ground. The gospel creates an ideal reading position, which actual readers are invited to adopt and which mirrors its ideological point of view.[4] The narrative aims to elicit a total response from its readers, which will lead them to choose "light" and "life" over "darkness" and "death," that is, to respond positively to Jesus and to accept his messianic identity. But whereas the concluding statement of the gospel (20:30–31) hints at the blessedness accruing to those who *do* believe, the fate of those characters (and by extension, those real readers) who remain unconvinced of the gospel's message represents the negative facet of this persuasive design. They function to dissuade the reader from replicating their response to Jesus. Often (and problematically) these negative characters are simply called "the Jews," and their collective hostility to Jesus builds as the narrative progresses.[5]

This essay will explore the gospel's array of persuasive techniques with a focused view towards explicating the issues stated above. First, I will present a brief theoretical overview of what is termed the "New Rhetoric," followed by the definition of concepts such as the implied and ideal readers that aim to explain the persuasive ends of narratives. This section will conclude with an assessment of the rhetorical dynamics present in the so-called thematic or didactic narrative. I will then move to the text of the Gospel of John and apply these insights to the text, with a focus upon how the gospel creates and shapes its implied reader, its narratee, and its ideal reader. I will give considerable attention to how, in this persuasive process, the gospel reader is invited to respond to "the Jews" (and other nonbelieving characters) as the "Other," and I will explore the implications of this invitation in light of the transferable potential of the text's meaning beyond the story-world of the narrative.

Narrative Persuasion and the New Rhetoric: Theoretical Soundings

It is common for scholars and students of literature to distinguish between the classical rhetoric of the ancient Greco-Roman world and the so-called

---

4. See "Point of View" by James L. Resseguie in this volume. Below I will define and discuss the terms *ideal reader* and *implied reader* in greater depth.

5. See below for more detail.

New Rhetoric.[6] Attention to the intrinsically persuasive nature of all narrative grew apace in the latter part of the twentieth-century, as critics sought not only to show *that* stories communicate but also to unravel *how* stories communicate and to what end.[7] Indeed, when the term rhetoric is used with reference to the analysis of narratives today, it is commonly understood as encompassing not so much the classical model of rational persuasion but the psychological paradigm by which language functions symbolically to "induce cooperation" in readers.[8]

This accepted distinction between classical rhetoric and the New Rhetoric—though now attenuated somewhat by those who highlight what both "rhetorics" have in common—developed over the course of centuries.[9] For W. B. Yeats and William Wordsworth, classical rhetoric was intractably disingenuous, combative, and antagonistic. Poetry, on the other hand, was conceived of as pure language: creative, emotive, and self-expressive.[10] The demise of classical (and neoclassical) rhetoric finds its advent in the romantics' contrast between the idealized power of poetry and the deadening restrictions of rule-bound rhetoric.[11] Yet the demise of classical rhetoric in contemporary literary studies persists also because classical rhetoric continues to be perceived as a system that failed to account for how language *worked*. Poetics therefore emerged in the 1920s–1930s as a means of investigating the "metaphoricality" of language. In the work of I. A. Richards, metaphoricality is a renewal of rhetoric's aims in that it is an attempt to determine how language

---

6. The term "New Rhetoric" was coined by Chaim Perelman and Lucie Olbrechts-Tytecha (*The New Rhetoric: A Treatise on Argumentation*, trans. John Wilkinson and Purcell Weaver [Notre Dame, IN: University of Notre Dame Press, 1969]). The term is otherwise often associated with the work of Kenneth Burke (see, e.g., *A Rhetoric of Motives* [Berkeley: University of California Press, 1969]).

7. See Wayne C. Booth, *The Rhetoric of Fiction*, 2nd ed. (Chicago: University of Chicago Press, 1983); Booth, *The Company We Keep: An Ethics of Fiction* (Berkeley: University of California Press, 1988).

8. Burke, *Rhetoric of Motives*, 261–62.

9. Cf. William M. Wright IV, "Greco-Roman Character Typing and the Presentation of Judas in the Fourth Gospel," *CBQ* 71 (2009): 545. See also John Rodden, "How Do Stories Convince Us? Notes towards a Rhetoric of Narrative," *College Literature* 35 (2008): 148–73.

10. Jennifer Richards, *Rhetoric* (London: Routledge, 2008), 102.

11. Ibid.

persuades.[12] Then, in the 1960's, linguistics came to be seen as a viable substitute for rhetoric, inasmuch as it conceived of itself as a functioning science that could predictably grasp the inner workings of language.[13] In its turn, structural linguistics experienced its own demise once poststructuralism was in the ascendant; linguistics came to take the place once occupied by classical rhetoric as a restrictive, rule-bound system combined with an overly optimistic means of systematizing discourse.[14] But additionally, poststructuralism broke with structural linguistics by insisting on the polyvalence of the "sign" and the instability of language.[15]

These intellectual advances signaled a shift in how rhetoric came to be understood. Language itself was deemed to be rhetorical—not just the metaphorical aspects of language (the tropes and figures of discourse) but *all* language as such. Rhetoric became synonymous with "rhetoricality," the latter term denoting something institutionally unbound and capable of manifesting "the groundless, infinitely ramifying character of discourse in the modern world."[16] Persuasiveness was thus incorporated back into language/poetics, as it were, not set apart from it in contradistinction. However, the supersession of structural linguistics by poststructuralism in the latter part of the twentieth century has not yielded to a sense of finality in literary studies, as though linguistic indeterminacy is the necessary end point of all theorizing. For rhetoric—and "rhetoricality"—of course implies the *persuasive* capacity of discourse, and persuasion in turn suggests *communication*: someone "acts" upon someone else.[17] Agency, whether authorial or otherwise, is central to communicative persuasion.[18]

---

12. I. A. Richards, *The Philosophy of Rhetoric* (New York: Oxford University Press, 1936).

13. See, e.g., Ferdinand de Saussure, *Course in General Linguistics*, ed. Charles Bally and Albert Sechehaye with Albert Reidlinger, trans. Wade Baskin (New York: McGraw-Hill, 1966).

14. Yet it remains that linguistics was self-presented as a "science" and rhetoric understood as a practice. See Roland Barthes, "The Old Rhetoric: An Aide-Mémoire," in *The Semiotic Challenge*, trans. Richard Howard (Oxford: Blackwell, 1988), 11–94.

15. See Terry Eagleton, *Literary Theory: An Introduction* (Oxford: Blackwell, 1983), 128–29.

16. John Bender and David E. Wellbery, "Rhetoricality: On the Modernist Return of Rhetoric," in *The Ends of Rhetoric: History, Theory, Practice*, ed. John Bender and David E. Wellbery (Stanford, CA: Stanford University Press, 1990), 25.

17. See Richards, *Rhetoric*, 147.

18. For a revision of the notions of agency and authorship in narrative after post-

The more circumscribed structuralism of recent narrative theory (otherwise called narratology) takes up this premise, namely, that narratives betray intentionality in their communicative design and that they set out to achieve a desired effect upon their readership. The New Rhetoric as applied to the study of fictional narratives has enjoyed an enduring and in-depth focus in recent research. Thus, James Phelan writes, "The rhetorical approach conceives of narrative as a purposive communicative act. In this view, narrative is not just a representation of events but is also itself an event—one in which someone is doing something with a representation of events."[19] Stories project a represented world that readers enter into; they temporarily inhabit that world, engage with its characters, and follow its plot, allowing themselves to be swayed by the story's teller.[20] It is in this relation between tellers, readers, and the represented world of the narrative that persuasion takes place.[21] The story's tellers reach out to their readers, trying to influence readers' emotions, thoughts, values, and responses.[22] The rhetorical approach to narrative thus also implies an ethical dimension, for it "attends to both an ethics of the told and an ethics of the telling."[23]

How do stories induce this kind of cooperation in readers? In *The Rhetoric of Fiction*, critic Wayne Booth postulates a narrative relation between the so-called implied author of a text and the implied audience (or implied reader). The implied author is the real author's "second self," created in the process of telling the story.[24] The implied author is a heuristic construct: it is the "version of him or herself the author constructs in writing the narrative"; it is emphatically not the real flesh-and-blood author of the narrative.[25] The correlative heuristic device is the implied

structuralism, see Seán Burke, *The Death and Return of the Author: Criticism and Subjectivity in Barthes, Foucault and Derrida*, 3rd ed. (Edinburgh: Edinburgh University Press, 2008).

19. James Phelan, "Rhetoric/Ethics," in *The Cambridge Companion to Narrative*, ed. David Herman (Cambridge: Cambridge University Press, 2007), 203.

20. Rodden, "How Do Stories Convince Us," 153.

21. See Phelan, "Rhetoric/Ethics," 203. The essay by Mark W. G. Stibbe in this volume ("Protagonist") distinguishes between "showing" and "telling" in narratives. By "telling" in this instance, I simply mean communication broadly conceived.

22. Phelan, "Rhetoric/Ethics," 203.

23. Ibid.

24. Booth, *Rhetoric of Fiction*, 71–72, 137.

25. Phelan, "Rhetoric/Ethics," 208. Cf. Seymour Chatman, *Story and Discourse: Narrative Structure in Fiction and Film* (Ithaca, NY: Cornell University Press, 1978), 148.

reader. This is the "mock" reader coded into the story and addressed by the implied author throughout.[26] The implied reader is a device that can be critically inferred from the text: it is a supremely "knowledgeable" reader, able to grasp and accept the rhetoric of the implied author.[27] In like manner, the implied reader is not the real, historically situated reader, although narrative persuasion is certainly advanced when real readers identify with the implied reader.[28]

Another level of complexity can be added to this theoretical dynamic when we add the concept of the narrator and its corollary, the narratee. The narrator is the "voice" that tells the story directly, either in commentary-like fashion or in asides.[29] The narrator's role varies: he or she can speak in the first-person—as a character somehow involved in the story—or in the third-person and thus be removed from the story-world.[30] The concept of the narratee indicates that the story requires a correlative "listener" who has "a pre-knowledge of some circumstances in the narrative and a basic non-knowledge of others."[31] Thus we have six constituents of narrative: a real author and a real reader, who are both extrinsic to the narrative text; an implied author and an implied reader, intrinsic to the text and relating to each other; and a narrator and a narratee, directly communicating with each other within the story-world of the text.[32]

---

26. Booth, *Rhetoric of Fiction*, 137. The term *implied reader* was coined by Wolfgang Iser (*Der implizite Leser: Kommunikationsformen des Romans von Bunyan bis Beckett* [Münich: Finch, 1972]).

27. See Ruth Sheridan, *Retelling Scripture: "The Jews" and the Scriptural Citations in John 1:19–12:15*, BibInt 110 (Leiden: Brill, 2012), 53, and the literature cited therein.

28. Ibid., 52.

29. Ibid., 54; see also R. Alan Culpepper, *Anatomy of the Fourth Gospel: A Study in Literary Design* (Minneapolis: Fortress, 1983), 16.

30. See Mieke Bal, *Narratology: Introduction to the Theory of Narrative*, 3rd ed., trans. Christine van Boheemen (Toronto: University of Toronto Press, 2009), 18–29. See also James Phelan, *Living to Tell about It: A Rhetoric and Ethics of Character Narration* (Ithaca, NY: Cornell University Press, 2005).

31. Geert Hallbäck, "The Gospel of John as Literature: Literary Readings of the Fourth Gospel," in *New Readings in John: Literary and Theological Perspectives; Essays from the Scandinavian Conference on the Fourth Gospel in Aarhus 1997*, ed. Johannes Nissen and Sigfred Pedersen, rev. ed., JSNTSup 182 (London: T&T Clark, 2004), 36.

32. See Chatman, *Story and Discourse*, 151.

Sometimes scholars blur the concepts of the implied and real reader of the text.[33] This is admittedly easy to do; some narratives convey such a forceful "code" for real readers that they almost demand ideological compliance. Hence, another category has emerged, that of the *ideal*, "paradigmatic," or "compliant" reader of a narrative. Such a reader *is* envisaged as a real, historically situated reader, and as something of a *bona fide* mirror of the narrative's heuristic, implied reader. The descriptor "ideal" designates not so much literary competence as willing adherence to the narrative's rhetorical point of view. The ideal reader is a *product* of narrative compliance; no narrative can force its perspective upon a real reader, and of course, even the most persuasive narratorial voices can meet with resistance. Yet, to the extent that any real reader identifies as completely as possible with a narrative's implied reader, the *ideal reader* emerges.

The ideal reader (or "ideal narrative audience") envisaged by literary critic Peter Rabinowitz is one of four different readers (or audiences).[34] These four audiences are distinguished by the types of *beliefs* they are expected to hold. This important point sets Rabinowitz's analytic model apart from the general model of the four-to-six constituents of narrative delineated above, as it bridges the domains of rhetoric and ethics.[35] Rabinowitz's ideal narrative audience "*agrees* with the narrator that certain events are *good* or that a particular analysis is *correct*, ... [and] is called upon to judge him [the narrator]."[36] The ideal narrative audience, in addition, always "believes the narrator, accepts his judgments, [and] sympathizes with his plight."[37] Not merely a perfectly aware and accepting *implied* constituent of the narrative, Rabinowitz's ideal narrative audience includes any real reader who genuinely complies with the narrator's point

33. Note the overlap in Brian Richardson, "Singular Text, Multiple Implied Readers," *Style* 41 (2007): 259–67. Pertaining to John's Gospel, we see the blurring of the implied reader with the real or intended reader in, for example, Culpepper, *Anatomy of the Fourth Gospel*, 224–25.

34. Peter J. Rabinowitz, "Truth in Fiction: A Reexamination of Audiences," *CI* 4 (1977): 126–28. The other three are: (1) the "actual audience," i.e., any real flesh-and-blood readers of a narrative at any given time; (2) the "authorial audience," i.e., the intended readership of the narrative; and (3) the "narrative audience," a concept approximating to the "implied reader" as defined by critics discussed above.

35. See Sheridan, *Retelling Scripture*, 56.

36. Rabinowitz, "Truth in Fiction," 135, emphasis added.

37. Ibid., 134.

of view. In that sense, Rabinowitz describes the ideal audience as one who "accepts uncritically" what the "narrator has to say."[38]

Do such actual, ideal readers exist? Surely they do, but on the whole, actual readers will assess the invitations for engagement with a narrative text with some degree of criticality. They may accept or reject the persuasive overtures of the narrator "in whole or in part."[39] Readers step into Rabinowitz's narrative audience—what Phelan calls the "observer position within the narrative world"—particularly in response to the story's characters.[40] Phelan considers narrative characterization to be central to the processes of the reader's engagement with a text and thus to the art of persuasion. He argues that by entering into Rabinowitz's audience positions, readers "develop interests and responses" that are "related to a particular component of the narrative."[41] For example, readers often respond to narrative characters in a mimetic sense, as if they were real people. Readers make judgments about characters on psychosocial grounds, such as emotiveness, desire, hope, expectation, satisfaction, and disappointment. Or readers might respond to characters in a thematic sense, interpreting them as "classes of people." Here, readers judge certain characters as emblematic of stereotypical groupings like the "corrupt aristocracy." The thematic response systematizes characters according to the cultural, ideological, or philosophical issues being addressed by the narrative.[42] Any one reader may respond to a narrative in both of these ways, just as multiple readers may respond in only one of these ways.

Although Phelan's schema relates to the components of *any* narrative, we could ask whether some narratives predominantly employ one of these components at the expense of others, particularly where characterization is concerned. John Rodden has theorized that the didactic novel, which employs an "argumentative" type of rhetoric by means of its primary focus on concepts and themes, subsumes characters and events into the author's larger objective to demonstrate a *case*.[43] Rodden supplies George Orwell's *1984* as the primary example of a didactic novel. Orwell's text incorporates characters into his narrative, but his overarching concern is to build an

---

38. Ibid.
39. Phelan, "Rhetoric/Ethics," 210.
40. Ibid.
41. Ibid.
42. Ibid., 210–11.
43. Rodden, "How Do Stories Convince Us," 152.

argument for evaluation and assent.[44] In such didactic texts, the implied "oratorical" voice can be intrusive, and the lack of "three-dimensional" characterization may be "unsatisfying."[45] Rodden likens the communicative exchange between the implied orator and the implied auditor to the typical courtroom interaction between "advocate and jury member, respectively."[46] The paradox is that although the implied orator of a didactic narrative often betrays a closer presence than the implied author of a traditional narrative, readers can become more wary or "on guard" of the implied orator's comparatively intrusive hand, prompting suspicion rather than trust.[47]

We can posit some overlap between what Phelan labelled the *thematic* response to a narrative's characters and Rodden's view of the function of the implied orator in didactic narratives. If the thematic concern of a narrative predominates to the point that it overrides character development, the ideal reader/auditor would be inclined to approach characters as "classes of people" or as symbols of some *idea* articulated by the implied orator. This can be ethically problematic when characters have a *mimetic* function *beyond* the story-world (that is, their presence is transferrable to the real world of the reader), and they potentially become fodder for stereotypes. The reader/auditor might ask, "Do the characters in the story *themselves* accept or reject the central theme or idea of the story?" This consideration would influence the ideal reader's evaluation of the story's characters. But, as mentioned, the heavy-handedness of didactic authority can lead a reader to resist the implied point of view in the narrative.[48]

The Gospel of John as a Persuasive Narrative

John's Gospel can be read through the theoretical lenses outlined in the previous section.[49] First, the implied reader of its narrative is certainly

44. Ibid., 155.

45. Ibid. For the didactic novel, Rodden substitutes the "implied orator" and the "implied auditor" for the more commonly accepted "author/reader" pair.

46. Ibid., 156.

47. Ibid., 157.

48. See Burke's notion of "demystification," i.e., resisting "identification" with a text's persuasive agenda; see *Rhetoric of Motives*, 22–25, 55, 58–59, 268–69.

49. A solid number of scholars have applied literary (or "narrative") criticism to the Gospel of John. Some seminal studies include Culpepper, *Anatomy of the Fourth Gospel*; Jeffrey Lloyd Staley, *The Print's First Kiss: A Rhetorical Investigation of the*

traceable, and thus the ideological point of view espoused by its implied author is obtainable. The reader implied by the gospel is one who is prepared to arrive at complete belief in Jesus as defined by the twin christological titles expressed in John 20:31, that Jesus is "Messiah" and "Son of God."[50] The gospel narrative presents the implied reader with an invitation to believe in its proclamation about Jesus in a variety of ways. These include the use of "recurring misunderstandings, sharp, witty irony, and profound, moving symbolism."[51] To take just one of these examples, Johannine irony contributes to the profile of the implied reader because it offers multivalent possibilities for understanding various words and phrases in the gospel: the surface or "fleshly" meaning coexists with the more subtle or spiritual meaning (see John 3:3–9). Where certain characters in the story may miss the subtle layer of meaning and so misunderstand the text's message about Jesus, the implied reader is formed by interpretive cues that prompt a deeper or genuine understanding of Jesus (see 4:11–13; 7:37–39; 12:34). Real readers, when taking up these cues and identifying with the implied reader, can move through the story with a sense of superiority to the unknowing characters, whose lack of understanding often foils their own understanding.[52]

The implied author's use of misunderstandings, irony, and "double meanings" all relate to his goal of *elevating* the implied reader at the expense of certain, unknowing characters in the story.[53] This is nowhere

---

Implied Reader in the Fourth Gospel, SBLDS 82 (Atlanta: Scholars Press, 1988); Stephen D. Moore, *Literary Criticism and the Gospels: The Theoretical Challenge* (New Haven: Yale University Press, 1989); Mark W. G. Stibbe, *John as Storyteller: Narrative Criticism and the Fourth Gospel*, SNTSMS 73 (Cambridge: Cambridge University Press, 1992); D. Francois Tolmie, *Jesus' Farewell to the Disciples: John 13:1–17:26 in Narratological Perspective*, BibInt 12 (Leiden: Brill, 1995); René Kieffer, "The Implied Reader in John's Gospel," in Nissen and Pedersen, *New Readings in John*, 47–65. Recently there has been a move toward reading Johannine characters from a literary-critical perspective; see Colleen M. Conway, *Men and Women in the Fourth Gospel: Gender and Johannine Characterization*, SBLDS 167 (Atlanta: Scholars Press, 1999); Susan E. Hylen, *Imperfect Believers: Ambiguous Characters in the Gospel of John* (Louisville: Westminster John Knox, 2009); see further the remaining literature cited in Christopher W. Skinner's essay ("Characterization") in this volume.

50. See Culpepper, *Anatomy of the Fourth Gospel*, 207.

51. Ibid., 7.

52. Ibid., 7, 152–99.

53. See Stibbe's essay in this volume ("Protagonist").

more evident than in the gospel's Prologue (1:1–18), where the implied reader is informed of Jesus's identity as the enfleshed "Word" of God (1:1–14) and the supreme mediator of "grace and truth" for humanity (1:17–18). The "glory" of the divine Word exists in the "flesh" of Jesus as the begotten Son (1:14–1:17). The remainder of the gospel narrates how characters either recognize the "glory" in the "flesh" of Jesus or misconstrue it. The implied reader effectively evaluates the response of various characters to Jesus based upon what has been revealed in the gospel's Prologue, which stands outside of, and prior to, the gospel story and thus benefits no actual character in the story.[54] Preeminently then, the gospel shapes its implied reader by distributing knowledge between characters and readers unevenly.[55] The implied author cues the implied reader into the correct interpretation of the story so that the reader is tutored to arrive at faith in Jesus.[56]

The textual relationship between the gospel's narrator and the narratee functions as part of its persuasive design.[57] The gospel's narrator is often equated in the scholarship with the so-called "beloved disciple"—a character in the story who witnesses the events narrated as well as testifying to their truth (13:23–25; 19:35; 21:20, 24).[58] R. Alan Culpepper has noted that the voice of the narrator is most explicitly present in the scripturally influenced "prolepses" (the intrusive, forward-looking commentaries on narrated events) that punctuate Jesus's public ministry (2:22; 7:39; 12:15).[59] It is also the case that, throughout the gospel, the narrator's presence is

---

54. See Culpepper, *Anatomy of the Fourth Gospel*, 89. Culpepper calls this "ironic" in that the gospel characters are striving to know what the reader has already learned in the Prologue.

55. The narrator as "focalizer" restricts knowledge of events to some characters and reveals it to others (or to the reader). In some narratives, the ideology of the focalizer is presented as "authoritative" while other ideologies or voices in the text are "subordinated" and "must be evaluated from it"; see Shlomith Rimmon-Kenan, *Narrative Fiction: Contemporary Poetics*, 2nd ed. (London: Routledge, 2002), 80.

56. See Robert Kysar, with Tom Thatcher, "John is Dead; Long Live John!" in *Anatomies of Narrative Criticism: The Past, Present, and Futures of the Fourth Gospel as Literature*, ed. Tom Thatcher and Stephen D. Moore, RBS 55 (Atlanta: Society Biblical Literature, 2008), 137–46.

57. See Culpepper, *Anatomy of the Fourth Gospel*, 16.

58. See James H. Charlesworth, *The Beloved Disciple: Whose Witness Validates the Gospel of John?* (Valley Forge, PA: Trinity Press International, 1995).

59. Culpepper, *Anatomy of the Fourth Gospel*, 7, 17.

bound up with the persuasive project of forging and fostering group identity.[60] The narrator often speaks in an inclusive, communally focused voice (1:14; 21:24), suggesting how the narrative hints at the personal history of a believing community.[61]

Yet the narratorial identity inscribed in the gospel and the history of the "Johannine community" are not the same.[62] The communally focused voice of the narrator can be likened to what literary theorist Uri Margolin has termed the "we-narratives."[63] The use of the first-person narrative voice (what we might call the "we-voice") is characteristic of "we-narratives." At first, the narratorial "we-voice" can potentially alienate the narratee (and thus, the real reader). If the reader can situate herself in the position of the narratee by means of an empathic identification with the "we-voice," however, the exclusiveness of the plural grammar is overcome; the reader assimilates the inclusive perspective and becomes part of the narrative's "in-group."

The gospel's "we-voice" is first heard in the Prologue, with the narrator announcing that "*we* have seen his [Jesus's] glory" (1:14a). The incarnate Word, identified as "the Father's only son" (1:14b), imparts grace to the narratorial "we-voice": "from his fullness, *we* have all received grace upon grace" (1:16).[64] Those who believe this become "children" of God (1:12), and they are brought into the "we-group" as those who are privy to the divine "glory" exhibited in Jesus. In the gospel narrative proper, the

---

60. Ruth Sheridan, "Identity and Alterity in the Gospel of John," *BibInt* 22 (2014): 188–209.

61. Ibid., 194–95.

62. Seminal works include J. Louis Martyn, *History and Theology in the Fourth Gospel*, 3rd ed. (Louisville: Westminster John Knox, 2003); Wayne A. Meeks, "The Man from Heaven in Johannine Sectarianism," *JBL* 91 (1972): 44–72; Raymond E. Brown, *The Community of the Beloved Disciple: The Life, Loves and Hates of an Individual Church in New Testament Times* (New York: Paulist, 1979); D. Moody Smith, *John among the Gospels: The Relationship in Twentieth Century Research* (Minneapolis: Fortress, 1992).

63. Uri Margolin, "Person," in *Routledge Encyclopedia of Narrative Theory*, ed. David Herman, Manfred Jahn, and Marie-Laure Ryan (London: Routledge, 2005), 422–23; Margolin, "Telling in the Plural: From Grammar to Ideology," *Poetics Today* 21 (2000): 591–618.

64. The Greek construction *charin anti charitos* has occasioned much debate. See Ruth Edwards, "Χάριν ἀντὶ χάριτος (John 1:16): Grace and Law in the Johannine Prologue," *JSNT* 32 (1988): 3–15.

"we-voice" of the narrator sometimes merges with the speaking voice of the character Jesus, a tactic that serves to reinforce the credibility of the narrator. For example, in 3:11, Jesus tells Nicodemus: "*we* speak of what *we* know, and testify to what *we* have seen, but you [pl.] do not receive our testimony." This group of concepts (speaking, knowing, testifying, seeing, and the rejection of testimony) echoes the narrator's claims in the Prologue, where the Word was rejected by "his own" (1:10) and where both John the Baptizer and the narratorial "we-voice" testified to—or "saw"— the Word's glory (1:6, 14–15). Other characters in the gospel who receive Jesus positively also adopt the "we-voice," suggesting their correspondence to the narrator's point of view. These include the Samaritans (4:42), Peter (6:69), and Mary of Magdala (20:2c; yet, see also 20:13b).[65] Readers are invited to evaluate the response of these characters in light of the narrator's rhetorical use of the "we-voice" and to effectively join their ranks by becoming part of the same inclusive community of faith.

The narrator also serves as a reliable support for the testimony of the anonymous individual witnessing the flow of blood and water from Jesus's pierced side at the crucifixion (19:35). Whereas, in the Prologue, it was the "we-voice" that testified to having seen Jesus's "glory" (1:14), at the cross the narrator tells us that it was "he who saw this" (*ho eōrakōs*) who "has testified" (*memarturēken*) (19:35a). Another voice emerges, insisting that this individual's testimony is true and even going so far as to comment upon his self-knowledge: "and he knows that he tells the truth" (19:35b). The narrator thus knows two things: that the eyewitness's testimony is true and that the eyewitness himself knows his own testimony is true. The narrator declares that the eyewitness has testified "so that you [pl.] also may believe" (19:35a), thus anticipating the climactic "purpose" statement of the gospel (20:31). But it also ties in with the conclusion of the gospel's epilogue, when the narrator identifies the "beloved disciple" as the one "who is testifying [*ho marturōn*] to these things ... and *we* know that his testimony is true" (21:24b). The narrator's use of the "we-voice," as well as his insight into the truth of other character's testimony or the validity of their self-knowledge, accords with his status as a fully reliable narrator.

Significantly, the narratorial use of the first-person plural functions to create an "us" and—implicitly—to define a "them."[66] Other character

---

65. Sheridan, "Identity and Alterity," 199.

66. See Judith Lieu, "Us or You? Persuasion and Identity in 1 John," *JBL* 127 (2008): 805–19.

groups also use the first-person plural but in ways that contest the words and actions of Jesus. Thus, for example, "the Jews" reply to Jesus's offer of "freedom" (8:31–32) with the statement, "*we* are children of Abraham and have never been enslaved to anyone" (8:33; see further 8:41, 48, 52; 19:7, 15). From a narratorial perspective, the group identities represented by these characters are not to be trusted, neither are the characters' responses to be replicated by real readers. Indeed, the rhetoric of the "we-voice" is something of a double-edged sword, so that the plural grammar of groups who contest and condemn Jesus operates as a *dissuasive* device that guides the narratee (as well as the implied and real reader) away from the point of view represented by their speech and/or action.

This facet of John's narrative leads us into an appreciation of how the gospel shapes an *ideal* or "compliant" reader. Recall that Rabinowitz's ideal reader is a real, historically situated reader, defined by *beliefs, judgments,* and *sympathies*: belief in the narrator's ideological point of view, assenting judgment in the (assumed) "good" nature of the events presented, and sympathetic engagement with the authorial voice and/or narrative protagonist.[67] Rabinowitz's "ideal" reader receives the narrative's presentation of events at face value, on the basis of a sympathetic belief in its inner truth—not on the basis of an empirical verification of its historical truth (although many readers of John's Gospel would read its narrative with sympathetic belief *and* possibly an embrace of its perceived historical truth). This is to approach the text with the kind of openness (or "uncritical" stance) appropriate to a trusting relationship, and hence Rabinowitz's theory bridges rhetoric and ethics. As Booth explained, the appropriate metaphor governing an ethical engagement with any given narrative is that of "relationship" or "friendship."[68]

Adele Reinhartz has applied Booth's ethical criticism to the Gospel of John in the most comprehensive manner to date.[69] Reinhartz understands the gospel's overtures to the (real) reader as an invitation to a metaphorical "friendship" with the narrator. The basis of the invitation to friendship is the proffering of a "gift"—"eternal life" in Jesus's name (20:31). But the offer is cast in "ethical terms," so that those characters who reject Jesus's gift of eternal "life" and "light" are judged negatively by the narrator (they

---

67. Rabinowitz, "Truth in Fiction," 141.

68. Booth, *Company We Keep,* 169–82.

69. Reinhartz, *Befriending the Beloved Disciple*; and see the detailed discussion in Sheridan, *Retelling Scripture,* 62–67.

"do evil deeds," "hate the light and avoid it" [3:20]), but those characters who accept the gift are judged positively (they "do what is true," "come into the light," and their deeds are "done in God" [3:21]).[70] This system establishes the narrative's "rhetoric of binary opposition," a terse dualism that overflows to real readers of the story. One group of readers, aligning themselves with the characters who accept Jesus, will find themselves nourished by the text's metaphorical "friendship"; but another group of readers, perhaps empathizing with those characters who cannot (or will not) receive Jesus's words, find themselves consigned "to the role of the Other."[71]

Rabinowitz's concept of the ideal reader resonates well with John's ethical dualism. The reader who (1) assents to the implied author's point of view and depiction of narrative events, (2) believes in the text's theological message, and (3) sympathizes with the story's protagonist, even while judging its antagonists, will become an "ideal" reader. Reinhartz's term is the *compliant* reader.[72] Due to the binary structure of the gospel's rhetoric, adopting a compliant reading of the text can lead to positioning the characters in the story who are inimical to Jesus as the "Other."[73] As discussed above, the gospel's antagonistic characters are most frequently grouped together as "the Jews" or "the Pharisees" (8:12–21; compare with 9:13–17); they speak with their distinctively collective "voices," offering a counter-narrative to the dominant one espoused by the implied author and the narrator. The issue is complicated by the fact that John's "ethical dualism" operates on both the narrative-historical and theological plane.[74] The gospel's ostensibly historical narrative induces compliance in the ideal reader insofar as it is presented as something to be accepted on its own terms, conveyed through the generic medium of narrative historiography, thus approaching verisimilitude. On this level, the ideal (or compliant) reader is enjoined to negatively evaluate "the Jews" who are depicted as hostile toward Jesus, as refusing to believe in him, and as actively seeking his death (1:19; 2:28; 3:25; 5:10, 15–16, 18; 6:41, 52; 7:1, 11, 13, 20; 8:31, 37, 40, 48, 52, 57; 9:18, 22; 10:24, 31, 33; 11:8, 53–54; 18:28–32, 35–38; 19:7,

---

70. Reinhartz, *Befriending the Beloved Disciple*, 25.

71. Ibid., 25, 20.

72. Actually, Reinhartz identifies four "reading positions": compliant, resistant, sympathetic, and engaged; see discussion of each in *Befriending the Beloved Disciple*, 54–80, 81–98, 99–130, 131–59, respectively.

73. Ibid., 54–80.

74. See Reinhartz, *Befriending the Beloved Disciple*, 32–42.

12, 14, 38; 20:19).[75] And on the theological plane, "the Jews" as a group
are connotatively associated with traits that the narrator would have us
understand as arising from a love of "darkness" and "evil" (see 3:19–21).[76]
The way that the mythological aspect of the gospel intersects with its historiographical presentation certainly compounds the force of the Jews'
pejorative characterization. Furthermore, the gospel's soteriology is also
framed around "contrasting states of being, such as light/darkness, life/
death, from above/below, being from God or not being from God."[77] These
"states of being" give rise to contrasting activities with respect to Jesus and
God, such as believing or not believing, loving or hating.[78] Overwhelm-
ingly, "the Jews" (and "the Pharisees") inhabit the underside of this soteriological schema: they reject Jesus, who is the "light" (8:12–21), and so
they live in darkness (12:37) and blindness (9:40–41). The Jews do not
"see" (5:38) or "know" (8:55) God, for they do not receive Jesus (8:42–43).
The come "from below" (8:23), are fathered by the devil (8:44), and will
"die in their sin" (8:24; cf. 9:13–17).[79]

John's Gospel "works" to persuade—or in the words of Kenneth
Burke, to "induce symbolic cooperation" in its readers—by weaving stereotyped characterization into its structured mythology about the historical figure of Jesus.[80] Compliance therefore comes by way of what Burke
calls "identification," but in John's narrative, a compliant reading neces-

75. While the broader picture developed in the gospel is slightly more nuanced—
"positive" uses of the term *hoi Ioudaioi* do occur (4:9, 22; see also 3:2; 4:31; 8:31
[maybe]; 11:8; 12:11), as well as "neutral" uses (2:6, 13; 5:1; 6:4; 11:55)—the negative usages outweigh these others. See Stephen G. Wilson, *Related Strangers: Jews and
Christians, 70–170 CE* (Minneapolis: Fortress, 1995), 74.

76. Sheridan, *Retelling Scripture*, 3–4. See Judith M. Lieu, "Anti-Judaism, 'the
Jews', and the Worlds of the Fourth Gospel," in *The Gospel of John and Christian Theology*, ed. Richard Bauckham and Carl Mosser (Grand Rapids: Eerdmans, 2008), 171:
"Whenever the [gospel] narrative moves towards hostility it also moves towards the
use of *hoi Ioudaioi*." It is accepted that the Jews receive the most consistently negative
characterization in the gospel as Jesus's stereotyped antagonists; cf. Gerry Wheaton,
The Role of Jewish Feasts in John's Gospel, SNTSMS 162 (Cambridge: Cambridge University Press, 2015), 43; but see Wheaton's more cautious assessment on 45.

77. Adele Reinhartz, "'Jews' and Jews in the Fourth Gospel," in *Anti-Judaism and
the Fourth Gospel*, ed. Reimund Bieringer, Didier Pollefeyt, and Frederique Vandecasteele-Vanneuville (Louisville: Westminster John Knox, 2001), 215.

78. Ibid.

79. Sheridan, *Retelling Scripture*, 65.

80. Burke, *Rhetoric of Motives*, 262.

sarily involves *dis*-identification from characters that reject of the gift of eternal life presumably present in Jesus.[81] This accords with Mark Stibbe's notion of the "paradigmatic reader" of the gospel, as one who "does not resist the narrator."[82] The "paradigmatic reader" accepts all that is claimed about Jesus on the christological level (1:14; 10:30; 11:27; 20:31), and he or she receives the gift of "life" (1:3–4; 3:16; 5:24; 10:10; 17:1–3) without coming to judgment (3:17; 5:24).[83] The paradigmatic reader understands that characters such as "the Jews" function as negative exemplars of the kind of faith response to Jesus that the gospel calls forth from its readers.[84]

It is worth considering the foregoing in light of what Phelan identified as the "thematic" response of the reader to characters. Recall that this response occurs when readers approach characters as "classes of people," as symbolic or emblematic of one or more of the narrative's central themes.[85] The gospel's "compliant reader" would have no trouble fitting "the Jews" into the fabricated role of the antagonists or villains. But more pertinently, it is their association with "all the negative categories and images in the gospel: the world, sin, the devil, darkness, blindness and death," that can lead the reader into the kind of "thematic" response articulated by Phelan.[86] Rudolf Bultmann's existentialist overlay to his classic exegesis of the gospel only partially accounts for his understanding that "the Jews" play a representative or symbolic function in the narrative.[87] It is the *kind* of thematic narrative exemplified by the gospel that potentially permits readers to respond to the pejoratively depicted characters in this way; certainly "the Jews"—and most other characters in the story-world—are not as amena-

---

81. A compliant reading of John's Gospel entails that one understand "the Jews" to represent "the forces that stand in opposition to Jesus and hence to God" (Reinhartz, *Befriending the Beloved Disciple*, 70), indicating how Johannine anti-Judaism is not chimerical but inscribed into the persuasive design of the reading process.

82. Stibbe, *John as Storyteller*, 16.

83. Ibid.

84. Sheridan, *Retelling Scripture*, 99. Jerome Neyrey even claims that the gospel's characters are drawn in such a way as to arouse particular emotions in readers who will "hate" or "bear contempt" towards those characters who reject Jesus or try to kill him. See Neyrey, " 'In Conclusion …': John 12 as Rhetorical *Peroratio*," *BTB* 37 (2007): 101–13.

85. Phelan, "Rhetoric/Ethics," 210–11.

86. Culpepper, *Anatomy of the Fourth Gospel*, 129.

87. Rudolf Bultmann, *The Gospel of John: A Commentary*, trans. G. R. Beasley-Murray (Philadelphia: Westminster, 1971).

ble to Phelan's mimetic response, that is, to being assessed as "realistic" people with full, inner lives. The gospel's characters are relatively "flat," so to speak, and thus open to stereotyped character reconstructions.[88]

This leads us back to Rodden's theory of the kind of rhetoric operative in didactic novels, which subsume characters into the larger objective of arguing a "case" to be assessed by the reader.[89] The implied orator, we will recall, establishes characters and events in the story as ripe for evaluation and judgment, almost like readers are jurors in a courtroom trial. This metaphor is indeed apt. John's narrative has been frequently understood as forensic in function, with Jesus standing "trial" throughout the period of his public ministry before the Jews and the Pharisees, as he presents his "case" with witnesses and evidence (5:19–47; 7:1–8:59; 10:22–38).[90] The narrated disputes between Jesus and the Jews are crafted in such a way as to persuade the reader "of the justice of Jesus's cause."[91] The purpose is for the reader to come to a verdict about Jesus, one way or the other.[92] The "implied orator" (to borrow Rodden's phrase) of John's "thematic" narrative, when seen in this light, is quite heavy-handed. The reader either accepts Jesus or rejects him and can evaluate the narrative characters only on this same basis. The consequences of rejecting Jesus are nothing short of "death in sin" (8:24) or of "judgment on the last day" (12:48).

But what if, in view of this very insistence, the reader is led to resist the narrator? Against the gospel's ideal, "compliant" reader, Reinhartz posits the "resistant" reader who reads the story "from the point of view of the Other."[93] At the very least, it is to allow that "the Jews" (and other rejecting characters) are victims of the implied author's polarized rhetoric.[94] Performing a resistant reading means critically considering the legitimacy of the Jews' counter-claims: their right to dispute Jesus's perceived activity of "making himself god," although a man (see chapter 5; 10:33), and their

---

88. On the "round" versus "flat" distinction in characterization theory, see E. M. Forster, *Aspects of the Novel* (New York: Harcourt, 1927), 73–81.

89. Rodden, "How Do Stories Convince Us?" 152.

90. Anthony E. Harvey, *Jesus on Trial: A Study in the Fourth Gospel* (London: SPCK, 1976), 16, see also 14.

91. Harvey, *Jesus on Trial*, 15. See also Andrew T. Lincoln, *Truth on Trial: The Lawsuit Motif in the Fourth Gospel* (Peabody, MA: Hendrickson, 2000).

92. Harvey, *Jesus on Trial*, 17.

93. Reinhartz, *Befriending the Beloved Disciple*, 81.

94. Ibid., 87.

genuine claim to be "free" (8:32–33).[95] A resistant reading understands
the community "history" behind the text as producing a biased, one-sided
picture of what was, no doubt, a two-sided debate between two parties.
The legitimacy of the Jews' "voice"—almost wholly sidelined by the gospel's polemic—is recovered in a resistant reading.[96] The importance of this
cannot be overstated: a wholehearted, "compliant" or "thematic" response
to "the Jews" in John's Gospel is made ethically problematic because the
term "the Jews" designates a real group of people today, with potentially
transferrable meaning beyond the narrative. Returning to Phelan's schema,
this could be rephrased as saying that "the Jews" in John have a *mimetic*
function *beyond* the story-world, and thus *real* Jews can be potentially stereotyped on the basis of the gospel's anti-Jewish perspective. A study of
the gospel's persuasive design therefore ought to trace not only the mecha-
nisms by which the reader is called to sympathize with its presentation of
Jesus but also the means by which rhetorical identification can, and perhaps should, be avoided.

---

95. Ibid., 93.
96. See Sheridan, *Retelling Scripture*, 66.

13

Closure

Francis J. Moloney

Tracing *how* John draws his narrative to closure is fraught with challenges, due to the unresolved debate concerning *where* his story ended. For many scholars and commentators, the words of the narrator to the audience in 20:30–31 mark the end of the original Johannine Gospel.[1] Increasingly, however, interpreters regard 21:1–25 as part of the original gospel. Most contemporary literary critics insist on the importance of interpreting a narrative in the form that it has come down to us over almost two thousand years. They regard the final chapter as an integral part of the story that must be taken into account in assessing Johannine theology and Christology and also in tracing "how John works."[2] There are ongoing themes

---

1. It is widely claimed that there is no evidence of a manuscript tradition without 21:1–25, but Michael Lattke ("Joh. 20:30f als Buchschluß," *ZNW* 78 [1987]: 288–92) has suggested that Tertullian knew a Fourth Gospel that ended with 20:30–31. Philip W. Comfort (*The Quest for the Original Text of the New Testament* [Grand Rapids: Baker, 1992], 157–66) argues that the scribes of P[5] and P[75] would have had to add two extra pages to contain 21:1–25. J. K. Elliott, in his review of Comfort's book (*NovT* 36 [1994]: 284–87), rightly remarks: "As both of these manuscripts are fragmentary it seems risky to argue that there is textual evidence for a chapter 20 edition of the Fourth Gospel on these grounds" (286). Such fragmentary evidence cannot be claimed as sure grounds for the way an original might have ended. Too much of Comfort's argument historicizes why and when the gospel was written (see *Quest for the Original Text*, 164–66). There is increasing interest in Coptic manuscripts that may close with John 20. See, for example, Gesa Schenke, "Das Erscheinen Jesu vor den Jüngern und der ungläubige Thomas: Johannes 20,19–31," in *Coptica—Gnostica—Manichaica: Mélanges offerts à Wolf-Peter Funk*, ed. Louis Painchaud and Paul-Hubert Poirier, BCNHSE 7 (Québec: University of Laval Press; Leuven: Peeters, 2006), 893–904.

2. For a survey of recent scholarship, see R. Alan Culpepper, "Designs for the

across John 1–20 and John 21,[3] and unresolved problems from 1:1–20:31 are dealt with in 21:1–25.[4]

Five significant characters who have appeared earlier in the narrative are the key players in 20:1–31: Peter (1:40–44; 6:8, 68–69; 13:6–10, 24, 36–38; 18:10–11, 15–18, 25–27), the Disciple whom Jesus loved (1:35 [?]; 13:23–25; 18:15–16 [?]; 19:25–27), Mary Magdalene (19:25), the disciples (passim), and Thomas (11:16; 14:5). Other characters appear in John 21 (Thomas, Nathanael, and the sons of Zebedee [vv. 2–3, 5–14]), but they are marginal. Peter and the Beloved Disciple continue to play major roles (Peter in vv. 2–3, 7, 11, 15–21; the Beloved Disciple in vv. 7, 20–24) returning from the obscurity of their respective homes (see 20:10: *apēlthon oun palin autous hoi mathētai*); one is appointed shepherd (Peter, 21:15–18) and the other, witness (the Beloved Disciple, 21:24).[5] Another element in John 20–21 is the "voice" of the narrator. In 20:1–31, by means of direct communications between the implied author and the implied reader in verse 9, and in the final statement of the purpose of this writing in verses 30–31, the narrator plays a role that subordinates the characters *in the story* to the narrative rhetoric of John 20:1–31, aimed at the reader/

Church in the Imagery of John 21:1–14," in *Imagery in the Gospel of John: Terms, Forms, Themes, and Theology of Johannine Figurative Language*, ed. Jörg Frey, Jan G. van der Watt, and Ruben Zimmermann, WUNT 200 (Tübingen: Mohr Siebeck, 2006), 369–73.

3. See, for example, Mark W. G. Stibbe, *John*, Readings: A New Biblical Commentary (Sheffield: JSOT Press, 1993), 207–208; Martin Hasitschka, "The Significance of the Resurrection Appearance in John 21," in *The Resurrection of Jesus in the Gospel of John*, ed. Craig R. Koester and Reimund Bieringer, WUNT 222 (Tübingen: Mohr Siebeck, 2008), 311–28.

4. See, for example, Jean Zumstein, "Die Endredaktion des Johannesevangeliums (am Beispiel von Kapitel 21)," in *Kreative Erinnerung: Relecture und Auslegung im Johannesevangelium*, ed. Jean Zumstein, 2nd ed., ATANT 84 (Zurich: TVZ, 2004), 291–315.

5. For guides to contemporary interest in Johannine characters and characterization, see Christopher W. Skinner, "Characters and Characterization in the Gospel of John: Reflections on the *Status Quaestionis*," in *Characters and Characterization in the Gospel of John*, ed. Christopher W. Skinner, LNTS 461 (London: T&T Clark, 2013), xvii–xxxii; and Steven A. Hunt, D. Francois Tolmie, and Ruben Zimmermann, "An Introduction to Character and Characterization in John and Related New Testament Literature," in *Character Studies in the Fourth Gospel: Narrative Approaches to Seventy Figures in John*, ed. Steven A. Hunt, D. Francois Tolmie, and Ruben Zimmermann, WUNT 314 (Tübingen: Mohr Siebeck, 2013), 1–33.

listener.[6] The same must be said for the voice of the narrator in 21:1–25 (especially verse 25).

LITERARY CONSIDERATIONS

Literary theory surrounding "endings" has not been extensively applied to biblical narratives, despite the epoch-making study of Barbara Herrnstein Smith on closure in poetry, the more recent study of narrative closure in antiquity by Massimo Fusillo, and others.[7] The variety and sometimes puzzling nature of the "endings" of New Testament narratives makes it difficult to formulate a theory about them in their contemporary rhetorical, literary, and theological contexts. Morna Hooker has elegantly shown that all the gospel "endings" serve as "invitations to discipleship," but the authors of Mark, Matthew, Luke, John, and Acts do this in very different ways.[8]

---

6. Until recent times, interpreters focused upon "the reader" of a written text. Some contemporary critics focus upon "the listener," given the limited literacy of early Christians. I respect both positions with my expression "reader/listener." Important scholars have pointed to the dangers, and even the errors, of this recent approach. See especially, Larry W. Hurtado, "Oral Fixation and New Testament Studies? 'Orality', 'Performance' and Reading Texts in Early Christianity," *NTS* 60 (2014): 321–40; Udo Schnelle, "Das frühe Christentum und die Bildung," *NTS* 61 (2015): 113–43.

7. Barbara Herrnstein Smith, *Poetic Closure: A Study of How Poems End* (Chicago: University of Chicago Press, 1968); Massimo Fusillo, "How Novels End: Some Patterns of Closure in Ancient Narrative," in *Classical Closure: Reading the End in Greek and Latin Literature*, ed. Deborah H. Roberts, Francis M. Dunn, and Don Fowler (Princeton: Princeton University Press, 1997), 209–27. A number of essays in this collection may be of interest to the reader, especially Fowler, "Second Thoughts on Closure," 3–22. See further, R. Alan Culpepper, "John 21:24–25: The Johannine *Sphragis*," in *John, Jesus, and History, Volume 2: Aspects of Historicity in the Fourth Gospel*, ed. Paul N. Anderson, Felix Just, and Tom Thatcher, ECL 2 (Atlanta: Society of Biblical Literature, 2009), 342–59, who provides a helpful summary of the work of Fusillo. On closure in the Fourth Gospel, see also Douglas Estes, *The Temporal Mechanics of the Fourth Gospel: A Theory of Hermeneutical Relativity in the Gospel of John*, BibInt 92 (Leiden: Brill, 2008), 99–130. On John 21, see Beverley R. Gaventa, "The Archive of Excess: John 21 and the Problem of Narrative Closure," in *Exploring the Gospel of John: In Honor of D. Moody Smith*, ed. R. Alan Culpepper and C. Clifton Black (Louisville: Westminster John Knox, 1996), 240–52. On Gaventa's essay, see Francis J. Moloney, *Glory Not Dishonor: Reading John 13–21* (Minneapolis: Fortress, 1998), 191–92.

8. Morna D. Hooker, *Endings: Invitations to Discipleship* (London: SCM, 2003). On the variety of "closures," see 1–10. All gospel "beginnings" can be regarded as a

There are several "closures" in the Fourth Gospel. John 1:18 looks back across 1:1–17 as the Prologue closes. Jesus's first days close with Jesus's request that the disciples look beyond their expectations to the promised revelation of the heavenly in the Son of Man (1:49–51). The second Cana miracle (4:46–54) rounds off and looks back across the responses to Jesus that have marked 2:1–4:45. Jesus's celebration of the Jewish feasts closes with the reason for his claim to be true bread, true light, living water, the light of the world, and the Good Shepherd who lays down his life for his friends: he and his Father are one (10:30; see v. 38); it closes further with a glance back the place where John was baptizing as the story began (10:40–42; see 1:28). The turn toward the cross closes with a summary of Jesus's ministry (12:44–50). Jesus's last night with his disciples climaxes in his prayer that all may be where he will be—united in love with the Father (17:24–26). Yet the reader/listener finds that the account of Jesus's death and resurrection has two endings: 20:30–31 and 21:25.

A further literary feature of the Fourth Gospel calls for attention: John's tendency to frame episodes. Widely recognized examples are the oneness between God and the Logos in 1:1 and the oneness between Father and the Son in 1:18; the Mosaic law used by "the Jews" to put Jesus on trial in 5:16–18 and Jesus's counterclaim that Moses accuses them in 5:45–47; the Cana miracles of 2:1–2 and 4:46–54 frame the beginnings of Jesus's ministry; a garden scene opens and closes the passion narrative (18:1–11; 19:38–42). The same feature appears at a macrolevel across the gospel. The best known is the oft-identified parallel between 1:1–18 and 20:30–31.[9] The public ministry is framed by references to the location and activity of John the Baptist (1:28 and 10:40–42). A number of commentators who argue in support of the originality of 21:1–25 point to an

---

form of literary "prologue" (Mark 1:1–13; Matt 1:1–4:17; Luke 1:1–4:15; John 1:1–18), while the "endings" defy a single *literary* classification. While Culpepper, "John 21:24–25," shows convincingly that Fusillo's assessment of the closure of ancient narratives applies to John 21:24–25, this cannot be claimed for the endings of Mark, Matthew, and Luke. For further studies on "closure" in biblical narrative, see Walter B. Crouch, *Death and Closure in Biblical Narratives* (New York: Lang, 2000); Susan Zeelander, *Closure in Biblical Narrative*, BibInt 111 (Leiden: Brill, 2012).

9. See, for example, George Mlakhuzhyil, *The Christocentric Literary Structure of the Fourth Gospel*, 2nd ed., AnBib 117 (Rome: Gregorian & Biblical, 2011), 137–52, who traces a chiastic parallelism between 1:1–2:11 and 20:30–31, and across the whole gospel.

"inclusion" between 1:19–51 and 21:1–25.[10] Following Howard Jackson, Richard Bauckham argues that "circling back" to the first appearance of the Beloved Disciple (1:35) as the story closes (21:7, 20–24) is a sign of eyewitness testimony.[11]

The Cana-to-Cana section of the gospel (2:1–4:54) opens the account of Jesus's public ministry. Across this literary unit, the reader/listener encounters a series of responses to the word of Jesus: the Mother of Jesus, "the Jews," Nicodemus, John the Baptist, the Samaritan woman, the Samaritan villagers, and the royal official. A description of "journeys of faith" *began the story* (2:1–4:54), and parallel "journeys of faith" *close the story* (20:1–29). But there is a difference. While in 2:1–4:54 eight *different* characters respond to Jesus in a variety of ways, four *foundational* characters move from no faith to belief in 20:1–31: the Disciple whom Jesus loved (20:2–10; 21:7, 20–24), Mary Magdalene (20:1–2, 11–18), the disciples (20:19–23; 21:12–14), and Thomas (20:24–29). In 21:1–25, the disciples, Peter, and the Beloved Disciple reappear, but there is no hint of any "journey of faith."

Following hard on the heels of Jesus's blessing of "those who have not seen and yet believe," this intervention from the narrator, explaining the purpose of the "writing," looks back to the disciple who believed without seeing Jesus (see v. 8), but who did not yet know "the Writing" (v. 9: *tēn graphēn*).[12] There is no such focus upon the faith experience of Peter and the Beloved Disciple in 21:1–25 nor upon the significance of "the Writing." Although the issue of faith is not totally absent (see vv. 7 [the

---

10. See, for example, René Kieffer, *Le monde symbolique de Saint Jean*, LD 137 (Paris: Cerf, 1989), 17, 90–95; Peter F. Ellis, *The Genius of John: A Compositional-Critical Commentary on the Fourth Gospel* (Collegeville, MN: Liturgical Press, 1984), 13–15, 310–12; Majella Franzmann and Michael Klinger, "The Call Stories of John 1 and John 21," *SVTQ* 36 (1992): 7–16.

11. Howard M. Jackson, "Ancient Self-Referential Conventions and Their Implications for the Authorship and Integrity of the Gospel of John," *JTS* 50 (1999): 1–34; Richard Bauckham, *Jesus and the Eyewitnesses: The Gospels as Eyewitness Testimony* (Grand Rapids: Eerdmans, 2006), 124–47. See, however, Culpepper, "John 21:24–25." He argues that 21:24–25, rather than indicating an eyewitness, serves as a *sphragis*, "a literary seal or certification of authority, in which an editor, speaking on behalf of the Johannine school, affirms the truthfulness of the community's Gospel" (363).

12. The English translation "yet" in v. 29 is part of the meaning of the adversative *kai*, set between the two aorist participles *mē idontes* and *pisteusantes*: not seeing, *yet* believing.

Beloved Disciples and Peter], 18–19 [Peter]), John is more interested in their *respective roles in the community* (vv. 15–18, 20–24).[13] The final reference to the writing of books (21:25), which is modeled upon 20:30–31 (especially v. 30) and directed to subsequent readers and listeners, does not instruct them that *this book* has been written to lead them deeper into faith in Jesus as the Christ, the Son of God.[14]

What follows pursues a literary approach to John 20–21, focusing upon the importance of the use of the final appearances of major characters from the narrative as a whole in an attempt to uncover how John brought his story to closure.[15] It will also devote attention to the "voice" of the narrator, especially in 20:9, 30–31, and 21:25.

---

13. It has been suggested that John 20 affirms the importance of "faith" (esp. vv. 30–31), while John 21 stresses the importance of "love" (esp. vv. 15–17). See R. Alan Culpepper, "Peter as Exemplary Disciple in John 21:15–19," *PRSt* 37 (2010): 165–78, for Peter's response as loving self-gift. But the love theme in 21:15–19 serves the vindication of Simon Peter rather than being the dominant theme of the chapter. On this, see the fine essay of Michael Labahn, "Peter's Rehabilitation (John 21:15–19) and the Adoption of Sinners: Remembering Jesus and Relecturing John," in Anderson, Just, and Thatcher, *John, Jesus, and History 2*, 335–48.

14. For a comparative study of 20:30–31 and 21:25, see George R. Beasley-Murray, *John*, WBC 36 (Waco, TX: Word, 1987), 416. For indications that 21:25 adopts a literary form used by other writers of the period, see Raymond E. Brown, *The Gospel according to John*, 2 vols., AB 29–29a (Garden City, NY: Doubleday, 1966–1970), 2:1130.

15. What follows is thus situated in the contemporary interest in Johannine characters and characterization, initiated by Raymond F. Collins, "The Representative Figures of the Fourth Gospel, Part I," *DRev* 94 (1976): 26–46, Collins, "The Representative Figures of the Fourth Gospel, Part II," *DRev* 94 (1976): 118–32, and further developed by R. Alan Culpepper, *Anatomy of the Fourth Gospel: A Study in Literary Design* (Minneapolis: Fortress, 1983), 101–48. More recently, see Cornelis Bennema, *Encountering Jesus: Character Studies in the Gospel of John*, 2nd ed. (Minneapolis: Fortress, 2014); Skinner, *Characters and Characterization*; Hunt, Tolmie, and Zimmermann, eds., *Character Studies in the Fourth Gospel*. For the characters in John 20–21, see David R. Beck, "'Whom Jesus Loved': Anonymity and Identity; Belief and Witness in the Fourth Gospel," in Skinner, *Characters and Characterization*, 221–39. See the following studies of the characters in John 20–21 in Hunt, Tolmie, and Zimmerman, *Character Studies*: Michael Labahn, "Simon Peter," 151–67; James L. Resseguie, "The Beloved Disciple," 537–49; Jean Zumstein, "The Mother of Jesus and the Beloved Disciple," 641–45; Jaime Clark-Soles, "Mary Magdalene," 626–40; Susan E. Hylen, "The Disciples," 214–27; Thomas Popp, "Thomas," 504–29.

THE CHARACTERS IN JOHN 20:1–31

The use of time should be taken into account in an assessment of the rhetorical use of the characters in 20:1–31.[16]

(1) The report of the experience of Peter and the Disciple whom Jesus loved (20:3–10) is recorded as something that happened in the past. They are dismissed from the story-world in verse 10. However, immediately prior to that dismissal, the use of the pluperfect tense (*ēideisan*) points to a past time, after which much has happened. The narrator reports that at that time "they did not yet know the Scripture." The expression contains the hint of a promise that one day they will come to that knowledge.[17] That experience is not recorded *within* 20:1–31.

(2) Mary Magdalene, the disciples, and Thomas experience a journey from lack of faith to a confession of Jesus recorded *within the time frame of the narrative*:

(2a) Mary Magdalene moves from a conviction that the body has been stolen (vv. 1–2, 11–16), to "her" being recognized by Jesus who prevents her from *clinging* to him (vv. 16–17), to her acceptance of a mission from the Risen Jesus (verse 18).

(2b) Although not as intense as the requests of Mary Magdalene and Thomas, the disciples experience the *physical* presence of Jesus: "He showed them his hands and his side" (v. 20).

(2c) Thomas is initially absent when the risen Jesus appears (v. 24), and he will not accept that Jesus has risen "unless" certain *physical* conditions are fulfilled (v. 25). Challenged by the appearance of Jesus (vv. 26–27), he confesses that Jesus is his Lord and God (v. 28).

With the exception of Peter and the Beloved Disciple, the experiences of faith in the risen Jesus resolved *within the narrative itself* are the result of *seeing* Jesus, and they are shot through with the physical. As the narrative closes, Jesus contrasts Thomas's arrival at faith on the basis of "sight" with those "who have not seen and yet believe" (vv. 24–29).[18] The aorist parti-

---

16. See especially Gerard Genette, *Narrative Discourse: An Essay in Method*, trans. Jane A. Lewin (Ithaca, NY: Cornell University Press, 1980), 86–160.

17. This is conveyed by the English translation "yet," rendering the temporal aspect of the Greek *oudepō*. See BDAG, s.v. *oudepō*.

18. For a very different reading of 20:24–29, see Popp, "Thomas," 513–23. Popp presents Thomas in an entirely positive light, suggesting that all he asks in his request to touch Jesus is the Easter experience had by Mary Magdalene and the other dis-

ciples describing "those who have not seen [*hoi mē idontes*] and yet believe [*kai pisteusantes*]" and the general context of these culminating words of Jesus indicate that they are directed to believers who live in the time after the return of Jesus to his Father (see 17:5; 20:17).[19] Those who are blessed belong to a later generation living in the period of the absence of Jesus. In other words, Jesus's blessing within the narrative is directed *forward* into a time and a situation that *lies beyond the limitations of the narrative*, to a time when the sight of Jesus, and the possibility of physical proximity, are no longer available.

Peter, the Disciple whom Jesus loved, Mary Magdalene, Thomas, and the rest of the disciples are characters *in the story*. As such, Peter and the Disciple whom Jesus loved cannot yet know the Scripture (*tēn graphēn*), as they are part of it. Within John 20, only the Disciple whom Jesus loved comes to faith without seeing Jesus (vv. 11–18). But this story was written (*gegraptai*, v. 31) for the readers and hearers *of this gospel* who believe without seeing.[20] Located in a *time outside the narrative*, they have it in hand; they are hearing it recited or watching its performance.[21] Only they are blessed (*makarioi*, v. 29). Peter and the Disciple whom Jesus loved disappear from the narrative as they return to their respective homes (v. 10), never to be heard of again within John 20.[22] Is it possible that John is giving a unique status to his "writing" that the *characters in the story* cannot yet know (v. 9), while the *recipients of the story* are instructed that

---

ciples. The beatitude of v. 29 includes Thomas, and thus the episode "presents the final amplification of touching the Risen One in John 20" (521). He adds that, "Thomas is on the highest peak of the Christological mountain of the Fourth Gospel" (527). This downplays the absence in v. 24, the conditionals in v. 25, closing with "I will not believe," and the author's pointing elsewhere (to those who cannot "touch" Jesus) with the beatitude of v. 29.

19. Unless otherwise stated, all translations of biblical texts are my own.

20. The temporal aspect of the perfect tense of the verb "has been written" also plays into the author's use of time. This book has been written in the past, but the perfect tense of the verb *gegraptai* indicates that it is still available, providing access to faith in Jesus and the life that comes from faith in his name.

21. See Francis J. Moloney, "'For as Yet They Did Not Know the Scripture' (John 20:9): A Study in Narrative Time," *ITQ* 79 (2014): 97–111.

22. Labahn, "Simon Peter," 162–63, rightly points to Peter's need for an encounter with the risen Lord. But he claims that it "is provided in a subsequent scene: 20:19–29, which leads him to post-Easter understanding." But Peter and the Beloved Disciple are decisively dismissed in v. 10. There is no indication in the narrative that Peter is present for vv. 19–29, whatever one makes of John 21.

they are hearing the Scripture (*tēn graphēn*), written (*gegraptai*) that they may believe that Jesus is the Christ, the Son of God, and believing have life in his name (vv. 30–31)?[23] Which "Scripture" is referred to in verse 9?[24]

Perhaps the readers of the Gospel of John accept that "the word" they hold in their hands is "the Scripture." This is something that the Disciple whom Jesus loved and Peter, key players in the drama of the narrative, "as yet" were not able to understand (20:9).[25] Such understanding will be provided for the readers of the story "later" (v. 29).[26] That will be made clear in verses 29–31. A candidate for the "Scripture" that Peter and the Disciple whom Jesus loved did *not yet* know (v. 9) is the Johannine story. It was

---

23. Other recent scholars, on somewhat different grounds, have suggested this possibility. See Andreas Obermann, *Die christologische Erfüllung der Schrift im Johannesevangelium: Eine Untersuchung zur johanneischen Hermeneutik anhand der Schriftzitate*, WUNT 2/83 (Tübingen: Mohr Siebeck, 1996), 409–22, esp. 418–22; Klaus Scholtissek, "'Geschrieben in diesem Buch' (Joh 20,30): Beobachtungen zum kanonischen Anspruch des Johannesevangeliums," in *Israel und seine Heilstradition im Johannesevangelium: Festgabe für Johannes Beutler SJ zum 70. Geburtstag*, ed. Michael Labahn, Klaus Scholtissek, and Angelika Strottman (Paderborn: Schöningh, 2004), 207–26, esp. 219–24; Michael Labahn, "Jesus und die Autorität der Schrift im Johannesevangelium: Überlegungen zu einem spannungsreichen Verhältnis," in Labahn, Scholtissek, and Strottman, *Israel und seine Heilstradition*, 185–206. See the excellent summary of Obermann's work in Ruth Sheridan, *Retelling Scripture: "The Jews" and the Scriptural Citations in John 1:19–12:15*, BibInt 110 (Leiden: Brill, 2012), 27–32.

24. For a result of a survey of scholarly opinion see Craig S. Keener, *The Gospel of John: A Commentary*, 2 vols. (Peabody, MA: Hendrickson, 2003), 2:1184: "The Scripture to which John refers is unclear here."

25. For more detail, see Moloney, "A Study in Narrative Time," 104–7. For a response to this essay, see Brendan Byrne, "A Step Too Far: A Critique of Francis Moloney's Understanding of 'the Scripture' in John 20:9," *ITQ* 80 (2015): 149–56. Byrne's response reflects a lack of care over the shift of focus in the use of "had been written" in 1:19–12:16, in support of christological claims, and the "fulfilment" of Scripture from 12:38–19:37 (reaching its high point in 19:30), a tendency to read John as if he was Paul, and a lack of appreciation of the uniqueness of the Fourth Gospel's claim to be the word about "the Word." Byrne's work on John is always informative (see, for example, his *Life Abounding: A Reading of John's Gospel* [Collegeville, MN: Liturgical Press, 2015]), but often lacks a depth of appreciation of Johannine nuance and uniqueness.

26. On the "narrative tension," pointing the reader/listener to the *dénouement* of the Johannine version of Jesus's death and resurrection, see Francis J. Moloney, *Love in the Gospel of John: An Exegetical, Theological, and Literary Study* (Grand Rapids: Baker Academic, 2013), 71–98.

impossible for them to know this Scripture because they are characters *in the story* and thus *not yet* (*oudepō*) readers or hearers *of the story*. As such, the "Scripture" of the Gospel of John is not available to the Disciple whom Jesus loved. But he has been presented as the first disciple to come to belief in the risen Jesus, *even though he does not see Jesus*.

The response of the other individual foundational disciples—one a woman (20:1–2, 10–18) and the other a man (20:24–29)—is strikingly different from that of the Disciple whom Jesus loved. They seek to establish a "fleshly" contact with the Jesus they can see and touch (see especially 20:16–17, 25, 27). The same must be said for the disciples. Informed that Jesus is now the risen Lord (v. 18), they also "see" Jesus and are shown the physical evidence of his hands and his side (vv. 19–20). They are to be his sent ones, the bearers of his word (see 18:21), and whoever receives them will receive Jesus and the one who sent him (13:20). It is to that "later" world, however, touched by the witness and the critical presence of the disciples (vv. 19–23), that Jesus directs his final blessing (v. 29).[27]

The Voice of the Narrator in John 20:30–31

Turning away from Thomas, Jesus's final words in John 20 are directed to later generations of readers and hearers, those who have not seen Jesus but still believe (v. 29). The narrator then tells them why he wrote this book (vv. 30–31). Looking back across the faith journeys recorded in the episodes of the Disciple whom Jesus loved, Mary Magdalene, the disciples gathered behind closed doors, and Thomas, there is an important link between Jesus's final blessing of those who do not see and yet believe (v. 29) and the experience of the Disciple whom Jesus loved: he also did not see, yet he believed (v. 8). This is what it means to be a disciple whom Jesus loves.[28] The author, in fact, suggests that later generations, those who do

---

27. Against Popp, "Thomas," 515–23, who includes Thomas in the beatitude of v. 29. Although she does not devote detailed attention to the disciples in 20:19–23, Hylen reacts to the widespread notion that they are examples of true faith. She shows that as "characters" in the Johannine narrative, the disciples remain "ambiguous." They "are people who always seek to gain understanding" ("Disciples," 226).

28. See Brendan Byrne, "The Faith of the Beloved Disciple and the Community in John 20," *JSNT* 23 (1985): 83–97. See also Barnabas Lindars, *The Gospel of John*, NCB (London: Oliphants, 1972), 602: "He (the author) is concerned that *the reader* should believe, and sets the Disciple whom Jesus loved before him as the first example for him to follow."

not see and yet believe (v. 29), have an advantage. They have been provided with "the Writing" that Peter and the Disciple whom Jesus loved did not yet know (v. 9).

Jesus did many signs, but they have not been *written* (*gegrammena*) in this book (v. 30). There is a purpose behind the selection of the signs that has been *written* (*gegraptai*) "so that *you* [later generations of disciples who have not seen, but have this story], may believe that Jesus is the Christ, the Son of God, and that believing you may have life in his name" (v. 31). This "Writing," *not yet* available for the Disciple whom Jesus loved (v. 9), is available to those who are reading John's story of Jesus and in the ears and hearts of those who are hearing it or seeing it performed. Their blessing (v. 29) is part of John's rhetoric of persuasion.[29] Living in the time of the absence of the physical Jesus, they are in a more advantageous position than those who had access to his bodily presence: Mary Magdalene, the disciples, and Thomas. They also have an advantage over Peter and the Disciple whom Jesus loved, who returned to their homes, not yet knowing "the Scripture" (*tēn graphēn*) that Jesus must rise from the dead (vv. 9–10). They have "the Writing" (*tēn graphēn*, v. 9), *written* for them (*gegraptai*, vv. 30–31).

THE CHARACTERS IN JOHN 21

John has dismissed Peter and the Beloved Disciple (20:10), but they return to play key roles in 21:1–25.[30]

(1) Peter has lost interest in what has gone before: "I am going fishing" (21:3). When he is informed by the Beloved Disciple that the personal calling to the fishermen from the shore "is the Lord," he leaps into the water (v. 7), and he hauls the net ashore when Jesus asks for some of the fish (v. 11). The reader/listener recognizes such actions as typical of his enthusiasm (see 6:66–69; 13:6–10, 36–38) but knows that he has failed (18:15–18, 25–27). On the basis of a threefold profession that he loves Jesus "more than these," Peter reverses his abandoning of the Jesus-story (vv. 1–3).[31]

---

29. See the essay "Persuasion" by Ruth Sheridan in this volume.

30. For a more detailed analysis of the role of Peter and the Beloved Disciple in John 21, see Moloney, *Love in the Gospel of John*, 176–89.

31. See Francis J. Moloney, *The Resurrection of the Messiah: A Narrative Commentary on the Resurrection Accounts of the Fourth Gospel* (New York: Paulist, 2013), 121–22, 134 n. 63.

He is appointed the shepherd of Jesus's flock, symbolized by the catch of many fish and the fact that the net is not torn apart (see 19:23–25a).[32] The narrator's comment in verse 19a, catching up themes and words that spoke of the future death of Jesus (see 12:33; 18:32), informs the reader/listener that Peter will lose his life in a fashion that matches the death of Jesus (vv. 15–18).[33]

(2) The Beloved Disciple's actions are minimal and entirely positive, as his role is never ambiguous. He is not mentioned in the original group of disinterested fishermen in verses 1–2, and he thus appears on the scene surprisingly in verse 7 where he informs those disciples: "It is the Lord." Peter responds (vv. 7–18), but as he "follows" Jesus (v. 19), he turns and asks a question that bothered those who were reading and hearing this story. Seeing the Beloved Disciple also "following," he asks "What about this man?" (vv. 20–21). This is a pivotal question on the final page of a story where Peter has always been a leader (1:41–42; 6:67–69; 20:2–10), albeit a somewhat ambiguous one (13:6–11; 18:15–18, 25–27). Whenever Peter and the Beloved Disciple appear together, the former is always upstaged by the latter (13:22–25; 18:15–18; 20:2–10). The Johannine community is asking the question placed on the lips of Peter: "What about this man?" (21:21). Addressing the world *outside the text*, in a period *after* the death of Peter (vv. 18–19) and *after* the death of the Beloved Disciple (vv. 22–23), the narrator answers the question of verse 21: what about this man? The Beloved Disciple is their witness; the one who has written these things, through whom they have received their authoritative Jesus-story (v. 24).

John 21 has provided a response to the unresolved question of the respective roles of Peter and the Beloved Disciple.[34] Another "resolution," however, that is seldom noticed is the bleak situation of the two foundational disciples who "as yet did not know the Scripture" (20:9). The story

---

32. For a comprehensive study in support of this claim, see Culpepper, "Designs for the Church," 369–402.

33. See Moloney, *Love in the Gospel of John*, 183–84. See also D. Francois Tolmie, "The (Not So) Good Shepherd: The Use of Shepherd Imagery in the Characterisation of Peter in the Fourth Gospel," in Frey, van der Watt, and Zimmermann, *Imagery in the Gospel of John*, 352–67, esp. 363–67.

34. For a more comprehensive survey of the many points of continuity and resolution between 1:1–20:31 and 21:1–25, see Francis J. Moloney, "John 21 and the Johannine Story," in *Anatomies of Narrative Criticism: The Past, Present, and Futures of the Fourth Gospel as Literature*, ed. Tom Thatcher and Stephen D. Moore, RBS 55 (Atlanta: Society of Biblical Literature, 2008), 237–51.

of the subsequent Johannine church must be based on more solid authority than these disciples who disappeared from the story as they returned
home after their experiences at an empty tomb (20:9–10). The situation is
resolved in 21:15–24: Peter will profess unconditional love and eventually
experience a death that will glorify God (vv. 15–18). The Disciple whom
Jesus loved, who has also died, is the one who has "written these things"
(vv. 19–24). One is the authoritative shepherd and the other is the witness.[35]

CONCLUSION

John is not *primarily* interested in the "character" or the "characterization"
of the Beloved Disciple, Peter, Mary Magdalene, Thomas, or the disciples
in John 20–21. His gospel is directed to its audience, those who have not
seen, yet believed (20:29).[36] It is at this point that John 21 falters in its role
as "closure" for the Johannine story. There are many indications across 1:1–
20:31 that this gospel has been written for those who do not see yet believe,
*readers and listeners who receive the text but who experience the absence of
Jesus.* This is especially clear in the Johannine use of sacramental material
(3:3–5; 6:51–58; 13:1–38; 19:31–37),[37] its teaching on the Paraclete (14:16,
25–26; 15:26–27; 16:7–11, 12–15),[38] the need for Jesus to depart (14:1–4,
27–31; 16:4–7, 16, 19–21, 28), and in such editorial interventions as 1:1–18
and 19:35.[39]

In 21:1–25, Mary Magdalene, Thomas and the disciples do not play a
role. The issue of believing without seeing has disappeared from the Johannine rhetorical agenda, and thus the faith experience of these foundational

---

35. See Moloney, *Resurrection of the Messiah*, 121–26; D. Moody Smith, "When
Did the Gospels Become Scripture?" *JBL* 119 (2000): 12–13.

36. As R. Alan Culpepper, "The Weave of the Tapestry: Character and Theme in
John," in Skinner, *Characters and Characterization*, correctly observes: "In a sense,
each of the characters is a 'plot functionary,' and it is important to take note of the ways
characterization, theme development and the rhetorical design of the gospel narrative
are intertwined" (35).

37. Francis J. Moloney, "When Is John Talking about Sacraments?" *ABR* 30
(1982): 10–33.

38. Francis J. Moloney, "The Gospel of John: A Story of Two Paracletes," in *The
Gospel of John: Text and Context*, ed. Francis J. Moloney, BibInt 72 (Leiden: Brill,
2005), 241–59.

39. On 19:35, see Moloney, *Gospel of John*, 505–6, 509. It is important to recognize
that 1:1–18 is a massive authorial intervention directed to readers and listeners.

figures is unimportant. But Jesus must return to the story to bring Peter
and the Beloved Disciple out of their homes (see 20:10), to establish them
respectively as shepherd (Peter) and witness (Beloved Disciple). In 20:17–
18, the risen Jesus spoke of his imminent return to his Father but that
has been postponed in 21:1–23. John must address readers and listeners
about a matter of concern: the nature of the community (vv. 3–18) and the
respective roles of Peter (vv. 15–18) and the Beloved Disciple (v. 20–24).

John's story *of Jesus* ended in 20:30–31, but that was not the end of
the story *of the Johannine disciples*. The implied author whose narrative,
christological, and theological strategies direct the rhetoric of 1:1–20:31
wanted to convince readers that the Scriptures had been fulfilled in the
glorification of Jesus through his death and resurrection (19:23–37, esp.
vv. 28–30), and he had left the *graphē* of his story of Jesus as a witness to
that fulfillment (20:9, 30–31). What had been selected from the tradition
had been "written" that all who did not see might believe in Jesus as the
Christ, the Son of God, and have life in his name (20:30–31).[40] But, as we
know from subsequent Johannine literature (1, 2 and 3 John), the Johannine disciples were troubled by the unanswered questions concerning the
nature and mission of the community as well as questions of leadership
and authority.[41] The story of Jesus had come to an end, but another story
had begun. The implied author of John 21 called upon other Johannine
traditions concerning the risen Jesus to generate that story.[42]

The addition of the epilogue was pastorally effective, as the ongoing
presence of John 21 within Christian literature indicates. But it has altered

40. See Francis J. Moloney, "The Gospel of John as Scripture," *CBQ* 67 (2005):
454–68.

41. This sentence accepts that the Johannine letters appeared after the Fourth
Gospel. Although widely accepted, especially in the light of the authoritative work of
Raymond E. Brown (*The Epistles of John*, AB 30 [Garden City, NY: Doubleday, 1982],
47–115), this position is by no means universal. For a good example of the contemporary debate, see R. Alan Culpepper and Paul N. Anderson, eds., *Communities in Dispute: Current Scholarship on the Johannine Epistles*, ECL 13 (Atlanta: SBL Press, 2014),
especially Culpepper, "The Relationship between the Gospel of John and 1 John,"
95–122. The most comprehensive recent challenge has come from Udo Schnelle, "Die
Reihenfolge der johanneischen Schriften," *NTS* 57 (2013): 114–44.

42. See William S. Vorster, "The Growth and Making of John 21," in *The Four Gos-
pels 1992: Festschrift Frans Neirynck*, ed. Frans van Segbroek, Christopher M. Tuckett,
Gilbert Van Belle, and Jos Verheyden, 3 vols., BETL 100 (Leuven: Leuven University
Press, 1992), 2207–14.

an important element in the rhetoric of the earlier narrative. A post-Easter Christian reader has been led from 1:1 to 20:31 to see the blessedness of the one who believes in Jesus as the Christ the Son of God and has life in his name because of what has been "written" (20:30–31), despite the *absence* of Jesus.[43] In an ideal world, there is no need for the return of the ascended Jesus to guide the church with Peter, the Beloved Disciple, and the other disciples. Jesus has ascended to the Father to establish a new situation where his disciples are his brethren, children of God (see 1:12; 20:17).[44] Another Paraclete is with the followers of Jesus and will be with them (see 14:16–17, 25–26; 16:7–11, 12–14) until Jesus returns to take them to his Father's dwelling place (see 14:2–3, 18–24).

But Johannine disciples do not live in an ideal world. Despite the importance of "departure" and "absence" for the Christology of John 1:1–20:31, they need instructions from the risen Lord, still present, to guide them as they live the in-between-time.[45] Thus the Fourth Gospel appeared in its present form: John 1:1–21:25. Behind John 1–21 lie two implied authors communicating slightly different points of view through the voice of a single narrator.[46] John 21:25 hints that the early Christian community which listened to and read John 1:1–20:31, despite its conviction that "the world itself could not contain the books that would be written" (21:25), experienced the need to add more to the story it already had as a treasured part of its story-telling tradition.

---

43. I have come to regard 21:1–25 as a "necessary epilogue," but I suggest that John 1:1–20:31 has an internal rhetoric of its own (i.e., without 21:1–25), in leaving the questions of community and leadership (Simon Peter and the Beloved Disciple) unanswered. This rhetoric matches the closure of the Gospel of Mark in 16:8, inviting post-Easter disciples to "fill the gaps" in their response to the presence of the risen Jesus. On this, see Francis J. Moloney, *The Gospel of Mark: A Commentary* (Grand Rapids: Baker Academic, 2012), 339–54.

44. See Frances Back, *Gott als Vater der Jünger im Johannesevangelium*, WUNT 2/336 (Tübingen: Mohr Siebeck, 2012), 1–24, 195–99.

45. Aptly caught by Hooker, *Endings*, 80: "There is something odd about John's ending; whereas in Mark the risen Christ never made an appearance, in John he never departs."

46. On this notion of two implied authors writing for a single readership, see Zumstein, "Endredaktion des Johannesevangeliums," 288–90.

14

AUDIENCE

Edward W. Klink III

Every story is written for an audience. Every story seeks to capture its audience, directing them along an intended textual path and sharing with them a purposeful communication. The story told by the Gospel of John is no different. John speaks *about* a topic, the life and ministry of Jesus, but also *to* an audience, one for whom Jesus is intended to be made both relevant and personal. Since an audience is implied whenever a text is created, it becomes an essential component in its interpretation. To interpret John, then, is to interpret its use of audience.

THE AUDIENCE(S) OF JOHN

Before we explore how John uses audience, it is worth surveying briefly the various ways John's audience can be conceived.

Original Audience

The early church had several traditions regarding the origins of the gospels, including the audience for whom they were written. Over the last century, however, those traditions have been developed so as to take on a life of their own. Gospels research now considers it axiomatic that the four evangelists wrote for and in response to their own particular Christian communities. In the last few decades, elaborate reconstructions of the four gospel communities have been proposed using technical reading techniques that attempt to get "behind the text" of each gospel. The quest for the historical Jesus that occupied much of the nineteenth century largely gave way to the quest for the early church in the twentieth century.[1] The basic assumption is that by discovering the identity of the historical audience and its social-historical location, each gospel can be rightly interpreted according to its original occasion and intended purpose.

While all four gospels have been interpreted through the lens of their reconstructed audience, the uniqueness of the Gospel of John has almost required that it receive the most robust and detailed reconstruction of its audience, what is now commonly called the "Johannine community."[2] It is impossible to separate the reconstructions of the gospel's audience from its authorship, source, and origin issues or, in fact, from the rest of the Johannine literature. Once the majority of critical scholarship held that John the apostle may not be the author, as was traditionally believed, then a wave of varying theories were presented in its place, leading to the current reconstructions of the audience.

There has been a growing criticism of the interpretive theory of gospel audience reconstructions.[3] This critique of what had been a general consensus has led to a methodological debate over the audience of the gospels and an evaluation of the appropriate methods for interpreting the gospels.[4] Each of the gospels has received a level of evaluation regarding the warrant of reconstructing a particular audience, including the Gospel of John.[5] As much as the old consensus (community reconstruction) has been given a sharp rebuke in regard to method and presupposition, it has hardly been rejected outright. If anything, the audience debate has simply brought a bit more balance to the use of the theories and approaches

---

1. See Thomas L. Brodie, *The Quest for the Origin of John's Gospel: A Source-Oriented Approach* (New York: Oxford University Press, 1992), vii–viii, 5–21, 137–52.

2. See Edward W. Klink III, *The Sheep of the Fold: The Audience and Origin of the Gospel of John*, SNTSMS 141 (Cambridge: Cambridge University Press, 2007), 24–35.

3. The challenge started with the book by Richard Bauckham, ed., *The Gospels for All Christians: Rethinking the Gospel Audiences* (Grand Rapids: Eerdmans, 1998).

4. For an overview of the original audience debate, see Edward W. Klink III, "Gospel Audience and Origin: The Current Debate," in *The Audience of the Gospels: The Origin and Function of the Gospels in Early Christianity*, ed. Edward W. Klink III, LNTS 353 (London: T&T Clark, 2010), 1–26.

5. For a recent survey of the Johannine audience debate, see Wally V. Cirafesi, "The Johannine Community Hypothesis (1968–Present): Past and Present Approaches and a New Way Forward," *CurBR* 12 (2014): 173–93. See also Jonathan Bernier, *Aposynagōgos and the Historical Jesus in John: Rethinking the Historicity of the Johannine Expulsion Passages*, BibInt 122 (Leiden: Brill, 2013).

applied to the interpretation of the gospels. Even those who see a wider audience intended by the author(s) of the gospels are clearly interested in the historical audience of John, the audience connected to the origin of the gospel.

Extended Audience

The argument for a wider, original audience matches the use of the gospels shortly after their creation. From their inception, the function and use of the gospels in early Christianity reflects an extended audience. At a fairly early date, the gospels had authority in Christian circles and were used in the worship services of the earliest churches. It can even be suggested that the gospels were intended to function in the manner in which they are now used—as Scripture or as the continuation of the Jewish Scripture. "The early Christian claim that the narrative and prophecies of old are fulfilled and continued in Jesus and the church prefigures, even perhaps demands, the production of more scripture.... Such scripture is required to explain this not first of all to outsiders but rather to Christians themselves. It becomes an essential part of their identity and self-understanding."[6] The gospels were likely perceived and designed for the purpose of proclaiming that Jesus was the fulfillment of Scripture. Their placement beside the older, Jewish Scriptures in worship, certainly as early as the mid-second century but probably much earlier, was likely the continuation of a long-standing process of uniting the Jewish and Christian Scriptures into one unified collection.[7]

This historical argument for an extended audience suggests that John was envisioning a readership and functionality beyond its original audience. The gospel was likely viewed as a "narrative statement" intending to educate insiders and invite outsiders into the life of the Christian God through Jesus Christ.[8] In fact, readers have frequently argued that rather than serving insiders, the Fourth Gospel was intended "in the first place, not so much

---

6. D. Moody Smith, "When Did the Gospels Become Scripture?" *JBL* 119 (2000): 3–20 (12).

7. Bruce Metzger, *The Canon of the New Testament: Its Origin, Development, and Significance* (Oxford: Clarendon, 1987), 6.

8. C. F. D. Moule, "The Intention of the Evangelists," in *The Phenomenon of the New Testament: An Inquiry into the Implications of Certain Features of the New Testament*, SBT 2/1 (London: SCM, 1967), 101.

[for] Christians who need a deeper theology, as [for] non-Christians who are concerned about eternal life and the way to it, and may be ready to follow the Christian way if this is presented to them in terms that are intelligibly related to their previous religious interests and experience."[9] In this way, then, even from the start the Gospel of John was intending an expansive audience, for whom the gospel served to invite and establish an identity that was uniquely Christian. Averil Cameron even suggests that "if ever there was a case of the construction of reality through text, such a case is provided by early Christianity.... Christians built themselves a new world."[10] The Gospel of John must be understood as having participated in the unique "Christian" creation of a new identity, viewing themselves as a new *genus*, neither Jew nor Greek but a third "race."[11] From its inception, it can be argued, the Gospel of John was addressing a much larger and inclusive audience.

Contemporary Audience

A final audience of John is the contemporary audience, which can take one of two forms. At its most basic level, the Gospel of John is a text from antiquity that is recognized as an artifact that has historical, cultural, and literary value. This form of contemporary audience would view John as an artifact with academic significance, recognizing the text in a morally and religiously neutral fashion and simply as a relic from the past. Its continued use for religious purposes is also of academic value from a social-cultural vantage point.

The religious use of John creates another form of a contemporary audience. From the perspective of the Christian tradition and faith, the contemporary reader of the Gospel of John also functions as the gospel's intended audience, by means of its divinely authorized status as God's word for the Christian church. The extended audience implicit in the original

---

9. C. H. Dodd, *The Interpretation of the Fourth Gospel* (Cambridge: Cambridge University Press, 1953), 9. For an applied example, see Stephen Motyer, *Your Father the Devil? A New Approach to John and "the Jews,"* PBTM (Carlisle: Paternoster, 1997), 212. Cf. Ruth Sheridan, *Retelling Scripture: The "Jews" and the Scriptural Citations in John 1:19–12:15*, BibInt 110 (Leiden: Brill, 2012), 37–46.

10. Averil Cameron, *Christianity and the Rhetoric of Empire: The Development of Christian Discourse*, SCL 55 (Berkeley: University of California Press, 1991), 21.

11. Judith M. Lieu, *Neither Jew Nor Greek? Constructing Early Christianity*, SNTW (Edinburgh: T&T Clark, 2003), 183–84.

intentions of the gospel were received and reflected in the incorporation of the Fourth Gospel into the Christian Scriptures. As much as this reception is historical, it has also been received by a perceived doctrinal authority. This form of contemporary audience would view John less as an artifact and more as a living expression of the voice of God. The text would not be viewed as morally or religiously neutral but as giving explicit instruction for faith and for daily life. The gospel, therefore, becomes relevant in practical and personal ways.

The Implied Audience (or Reader) of a Text

It would be a mistake, however, to conceive of audience as merely external to or outside of John. From the start, the interpretation of a text is the negotiation between the author, the composition, and the audience. We cannot separate the author from the audience; they are in an interwoven, symbiotic relationship; an interaction of both giving and receiving. A text does not "work" until the audience works it out: irony, humor, riddles, force of an argument, and the rest.[12] Although different from a live performance, where the presentation can adjust to the responses of the audience, the author of a text creates a presentation that not only assumes an audience but even includes them in its portrayal and processes.[13]

Narrative approaches to interpretation have often been used alongside historical approaches to give definition to the audience a text would have expected. Traditionally, the reader was a detached observer of authorial intention or the verbal sense, but this is no longer the case.[14] Although we will not discuss the various theories of reading proposed by postmodern literary theory, we will certainly use one aspect of that discussion: the implied reader.[15] Narrative criticism's use and application of the implied

---

12. David Rhoads, "Performance Criticism: An Emerging Methodology in Second Testament Studies, Part I," *BTB* 36 (2006): 9.

13. John Goldingay, "How Far Do Readers Make Sense? Interpreting Biblical Narrative," *Them* 18 (1993): 5–10.

14. Kevin J. Vanhoozer, *Is There a Meaning in This Text? The Bible, the Reader, and the Morality of Literary Knowledge* (Grand Rapids: Zondervan, 1998), 149.

15. Narrative discussions are often based on a certain concept of the text. As defined by R. Alan Culpepper, *Anatomy of the Fourth Gospel: A Study in Literary Design* (Minneapolis: Fortress, 1983), 5: "The Gospel as it stands rather than its sources, historical background, or themes is the subject of this study."

reader has added a missing dimension in biblical studies research, especially in the gospels.[16]

Although it comes in various forms, reader-response criticism is concerned with what the text *does* to the reader.[17] Said another way, it is interested in focusing on the way in which the reader has an involved response to the text. What change in outlook does the text effect in the reader? How does the text bring about such change? In short, "reader-response criticism focuses on readers' reading and the dynamics involved in readers' assembling the meaning of a text."[18] While historians often use the category of "audience," literary critics use an array of terms to describe the text's designated reader: implied reader, informed reader, and ideal reader, to name a few. At times, the stance of the reader is made to be *in the text* (that is to say, a reader construct of the text; a property of the text's meaning) or *over the text* (that is, a real reader with complete dominance of meaning, freed from authorial intention). For our purposes, a more useful approach will be to explore a stance of the reader in which the reading audience has a dialectical relationship *with the text*. This reader interacts with the text in the production of its meaning. According to Wolfgang Iser, there are "gaps" or areas of "indeterminancy" in a text that must be filled in or "realized" by the reader. Iser gives a helpful analogy of this by depicting two people gazing at the night sky: "Both [may] be looking at the same collection of stars, but one will see the image of a plough, and the other will make out a dipper. The 'stars' in a literary text are fixed; the lines that join them are variable."[19]

Narrative critics do not agree on the exact identity of the reader of the text, but the results for biblical narrative criticism are functionally the same. Mark Allan Powell speaks of an "implied reader who is presupposed by the text" and "distinct from any real, historical reader."[20] For Powell the

---

16. The history of the application of literary criticism to the study of the gospels is well known. For a general survey of the method in application to the New Testament, see William A. Beardslee, *Literary Criticism of the New Testament*, GBS (Philadelphia: Fortress, 1970).

17. James L. Resseguie, *Narrative Criticism of the New Testament: An Introduction* (Grand Rapids: Baker Academic, 2005), 30.

18. Ibid.

19. Wolfgang Iser, *The Implied Reader: Patterns of Communication in Prose Fiction from Bunyan to Beckett* (Baltimore: John Hopkins University Press, 1974), 282.

20. Mark Allan Powell, *What Is Narrative Criticism?*, GBS (Minneapolis: Fortress, 1990), 19.

implied reader is ideal in that she can read the text as an (implied) author intended the text to be read; she can connect correctly the lines that join the stars, to use Iser's analogy. Jack Dean Kingsbury defines the implied reader as "no flesh-and-blood person of any century. Instead, it refers to an imaginary person who is to be envisaged ... as responding to the text at every point with whatever emotion, understanding, or knowledge the text ideally calls for."[21] In both definitions, the competent readers who are not only familiar with the literary, historical, social-cultural, and linguistic assumptions of the intended audience, but also they are able to see and understand the clues in the text that direct the readers through the text's meaningful communication.

IMPLIED AUDIENCE AS A CATEGORY FOR INTERPRETING JOHN

By using the category of "implied reader" as a tool for interpretation, we may begin to explore how the Gospel of John directs or shows its intention to a competent reading audience. When we speak of John's implied reader (or audience, the terms can be used interchangeably for our purposes), we are speaking of the audience with whom the text of John is engaged in intentional communication. This audience is not a real, historical audience—original or contemporary—but the audience anticipated by the narrative's own design. In short, the implied audience is the role or persona provided in the text for the reader.[22] This role or persona serves to guide the reading of the gospel and direct its interpretation.

It is important to note that we are not using the implied audience to uncover or reconstruct the audience implied at the time of its origin. That is often the goal of historically-oriented biblical criticism we discussed above. Rather, we are using the implied audience to uncover the implied reading assigned to the audience. Said another way, we are not

---

21. Jack Dean Kingsbury, *Matthew as Story* (Philadelphia: Fortress, 1986), 28.

22. Robert M. Fowler, "Who Is 'the Reader' in Reader Response Criticism?" *Semeia* 31 (1985): 10. Cf. Seymour Chatman, *Story Discourse: Narrative Structure in Fiction and Film* (Ithaca, NY: Cornell University Press, 1978), 151. See also Wayne C. Booth, *The Rhetoric of Fiction*, 2nd ed. (Chicago: University of Chicago Press, 1983), 429, who uses the term "the postulated reader"; Peter J. Rabinowitz, "Truth in Fiction: A Reexamination of Audiences," *CI* 4 (1977): 121–41, who only speaks of the "authorial audience" (126); and Gerald Prince, *Narratology: The Form and Function of Narrative* (Berlin: Mouton, 1982), who uses the term "virtual reader."

trying to identify the expected reader but to identify the *expected reading* intended for the reader, whoever he or she may be.[23] Our goal is not to define who first read the gospel, for example, but how the gospel is supposed to be read. Thus, the implied audience becomes a category that guides interpretation.

So how does the implied audience function as a category for interpreting a text like John? The category of implied audience highlights the literary competence expected by the text itself. A reader's literary competence requires (1) *knowledge* of the type of genre of literature, (2) *skill* to follow rhetorical moves within the narrative and understand how to interpret the story in ways consistent with its genre, and (3) *commitment* to know certain things, believe certain things, or espouse certain things.[24] Knowledge of the text's genre simply means that the reader understands what kind of communication the text is intending to perform, whereas skill assumes the reader can handle the communicative maneuvers the text performs. For example, a level of skill is needed to understand when irony is intended and how it is intending to direct the meaning of the text. A commitment to beliefs and values are especially significant, as they may be more subtle and therefore go undetected. For example, the authority of the Old Testament/Jewish Scriptures is assumed or implied in John without being stated in propositional form.

An expected reading of John, then, would match the reading implied by the narrative's own direction by resigning its interpretation to the knowledge of, skill in, and commitment to the text itself. In a very real sense, the readers are expected to unite themselves to the implied reader or at least to see what the implied reader is expected to see, even if the real reader does not agree with the commitment assumed by the text.

John's Use of Audience

It is one thing to talk about how a text uses audience; it is another thing to show what it actually looks like in practice. For the remainder of this essay, we will show examples in John where the implied audience is given direction by the narrative for interpretation. While there are several other examples that could have been selected, we have chosen three that depict

---

23. Mark Allan Powell, *Chasing the Eastern Star: Adventures in Biblical Reader-Response Criticism* (Louisville: Westminster John Knox, 2001), 8.

24. Ibid., 72.

the ways John uses audience, with each reflecting either the *knowledge*, *skill*, or *commitment* required of a literary-competent reading audience. It is also worth admitting that our interpretations of the expected readings cannot be equated with the actual expected reading. While our interpretation might rightly see a narrative maneuver, we might inappropriately draw out its expectation and application. Again, to use Iser's analogy, we might rightly see the fixed stars in the sky but do a poor job of drawing meaningful lines between them. The following can be described as a partial commentary on John's use of audience.[25]

Orientation: The Prologue (1:1–18)

A reader's literary competence requires knowledge of the type of genre of literature. This extends not only to the work as a whole—for John, a Greco-Roman biography—but also subgenres and their literary functions within a narrative like John.[26] A clear example of this is the beginning of John, the Prologue (1:1–18).

The beginning of narratives, often in the form of a preface or prologue, provide information regarding purpose, method, and contents; they offer key information needed to understand the rest of the narrative.[27] While all types of narrative beginnings are important, prologues had a uniquely dramatic force in ancient writings. Reminiscent of the openings of classic dramas, prologues were often used to introduce the important characters in the narrative, situate them within the story, and give some understanding of their importance. John clearly does this with the character of his biography.

But there is a further function of prologues that is very important: prologues would project the plot by explaining both seen and unseen forces within the action. Morna Hooker explains this function: "It was customary for the Greek dramatist to introduce the theme of his play in a 'prologue,' which provided members of his audience with the vital information that would enable them to comprehend the plot, and to understand the

---

25. For a fuller commentary on each of the following three texts, see Edward W. Klink III, *John*, ZECNT 4 (Grand Rapids: Zondervan, 2016).

26. Further, see "Genre" by Harold W. Attridge in this volume.

27. See Morna D. Hooker, "Beginnings and Endings," in *The Written Gospel*, ed. Markus Bockmuehl and Donald A. Hagner (Cambridge: Cambridge University Press, 2005), 184.

unseen forces—the desires and plans of the gods—which were at work in the story."[28] While John does not reveal the desires and plans of the gods, he does, in dramatist fashion, explain the desires and plans of *the* God. The prologue, in this sense, prescribes the reader's comprehension of the plot and explains the behind-the-scene activities of God. This is no mere background issue, for it is rooted in the narrative's own emplotment, but it is also not merely theological abstraction, for it is connected to real events described by the narrative. What is explained is the "unseen forces" that are at work in and around the real events described by the narrative. Thus, the prologue is guiding the reader to see the invisible (God) in the visible (historical persons and events).

Interestingly, it was common in classic prologues that the deliverer of the prologue, often a character in the play (or in our case, the narrator), "would continue to comment on the action of subsequent scenes."[29] The prologue, therefore, not only introduces the plot, characters, and unseen forces of the narrative to the reader but also introduces the "narratee," the person inside the text to whom the narrator is speaking and who has a privileged position in relation to the story being told. The narratee sits beside the narrator and watches the action from the narrator's vantage point and its interpretive insights.

It is in this way that the prologue provides an important orientation to the reader. For example, the prologue explains to the reader that John has two narrative strands that, though distinct, are ultimately unified in the gospel's emplotment. This two-strand plot is related to each of the forces discussed above: the visible (historical persons and events) and the invisible (God). Neither strand of the plot is complete on its own; in fact, each strand is supported by the other. This is vital information that the prologue reveals to the reader. This is what the prologue is prescribing for the reader and what must be understood if the remainder of the gospel's message is to be grasped.

The prologue explains to the reader that the forthcoming story needs more than a historical orientation; it also needs what Adele Reinhartz calls a cosmological orientation.[30] The vast majority of the narrative is set in the early first century CE in Palestine. Thus, this story is historical in that

---

28. Ibid., 186.

29. Ibid.

30. Adele Reinhartz, *The Word in the World: The Cosmological Tale in the Fourth Gospel*, SBLMS 45 (Atlanta: Scholars Press, 1992).

it deals with Jesus in history. Without taking away the nature of emplot-ment, the historical story is clearly meant to be read as a true account of what really happened (cf. 21:24). Reinhartz argues that the historical story is "accessible to all readers of the Fourth Gospel and might be described as the primary 'signified' or content towards which the gospel as signifier is generally thought to point."[31]

At the same time, according to Reinhartz, "specific hints in the Gospel intimate that its story goes well beyond the temporal and geographical boundaries."[32] One need not look further in the narrative than 1:1. From the very beginning, the story told by the Fourth Evangelist is the story of the Word who was with God and was God. The setting of this second story is not Palestine in the first century but the cosmos in eternity itself. Inter-estingly, the cosmological story is the very first thing introduced to the reader. Since the prologue is intended to guide the reader "to comprehend the plot" and "to understand the unseen forces," it is clear that the cosmo-logical story is central to the cumulative story told by the Fourth Gospel. The cosmological story is not in conflict with the historical story but func-tions as the meta-story, the narrative framework in which the events of the historical story take place. Even more, the events of the historical story are defined and explained by the cosmological story; without the cosmologi-cal story, the historical story would be incomplete.

The audience is expected to read the rest of John through the pro-logue's spectacles, seeing in every historical scene or moment not merely Jesus the Jew but Jesus the Word-became-flesh, who was with God in the beginning. This orientation is essential to a right reading of the gospel, a reading that requires a particular reading competence that recognizes and utilizes the generic conventions of the text. By beginning with a formal prologue, John creates a superior position for the audience to use to grasp the fullest perspective of the story about to be presented.

Narration: The Cleansing of the Temple (2:12–25)

A reader's literary competence also requires skill to follow rhetorical moves within the narrative and understand how to interpret the story in ways consistent with its genre. While numerous examples could be given

31. Ibid., 2.
32. Ibid.

in John, one clear example is the cleansing of the temple by Jesus in 2:12–25. The orientation given by the prologue is intended to be still in effect for the reader. The reading audience is well aware that Jesus is more than he is perceived to be by the historical audience. Even more, the scene in the temple is intended to evoke a sense of irony, as the Lord himself stands unnoticed as such and rejected by what should be his most intimate worshippers and faithful supporters.

The readers are also expected to be able to understand the perspectives of the various characters in the narrative. That is, the reading audience should simultaneously understand the perspective of the religious authorities in the temple (the historical perspective, per the prologue), that Jesus is challenging their God-given authority and the institution of the temple itself by his actions; and at the same time, they should understand the perspective of Jesus (the cosmological perspective, per the prologue), that he is the actual and final authority, the true high priest, and the "Tabernacling One" (1:14), who is the very embodiment and therefore replacement of the temple.

The context of the scene is important to a right reading. According to John, when Jesus entered the temple at Passover, he reacted strongly to the business being made of his Father's house and removed the traders and their animals from the place. At their removal, Jesus concludes by giving the reason for his action. By giving the reasoning last, John has made sure that we get the explanation like a commentary on the action of judgment already accomplished.

The narrator is quick to add an important statement to the readers, befitting the relationship established between the author (narrator) and audience (narratee). The comment is entirely outside the time frame of the story, matching the cosmological insights introduced by the prologue. The audience is given later-date insights into the scene at hand. By referring to a later remembrance of the disciples, along with a statement of Jesus that echoes Scripture (Ps 69), the narrator creates a triangulation for the audience that places them interactively between Scripture (past), Jesus (present), and their future understanding of the truth. John uses the audience as the fulcrum point, which offers the interpretive balance of all three.

The scene transitions to a challenge-style dialogue between Jesus and the religious authorities, who demand that Jesus authenticate his authoritative actions by means of a miraculous sign, proving the confirmation of God on his person and work. Without any hesitation or pushback, Jesus agrees to the demand and states directly the proof of his authority. But the temple about which he speaks seems inconceivable to the authorities: "this temple" and "in three days." The audience, like the historical listeners, is struck by the audacity of the claim. The Jews mock Jesus's brazen claim— and rightly so. Although the narrator will explain below that by means of his statement Jesus is referring to himself, the reader must not miss that Jesus's statement taken on its own is referring to the temple structure. Only this explains the response of the Jews and, therefore, the need for the narrator to give an explanation.

To fault the Jews for taking Jesus's statement too literally, as some interpreters do, is to misunderstand the message of the narrative. The rhetorical force of John is dependent upon this truly referring to one thing and yet also to another. For this reason, the Jews heard correctly what Jesus was saying and gave a response intending to reject the sign as well as to shame the challenger. To interpret this as anything other than a defeating counterclaim by the Jews is to misunderstand the pericope. Jesus is talking about *the* temple, and they do hear him correctly. But in this scene the temple is eclipsed by *the* temple (1:14), and both need to be in view. The reader is supposed to see two temples, not one, with the former now made entirely obsolete. The reader is supposed to have heard a valid defense of the old temple. Quite simply, the misunderstanding is not to understand that the Jews are defending the wrong temple. It is in this way that John uses the audience.

John uses the audience's dual understanding to magnify the true temple. In fact, the narrator's self-insertion in 2:21 suggests the historical characters did not see what the readers can see. The counterresponse by the Jews and, therefore, the absence of a response by Jesus, is fully intended to signify that Jesus lost the challenge. In a culture built on the foundational social values of honor and shame, Jesus was given shame. Jesus did not respond because no response was warranted; in the eyes of the temple authorities, in the eyes of any bystanders, and even in the eyes of the disciples, as verse 22 will explain, Jesus was shamed. This is the only honor contest recorded in the gospels where the verdict was not declared and, maybe more significantly, where Jesus was not (publically) victorious.[33] Such a conclusion is not based entirely upon sociological insights or even the silence of the narrative but on the explanation provided by the

---

33. E. Randolph Richards, "An Honor/Shame Argument for Two Temple Clearings," *TrinJ* 29 (2008): 35.

narrator. The narrator provides the necessary ("unseen") insight that no one else saw: Jesus was not referring to the Jewish temple but to the temple of his body.

Finally, 2:22 makes clear that the disciples came to see what the readers had already seen, that the word of God (the Scripture) and the Word of God (the Son) were both speaking to the true proof or sign: the death and resurrection of Jesus. Again, John uses the audience to anchor the truth of Jesus's message and work. The audience becomes a participatory witness to the truth that the death and resurrection of Jesus is the ultimate temple cleansing; and the temple of his body is a full replacement of the temple of the Jews, the dwelling of God with humanity. This narration is essential to a right reading of the gospel, a reading that requires a particular reading competence that recognizes and follows the rhetorical maneuvers of the text.

Reception: The Narrative Intention of the "Absent Thomas" (20:24–31)

A reader's literary competence also requires commitment to know certain things, believe certain things, or espouse certain things. While several examples could be given regarding beliefs about God and humanity that have religious implications, the conclusion of the Gospel of John offers its own direction of belief to the audience, guiding how the reader is expected to receive both the text and its message.

It is common for the focus of John 20:24–31 to be placed on Thomas as the one who "doubted" Jesus. But this common interpretation misplaces the intention of the scene. All the disciples except for Thomas were present when Jesus first appeared to his disciples (20:19–23). In the next scene in the gospel when Thomas rejoins the disciples (20:24–25), the disciples provide a unified and emphatic witness to what they have seen, "we have seen the Lord." Thomas, however, makes clear that he will not believe without physical evidence that is particularly concrete: the wounds from the crucifixion. While Thomas's request might seem absurd for its detail, it also serves to declare the eyewitness account of the disciples as absurd. The very disciples who had just been sent with the Spirit-empowered authority of the Lord to announce his person and work to the world (20:21–23) were immediately rejected by one of their own, even more, by one who had already exhibited belief in Jesus. The conflict presented here is not primarily about *what* Thomas believes but about the *warrant* Thomas requires to believe. The question the gospel now poses to the reading-audience is the following: *How* is the Lord encountered in his physical absence?

When Jesus appears again and confronts Thomas (20:26–28), the immediate context, especially the emphasis placed upon the disciples' witness (20:25), suggests that Jesus's rebuke of Thomas is not for what he had yet to see in him but for what he had already seen (and yet failed to believe) through them. Jesus's appearance to Thomas is not intended to confirm Thomas's faith but to confirm the original testimony of the disciples. In the providence of God, Thomas's absence allowed him to function as an example of a future believer, who had to rely on the testimony of the disciples as eyewitnesses of the person and work of Jesus Christ. In this way, the reader is given a comparable analogy for their own belief and reception of the apostolic witness. It is no wonder that the author/narrator decided to place the gospel's purpose statement (20:30–31) immediately after this scene (20:24–29).

This makes sense of Jesus's closing statement to Thomas and the gospel proper in 20:29: "Because you have seen me you have believed. Blessed are those who have not seen and have believed." Jesus's rebuke of Thomas not only directs the reader to see what Thomas failed to do, but also to see what he has been reinstated to become. By his dismissal of the disciples' testimony, Thomas undercut his own role as an apostolic witness. For this reason Jesus reestablishes it, giving freight to the apostolic mission in the previous passage (20:19–23) and making clear that the apostolic ministry is a necessary ground upon which the mission of God will continue. In the gospel's opening chapter, John the Baptist was positioned in redemptive history to be the voice of both an Old Testament prophet and an apostle, for he transitioned from looking *for* him to looking *at* him (see 1:15). In the final chapter of the gospel proper, Thomas was also positioned by God in redemptive history to be the voice of both a disciple and an apostle, for he transitioned from being a witness *of* him to a witness *for* him. The Fourth Gospel is established upon this witness. In this way, the concluding statement of Jesus places the readers within the gospel's purview, making them participants in its authoritative and living witness. "From this moment the company no longer consists solely of eleven disciples gathered at that particular time and place; every reader of the Gospel who has faith, to the end of time, is included in Christ's final beatitude."[34]

Thomas functions in the gospel as the narrative-directed mediator between the disciples and all future audiences. John uses the very first

---

34. Dodd, *Interpretation of the Fourth Gospel*, 443.

audience—one of the original twelve disciples—to portray the experience of every other disciple to whom the message of Jesus Christ, and the
Gospel of John, would be presented. It is in this way, then, that John uses
audience, with the very first disciples speaking to, even representing, the
very last and everyone in between. In this gospel, the characters in the
gospel become the first of a kind of audience, both receiving and passing
along a witness that started with the original disciples. That is, the implied
reader of John becomes a real reader in that the implied reader can be used
as a functional category for "a mode of reading," through which the gospel
itself explains and constructs the kind of reader it not only assumes but
also desires.

John uses his audience like a character in the narrative who, after
receiving this text-based witness, is beckoned to respond in faith. Just as
the gospel begins with a disciple of Jesus (Andrew) seeking his brother
(Peter) and leads him to Jesus (1:41), so the gospel ends with a disciple of
Jesus (the Beloved Disciple) leading a brother or sister (the reader) to Jesus.
Ultimately, the mysterious identity of the Beloved Disciple is eclipsed in
narrative importance by his ministerial the role, a textual-based ministry,
and it is the reader who becomes the referent of this mystery as he or she
receives and believes the gospel's message. Since all disciples are sent by
Jesus, even this text-based ministry is an extension of the love of God (see
3:16) to the reader, an ongoing invitation to believe in Jesus Christ and
receive life in his name (20:30–31).

Conclusion

The identity of the original audience of the gospel has long been a mystery and, therefore, an attraction for readers, both in the academy and
the church. This attraction has had an ironic effect on the search for the
identity of the audience: rather than determining the original audience,
this attraction has often reflected more about the reader and their interpretive bent and interests. The mystery of Johannine audience is less the
circumstances of the original audience and more the manner in which
the gospel continues to procure an audience and, even more, continues
to speak to this audience with equal relevance. For this gospel, even more
than the other three, speaks directly to its audience, for whom the gospel
is expressly intended (20:30–31; cf. 21:24–25). By means of John's use of
audience, the reader of the gospel, like the earliest disciples, is confronted
by Jesus and asked, "What do you seek?" (1:38). Through the Fourth

Gospel, Jesus questions the reader and invites him or her to believe in him and to have life in his name (20:31)—that is, to become his disciple. Every reader of this gospel, no matter their relation to God and stage of their Christian walk, is beckoned to "come and see" (1:39, 46).

.

15

Culture*

Charles E. Hill

As even the casual reader knows, there is something different about John's Gospel. No, there are lots of things about it that are different. Many of the literary traits that help make John's Gospel what it is and which serve to differentiate it from other books and even from other gospels have been identified and explored in the present volume. Genre, style, time and space, imagery, characterization, protagonist, plot, point of view, use of Scripture, rhetoric, persuasion, closure, audience: each plays a part in shaping the story of the gospel, helping to reveal "how John works."

But can we know, or even reasonably presume, that it actually did "work" in its immediate environment? Can we know if it connected, not simply to a reconstructed, imaginary, or "implied reader," a reader assumed to be alert to its literary character, but to real ones? Our intention in considering John's use of "culture" is to explore this topic a bit.

From one perspective, we may view an author's decisions to include anything more than the most incidental or artificial references to cultural elements in any narrative, along with the ways in which he or she employs these references, as conscious, literary decisions. Thus they may be analyzed alongside other literary choices an author makes. When an author decides to include, for instance, references to family, common meals, religious ceremonies, or the titles of government officials, such "cultural signifiers" in a narrative generally serve to add realism to the narrative. At

---

*This article is dedicated to the 142 students of Garissa University College, Kenya, murdered for being Christians on April 2, 2015, and to the twenty-one Egyptian Coptic Christians beheaded in early February 2015. "And if I go and prepare a place for you, I will come again and will take you to myself, that where I am you may be also" (John 14:3).

least ostensibly, they add the impression of historicity to the account (even if they are actually fictional). Cultural elements often invoke experiences shared by author and reader and usually by other groups of people as well. Cultural elements in literature could be references to everyday experiences, such as eating (with all its associated cultural trappings), working (in the various human labors or professions), sleeping, or occasional experiences, such as weddings, cultic activities, burials, and feasts. They include references to political entities and realities, religious or educational institutions, norms, customs, or beliefs that relate to gender, family, social status, and the like. They include expressions of the arts. Humanly-constructed features of the physical landscape, such as temples, synagogues, homes, gardens, roads, and so forth, even features of the natural landscape that are named and given significance by humans, are also markers of human culture that communicate as such.

Taken in this way, the category of "culture" includes such things as the particular human language used in communication (Jesus, presumably, spoke mostly in Aramaic but the gospel is written in Greek). From another perspective, then, even the *literary* characteristics of John's Gospel considered in previous chapters of this book belong to the communicative aspects of the common culture in which John and his first readers lived. The Gospel of John itself, in its literary individuality, is a significant cultural artifact.

To summarize what I have been saying so far, the choice to incorporate a meaningful quantity of cultural elements in a written composition is a literary decision, hence the justification for a chapter on "culture" in a book about literary qualities of John. At the same time, literary decisions made for communicative purposes derive meaning from an existing cultural context. The cultural context for any writing is one that is mostly shared with the first audiences of the writing. This shared cultural space can then become the vantage point from which we may begin to observe the actual connections that John's Gospel made with its first readers as they engaged the story and its message about Jesus.

The following essay will consist of two parts. The first part will introduce some of the cultural features in John, with observations on the ways John uses them both to connect with and to instruct his readers. Then, taking the gospel's cultural elements as starting points, we will transition to the early reception of John to gain some idea of whether and how John "worked" with early readers in the first 100–150 years or so of its life. As a way to delimit and focus our study, this exploration by means of cultural elements in John will center on the explicitly named "signs" in the gospel,[1] each of which involves a number of cultural elements.

A SAMPLING OF CULTURAL ELEMENTS IN JOHN

Categories

Apropos to John's presentation, we might bring together cultural signifiers in the gospel under the rubrics of the common and the specific, that is, those that are shared across the Mediterranean subcultures of his day and those that are rather peculiar to the "host" culture of the story. The author is very much aware of this distinction, for he often takes the time to explain to the reader something specific to the culture of first-century Palestinian Judaism, something familiar to himself and to the actors in the story, but which he deems may be unfamiliar to many of his first readers. Thus, the six stone pots at the wedding feast in Cana are explained as being there "for the Jewish rites of purification" (2:6), and the woman at the well is surprised at Jesus's request, "For Jews do not associate with Samaritans" (4:9).[2]

The Ways Jesus and John Use Cultural Elements

We may suggest here three ways in which various facets of human culture are employed in John: to connect with the audience "casually" by means of the culturally familiar; to draw in the audience "formally" by means

---

1. The signs and their role in the gospel have generated a great deal of scholarly literature. The view that the author of the gospel made use of a preexisting "signs source," or "signs gospel," has been advocated for many decades, most elaborately by Robert Fortna in two major publications: *The Gospel of Signs: A Reconstruction of the Narrative Source Underlying the Fourth Gospel*, SNTSMS 11 (Cambridge: Cambridge University Press, 1970); *The Fourth Gospel and Its Predecessor: From Narrative Source to Present Gospel* (Philadelphia: Fortress, 1988). Others (e.g., Gilbert Van Belle, *The Signs Source in the Fourth Gospel: Historical Survey and Critical Evaluation of the Semeia Hypothesis*, BETL 116 [Leuven: Peeters, 1994]) have strongly contested this theory. Most scholars today regard the idea of a separate signs source as only a possibility and lay more stress on the finished literary form, no matter whether, or how many, sources were used. In any case, almost all will agree that the signs accomplished by Jesus play a strategic role in the plan of the finished gospel.

2. Unless otherwise stated, all translations of biblical texts are my own.

of explanations of what is culturally unfamiliar; and to teach spiritual or
theological truths about Jesus by the symbolic use of cultural features.

To Connect by Means of the Culturally Familiar

One way the gospel "works" is by fluidly linking its readers to a host of
familiar cultural realities, thus tapping into an assumed mutuality with its
readers. He refers to common activities such as drawing water (4:7), dip-
ping bread (13:26), banqueting (12:2), footwashing (13:5–12), and he uses
common ways of marking time, such as the numbering of the hours (1:39;
4:6; 5:52) and the rooster crow (13:38; 18:27). Such details help connect
readers to the realism of the narrative and further establish the relationship between reader and narrator. At times, John can assume a degree of
familiarity on the part of his readers even with certain aspects of Jewish
culture, as when, for instance, the Jewish Sabbath enters the narrative, the
temple is mentioned (2:13), or Jesus speaks to the Jews about "your" law
(8:17; 10:34; cf. 15:25), with no accompanying explanations.

To Educate by Means of the Culturally Unfamiliar

Perhaps another reason why John has worked so well, both in its immediate environment and with readers through the centuries, is that the
author is so attuned to the cultural differences that separate the participants in his narrative from many of his readers. This comes through
vividly when he pauses and addresses the reader in many explanatory
asides that occur throughout the gospel.[3] These have the effect of drawing readers in, letting them know that the author is aware of them and is
educating, enlightening, or mentoring them. Many of the asides have to
do with what could be considered cultural signifiers, such as translations
(1:38, 41, 42; 5:2; 20:16), notations on local landmarks ("Now there is in
Jerusalem by the Sheep Gate a pool ..." 5:2; 6:1; 7:37; 10:40: 11:1, 18; etc.)
or explanations of Jewish customs or ideals (2:6; 4:9; 19:40; etc.). John's
explanations show an author self-consciously extending the reach of his
message across cultures.

---

3. See, e.g., John J. O'Rourke, "Asides in the Gospel of John," *NovT* 31 (1979):
210–19.

To Symbolize Theological Truths

A third way the gospel uses cultural features is as *symbolic* types, pointing beyond themselves. Most of Jesus's famous "I am" statements relate to common cultural elements or experiences: Jesus is the bread of life (6:35, 48, 51), the light of the world (8:12; 9:5), the door of the sheep (10:7, 9), the good shepherd (10:11, 14), and the true vine (15:1, 5). Human birth becomes a metaphor for a spiritual conversion (3:3–12), the Jerusalem temple for Jesus's body (2:19–22). Common agricultural activities— sowing, reaping, pruning, and harvesting—are given new meanings (4:35–38; 15:1–2). The everyday acts of eating bread and drinking wine become scandalizing metaphors for following Jesus (6:33–58). In these and other cases, the reader needs Jesus's interpretive clue—"The words that I have spoken to you are spirit and life" (6:63)—or the narrator's instructive reminder—"Now this he said about the Spirit, whom those who believed in him were to receive, for as yet the Spirit was not given, because Jesus was not yet glorified" (7:39).

In what follows, I propose to look briefly at the seven named signs in the gospel and their cultural aspects. These signs and their cultural aspects will then lead to an introduction to the use of John's Gospel in the early church grouped according to several topics. This will only scratch the surface of early Christian use of John, but I hope nonetheless to indicate some sense of the culture-creating capacity of this gospel in the early church. These categories will be: marriage, persecution, Christology, devotion, heresy, art, and witness.

CULTURAL ASPECTS OF THE SIGNS AND THEIR APPROPRIATION IN THE SECOND CENTURY

The Wedding Feast at Cana (2:1–11)

Much of the social *realia* of the wedding feast that forms the setting for Jesus's first sign would have been familiar to readers in practically all contemporary subcultures: a bridegroom, a "master of the feast" (see Sir 32:1–2), servants, wine, and the centrality of the wedding meal.[4] Jesus uses

---

4. Ancient, written wedding invitations reveal the centrality not of the ceremony but of the feast, inviting the guest to "dine at the wedding of...." See S. R. Llewelyn,

this common social occasion in his parables (Matt 22:1–14; 25:1–13; Luke 12:36–38; 14:7–11), and it is the wedding supper of the Lamb to which the blessed are called in Rev 19:7–9. An aspect of particular Jewish culture, the six stone water jars for Jewish rites of purification, is explained to John's readers (2:6).

Early Appropriation: Marriage and Culture

The wedding at Cana and Jesus's turning of the water into wine at the feast are referenced in Christian literature as early as Ep. Apos. 5.1–3, from the first half of the second century. Two early sources view John's annotation that this was the "first" of Jesus's signs (2:11) as showing John's attention to the proper ordering of the events of the gospel (Eusebius, *Hist. eccl.* 3.24.11; Muratorian Fragment). Irenaeus refers to "the wondrous sign of the wine (*admiribile uini signum*)," showing that he perceived symbolic significance in the miraculous wine (*Haer.* 3.16.7).[5]

Early appropriation of this sign often had to do with affirming either the goodness of the creation of God—the water and the wine as among God's good gifts (Irenaeus, *Haer.* 3.11.5)—or the goodness of the institution of marriage. Christian marriage was both like and unlike marriage in the surrounding culture. Christians, according to one mid-second-century author, "are not distinguished from the rest of humanity by country, language, or custom"; they marry and have children, just like their neighbors, "but they do not expose their offspring. They share their food but not their wives" (Ep. Diogn. 5.4, 6–7). Because it is the only wedding Jesus is recorded as attending in the gospels, Tertullian understands Jesus's presence at the Cana feast to signify a moral law of *single* marriages (*Mon.* 8), as opposed to polygamy or even remarriage after the death of a spouse. Jerome followed this line of interpretation as well, but by the late fourth century the ascetic tradition in Christianity had advanced so far as to lead some to devalue the married state. The celibate Jerome would say, "it is only heretics who condemn marriage and tread underfoot the ordinance of God.... For the Church does not condemn marriage, but only subor-

---

ed., *A Review of the Greek Inscriptions and Papyri Published in 1986–87*, vol. 9 of *New Documents Illustrating Early Christianity* (Grand Rapids: Eerdmans, 2002), 82–98.

5. See Irenaeus, *Against the Heresies, Book 3*, trans. and annotated by Dominic J. Unger, introduction and further revisions by Irenaeus M. C. Steenberg, ACW 64 (New York: Paulist, 2012), 164–65 n. 54.

dinates it" (*Epist. 48, To Pammachius* 11). Subordinates it, that is, to the higher ideal of lifelong virginity. In any case, Jesus's presence at the wedding, and his choice to perform his first miracle there, have through the centuries served to safeguard[6] and exalt the institution, denoting Jesus's blessing and sanctifying of what the 1549 *Book of Common Prayer* called "the holy estate of Matrimonie."[7]

Healing of a Government Official's Son (4:46–54)

Coming as it does on the heels of Jesus's encounter with the Samaritan woman and the Samaritan townspeople, this story of Jesus performing another sign as he returns to Galilee extends Jesus's work beyond the boundaries of "orthodox," Judean[8] Jewish culture, centered in Jerusalem and its temple,[9] and it magnifies the proof that that he is "indeed the Savior of the world" (4:42).[10] The government official (*basilikos*) whose son Jesus heals from a distance in this episode was probably a servant of

---

6. Against, for instance, the Cathars of the twelfth through fourteenth centuries, who rejected marriage and procreation as moral evils. See, e.g., the expositions of the Cana passage by medieval preachers in David d'Avray, *Medieval Marriage Sermons: Mass Communication in a Culture without Print* (Oxford: Oxford University Press, 2001): a sermon by Pierre de Saint-Benoît (211), a sermon by Gérard de Mailly (249), a sermon by Guibert de Tournai (301).

7. An 1844 facsimile reprint, *The Book of Common Prayer: Printed by Whitchurch March 1549; Commonly called The First Book of Edward VI* (London: William Pickering, 1844), is viewable online at http://tinyurl.com/SBL0392b.

8. By using the term "Judean" here, I am not wading into the debate about whether, or how often, the term *Iudaioi* in John should be translated "Judeans" instead of "Jews." See, e.g., Malcolm Lowe, "Who Were the ΙΟΥΔΑΙΟΙ?" *NovT* 18 (1976): 101–30; Urban C. von Wahlde, "'The Jews' in the Gospel of John: Fifteen Years of Research (1983–1998)," *ETL* 76 (2000): 30–55. See also the interchange at http://tinyurl.com/SBL0392c. Here I am referring to the primacy that was often attached to Judea, as opposed to Galilee, due to the importance of Jerusalem, the temple and its priesthood, and the ruling body of the Jews, the Sanhedrin (cf. John 1:46; 7:41, 52).

9. Peter J. Judge, "The Royal Official and the Historical Jesus," in *John, Jesus, and History, Volume 2: Aspects of Historicity in the Fourth Gospel*, ed. Paul N. Anderson, Felix Just, and Tom Thatcher (Atlanta: Society of Biblical Literature, 2009), 86.

10. The actual ethnicity of the official is not specified (contrast Matt 8:5–13; Luke 7:1–10), and some have even argued that he was Jewish rather than gentile (John P. Meier, *Mentor, Message, and Miracles*, vol. 2 of *A Marginal Jew: Rethinking the Historical Jesus*, ABRL [New York: Doubleday, 1994], 721–22). What is specified and even prominent, however, is his title *basilikos*, and this links him with Herod and the

Herod Antipas the tetrarch, who is called *basileus* in Matt 14:9 and Mark 6:14. It was Herod who would have John the Baptizer arrested (John 3:24) and later beheaded (Mark 6:17, 21–29). Though there is no comparative sense of threat in this episode, we may still observe that Jesus's ministry is extended here even to one who represents a *potentially oppressive power*.

This sign, then, escorts us into the political realities of Jesus's day, realities that would remain very much a part of the situation of John's first readers for centuries to come. In John, this power has an intimate association with "the world," a world Jesus will later say will be prone to hate and persecute his disciples, as it hated and persecuted him (15:18, 20). Even Jesus's "own nation and the chief priests" (18:35) would at times join forces with this hostile world: "They will put you out of the synagogues," Jesus portends (16:2). But the ensuing warning, "Indeed, the hour is coming when whoever kills you will think he is offering service to God" (16:2), universalizes the prospective opposition.

Early Appropriations: Christians in Conflict with Culture

Despite attempts to live peaceably within Greco-Roman culture, Christians felt unable to accommodate certain aspects of it (again, the words of Diognetus, "They share their food but not their wives" [5.7]). Their resistance to the paraphernalia of pagan worship often led to turmoil.

During the joint reign of Marcus Aurelius and Lucius Verus (161–69 CE) or perhaps Septimius Severus (193–211 CE),[11] two men named Carpus and Papylus and a woman named Agathonice were tried and executed for refusing to venerate the gods. In his statement of defense, Carpus confessed that "the true worshippers, according to the Lord's divine instruction, those who worship God in spirit and in truth, take on the image of God's glory and become immortal with him, sharing in eternal life through the Word" (Martyrdom of Carpus, Papylus, and Agothonice 1.7).[12] As they faced the ultimate choice of life or death, of true worship

---

Roman power. The expression used for Nicodemus, "ruler of the Jews" (*archōn tōn Ioudaiōn*) is different.

11. On the dating of The Martyrdom of Carpus, Papylus, and Agathonice, see Jan den Boeft and Jan Bremmer, "Notiunculae Martyrologicae II," *VC* 36 (1982): 385.

12. Translation from Herbert Musurillo, *The Acts of the Christian Martyrs: Introduction, Texts, and Translations* (Oxford: Oxford University Press, 1972), 23.

or false worship, it was the words of Jesus from John's Gospel (4:24) that delivered strength and resolve.

A decade or so later, Christians in Gaul were subjected to public harassment, confiscation, arrests, and several brutal executions. In his account of the atrocities, one survivor reminded his fellow Christians that Jesus had predicted these very sufferings, citing words from John's Gospel:

> All men turned like beasts against us, so that even if any had formerly been lenient for friendship's sake they then became furious and raged against us, and there was fulfilled that which was spoken by our Lord, that the time will come when "whoever kills you will think that he is offering worship to God" (John 16:2). (Epistle of Vienne and Lyons, from Eusebius, *Hist. eccl.* 5.1.15)[13]

After the accession of Constantine, of course, things would change drastically for Christians in Roman society. Recent events in our own day, however, offer horrifying reminders that the "time" is still with us when some believe that the worship of their God justifies or even mandates the killing of Jesus's followers.

Healing a Paralytic at the Pool of Bethesda (5:1–18)

Readers throughout the empire would have been accustomed to the sight of the chronically ill and handicapped congregating at temples, sanctuaries, and shrines in search of divine cures. This was part of the common culture. It is something specific to Jewish religious culture, however, which sparks the immediate controversy in the aftermath of this sign. Jesus had healed this paralyzed man on the Sabbath (5:9).

It was Jesus's working on the Sabbath that, according to John 5:15, provoked certain leaders of his own people to persecute him. But it was Jesus's response to their opposition that was even more provocative and led to the first mention of the idea of killing him: "because not only was he breaking the Sabbath, but he was even calling God his own Father, making himself equal with God" (5:18). In chapter 10, after Jesus proclaims "I and the Father are one," his opponents will say "It is not for a good work that

---

13. Translation from C. E. Hill, "'The Orthodox Gospel': The Reception of John in the Great Church prior to Irenaeus," in *The Legacy of John: Second-Century Reception of the Fourth Gospel*, ed. Tuomas Rasimus, NovTSup 132 (Leiden: Brill, 2010), 242–43.

we are going to stone you but for blasphemy, because you, being a man, are making yourself God" (10:33).[14]

Early Appropriation: John's High Christology

It is hard to calculate the momentous ramifications that John's portrayal of Jesus had on Christians of the second century CE. For early apologists like Aristides of Athens, the author of the Epistle to Diognetus, Justin Martyr, Tatian, and Theophilus of Antioch, it was John's rich Christology that carried the weight for their presentations of a divine and human savior to outsiders who could not understand their devotion to a man who had been crucified. John's teachings featured prominently in their efforts to introduce and defend the religion of the Christians to the interested pagan (Diognetus), the skeptical Jew (Trypho), the educated elite, and the politically powerful (Hadrian by Aristides, the Senate by Justin).

Apparently drawing upon the self-testimony of Jesus in John 3:13 and 6:38, Aristides, in about 125 CE, informs the emperor Hadrian that this one called Jesus "came down from heaven" (*ap' ouranou katabas*).[15] Writing to "the Greeks," Clement of Alexandria praises the "Word, who alone is both God and man, the cause of all our good" (*Protr.* 1, written before 190 CE). Justin echoes Johannine language when he speaks of the preexistent Word (*ho Logos*), the only (*monos*) Son of God, the "only-begotten" (*monogenēs*) to the Father of all things (*Dial.* 105.1). The divine Logos was begotten by God in a peculiar manner,[16] Justin tells the emperor and Senate, and "was made flesh (*sarkopoiētheis*) and became man" (*1 Apol.* 32.10; see also 66.2; 87.2);[17] here too, Justin paraphrases the presentation in John 1:14 (*kai ho logos sarx egeneto*).[18]

---

14. Cf. Tertullian, *Adv. Jud.* 9, which conflates John 5:18 with 10:33 in a confused way.

15. See C. E. Hill, *The Johannine Corpus in the Early Church*, rev. ed. (Oxford: Oxford University Press, 2006), and Titus Nagel, *Die Rezeption des Johannesevangeliums im 2. Jahrhundert: Studien zu vorirenäischen Auslegung des vierten Evangeliums in christlicher und christlich gnostischer Literatur*, ABG 2 (Leipzig: Evangelische Verlagsanstalt, 2000), 118–19.

16. Justin, *1 Apol.* 21.1; 22.2; 23.2; similarly, Tatian, *Or. Graec.* 5.1–3; compare John 1:1, 12–13, 14, 18.

17. Cf. Justin, *1 Apol.* 5.4, "Reason himself took shape, and became man, and was called Jesus Christ."

18. See Hill, *Johannine Corpus*, 320–23; Hill, "Was John's Gospel among Justin's

So rudimentary for Christians was belief in Jesus's deity that by the beginning of the third century CE the view known as Monarchianism had sprung up, which held that Father, Son, and Holy Spirit were simply three modes by which the one God was manifest. Praxeas read Jesus's statements, "I and the Father are one" (10:30), "Whoever has seen me has seen the Father" (14:9), and "I am in the Father and the Father is in me" (14:10), in a way that identified the Son and the Father as numerically the same.[19] Tertullian's response, *Adversus Praxean*, was an expositional march through the Gospel of John, showing the Father, the Son, and the Spirit to be one divine essence but three distinct persons. Hippolytus pointed out that Jesus did not say "I and the Father *am* one" but "I and the Father *are* one" (*Noet.* 7). Here, as in practically all significant christological discussion that subsequently took place in the church, the Gospel of John was at center stage.

The Feeding of the Multitude (6:1–71)

The long and complex account of this miracle and its aftermath envelops a large number of elements from both common and Jewish religious culture. Features of the Galilean geographical landscape are named: "the Sea of Galilee, which is the Sea of Tiberias," an adjacent mountain, and the cities of Capernaum and Tiberias, the synagogue in Capernaum. The events take place when "the Passover, the feast of the Jews, was at hand" (6:4). The common Roman currency has a part in the story when "two hundred denarii" is said not to be enough to provide food for the large crowd (6:7).

These are all "incidentals"; the major use of culturally commonplace objects has to do with a symbolic use of food. Jesus charges the crowd, "Do not labor for the food that perishes, but for the food that endures to eternal life, which the Son of Man will give you" (6:27). When the crowd brings up God's feeding of Israel with manna in the wilderness and challenges Jesus to perform a work worthy of comparison, Jesus proclaims that he is the bread from heaven, the bread of God (*artos theou*), who has come down from heaven to give life to the world (6:33). He ultimately

Apostolic Memoirs?" in *Justin Martyr and His Worlds*, ed. Sara Parvis and Paul Foster (Minneapolis: Fortress, 2007), 89.

19. Mark DelCogliano, "The Interpretation of John 10:30 in the Third Century: Antimonarchian Polemics and the Rise of Grammatical Reading Techniques," *JTI* 6 (2012): 117–38.

presses the message home in a shocking application of this symbolism that was meant to offend and drive away the cynical sign-seekers: "Unless you eat the flesh of the Son of Man and drink his blood, you have no life in you. Whoever feeds on my flesh and drinks my blood has eternal life, and I will raise him up on the last day" (6:53–54 ESV).

Early Appropriations: Christian Devotion, Worship, and Liturgy

In about 107 CE, Ignatius, leader of the church in Antioch, Syria, was arrested and taken to Rome to be executed. As he and his captors passed through Asia Minor *en route* to the capital city, Ignatius wrote letters to Christians in the region. Ignatius's particular style of devotion to Jesus comes through in these letters and reveals its indebtedness to Johannine language and thoughts.[20] One passage is particularly rich in allusions to John 6:

> I take no pleasure in the food of corruption nor in pleasures of this life.
> I desire the bread of God, that is, the flesh of Christ who is of the seed of David; for drink I desire his blood, which is incorruptible love. (Ignatius, *Rom.* 7.3)

Here are clustered together four apparent allusions to John 6: the "food of corruption" (compare John's "food which perishes," 6:27), the bread of God (6:33),[21] uniquely identified with the flesh of Jesus (6:51), and Jesus's flesh and blood as food and drink (6:53, 54, 55, 56).[22] John would continue to play a large role in devotion, worship, and ritual observances of Christian groups throughout the second century. It was used in preaching, as we know from Melito of Sardis's *On the Passover* (25, 499, 501, 552, 656, 653–654, 701, 708), probably from the early 160s,[23] and at about the same time, from Justin's reference to the reading of the "memoirs of the apostles" in worship services in Rome (*1 Apol.* 67.3).

In one passage of Justin's first apology, Jesus's words to Nicodemus about the necessity of being "born of water and the Spirit" (John 3:5)

---

20. For instance, Ignatius refers to the Spirit not being deceived "because it knows whence it comes and whither it goes" (*Phld.* 7.1, from John 3:8).

21. The only occurrence of *artos theou* in the New Testament or LXX.

22. For more on this, see Hill, "Orthodox Gospel," 278–79.

23. See Hill, *Johannine Corpus*, 294–96.

ground a theological explanation of the church's rite of baptism (*1 Apol.* 61.4–5).[24] A half-century later, Tertullian would interpret these same words to mean that baptism with water was necessary for a person's salvation (*Bapt.* 12, 13). Others were arguing the opposite conclusion from John 4:2, where John informs us that Jesus himself did not perform baptisms, only his disciples did (*Bapt.* 11). All sides here were using the Gospel of John, as was apparently also the case during debates over the proper observance of Passover—for Christians the anniversary of Jesus's suffering and resurrection. Tertullian saw baptism indicated in another Johannine text, John 19:34–35, where the water that flowed from Jesus's side at the crucifixion signified baptism with water, and the blood signified a "second baptism," a baptism with blood, that is, martyrdom (*Bapt.* 16).

Healing of the Man Born Blind (9:1–41)

By healing the man born blind, Jesus teaches that he is the light of the world (9:5, 39–41). The story encompasses many aspects of common culture with which readers would have been familiar: the affliction of blindness, the poor or handicapped begging in public places, authorities in control of religious institutions and their membership (9:22, "put out of the synagogue"), and complications of parent-adult child relations. Prominent once again are Jewish elements by now familiar to the reader: another healing on the Sabbath, the antagonism of certain Pharisees, the synagogue, and Moses. One new feature of the Jerusalem landscape receives an explanation for outsiders: "the pool of Siloam (which means Sent)" (9:7). As was the case with the paralyzed man in chapter 5, it is the fact that the healing took place on the Sabbath that draws the scrutiny of the Pharisees.

This particular Sabbath activity carries other clear overtones of the original creation story from Gen 1 and 2 that would have struck chords within a Jewish culture. Jesus's reference to day and night in relation to the "works" of God (9:4), particularly in light of the later reference to the Sabbath, recalls God's work in the creation days of Gen 1. Jesus, calling himself "the light of the world," harks back to God's original "Let there

---

24. For the view that Justin is dependent not on John but on a "liturgical baptismal text" based on a tradition also known to the Johannine author, see A. J. Bellinzoni, *The Sayings of Jesus in the Writings of Justin Martyr*, NovTSup 17 (Leiden: Brill, 1967), 136–37. Against this view, see Hill, *Johannine Corpus*, 325–30; Hill, "Orthodox Gospel," 253–56.

be light" in Gen 1:3. Perhaps most evocatively, the means Jesus uses for healing, clay from made his saliva, recalls God's original formation of man from the dust of the ground. Thus there are overtones of Jesus as acting in cooperation with God in forming a new creation.

Early Appropriation: The Struggle between Orthodoxy and Heterodoxy

The first references we have to this sign simply allude to it as a historical incident, as one of the wonderful healings that Jesus performed (Justin, *1 Apol.* 22; *Dial.* 69; Melito of Sardis, *Pascha* 653–654). But in the struggle between competing interpretations of the Christian faith in the second century CE, this passage was one of a multitude that would be subjected to radically varying treatments. We may use it, then, as an introduction to the rival Christian cultures that were developing in the second century and their alternative approaches to John's Gospel.

The Gospel of John, which was probably not published until sometime in the last one or two decades of the first century CE,[25] was so early received as a primary source for Christian teaching about Jesus that it was used on practically all sides of Christian debate.[26] It was therefore soon subjected to multiple "reading strategies." A good deal of the strategy of the followers of Valentinus (mid- to late second century) involved the effort to find in the sacred texts typological reflections of the Valentinian "pleromatic myth."[27] This myth posited a fullness (*pleroma*) of thirty divine emanations, known as aeons, springing from a primal, unitary principle. In the first words of John's Gospel, "In the beginning was the Word.... In him was life, and that life was the light of men" (John 1:1–4), the Valentinians saw no less than five of their aeons named: Beginning, Word, Life, Light, and Man. They viewed the man born blind in John 9 as an allegory for the blindness/ignorance of the aeon named "Word," who was said to be ignorant of his own paternity (as accounted by Irenaeus, *Haer.* 2.17.9).

---

25. While some scholars have argued for an early date before the destruction of the Jerusalem temple in 70 CE and a few have posited a date as late as the middle of the second century, the vast majority believe the Gospel of John was published in its present form sometime between about 80–110 CE.

26. The Cerinthians and the Marcionites were among the few who seem to have avoided it.

27. As Irenaeus says, "they assert that the things which were done by the Lord were types of what took place in the Pleroma" (*Haer.* 2.23.2).

Irenaeus, in response, finds ridiculous the mere notion that a spiritual being within the divine fullness could be ignorant of his Father, to say nothing of the treatment of John 9. In a later portion of his treatise, Irenaeus returns to the healing of the blind man in order to establish, against his Valentinian opponents, the continuity of Christ's actions in creation and recreation. In doing so, Irenaeus picks up on the allusions to the Genesis creation account:

> To that man, however, who had been blind from his birth, He gave sight ... by an outward action ... that He might show forth the hand of God, that which at the beginning had moulded man.... Now the work of God is the fashioning of man. For, as the Scripture says, He made [man] by a kind of process: "And the Lord took clay from the earth, and formed man." Wherefore also the Lord spat on the ground and made clay, and smeared it upon the eyes, pointing out the original fashioning [of man], how it was effected, and manifesting the hand of God to those who can understand by what [hand] man was formed out of the dust. (Irenaeus, *Haer.* 5.15.2 [*ANF* 1:543])[28]

Valentinians and those often termed "gnostics" may have felt particularly at home with John's presentation of Jesus's divinity and heavenly origin (as many scholars have assumed). But so did the churches represented by Justin, Irenaeus, Clement, and Tertullian. It was the ability to assimilate and embrace John's equally impressive and equally integral statements of Jesus's humanity—that "The Word became flesh and dwelt among us" (1:14), that he wearied (4:6), that he wept (11:35), that he bled (19:34),[29] and that he rose bodily and *tangible* from the tomb (20:27)—that would ultimately ensure the viability of only one of these two competing cultures of reading and believing.[30]

---

28. See also Ambrose, *Vid.* 10.62, who also links this miracle to the first creation of mankind.

29. E.g., the author of Acts John 101.8–9, "You hear that I suffered, yet I suffered not; and that I suffered not, yet I did suffer; and that I was pierced, yet I was not lashed; that I was hanged, yet I was not hanged; that blood flowed from me, ye it did not flow."

30. See Hill, *Johannine Corpus*, "John and 'the Gnostics,'" 205–93.

The Raising of Lazarus (11:1–44)

The universal experience of death is attended in every human society by a host of cultural trappings. Palestinian Jewish burial and mourning practices may have differed in a number of ways from those of other subcultures around the Roman Empire (note John's explanatory aside in 19:40). But even these distinctives would have been easily comprehensible throughout the Mediterranean world.[31] John specifically mentions the body of the deceased being wrapped in linen strips and a face cloth and then its burial in a cave tomb, the mouth of which was covered by a stone (11:38). A customary period of mourning was still being kept four days after the burial (11:19, 31), and when he arrives, Jesus participates, allowing his love for his friend to move him to tears (11:35).

Early Appropriation: Hope Memorialized in Art

Apart from the resurrection of Jesus, the raising of Lazarus is certainly the most dramatic and remarkable of the signs in John's Gospel. Melito of Sardis exclaims, "the most unprecedented sign [sēmeion] ... a corpse roused from a tomb already four days old" (*Pascha* lines 551–52, cf. 656). This sign demonstrated Jesus's power to give life to the dead (see 5:21, 24, 25–29) and offered a stunning preview of that hour when "all who are in the tombs will hear his voice, and come out" (5:28–29). Quite naturally, then, Irenaeus cites the raising of Lazarus as proof of the future resurrection of the body (*Haer.* 5.13.1; cf. Clement, *Paed.* 2). Origen sees the same power at work in raising Lazarus as in the original creation of man (*Comm. Matt.* 12.2).

Another early appropriation of the Lazarus story demonstrates how John's Gospel began to change customs surrounding death, and at the same time it introduces us to another, relatively underexplored dimension in the cultural effects of John, namely, its influence in the visual and plastic arts. Here we briefly note a few of the early developments.

Church officials in Rome from at least the late second century CE managed sections of underground tombs now known as catacombs. Paintings depicting the raising of Lazarus appear no less than fifty-three times

---

31. See Bryon R. McCane, *Roll Back the Stone: Death and Burial in the World of Jesus* (Harrisburg, PA: Trinity Press International, 2003).

on Roman catacomb walls, three of which may date to as early as the end of the second century or the beginning of the third.[32] When the use of sarcophagi increased among modestly well-to-do Christians in the third century, the raising of Lazarus was a frequent theme used in ornamentation. As art historian Robin Jensen observes, "The sepulchral location of most of these Lazarus compositions suggests that the scene conveys a message of reassurance of resurrection, or life beyond death."[33]

Images representing the wedding at Cana from John 2, the Samaritan woman from John 4, the paralytic from John 5, Jesus as the Good Shepherd from John 10, are also contained in the catacombs. Early Christian art was not, of course, restricted to funerary settings. Tertullian mentions the use of communion chalices in Carthage painted with the image of "the Good Shepherd" (*Pud.* 7.4), a clear indication that John 10:11, 14 must have been the inspiration.[34] Perhaps the earliest securely datable piece of Christian art is a depiction of Jesus's healing of the paralytic in John 5 on the wall of a baptistery at Dura Europos, which must have been done before the city was destroyed in 256–57 CE.

Figure 1: Christ the Good Shepherd. Catacomb of Callistus. See http://tinyurl.com/SBL0392e.

Figure 2: Healing of the Paralytic. Dura Europos baptistery. Public Domain. Photo courtesy of Yale University Art Gallery. http://tinyurl.com/SBL0392f.

---

32. See A. G. Martimort, "L'iconographie des catacombs et la catéchèse antique," *Rivista di archaeologia cristiana* 25 (1949): 107; Hill, *Johannine Corpus*, 156–57.

33. Robin Margaret Jensen, *Understanding Early Christian Art* (London: Routledge, 2000), 170.

34. Hill, *Johannine Corpus*, 164.

The Resurrection of Jesus 20:1–21:25

The resurrection of Jesus is, of course, the climactic "sign" in the gospel. It is anticipated as such from chapter 2, where Jesus's answer to the demand for a sign is his enigmatic "Destroy this temple, and in three days I will raise it up," which is then interpreted by John, "he was speaking about the temple of his body" (2:19, 21). Jesus's resurrection becomes the occasion for Thomas's culminating response of faith: "My Lord and my God" (20:8). Cultural features special to John's account of Jesus's resurrection include a reiteration of certain Jewish burial customs already introduced, a translation of Mary's Aramaic word *rabboni*, "which means Teacher" (20:16), and the culturally suspect (as we shall see) appearance of Jesus to a woman (20:14–18).

Early Appropriations: Apologetic Witness in the Pagan World

As we have already observed, some strong currents of Greco-Roman culture were flowing against the fledgling religion of Christianity in its first centuries. But as Christianity gained a public presence and even benefitted from public defenses made by a number of advocates who belonged to the educated class, such as Aristides, Quadratus, Justin, and Theophilus, it also drew opponents from the same social circles.

To our knowledge, the first of these to write an entire treatise against Christianity was a philosopher named Celsus. His treatise, *The True Word* (already a poke at John 1:1?), penned sometime in the 160s or 170s, is also the first pagan work that signals an acquaintance with the written Gospel of John. Celsus's assault on the credibility of Christian claims that Jesus rose from the dead alludes to two aspects of John's unique account. Jesus, Christians say, "rose again, and showed the marks of his punishment, and how his hands were pierced with nails" (*Cels.* 2.55; 2.61; see John 20:20, 25, 27).[35] Then comes the taunt: "Who beheld this? A half-frantic [*paroistros*] woman, as you state, and some other one, perhaps, of those who were engaged in the same system of delusion." The "some other one," mentioned as almost an afterthought, is certainly Thomas, though there were, of course, others, as well. But Celsus is more interested in the

---

35. For more on Celsus's knowledge of John's Gospel, see Hill, *Johannine Corpus*, 309–11; Hill, "Orthodox Gospel," 249–52.

"half-frantic" woman, Mary Magdalene, a description, Origen is quick to point out, that was not made "by the history recording the fact" (probably it is Celsus's gloss on Mary's weeping) but only alleged by Celsus in order to disparage the claim (*Cels.* 2.60). In any case, what Celsus seizes upon is the absurdity of Christians relying upon the witness of a woman[36] and a woman who was under emotional duress, at that.

This reminds us how notable a thing it is that the Gospel of John is so candid about this cultural "vulnerability" (who would make this up?), not only here, but also in the case of the Samaritan woman in chapter 4, where John even notes that Jesus's male disciples "marveled that he was talking with a woman" (4:27).[37] The countercultural nature of Jesus's exchanges with these women was not missed by the author nor, as Celsus attests, by his early readers.

CONCLUSION

John's deliberate employment of so many cultural elements, both those relating to the common culture and those specific to Palestinian Jewish culture, may suggest that the world he reconstructs through his writing is not "merely literary" or imaginative or rhetorical. It converses with authentic, knowable, and known human, cultural environments. This further suggests the legitimacy of using cultural features of the narrative as conceptual pathways to circulate between John's world and that of his first readers. This approach seems to find confirmation in the lives and writings

---

36. Note Josephus's well-known addendum to the laws concerning witness in Deut 19, "From women let no evidence be accepted, because of the levity and temerity of their sex" (*A.J.* 4.219). While this attitude cannot have been monolithic (see Robert G. Maccini, *Her Testimony Is True: Women as Witnesses according to John*, JSNTSup 125 [Sheffield: Sheffield Academic, 1996], 63–97, for some of the complexities in rabbinic law), Craig Keener is probably correct in saying, "Most of Jesus' Jewish contemporaries held little esteem for the testimony of women; this reflects a broader Mediterranean limited trust of women's testimony and speech, also enshrined in Roman law" (Craig S. Keener, *The Gospel of John: A Commentary*, 2 vols. [Peabody, MA: Hendrickson, 2003], 2:1192). See his citation of both Jewish and Roman sources.

37. "A fictitious account of a faith-response to Jesus by a woman and the Samaritans would hardly persuade the living audience of the gospel to make a true faith-response to him." See Teresa Okure, *The Johannine Approach to Mission: A Contextual Study of John 4:1–42*, WUNT 2/31 (Tübingen: Mohr Siebeck, 1988), 188–89, cited approvingly by Maccini, *Her Testimony Is True*, 144.

of his first readers, who remained, as John and his immediate community did, very much invested in the structures of the world around them.

These readers connected with what John wrote about Jesus's signs and responded very much as he had hoped, with faith (20:31). Besides demonstrating Jesus's divine power and revealing his glory, Jesus's miracle at the wedding at Cana was read as an affirmation of creation and an honoring of the culturally primary institution of marriage. Believing readers in the second century received John's distinctive portrayal, through signs and the narrative, of Jesus as God's only Son, the Word become flesh. In many different contexts they reaffirmed both Jesus's deity and his humanity in the face of well-articulated alternatives, even seeking to preserve John's peculiar linguistic expressions for their theological formulations. John's portrait of Jesus deeply formed their piety and shaped their developing corporate, ritual observances. John quickly became part of the public face of Christianity amid controversy; friends spontaneously used it, foes could not avoid it. The words of Jesus in John's Gospel ministered courage and resolution when the controversy went beyond words to betrayal, trial, and the taking of Christian's lives. Christian hope and worship channeled artistic expression in new ways, ways influenced by John's Jesus.

In short, John worked.

BIBLIOGRAPHY

Abrams, Meyer H., and Geoffrey Galt Harpham. *A Glossary of Literary Terms.* 10th ed. Boston: Wadsworth, 2012.

Achtemeier, Paul J. "*Omne verbum sonat*: The New Testament and the Oral Environment of Late Western Antiquity." *JBL* 109 (1990): 3–27.

Akala, Adesola Joan. *The Son-Father Relationship and Christological Symbolism in the Gospel of John.* LNTS 505. London: Bloomsbury, 2014.

Alexander, Loveday. *Acts in Its Ancient Literary Context: A Classicist Looks at the Acts of the Apostles.* LNTS 298. Edinburgh: T&T Clark, 2005.

———. *The Preface to Luke's Gospel: Literary Convention and Social Context in Luke 1.1–4 and Acts 1.1.* SNTSMS 78. Cambridge: Cambridge University Press, 1993.

Alter, Robert. *The Art of Biblical Narrative.* London: Allen & Unwin, 1981.

Anderson, Paul N. "Aspects of Historicity in the Gospel of John: Implications for Investigations of Jesus and Archaeology." Pages 587–618 in *Jesus and Archaeology.* Edited by James H. Charlesworth. Grand Rapids: Eerdmans, 2006.

———. "Aspects of Interfluentiality between John and the Synoptics: John 18–19 as a Case Study." Pages 711–28 in *The Death of Jesus in the Fourth Gospel.* Edited by Gilbert Van Belle. BETL 200. Leuven: Peeters, 2007.

———. "Gradations of Symbolization in the Johannine Passion Narrative: Control Measures for Theologizing Speculation Gone Awry." Pages 157–94 in *Imagery in the Gospel of John: Terms, Forms, Themes, and Theology of Johannine Figurative Language.* Edited by Jörg Frey, Jan G. van der Watt, and Ruben Zimmermann. WUNT 200. Tübingen: Mohr Siebeck, 2006.

———. *The Riddles of the Fourth Gospel: An Introduction to John.* Minneapolis: Fortress, 2011.

Anderson, Paul N., Felix Just, and Tom Thatcher, eds. *John, Jesus, and History, Volume 1: Critical Appraisals of Critical Views.* SymS 44. Atlanta: Society of Biblical Literature, 2007.

———. *John, Jesus, and History, Volume 2: Aspects of Historicity in the Fourth Gospel.* ECL 2. Atlanta: Society of Biblical Literature, 2009.

Aristotle. *Art of Rhetoric.* Translated by J. H. Freese. LCL. Cambridge: Harvard University Press, 1926.

———. *The Complete Works of Aristotle: The Revised Oxford Translation.* Edited by Jonathan Barnes. 2 vols. Bollingen Series 71.2. Princeton: Princeton University Press, 1984.

———. *Nicomachean Ethics.* Translated by H. Rackham. LCL. Cambridge: Harvard University Press, 1926.

———. *The Physics.* 2 vols. Translated by Philip H. Wicksteed and Francis M. Cornford. LCL. Cambridge: Harvard University Press, 1934.

———. *Poetics.* Translated by Stephan Halliwell. LCL. Cambridge: Harvard University Press, 1999.

Ashton, John. *Understanding the Fourth Gospel.* 2nd ed. Oxford: Oxford University Press, 2007.

Attridge, Harold W. "Argumentation in John 5." Pages 188–99 in *Rhetorical Argumentation in Biblical Texts: Essays from the Lund Conference.* Edited by Anders Eriksson, Thomas Olbricht, and Walter Überlacker. ESEC 8. Harrisburg, PA: Trinity Press International, 2002.

———. "The Cubist Principle in Johannine Imagery: John and the Reading of Images in Contemporary Platonism." Pages 47–60 in *Imagery in the Gospel of John: Terms, Forms, Themes and Theology of Johannine Figurative Language.* Edited by Jörg Frey, Jan G. van der Watt, and Ruben Zimmermann. WUNT 200. Tübingen: Mohr Siebeck, 2006.

———. "Divine Sovereignty and Human Responsibility in the Fourth Gospel." Pages 183–99 in *Revealed Wisdom: Studies in Apocalyptic in Honour of Christopher Rowland.* Edited by John Ashton. AJEC 88. Leiden: Brill, 2014.

———. "An Emotional Jesus and Stoic Traditions." Pages 77–92 in *Stoicism in Early Christianity.* Edited by Tuomas Rasimus, Troels Engberg-Pedersen, and Ismo Dunderberg. Peabody, MA: Hendrickson, 2010.

———. *Essays on John and Hebrews.* Grand Rapids: Baker Academic, 2012.

———. "Genre Bending in the Fourth Gospel." *JBL* 121 (2002): 3–21.

———. "Historiography." Pages 157–184 in *Jewish Writings of the Second Temple: Apocrypha, Pseudepigrapha, Qumran Sectarian Writings, Philo, Josephus.* Edited by Michael E. Stone. CRINT 2.2. Philadelphia: Fortress, 1984.

———. *The Interpretation of Biblical History in the* Antiquitates Judaicae *of Flavius Josephus.* HDR 7. Missoula, MT: Scholars Press, 1976.

———.Josephus and His Works." Pages 185–232 in *Jewish Writings of the Second Temple: Apocrypha, Pseudepigrapha, Qumran Sectarian Writings, Philo, Josephus*. Edited by Michael E. Stone. CRINT 2.2. Philadelphia: Fortress, 1984.

———. "Plato, Plutarch, and John: Three Symposia about Love." Pages 367–78 in *Beyond the Gnostic Gospels: Studies Building on the Work of Elaine Pagels*. Edited by Eduard Iricinschi, Lance Jenott, Nicola Denzey Lewis, and Philippa Townsend. STAC 82. Tübingen: Mohr Siebeck, 2013.

———. "The Restless Quest for the Beloved Disciple." Pages 71–80 in *Early Christian Voices: In Texts, Traditions, and Symbols; Essays in Honor of François Bovon*. Edited by David H. Warren, Ann Graham Brock, and David W. Pao. BibInt 66. Leiden: Brill, 2003.

———. "Temple, Tabernacle, Time, and Space in John and Hebrews." *Early Christianity* 1 (2010): 261–74.

Back, Frances. *Gott als Vater der Jünger im Johannesevangelium*. WUNT 2/336. Tübingen: Mohr Siebeck, 2012.

Bakhtin, Mikhail M. *Chronotopos*. Translated by Michael Dewey. Frankfurt am Main: Suhrkamp, 2011.

———. "Forms of Time and of the Chronotope in the Novel: Notes towards a Historical Poetics." Pages 84–258 in *The Dialogic Imagination: Four Essays*. Edited by Michael Holquist. Translated by Caryl Emerson and Michael Holquist. Austin: University of Texas Press, 1981.

———. *Speech Genres and Other Late Essays*. Edited by Caryle Emerson and Michael Holquist. Translated by Vern W. McGee. Austin: University of Texas Press, 1986.

Bal, Mieke. *Narratology: Introduction to the Theory of Narrative*. 3rd ed. Translated by Christine van Boheemen. Toronto: University of Toronto Press, 2009.

Bar-Efrat, Shimon. *Narrative Art in the Bible*. Sheffield: Almond, 1989.

Barrett, C. K. "The Old Testament in the Fourth Gospel." *JTS* 48 (1947): 155–69.

Barthes, Roland. "L'effet de réel." *Communications* 11 (1968): 84–89.

———. "Introduction à l'analyse structurale du récit." *Communications* 8 (1966): 1–27.

———. "The Old Rhetoric: An Aide-Mémoire." Pages 11–94 in *The Semiotic Challenge*. Translated by Richard Howard. Oxford: Blackwell, 1988.

Bauckham, Richard, ed. *The Gospels for All Christians: Rethinking the Gospel Audiences*. Grand Rapids: Eerdmans, 1998.

———. "Historiographical Characteristics of the Gospel of John." *NTS* 53 (2007): 17–36. Repr., pages 93–112 in *The Testimony of the Beloved Disciple: Narrative, History, and Theology in the Gospel of John*. Grand Rapids: Baker, 2007.

———. *Jesus and the Eyewitnesses: The Gospels as Eyewitness Testimony*. Grand Rapids: Eerdmans, 2006.

Beardslee, William A. *Literary Criticism of the New Testament*. GBS. Philadelphia: Fortress, 1970.

Beasley-Murray, George R. *John*. WBC 36. Waco, TX: Word, 1987.

Beck, David R. *The Discipleship Paradigm: Readers and Anonymous Characters in the Fourth Gospel*. BibInt 27. Leiden: Brill, 1997.

———. "The Narrative Function of Anonymity in Fourth Gospel Characterization." *Semeia* 63 (1993): 143–58.

———. " 'Whom Jesus Loved': Anonymity and Identity; Belief and Witness in the Fourth Gospel." Pages 221–39 in *Characters and Characterization in the Gospel of John*. Edited by Christopher W. Skinner. LNTS 461. London: T&T Clark, 2013.

Beck, Mark. "Plutarch." Pages 441–62 in *Space in Ancient Greek Literature: Studies in Ancient Greek Narrative*. Edited by Irene J. F. de Jong. MnSup 339. Leiden: Brill, 2012.

Bellinzoni, A. J. *The Sayings of Jesus in the Writings of Justin Martyr*. NovTSup 17. Leiden: Brill, 1967.

Bender, John, and David E. Wellbery. "Rhetoricality: On the Modernist Return of Rhetoric." Pages 3–39 in *The Ends of Rhetoric: History, Theory, Practice*. Edited by John Bender and David E. Wellbery. Stanford, CA: Stanford University Press, 1990.

Bennema, Cornelis. "A Comprehensive Approach to Understanding Character in the Gospel of John." Pages 36–58 in *Characters and Characterization in the Gospel of John*. Edited by Christopher W. Skinner. LNTS 461. London: T&T Clark, 2013.

———. *Encountering Jesus: Character Studies in the Gospel of John*. 2nd ed. Minneapolis: Fortress, 2014.

———. "Judas (the Betrayer): The Black Sheep of the Family." Pages 360–72 in *Character Studies in the Fourth Gospel: Narrative Approaches to Seventy Figures in John*. Edited by Steven A. Hunt, D. Francois Tolmie, and Ruben Zimmermann. WUNT 314. Tübingen: Mohr Siebeck, 2013.

———. *A Theory of Character in New Testament Narrative*. Minneapolis: Fortress, 2014.

———. "A Theory of Character in the Fourth Gospel with Reference to Ancient and Modern Literature." *BibInt* 17 (2009): 375–421.

Bergmeier, Roland. "Die Bedeutung der Synoptiker für das johanneische Zeugnisthema: Mit einem Anhang zum Perfekt-Gebrauch im vierten Evangelium." *NTS* 52 (2006): 458–83.

Berlin, Adele. *Poetics and Interpretation of Biblical Narrative*. Winona Lake, IN: Eisenbrauns, 1994.

Bernier, Jonathan. Aposynagōgos *and the Historical Jesus in John: Rethinking the Historicity of the Johannine Expulsion Passages*. BibInt 122. Leiden: Brill, 2013.

Beutler, Johannes. *Do Not Be Afraid: The First Farewell Discourse in John's Gospel*. NTSCE 6. Frankfurt am Main: Lang, 2011. Translation of *Habt keine Angst: Die erste johanneische Abschiedsrede (Joh 14)*. SBS 116. Stuttgart: Katholisches Bibelwerk, 1984.

———. *Judaism and the Jews in the Gospel of John*. SubBi 30. Rome: Pontifical Biblical Institute, 2006.

Blank, Josef. *Krisis: Untersuchungen zur johanneischen Christologie und Eschatologie*. Freiburg: Lambertus, 1964.

Bloomer, W. Martin. "The Ancient Child in School." Pages 447–56 in *The Oxford Handbook on Childhood and Education in the Classical World*. Edited by Judith Evans Grubbs and Tim Parkin. Oxford: Oxford University Press, 2013.

Boeft, Jan den, and Jan Bremmer. "Notiunculae Martyrologicae II." *VC* 36 (1982): 383–402.

The Book of Common Prayer: Printed by Whitchurch March 1549; Commonly called The First Book of Edward VI. London: William Pickering, 1844. http://tinyurl.com/SBL0392b.

Booth, Wayne C. *The Company We Keep: An Ethics of Fiction*. Berkeley: University of California Press, 1988.

———. *The Rhetoric of Fiction*. 2nd ed. Chicago: University of Chicago Press, 1983.

Borgen, Peder. *Bread from Heaven: An Exegetical Study of the Concept of Manna in the Gospel of John and the Writings of Philo*. NovTSup 10. Leiden: Brill, 1965.

Boring, M. Eugene, Klaus Berger, and Carsten Colpe, eds. *Hellenistic Commentary to the New Testament*. Nashville: Abingdon, 1995.

Bosenius, Bärbel. *Der literarische Raum des Markusevangeliums*. WMANT 140. Neukirchen-Vluyn: Neukirchener Verlag, 2014.

Bowie, A. M. "Aristophanes." Pages 359–73 in *Space in Ancient Greek Literature: Studies in Ancient Greek Narrative*. Edited by Irene J. F. de Jong. MnSup 339. Leiden: Brill, 2012.

Boyarin, Daniel. "The Gospel of the Memra: Jewish Binitarianism and the Prologue to John." *HTR* 94 (2001): 243–84.

Boyd, William. *Solo: A James Bond Novel*. London: Vintage, 2014.

Bradley, Keith R. *Discovering the Roman Family: Studies in Roman History*. Oxford: Oxford University Press, 1991.

Brant, Jo-Ann A. *Dialogue and Drama: Elements of Greek Tragedy in the Fourth Gospel*. Peabody, MA: Hendrickson, 2004.

——. "Divine Birth and Apparent Parents: The Plot of the Fourth Gospel." Pages 199–217 in *Ancient Fiction and Early Christian Narrative*. Edited by Ronald F. Hock, J. Bradley Chance, and Judith Perkins. SymS 6. Atlanta: Scholars Press, 1998.

——. *John*. PCNT. Grand Rapids: Baker Academic, 2011.

Bratcher, Robert G., ed. *Old Testament Quotations in the New Testament*. London: United Bible Societies, 1967.

Brodie, Thomas L. *The Gospel according to John: A Literary and Theological Commentary*. Oxford: Oxford University Press, 1993.

——. *The Quest for the Origin of John's Gospel: A Source-Oriented Approach*. New York: Oxford University Press, 1992.

Broer, Ingo. "Knowledge of Palestine in the Fourth Gospel?" Pages 83–90 in *Jesus in Johannine Tradition*. Edited by Robert T. Fortna and Tom Thatcher. Louisville: Westminster John Knox, 2011.

Brooke, George J. "Genre Theory, Rewritten Bible and Pesher." *DSD* 17 (2010): 361–86.

——. "Reading, Searching and Blessing: A Functional Approach to the Genres of Scriptural Interpretation in the Yahad." Pages 140–56 in *The Temple in Text and Tradition: A Festschrift in Honour of Robert Hayward*. Edited by R. Timothy McLay. LSTS 83. London: Bloomsbury, 2014.

Brooks, Peter. *Reading for the Plot: Design and Intention in Narrative*. Cambridge: Harvard University Press, 1984.

Brown, Peter. *Authority and the Sacred: Aspects of the Christianisation of the Roman World*. Cambridge: Cambridge University Press, 1995.

Brown, Raymond E. *The Community of the Beloved Disciple: The Life, Loves and Hates of an Individual Church in New Testament Times.* New York: Paulist, 1979.

——. *The Epistles of John.* AB 30. Garden City, NY: Doubleday, 1982.

——. *The Gospel according to John.* 2 vols. AB 29–29A. Garden City, NY: Doubleday, 1966–1970.

——. *An Introduction to the Gospel of John.* Edited by Francis J. Moloney. New York: Doubleday, 2003.

Bultmann, Rudolf. *The Gospel of John: A Commentary.* Translated by G. R. Beasley-Murray. Philadelphia: Westminster, 1971.

Burke, Kenneth. *A Rhetoric of Motives.* Berkeley: University of California Press, 1969.

Burke, Seán. *The Death and Return of the Author: Criticism and Subjectivity in Barthes, Foucault and Derrida.* 3rd ed. Edinburgh: Edinburgh University Press, 2008.

Burnett, Fred W. "Characterization and Reader Construction of Characters in the Gospels." *Semeia* 63 (1993): 3–78.

Burridge, Richard. "Gospels." Pages 432–44 in *The Oxford Handbook of Biblical Studies.* Edited by J. W. Rogerson and Judith M. Lieu. Oxford: Oxford University Press, 2006.

——. *What Are the Gospels? A Comparison with Greco-Roman Biography.* 2nd. rev. ed. Grand Rapids: Eerdmans, 2004.

Byrne, Brendan. "The Faith of the Beloved Disciple and the Community in John 20." *JSNT* 23 (1985): 83–97.

——. *Life Abounding: A Reading of John's Gospel.* Collegeville, MN: Liturgical Press, 2014.

——. "A Step Too Far: A Critique of Francis Moloney's Understanding of 'the Scripture' in John 20:9." *ITQ* 80 (2015): 149–56.

Byrskog, Samuel. *Story as History—History as Story: The Gospel Tradition in the Context of Ancient Oral History.* WUNT 123. Tübingen: Mohr Siebeck, 2000.

Cameron, Averil. *Christianity and the Rhetoric of Empire: The Development of Christian Discourse.* SCL 55. Berkeley: University of California Press, 1991.

Carter, Warren. *John and Empire: Initial Explorations.* London: T&T Clark, 2008.

Cassirer, Ernst. "Mythischer, ästhetischer und theoretischer Raum [1931]." Pages 93–119 in *Symbol, Technik, Sprache: Aufsätze aus den Jahren*

1927–1933. Edited by Ernst Wolfgang Orth and John Michael Krois. Hamburg: Meiner, 1985.

Charlesworth, James H. *The Beloved Disciple: Whose Witness Validates the Gospel of John?* Valley Forge, PA: Trinity Press International, 1995.

Chatman, Seymour. *Story and Discourse: Narrative Structure in Fiction and Film.* Ithaca, NY: Cornell University Press, 1978.

Chennattu, Rekha M. *Johannine Discipleship as a Covenant Relationship.* Peabody, MA: Hendrickson, 2006.

———. "The Word Became Flesh (John 1:1–18): A Cross-Cultural/Religious Expression of the Divine." Pages 43–51 in *Cross-Cultural Encounter: Experience and Expression of the Divine.* Edited by Mohan Doss and Andreas Vonach. Innsbruck: Innsbruck University Press, 2009.

Chibici-Revneanu, Nicole. *Die Herrlichkeit des Verherrlichten.* WUNT 2/231. Tübingen: Mohr Siebeck, 2007.

Chura, Patrick. "Prolepsis and Anachronism: Emmet Till and the Historicity of *To Kill a Mockingbird.*" *SLJ* 32 (2000): 1–26.

Cicero. *De Oratore.* Translated by E. W. Sutton and H. Rackham. LCL. Cambridge: Harvard University Press, 1959–1960.

[Cicero]. *Rhetorica ad Herennium.* Translated by Harry Caplan. LCL. Cambridge: Harvard University Press, 1964.

Cirafesi, Wally V. "The Johannine Community Hypothesis (1968–Present): Past and Present Approaches and a New Way Forward." *CurBR* 12 (2014): 173–93.

Clark-Soles, Jaime. "Mary Magdalene." Pages 626–40 in *Character Studies in the Fourth Gospel: Narrative Approaches to Seventy Figures in John.* Edited by Steven A. Hunt, D. Francois Tolmie, and Ruben Zimmermann. WUNT 314. Tübingen: Mohr Siebeck, 2013.

Cohn, Dorrit. *Transparent Minds: Narrative Modes for Presenting Consciousness in Fiction.* Princeton: Princeton University Press, 1978.

Collins, Adela Yarbro. *Is Mark's Gospel a Life of Jesus? The Question of Genre.* Milwaukee: Marquette University Press, 1990.

———. *Mark: A Commentary.* Hermeneia. Minneapolis: Fortress, 2007.

Collins, John J. *The Apocalyptic Imagination: An Introduction to Jewish Apocalyptic Literature.* 2nd ed. Grand Rapids: Eerdmans, 1998.

Collins, Raymond F. "Representative Figures." Pages 1–45 in *These Things Have Been Written: Studies on the Fourth Gospel.* LTPM 2. Leuven: Peters; Grand Rapids: Eerdmans, 1990.

———. "The Representative Figures of the Fourth Gospel, Part I." *DRev* 94 (1976): 26–46.

———. "The Representative Figures of the Fourth Gospel, Part II." *DRev* 94 (1976): 118–32.

———. *These Things Have Been Written: Studies on the Fourth Gospel.* LTPM 2. Leuven: Peeters; Grand Rapids: Eerdmans, 1990.

Coloe, Mary L. *God Dwells in Us: Temple Symbolism in the Fourth Gospel.* Collegeville, MN: Liturgical Press, 2001.

———. "The Mother of Jesus: A Woman Possessed." Pages 202–13 in *Character Studies in the Fourth Gospel: Narrative Approaches to Seventy Figures in John.* Edited by Steven A. Hunt, D. Francois Tolmie, and Ruben Zimmermann. WUNT 314. Tübingen: Mohr Siebeck, 2013.

———. "The Structure of the Johannine Prologue and Genesis 1." *ABR* 45 (1997): 40–55.

———. "Theological Reflections on Creation in the Gospel of John." *Pacifica* 24 (2011): 1–12.

———. "Witness and Friend: Symbolism Associated with John the Baptiser." Pages 319–32 in *Imagery in the Gospel of John: Terms, Forms, Themes, and Theology of Johannine Figurative Language.* Edited by Jörg Frey, Jan G. van der Watt, and Ruben Zimmermann. WUNT 200. Tübingen: Mohr Siebeck, 2006.

———. "The Woman of Samaria: Her Characterization, Narrative, and Theological Significance." Pages 182–96 in *Characters and Characterization in the Gospel of John.* Edited by Christopher W. Skinner. LNTS 461. London: T&T Clark, 2013.

Comfort, Philip W. *The Quest for the Original Text of the New Testament.* Grand Rapids: Baker, 1992.

Conway, Colleen M. *Behold the Man: Jesus and Greco-Roman Masculinity.* Oxford: Oxford University Press, 2008.

———. *Men and Women in the Fourth Gospel: Gender and Johannine Characterization.* SBLDS 167. Atlanta: Scholars Press, 1999.

———. "Speaking through Ambiguity: Minor Characters in the Fourth Gospel." *BibInt* 10 (2002): 324–41.

Copenhaver, Brian. *Hermetica: The Corpus Hermeticum and the Latin Asclepius in a New English Translation.* Cambridge: Cambridge University Press, 1992.

Corazza, Eros. "Temporal Indexicals and Temporal Terms." *Synthese* 130 (2002): 441–60.

Corbeill, Anthony. "Education in the Roman Republic: Creating Traditions." Pages 261–87 in *Education in Greek and Roman Antiquity.* Edited by Yun Lee Too. Leiden: Brill, 2001.

Corrigan, John. "Spatiality and Religion." Pages 157–72 in *The Spatial Turn: Interdisciplinary Perspectives*. Edited by Barney Warf and Santa Arias. London: Routledge, 2009.

Criboire, Raffaella. *Gymnastics of the Mind: Greek Education in Hellenistic and Roman Egypt*. Princeton: Princeton University Press, 2001.

Crouch, Walter B. *Death and Closure in Biblical Narratives*. New York: Lang, 2000.

Culler, Jonathan. "Omniscience." *Narrative* 12 (2004): 22–34.

Culpepper, R. Alan. *Anatomy of the Fourth Gospel: A Study in Literary Design*. Minneapolis: Fortress, 1983.

———. "Designs for the Church in the Imagery of John 21:1–14." Pages 369–402 in *Imagery in the Gospel of John: Terms, Forms, Themes, and Theology of Johannine Figurative Language*. Edited by Jörg Frey, Jan G. van der Watt, and Ruben Zimmermann. WUNT 200. Tübingen: Mohr Siebeck, 2006.

———. *The Gospel and Letters of John*. Interpreting Biblical Texts. Nashville: Abingdon, 1998.

———. "John 21:24–25: The Johannine *Sphragis*." Pages 342–59 in *John, Jesus, and History Volume 2: Aspects of Historicity in the Fourth Gospel*. Edited by Paul N. Anderson, Felix Just, and Tom Thatcher. ECL 2. Atlanta: Society of Biblical Literature, 2009.

———. "Peter as Exemplary Disciple in John 21:15–19." *PRSt* 37 (2010): 165–78.

———. "The Plot of John's Story of Jesus." *Int* 49 (1995): 347–58.

———. "The Relationship between the Gospel of John and 1 John." Pages 95–122 in *Communities in Dispute: Current Scholarship on the Johannine Epistles*. Edited by R. Alan Culpepper and Paul N. Anderson. ECL 13. Atlanta: SBL Press, 2014.

———. "The Weave of the Tapestry: Character and Theme in John." Pages 18–35 in *Characters and Characterization in the Gospel of John*. Edited by Christopher W. Skinner. LNTS 461. London: T&T Clark, 2013.

Culpepper, R. Alan, and Paul N. Anderson, eds. *Communities in Dispute: Current Scholarship on the Johannine Epistles*. ECL 13. Atlanta: SBL Press, 2014.

Danto, Arthur C. *Narration and Knowledge: Including the Integral Text of Analytical Philosophy of History*. New York: Columbia University Press, 1985.

Daube, David. "Rabbinic Methods of Interpretation and Hellenistic Rhetoric." *HUCA* 22 (1949): 239–64.

Davidsen, Ole. "The Lord, the Lamb, and the Lover: The Gospel of John as a Mixture of Spiritualized Narrative Genres." Pages 125–56 in *The Gospel of John as Genre Mosaic.* Edited by Kasper Bro Larsen. SANt 3. Göttingen: Vandenhoeck & Ruprecht, 2015.

D'Avray, David. *Medieval Marriage Sermons: Mass Communication in a Culture without Print.* Oxford: Oxford University Press, 2001.

DelCogliano, Mark. "The Interpretation of John 10:30 in the Third Century: Antimonarchian Polemics and the Rise of Grammatical Reading Techniques." *JTI* 6 (2012): 117–38.

Dennerlein, Katrin. *Narratologie des Raumes.* Narratologia 22. Berlin: de Gruyter, 2009.

Derrida, Jacques. "The Law of Genre." *CI* 7 (1980): 55–81.

Dionysius of Halicarnassus. *On Thucydides.* Translated by W. Kendrick Pritchett. Berkeley: University of California Press, 1975.

Dodd, C. H. *The Interpretation of the Fourth Gospel.* Cambridge: Cambridge University Press, 1953.

Doležel, Lubomír. *Possible Worlds of Fiction and History: The Postmodern Stage.* Baltimore: John Hopkins University Press, 2010.

Döring, Jörg, and Tristan Thielmann. "Einleitung: Was lesen wir im Raume? Der Spatial Turn und das geheime Wissen der Geographen." Pages 7–45 in *Spatial Turn: Das Raumparadigma in den Kultur- und Sozialwissenschaften.* Edited by Jörg Döring and Tristan Thielmann. Bielefeld: transcript, 2008.

Dronsch, Kristina. "Der Raum des Geistes: Die topographische Struktur der Rede vom Geist im Johannesevangelium." *ZNT* 13 (2010): 38–45.

Duke, Paul D. *Irony in the Fourth Gospel.* Atlanta: John Knox, 1985.

Dunn, James D. G. *Jesus Remembered.* Vol. 1 of *Christianity in the Making.* Grand Rapids: Eerdmans, 2003.

Eagleton, Terry. *Literary Theory: An Introduction.* Oxford: Blackwell, 1983.

Earman, John, and Richard M. Gale. "Time." Pages 920–22 in *The Cambridge Dictionary of Philosophy.* Edited by Robert Audi. 2nd ed. Cambridge: Cambridge University, 1999.

Edwards, Ruth. "Χάριν ἀντὶ χάριτος (John 1:16): Grace and Law in the Johannine Prologue." *JSNT* 32 (1988): 3–15.

Elliott, J. K. "Κηφᾶς: Σίμων Πέτρος: ὁ Πέτρος: An Examination of New Testament Usage." *NovT* 14 (1972): 241–56.

———. Review of *The Quest for the Original Text of the New Testament,* by Philip W. Comfort. *NovT* 36 (1994): 284–87.

Ellis, Peter F. *The Genius of John: A Compositional-Critical Commentary on the Fourth Gospel.* Collegeville, MN: Liturgical Press, 1984.

English, Adam C. "Feeding Imagery in the Gospel of John: Uniting the Physical and the Spiritual." *PRSt* 28 (2001): 203–14.

Estes, Douglas. *The Questions of Jesus in John: Logic, Rhetoric and Persuasive Discourse.* BibInt 115. Leiden: Brill, 2013.

———. "Rhetorical *Peristaseis* (Circumstances) in the Prologue of John." Pages 191–207 in *The Gospel of John as Genre Mosaic.* Edited by Kasper Bro Larsen. SANt 3. Göttingen: Vandenhoeck & Ruprecht, 2015.

———. *The Temporal Mechanics of the Fourth Gospel: A Theory of Hermeneutical Relativity in the Gospel of John.* BibInt 92. Leiden: Brill, 2008.

Farrell, Joseph. "Classical Genre in Theory and Practice." *NLH* 34 (2003): 383–408.

Fauconnier, Gilles. *Mental Spaces: Aspects of Meaning Construction in Natural Language.* Cambridge, MA: MIT Press, 1985. Repr., Cambridge: Cambridge University Press, 1994.

Felton, Tom, and Tom Thatcher. "Stylometry and the Signs Gospel." Pages 209–18 in *Jesus in Johannine Tradition.* Edited by Robert T. Fortna and Tom Thatcher. Louisville: Westminster John Knox, 2001.

Forster, E. M. *Aspects of the Novel.* New York: Harcourt, 1927.

Fortna, Robert T. *The Fourth Gospel and Its Predecessor: From Narrative Source to Present Gospel.* Philadelphia: Fortress, 1988.

———. *The Gospel of Signs: A Reconstruction of the Narrative Source Underlying the Fourth Gospel.* SNTSMS 11. Cambridge: Cambridge University Press, 1970.

Fowler, Alastair. *Kinds of Literature: An Introduction to the Theory of Genres and Modes.* Oxford: Clarendon, 1982.

Fowler, Don. "Second Thoughts on Closure." Pages 3–22 in *Classical Closure: Reading the End in Greek and Latin Literature.* Edited by Deborah H. Roberts, Francis M. Dunn, and Don Fowler. Princeton: Princeton University Press, 1997.

Fowler, Robert M. "Who Is 'the Reader' in Reader Response Criticism?" *Semeia* 31 (1985): 5–23.

Frank, Michael C., and Kirsten Mahlke. Epilogue to *Chronotopos*, by Mikhail M. Bakhtin. Translated by Michael Dewy. Frankfurt am Main: Suhrkamp, 2011.

Franzmann, Majella, and Michael Klinger. "The Call Stories of John 1 and John 21." *SVTQ* 36 (1992): 7–16.

Freed, Edwin D. *Old Testament Quotations in the Gospel of John*. NovTSup 11. Leiden: Brill, 1965.

Frey, Jörg. *Die johanneische Eschatologie II: Das johanneische Zeitverständnis*. WUNT 110. Tübingen: Mohr Siebeck, 1998.

———. "Love-Relations in the Fourth Gospel: Establishing a Semantic Network." Pages 171–98 in *Repetitions and Variations in the Fourth Gospel: Style, Text, Interpretation*. Edited by Gilbert Van Belle, Michael Labahn, and Petrus Maritz. BETL 223. Leuven: Peeters, 2009.

Frey, Jörg, Jan G. van der Watt, and Ruben Zimmermann, eds. *Imagery in the Gospel of John: Terms, Forms, Themes and Theology of Johannine Figurative Language*. WUNT 200. Tübingen: Mohr Siebeck, 2006.

Friedman, Norman. "Point of View in Fiction: The Development of a Critical Concept." *PMLA* 70 (1955): 1160–84.

Frow, John. *Genre: The New Critical Idiom*. London: Routledge, 2006.

Frye, Northrop. *The Great Code: The Bible and Literature*. London: Routledge & Kegan Paul, 1981.

Fusillo, Massimo. "How Novels End: Some Patterns of Closure in Ancient Narrative." Pages 209–27 in *Classical Closure: Reading the End in Greek and Latin Literature*. Edited by Deborah H. Roberts, Francis M. Dunn, and Don Fowler. Princeton: Princeton University Press, 1997.

Garský, Zbynek. *Das Wirken Jesu in Galiläa bei Johannes: Eine strukturale Analyse der Intertextualität des vierten Evangeliums mit den Synoptikern*. WUNT 2/325. Tübingen: Mohr Siebeck, 2012.

Gaventa, Beverley R. "The Archive of Excess: John 21 and the Problem of Narrative Closure." Pages 240–52 in *Exploring the Gospel of John: In Honor of D. Moody Smith*. Edited by R. Alan Culpepper and C. Clifton Black. Louisville: Westminster John Knox, 1996.

Genette, Gérard. *Narrative Discourse: An Essay in Method*. Translated by Jane E. Lewin. Ithaca, NY: Cornell University Press, 1980.

Gilhuly, Kate, and Nancy Worman. "Introduction." Pages 1–20 in *Space, Place, and Landscape in Ancient Greek Literature and Culture*. Edited by Kate Gilhuly and Nancy Worman. Cambridge: Cambridge University Press, 2014.

———, eds. *Space, Place, and Landscape in Ancient Greek Literature and Culture*. Cambridge: Cambridge University Press, 2014.

Glad, Clarence E. *Paul and Philodemus: Adaptability in Epicurean and Early Christian Psychagogy*. NovTSup 81. Leiden: Brill, 1995.

Gleason, Maud W. *Making Men: Sophists and Self-Presentation in Ancient Rome*. Princeton: Princeton University Press, 1995.

Gniesmer, Dirk F. *In den Prozeß verwickelt: Erzähltextanalytische und text-pragmatische Erwägungen zur Erzählung vom Prozeß Jesu vor Pilatus (Joh 18,28–19,16a.b.).* EHS 23/688. Frankfurt am Main: Lang, 2000.

Goldingay, John. "How Far Do Readers Make Sense? Interpreting Biblical Narrative." *Them* 18 (1993): 5–10.

Gorman, Heather M. *Interweaving Innocence: A Rhetorical Analysis of Luke's Passion Narrative (Luke 22:66–23:49).* Eugene, OR: Pickwick, 2015.

Gotschall, Jonathan. *The Storytelling Animal: How Stories Make Us Human.* Boston: Houghton Mifflin Harcourt, 2012.

Gourgues, Michel. "Le paraclet, l'esprit de vérité: Deux désignations, deux fonctions." Pages 83–108 in *Theology and Christology in the Fourth Gospel: Essays by the Members of the SNTS Johannine Writings Seminar.* Edited by Gilbert Van Belle, Jan G. van der Watt, and P. Maritz. BETL 184. Leuven: Leuven University Press, 2005.

Grappe, Christian. "Du sanctuaire au jardin: Jésus, nouveau et véritable Temple dans le quatrième évangile." Pages 285–94 in *Studien zu Matthäus und Johannes: Festschrift für Jean Zumstein zu seinem 65. Geburtstag / Études sur Mattheu et Jean: Mélanges offerts à Jean Zumstein pour son 65e anniversaire.* Edited by Andreas Dettwiler and Uta Poplutz. ATANT 97. Zürich: Theologischer, 2009.

Gregory, Andrew F., and C. Kavin Rowe. *Rethinking the Unity and the Reception of Luke and Acts.* Columbia: University of South Carolina Press, 2010.

Greimas, A. J. *Structural Semantics: An Attempt at a Method.* Lincoln: University of Nebraska Press, 1983.

Greimas, A. J., and J. Courtés. "The Cognitive Dimension of Narrative Discourse." *NLH* 8 (1976): 433–47.

———. *Semiotics and Language: An Analytical Dictionary.* Advances in Semiotics. Bloomington: Indiana University Press, 1982.

Gundry, Robert H. "In My Father's House Are Many Μοναί (John 14,2)." *ZNW* 58 (1967): 68–72.

Günzel, Stephan. "Spatial Turn—Topographical Turn—Topological Turn: Über die Unterschiede zwischen Raumparadigmen." Pages 220–37 in *Spatial Turn: Das Raumparadigma in den Kultur-und Sozialwissenschaften.* Edited by Jörg Döring and Tristan Thielmann. Bielefeld: transcript, 2008.

Haenchen, Ernst. *Das Johannesevangelium: Ein Kommentar.* Tübingen: Mohr Siebeck, 1980.

Hägg, Thomas. *The Art of Biography in Antiquity*. Cambridge: Cambridge University Press, 2012.

Hallbäck, Geert. "The Gospel of John as Literature: Literary Readings of the Fourth Gospel." Pages 31–46 in *New Readings in John: Literary and Theological Perspectives; Essays from the Scandinavian Conference on the Fourth Gospel in Aarhus 1997*. Edited by Johannes Nissen and Sigfred Pedersen. Rev. ed. JSNTSup 182. London: T&T Clark, 2004.

Hamid-Khani, Saeed. *Revelation and Concealment of Christ: A Theological Inquiry into the Elusive Language of the Fourth Gospel*. WUNT 2/120. Tübingen: Mohr Siebeck, 2000.

Hanson, A. T. "John's Use of Scripture." Pages 358–79 in *The Gospels and the Scriptures of Israel*. Edited by Craig A. Evans and W. Richard Stegner. JSNTSup 104. SSEJC 3. Sheffield: Sheffield Academic, 1994.

Harvey, Anthony E. *Jesus on Trial: A Study in the Fourth Gospel*. London: SPCK, 1976.

Harvey, W. J. *Character and the Novel*. Ithaca, NY: Cornell University Press, 1965.

Hasitschka, Martin. "The Significance of the Resurrection Appearance in John 21." Pages 311–28 in *The Resurrection of Jesus in the Gospel of John*. Edited by Craig R. Koester and Reimund Bieringer. WUNT 222. Tübingen: Mohr Siebeck, 2008.

Hearon, Holly E. "The Storytelling World of the First Century and the Gospels." Pages 21–35 in *The Bible in Ancient and Modern Media: Story and Performance*. Edited by Holly E. Hearon and Philip Ruge-Jones. Eugene, OR: Cascade, 2009.

Heath, Malcom. "Theon and the History of the Progymnasmata." *GRBS* 43 (2002): 129–60.

Hemelrijk, Emily A. *Matrona Docta: Educated Women in the Roman Élite from Cornelia to Julia Domna*. London: Routledge, 1999.

Hemer, Colin J. *The Book of Acts in the Setting of Hellenistic History*. WUNT 49. Tübingen: Mohr Siebeck, 1989.

Hengel, Martin. "The Old Testament in the Fourth Gospel." Pages 380–95 in *The Gospels and the Scriptures of Israel*. Edited by Craig A. Evans and W. Richard Stegner. JSNTSup 104. SSEJC 3. Sheffield: Sheffield Academic, 1994.

Herman, David. "Toward a Formal Description of Narrative Metalepsis." *JLS* 26 (1997): 132–52.

Herodotus. *The Persian Wars*. 4 vols. Translated by A. D. Godley. LCL. Cambridge: Harvard University Press, 1920–1925.

Higdon, David Leon. *Time and English Fiction*. Totowa, NJ: Rowman and Littlefield, 1977.

Hill, Charles E. *The Johannine Corpus in the Early Church*. Rev. ed. Oxford: Oxford University Press, 2006.

———. "'The Orthodox Gospel': The Reception of John in the Great Church prior to Irenaeus." Pages 233–300 in *The Legacy of John: Second-Century Reception of the Fourth Gospel*. Edited by Tuomas Rasimus. NovTSup 132. Leiden: Brill, 2010.

———. "Was John's Gospel among Justin's *Apostolic Memoirs?*" Pages 88–94 in *Justin Martyr and His Worlds*. Edited by Sara Parvis and Paul Foster. Minneapolis: Fortress, 2007.

Hillel, Vered. *Testaments of the Twelve Patriarchs: Structure, Source, Composition*. Lewiston, NY: Mellen, 2013.

Hirsch-Luipold, Rainer. "Klartext in Bildern." Pages 61–102 in *Imagery in the Gospel of John: Terms, Forms, Themes, and Theology of Johannine Figurative Language*. Edited by Jörg Frey, Jan G. van der Watt, and Ruben Zimmermann. WUNT 200. Tübingen: Mohr Siebeck, 2006.

Hock, Ronald F. "Homer in Greco-Roman Education." Pages 56–77 in *Mimesis and Intertextuality in Antiquity and Christianity*. Edited by Dennis R. MacDonald. SAC. Harrisburg, PA: Trinity Press International, 2001.

Holmesland, Oddvar. "Structuralism and Interpretation: Ernest Hemingway's 'Cat in the Rain.'" Pages 58–72 in *New Critical Approaches to the Short Stories of Ernest Hemingway*. Edited by Jackson J. Benson. Durham, NC: Duke University Press, 1990.

Hooker, Morna D. "Beginnings and Endings." Pages 184–202 in *The Written Gospel*. Edited by Markus Bockmuehl and Donald A. Hagner. Cambridge: Cambridge University Press, 2005.

———. *Endings: Invitations to Discipleship*. London: SCM, 2003.

Huber, Konrad. "Theologie als Topologie: Bemerkungen zum Raumkonzept von Joh 1,43–51." *ZKT* 121 (1999): 300–310.

Huitink, Luuk, and Jan W. van Henten. "Josephus." Pages 199–217 in *Space in Ancient Greek Literature: Studies in Ancient Greek Narrative*. Edited by Irene J. F. de Jong. MnSup 339. Leiden: Brill, 2012.

Hunt, Steven A., D. Francois Tolmie, and Ruben Zimmerman, eds. *Character Studies in the Fourth Gospel: Narrative Approaches to Seventy Figures in John*. WUNT 314. Tübingen: Mohr Siebeck, 2013.

———. "An Introduction to Character and Characterization in John and Related New Testament Literature." Pages 1–33 in *Character Studies in the Fourth Gospel: Narrative Approaches to Seventy Figures in John.* Edited by Steven A. Hunt, D. Francois Tolmie, and Ruben Zimmerman. WUNT 314. Tübingen: Mohr Siebeck, 2013.

Hurtado, Larry W. "Oral Fixation and New Testament Studies? 'Orality', 'Performance' and Reading Texts in Early Christianity." *NTS* 60 (2014): 321–40.

Hylen, Susan E. "The Disciples." Pages 214–27 in *Character Studies in the Fourth Gospel: Narrative Approaches to Seventy Figures in John.* Edited by Steven A. Hunt, D. Francois Tolmie, and Ruben Zimmermann. WUNT 314. Tübingen: Mohr Siebeck, 2013.

———. *Imperfect Believers: Ambiguous Characters in the Gospel of John.* Louisville: Westminster John Knox, 2009.

Irenaeus. *Against the Heresies, Book 3.* Translated and annotated by Dominic J. Unger with an introduction and further revisions by Irenaeus M. C. Steenberg. ACW 64. New York: Paulist, 2012.

Iser, Wolfgang. *The Implied Reader: Patterns of Communication in Prose Fiction from Bunyan to Beckett.* Baltimore: Johns Hopkins University Press, 1978. Translation of *Der implizite Leser: Kommunikationsformen des Romans von Bunyan bis Beckett.* Münich: Finch, 1972.

Iverson, Kelly R. *Gentiles in the Gospel of Mark: "Even the Dogs Under the Table Eat the Children's Crumbs."* LNTS 339. London: T&T Clark, 2007.

Jackson, Howard M. "Ancient Self-Referential Conventions and Their Implications for the Authorship and Integrity of the Gospel of John." *JTS* 50 (1999): 1–34.

Jensen, Robin Margaret. *Understanding Early Christian Art.* London: Routledge, 2000.

Jong, Irene J. F. de. "Homer." Pages 21–38 in *Space in Ancient Greek Literature: Studies in Ancient Greek Narrative.* Edited by Irene J. F. de Jong. MnSup 339. Leiden: Brill, 2012

———. "Narratological Theory on Space." Pages 1–18 in *Space in Ancient Greek Literature: Studies in Ancient Greek Narrative.* Edited by Irene J. F. de Jong. MnSup 339. Leiden: Brill, 2012.

———, ed. *Space in Ancient Greek Literature: Studies in Ancient Greek Narrative.* MnSup 339. Leiden: Brill, 2012.

Judge, Peter J. "The Royal Official and the Historical Jesus." Pages 83–92 in *John, Jesus, and History, Volume 2: Aspects of Historicity in the Fourth Gospel.* Edited by Paul N. Anderson, Felix Just, and Tom Thatcher. Atlanta: Society of Biblical Literature, 2009.

Kähler, Martin. *The So-Called Historical Jesus and the Historic, Biblical Christ.* Translated by Carl E. Braaten. Philadelphia: Fortress, 1964.

Karakolis, Christos. "'Across the Kidron Brook, There Was a Garden' (John 18:1): Two Old Testament Allusions and the Theme of the Heavenly King in the Johannine Passion Narrative." Pages 751–60 in *The Death of Jesus in the Fourth Gospel.* Edited by Gilbert Van Belle. BETL 200. Leuven: Leuven University Press, 2007.

Käsemann, Ernst. *The Testament of Jesus: A Study of the Gospel of John in Light of Chapter 17.* NTL. London: SCM, 1968.

Keener, Craig S. *Introduction and 1:1–2:47.* Vol. 1 of *Acts: An Exegetical Commentary.* Grand Rapids: Baker, 2012.

———. *The Gospel of John: A Commentary.* 2 vols. Peabody, MA: Hendrickson, 2003.

Kennedy, George A, trans. *Progymnasmata: Greek Textbooks of Prose Composition and Rhetoric.* WGRW 10. Atlanta: Society of Biblical Literature, 2003.

Kieffer, René. "The Implied Reader in John's Gospel." Pages 47–65 in *New Readings in John: Literary and Theological Perspectives; Essays from the Scandinavian Conference on the Fourth Gospel in Aarhus 1997.* Edited by Johannes Nissen and Sigfred Pedersen. Rev. ed. JSNTSup 182. London: T&T Clark, 2004.

———. *Le monde symbolique de Saint Jean.* LD 137. Paris: Cerf, 1989.

Kingsbury, Jack Dean. *Matthew as Story.* Philadelphia: Fortress, 1986.

Kirk, Alan, and Tom Thatcher, eds. *Memory, Tradition, and Text: Uses of the Past in Early Christianity.* SemeiaSt 52. Atlanta: Society of Biblical Literature, 2005.

Klassen, William. *Judas: Betrayer or Friend of Jesus?* Minneapolis: Fortress, 1996.

Klink, Edward W., III. "Gospel Audience and Origin: The Current Debate." Pages 1–26 in *The Audience of the Gospels: The Origin and Function of the Gospels in Early Christianity.* Edited by Edward W. Klink III. LNTS 353. London: T&T Clark, 2010.

———. *John.* ZECNT 4. Grand Rapids: Zondervan, 2016.

———. *The Sheep of the Fold: The Audience and Origin of the Gospel of John.* SNTSMS 141. Cambridge: Cambridge University Press, 2007.

Koch, Christiane. "'Es war aber an dem Ort ein Garten' (Joh 19,41): Der Garten als bedeutsames Erzählmotiv in den johanneischen Passions- und Auferstehungstexten." Pages 229–38 in *Im Geist und in der Wahrheit: Studien zum Johannesevangelium und zur Offenbarung des*

Johannes sowie andere Beiträge; Festschrift für Hasitschka zum 65. Geburtstag. Edited by Konrad Huber and Boris Repschinski. Münster: Aschendorff, 2008.

Koester, Craig R. *Symbolism in the Fourth Gospel: Meaning, Mystery, Community.* 2nd ed. Minneapolis: Fortress, 2003.

———. "Topography and Theology in the Gospel of John." Pages 436–48 in *Fortunate the Eyes That See: Essays in Honor of David Noel Freedman in Celebration of His Seventieth Birthday.* Edited by Astrid B. Beck, Andrew H. Bartelt, Paul R. Raabe, and Chris A. France. Grand Rapids: Eerdmans, 1995.

———. "What Does It Mean to Be Human? Imagery and the Human Condition in John's Gospel." Pages 403–20 in *Imagery in the Gospel of John: Terms, Forms, Themes, and Theology of Johannine Figurative Language.* Edited by Jörg Frey, Jan G. van der Watt, and Ruben Zimmermann. WUNT 200. Tübingen: Mohr Siebeck, 2006.

Kovacs, Judith L. "'Now Shall the Ruler of This World Be Driven Out': Jesus' Death as Cosmic Battle in John 12:30–36." *JBL* 114 (1995): 227–47.

Krieger, Norbert. "Fiktive Orte der Johannes-Taufe." *ZNW* 45 (1954): 121–23.

Kukkonen, Karin. "Plot." In *The Living Handbook of Narratology.* Edited by Peter Hühn, Jan Christoph Meister, John Pier, and Wolf Schmid. Hamburg: Hamburg University. http://tinyurl.com/SBL0392a.

Kundsin, Karl. *Topologische Überlieferungsstoffe im Johannes-Evangelium.* FRLANT 22. Göttingen: Vandenhoeck & Ruprecht, 1925.

Kurek-Chomycz, Dominika A. "The Fragrance of Her Perfume: The Significance of Sense Imagery in John's Account of the Anointing in Bethany." *NovT* 52 (2010): 334–54.

Kysar, Robert. "The Making of Metaphor: Another Reading of John 3:1–15." Pages 21–42 in *"What Is John?" Volume 1: Readers and Readings of the Fourth Gospel.* Edited by Fernando F. Segovia. SymS 3. Atlanta: Scholars Press, 1996.

Kysar, Robert, with Tom Thatcher. "John Is Dead; Long Live John!" Pages 137–46 in *Anatomies of Narrative Criticism: The Past, Present, and Futures of the Fourth Gospel as Literature.* Edited by Tom Thatcher and Stephen D. Moore. RBS 55. Atlanta: Society of Biblical Literature, 2008.

Labahn, Michael. "Jesus und die Autorität der Schrift im Johannesevangelium: Überlegungen zu einem spannungsreichen Verhältnis." Pages

185–206 in *Israel und seine Heilstradition im Johannesevangelium: Festgabe für Johannes Beutler SJ zum 70. Geburtstag*. Edited by Michael Labahn, Klaus Scholtissek, and Angelika Strottman. Paderborn: Schöningh, 2004.

———. "Peter's Rehabilitation (John 21:15–19) and the Adoption of Sinners: Remembering Jesus and Relecturing John." Pages 335–48 in *John, Jesus, and History, Volume 2: Aspects of Historicity in the Fourth Gospel*. Edited by Paul N. Anderson, Felix Just, and Tom Thatcher. ECL 2. Atlanta: Society of Biblical Literature, 2009.

———. "Simon Peter." Pages 151–67 in *Character Studies in the Fourth Gospel: Narrative Approaches to Seventy Figures in John*. Edited by Steven A. Hunt, D. Francois Tolmie, and Ruben Zimmermann. WUNT 314. Tübingen: Mohr Siebeck, 2013.

Labahn, Michael, and Manfred Lang. "Johannes und die Synoptiker: Positionen und Impulse seit 1990." Pages 443–516 in *Kontexte des Johannesevangeliums: Das vierte Evangelium in religions-und traditionsgeschichtlicher Perspektive*. Edited by Jörg Frey and Udo Schnelle. WUNT 175. Tübingen: Mohr Siebeck, 2004.

Lacomara, A. "Deuteronomy and the Farewell Discourse (John 13:31–16:33)." *CBQ* 36 (1974): 65–84.

Lang, Manfred. *Johannes und die Synoptiker: Eine redaktionsgeschichtliche Analyse von Joh 18–20 vor dem markinischen und lukanischen Hintergrund*. FRLANT 182. Göttingen: Vandenhoeck & Ruprecht, 1999.

Lanser, Susan Sniader. *The Narrative Act: Point of View in Prose Fiction*. Princeton: Princeton University Press, 1981.

Larsen, Kasper Bro, ed. *The Gospel of John as Genre Mosaic*. SANt 3. Göttingen: Vandenhoeck & Ruprecht, 2015.

———. "Narrative Docetism: Christology and Storytelling in the Gospel of John." Pages 346–355 in *The Gospel of John and Christian Theology*. Edited by Richard Bauckham and Carl Mosser. Grand Rapids: Eerdmans, 2008.

———. *Recognizing the Stranger: Recognition Scenes in the Gospel of John*. BibInt 93. Leiden: Brill, 2008.

Lattke, Michael. "Joh. 20:30f als Buchschluß." *ZNW* 78 (1987): 288–92.

Layton, Bentley. *The Gnostic Scriptures: A New Translation with Annotations and Introductions*. Garden City, NY: Doubleday, 1983.

Lee, Dorothy A. *Flesh and Glory: Symbol, Gender, and Theology in the Gospel of John*. New York: Crossroad, 2002.

———. "The Gospel of John and the Five Senses." *JBL* 129 (2010): 115–27.

———. "Paschal Imagery in the Gospel of John: A Narrative and Symbolic Reading." *Pacifica* 24 (2011): 13–28.

———. *The Symbolic Narratives of the Fourth Gospel: The Interplay of Form and Meaning.* JSNTSup 95. Sheffield: JSOT Press, 1994.

———. "Witness in the Fourth Gospel: John the Baptist and the Beloved Disciple as Counterparts." *ABR* 61 (2013): 1–17.

Lee, H. D. P. *Zeno of Elea.* CCS. Cambridge: Cambridge University, 1936.

Lee, Margaret Ellen, and Bernard Brandon Scott. *Sound Mapping the New Testament.* Salem, OR: Polebridge, 2009.

Leroy, Herbert. *Rätsel und Missverständnis: Ein Beitrag zur Formgeschichte des Johannesevangeliums.* BBB 30. Bonn: Hanstein, 1968.

Lessing, Gotthold Ephraim. "Laokoon oder Über die Grenzen der Malerei und Poesie [1766]." Pages 7–187 in vol. 6 of *Werke.* Munich: Hanser, 1974.

Lewis, Karoline M. *Rereading the "Shepherd Discourse": Restoring the Integrity of John 9:39–10:21.* StBibLit 113. New York: Lang: 2008.

Lieberman, Saul. *Hellenism in Jewish Palestine: Studies in the Literary Transmission, Beliefs and Manners of Palestine in the I Century B.C.E.–IV Century C.E.* TS 18. New York: Jewish Theological Seminary of America, 1962.

Lieu, Judith M. "Anti-Judaism, 'the Jews,' and the Worlds of the Fourth Gospel." Pages 168–82 in *The Gospel of John and Christian Theology.* Edited by Richard Bauckham and Carl Mosser. Grand Rapids: Eerdmans, 2008.

———. *Neither Jew Nor Greek? Constructing Early Christianity.* SNTW. Edinburgh: T&T Clark, 2003.

———. "Us or You? Persuasion and Identity in 1 John." *JBL* 127 (2008): 805–19.

Lincoln, Andrew T. *The Gospel according to Saint John.* BNTC. Peabody, MA: Hendrickson, 2005.

———. "Trials, Plots and the Narrative of the Fourth Gospel." *JSNT* 17 (1995): 3–29.

———. *Truth on Trial: The Lawsuit Motif in the Fourth Gospel.* Peabody, MA: Hendrickson, 2000.

Lindars, Barnabas. *The Gospel of John.* NCB. London: Oliphants, 1972.

Llewelyn, S. R., ed. *A Review of the Greek Inscriptions and Papyri Published in 1986–87.* Vol. 9 of *New Documents Illustrating Early Christianity.* Grand Rapids: Eerdmans, 2002.

Lloyd, M. "Euripides." Pages 341–58 in *Space in Ancient Greek Literature: Studies in Ancient Greek Narrative*. Edited by Irene J. F. de Jong. MnSup 339. Leiden: Brill, 2012.

Löschnigg, Martin. "Scene and Summary." Pages 576–77 in *Routledge Encyclopedia of Narrative Theory*. Edited by David Herman, Manfred Jahn, and Marie-Laure Ryan. New York: Routledge, 2005.

Lotman, J. M. "O semiosfere." *Sign Systems Studies* 17 (1984): 5–23.

———. "Point of View in a Text." *NLH* 6 (1975): 339–52.

———. *The Structure of the Artistic Text*. Michigan Slavic Contributions 7. Ann Arbor: University of Michigan Press, 1977.

Lowe, Malcolm. "Who Were the ΙΟΥΔΑΙΟΙ?" *NovT* 18 (1976): 101–30.

Lowenthal, David. *The Past Is a Foreign Country*. Cambridge: Cambridge University, 1985.

Lucian. Translated by K. Kilburn. 8 vols. LCL. Cambridge: Harvard University Press, 1959.

Lundhaug, Hugo. *Images of Rebirth: Cognitive Poetics and Transformational Soteriology in the* Gospel of Philip *and the* Exegesis on the Soul. NHMS 73. Leiden: Brill, 2010.

Maccini, Robert G. *Her Testimony Is True: Women as Witnesses according to John*. JSNTSup 125. Sheffield: Sheffield Academic, 1996.

MacRae, George W. "Theology and Irony in the Fourth Gospel." Pages 83–96 in *The Word in the World: Essays in Honour of Frederick L. Moriarty, S. J.* Edited by Richard J. Clifford and George W. MacRae. Cambridge, MA: Weston College Press, 1973.

Malbon, Elizabeth Struthers. "The Major Importance of Minor Characters in Mark." Pages 58–86 in *The New Literary Criticism and the New Testament*. Edited by Elizabeth Struthers Malbon and Edgar V. McKnight. JSNTSup 109. Sheffield: Sheffield Academic, 1994.

———. "Narrative Criticism: How Does the Story Mean?" Pages 1–40 in *In the Company of Jesus: Characters in Mark's Gospel*. Louisville: Westminster John Knox, 2000.

Margolin, Uri. "Person." Pages 422–23 in *Routledge Encyclopedia of Narrative Theory*. Edited by David Herman, Manfred Jahn, and Marie-Laure Ryan. London: Routledge, 2005.

———. "Telling in the Plural: From Grammar to Ideology." *Poetics Today* 21 (2000): 591–618.

Marincola, John. *Authority and Tradition in Ancient Historiography*. Cambridge: Cambridge University Press, 1997.

Maritz, Petrus, and Gilbert Van Belle. "Imagery of Eating and Drinking in John 6:35." Pages 333–52 in *Imagery in the Gospel of John: Terms, Forms, Themes, and Theology of Johannine Figurative Language.* Edited by Jörg Frey, Jan G. van der Watt, and Ruben Zimmermann. WUNT 200. Tübingen: Mohr Siebeck, 2006.

Martin, Wallace. *Recent Theories of Narrative.* Ithaca, NY: Cornell University Press, 1986.

Martínez, Matias, and Michael Scheffel. *Einführung in die Erzähltheorie.* 9th ed. Munich: Beck, 2012.

Martimort, A. G. "L'iconographie des catacombs et la catéchèse antique." *Rivista di archaeologia cristiana* 25 (1949): 105–14.

Martyn, J. Louis. *History and Theology in the Fourth Gospel.* 3rd ed. Louisville: Westminster John Knox, 2003.

McCaffrey, James M. *The House with Many Rooms: The Temple Theme in Jn. 14,2–3.* AnBib 114. Rome: Pontifical Institute, 1988.

McCane, Bryon R. *Roll Back the Stone: Death and Burial in the World of Jesus.* Harrisburg, PA: Trinity Press International, 2003.

McConnell, James R., Jr. *The Topos of Divine Testimony in Luke-Acts.* Eugene, OR: Pickwick, 2014.

Meeks, Wayne A. "Galilee and Judea in the Fourth Gospel." *JBL* 85 (1966): 159–69.

———. "The Man from Heaven in Johannine Sectarianism." *JBL* 91 (1972): 44–72.

Meier, John P. *Mentor, Message, and Miracles.* Vol. 2 of *A Marginal Jew: Rethinking the Historical Jesus.* ABRL. New York: Doubleday, 1994.

Menken, Maarten J. J. *Old Testament Quotations in the Fourth Gospel: Studies in Textual Form.* CBET 15. Kampen: Kok Pharos, 1996.

Metzger, Bruce M. *The Canon of the New Testament: Its Origin, Development, and Significance.* Oxford: Clarendon, 1987.

———. *A Textual Commentary on the Greek New Testament: A Companion Volume to the United Bible Societies' Greek New Testament.* 3rd ed. London: United Bible Societies, 1971.

Mlakhuzhyil, George. *The Christocentric Literary Structure of the Fourth Gospel.* 2nd ed. AnBib 117. Rome: Gregorian & Biblical, 2011.

Moloney, Francis J. *Belief in the Word: Reading John 1–4.* Minneapolis: Fortress, 1993.

———. "'For As Yet They Did Not Know the Scripture' (John 20:9): A Study in Narrative Time." *ITQ* 79 (2014): 97–111.

————. *Glory Not Dishonor: Reading John 13–21*. Minneapolis: Fortress, 1998.

————. *The Gospel of John*. SP 4. Collegeville, MN: Liturgical Press, 1998.

————. "The Gospel of John as Scripture." *CBQ* 67 (2005): 454–68.

————. "The Gospel of John: A Story of Two Paracletes." Pages 241–59 in *The Gospel of John: Text and Context*. Edited by Francis J. Moloney. BibInt 72. Leiden: Brill, 2005.

————. *The Gospel of John: Text and Context*. BibInt 72. Leiden: Brill, 2005.

————. *The Gospel of Mark: A Commentary*. Grand Rapids: Baker Academic, 2012.

————. "John 21 and the Johannine Story." Pages 237–51 in *Anatomies of Narrative Criticism: The Past, Present, and Futures of the Fourth Gospel as Literature*. Edited by Tom Thatcher and Stephen D. Moore. RBS 55. Atlanta: Society of Biblical Literature, 2008.

————. *Love in the Gospel of John: An Exegetical, Theological, and Literary Study*. Grand Rapids: Baker Academic, 2013.

————. *The Resurrection of the Messiah: A Narrative Commentary on the Resurrection Accounts of the Fourth Gospel*. New York: Paulist, 2013.

————. *Signs and Shadows: Reading John 5–12*. Minneapolis: Fortress, 1996.

————. "When Is John Talking about Sacraments?" *ABR* 30 (1982): 10–33.

Moore, Stephen D. *Literary Criticism and the Gospels: The Theoretical Challenge*. New Haven: Yale University Press, 1989.

Morgan-Wynne, John. *The Cross in the Johannine Writings*. Eugene, OR: Pickwick, 2011.

Motyer, Stephen. *Your Father the Devil? A New Approach to John and "the Jews."* PBTM. Carlisle: Paternoster, 1997.

Moule, C. F. D. "The Intention of the Evangelists." Pages 100–114 in *The Phenomenon of the New Testament: An Inquiry into the Implications of Certain Features of the New Testament*. SBT 2/1. London: SCM, 1967.

Musurillo, Herbert. *The Acts of the Christian Martyrs: Introduction, Texts, and Translations*. Oxford: Oxford University Press, 1972.

Myers, Alicia D. *Characterizing Jesus: A Rhetorical Analysis on the Fourth Gospel's Use of Scripture in Its Presentation of Jesus*. LNTS 458. London: T&T Clark, 2012.

————. "'In the Father's Bosom': Breastfeeding and Identity Formation in John's Gospel." *CBQ* 76 (2014): 481–97.

————. "'Jesus Said to Them': The Adaptation of Juridical Rhetoric in John 5:19–47." *JBL* 132 (2013): 415–30.

Nagel, Titus. *Die Rezeption des Johannesevangeliums im 2. Jahrhundert: Studien zu vorirenäischen Auslegung des vierten Evangeliums in christlicher und christlich gnostischer Literatur.* ABG 2. Leipzig: Evangelische Verlagsanstalt, 2000.

Najman, Hindy. "The Idea of Biblical Genre: From Discourse to Constellation." Pages 307–22 in *Prayer and Poetry in the Dead Sea Scrolls and Related Literature: Essays in Honor of Eileen Schuller on the Occasion of Her 65th Birthday.* Edited by Jeremy Penner, Ken M. Penner, and Cecilia Wassen. STDJ 98. Leiden: Brill, 2012.

Nässelqvist, Dan. *Public Reading in Early Christianity: Lectors, Manuscripts, and Sound in the Oral Delivery of John 1–4.* NovTSup 163. Leiden: Brill, 2016.

Nelles, William. *Frameworks: Narrative Levels and Embedded Narrative.* AUS 19/33. New York: Lang, 1997.

Newsom, Carol. "Pairing Research Questions and Theories of Genre: A Case Study of the Hodayot." *DSD* 17 (2010): 270–88.

———. "Spying Out the Land: A Report from Genology." Pages 437–50 in *Seeking Out the Wisdom of the Ancients: Essays Offered to Honor Michael V. Fox on the Occasion of His Sixty-Fifth Birthday.* Edited by Ronald L. Troxel, Kelvin G. Friebel, and Dennis R. Margy. Winona Lake, IN: Eisenbrauns, 2005.

Neyrey, Jerome H. *The Gospel of John in Cultural and Rhetorical Perspective.* Grand Rapids: Eerdmans, 2009.

———. "'In Conclusion…': John 12 as Rhetorical *Peroratio.*" *BTB* 37 (2007): 101–13.

———. "Spaces and Places, Whence and Whither, Homes and Rooms: 'Territoriality' in the Fourth Gospel." *BTB* 32 (2002): 60–74.

Nicolai, Roberto. *La storiografia nell' educazione antica.* Biblioteca di materiali e discussioni per l'analisi dei testi classici 10. Pisa: Giardini, 1992.

Nielsen, Jesper Tang. "The Narrative Structures of Glory and Glorification in the Fourth Gospel." *NTS* 56 (2010): 343–66.

Nünlist, René. "Some Ancient Views on Narrative, Its Structure and Working." Pages 156–74 in *Defining Greek Narrative.* Edited by Douglas Cairns and Ruth Scodel. ELS 7. Edinburgh: Edinburgh University Press, 2014.

Obermann, Andreas. *Die christologische Erfüllung der Schrift im Johannesevangelium: Eine Untersuchung zur johanneischen Hermeneutik anhand der Schriftzitate.* WUNT 2/83. Tübingen: Mohr Siebeck, 1996.

O'Day, Gail R. "John." Pages 381–93 in *The Women's Bible Commentary*. Edited by Carol A. Newsom and Sharon H. Ringe. Expanded ed. Louisville: Westminster John Knox, 1998.

———. *Revelation in the Fourth Gospel: Narrative Mode and Theological Claim*. Philadelphia: Fortress, 1986.

Okure, Teresa. *The Johannine Approach to Mission: A Contextual Study of John 4:1–42*. WUNT 2/31. Tübingen: Mohr Siebeck, 1988.

Oliver, Charles M. *Ernest Hemingway A to Z: The Essential Reference to the Life and Work*. New York: Checkmark, 1999.

O'Rourke, John J. "Asides in the Gospel of John." *NovT* 31 (1979): 210–19.

Painter, John. "The Earth Made Whole: John's Rereading of Genesis." Pages 65–84 in *Word, Theology, and Community in John*. Edited by John Painter, R. Alan Culpepper, and Fernando F. Segovia. St. Louis: Chalice, 2002.

Parsenios, George L. *Departure and Consolation: The Johannine Farewell Discourses in Light of Greco-Roman Literature*. NovTSup 117. Leiden: Brill, 2005.

———. *Rhetoric and Drama in the Johannine Lawsuit Motif*. WUNT 258. Tübingen: Mohr Siebeck, 2010.

Parsons, Mikeal C. *Body and Character in Luke and Acts: The Subversion of Physiognomy in Early Christianity*. 2nd ed. Waco, TX: Baylor University Press, 2011.

Parsons, Mikeal, and Richard I. Pervo. *Rethinking the Unity of Luke and Acts*. Minneapolis: Fortress, 1993.

Pastorelli, David. *Le Paraclet dans le corpus johannique*. BZNW 142. Berlin: de Gruyter, 2006.

Perelman, Chaim, and Lucie Olbrechts-Tytecha. *The New Rhetoric: A Treatise on Argumentation*. Translated by John Wilkinson and Purcell Weaver. Notre Dame, IN: University of Notre Dame Press, 1969.

Perkins, Pheme. *Gnosticism and the New Testament*. Minneapolis: Fortress, 1993.

Pervo, Richard I. *Acts*. Hermeneia. Minneapolis: Fortress, 2009.

———. *Profit with Delight: The Literary Genre of the Acts of the Apostles*. Philadelphia: Fortress, 1987.

Petersen, Silke. "Ich-bin-Worte als Metaphern." Pages 121–38 in *Imagery in the Gospel of John: Terms, Forms, Themes, and Theology of Johannine Figurative Language*. Edited by Jörg Frey, Jan G. van der Watt, and Ruben Zimmermann. WUNT 200. Tübingen: Mohr Siebeck, 2006.

Phelan, James. *Experiencing Fiction: Judgments, Progressions, and the Rhetorical Theory of Narrative.* Columbus: Ohio State University Press, 2007.

———. *Living to Tell about It: A Rhetoric and Ethics of Character Narration.* Ithaca, NY: Cornell University Press, 2005.

———. "Rhetoric/Ethics." Pages 203–16 in *The Cambridge Companion to Narrative.* Edited by David Herman. Cambridge: Cambridge University Press, 2007.

Piatti, Barbara, and Lorenz Hurni. "Mapping the Ontologically Unreal: Counterfactual Spaces in Literature and Cartography." *The Cartographic Journal* 46 (2009): 333–42.

Plato. *Republic.* Edited and translated by Chris Emlyn-Jones and William Preddy. 2 vols. LCL. Cambridge: Harvard University Press, 2013.

Playhoust, Catherine A. "Lifted Up from the Earth: The Ascent of Jesus and the Heavenly Ascent of Christians." PhD diss., Harvard University, 2006.

Plutarch. *Lives.* Translated by Bernadotte Perrin. 11 vols. LCL. Cambridge: Harvard University Press, 1967–75.

Polybius. *The Histories.* Translated by W. R. Paton. 6 vols. LCL. London: Heinemann; Cambridge: Harvard University Press, 1922.

Popkes, Enno Ezard. "Exkurs: Die sukzessive Entfaltung des Prädestinationsgedankens im Erzählverlauf des Johannesevangeliums." Pages 204–11 in *Die Theologie der Liebe Gottes in den johanneischen Schriften: Zur Semantik der Liebe und zum Motivkreis des Dualismus.* WUNT 2/197. Tübingen: Mohr Siebeck, 2005.

Poplutz, Uta. "Das Drama der Passion: Eine Analyse der Prozesserzählung Joh 18,28–19,16a unter Berücksichtigung dramentheorethischer Gesichtspunkte." Pages 769–82 in *The Death of Jesus in the Fourth Gospel.* Edited by Gilbert Van Belle. BETL 200. Leuven: Leuven University Press, 2007.

———. "Paroimia und Parabolē." Pages 103–20 in *Imagery in the Gospel of John: Terms, Forms, Themes, and Theology of Johannine Figurative Language.* Edited by Jörg Frey, Jan G. van der Watt, and Ruben Zimmermann. WUNT 200. Tübingen: Mohr Siebeck, 2006.

Popp, Thomas. "Thomas." Pages 504–29 in *Character Studies in the Fourth Gospel: Narrative Approaches to Seventy Figures in John.* Edited by Steven A. Hunt, D. Francois Tolmie, and Ruben Zimmermann. WUNT 314. Tübingen: Mohr Siebeck, 2013.

Porter, Stanley E. "Study of John's Gospel: New Directions or the Same Old Paths?" Pages 277–306 in *Linguistic Analysis of the Greek New Testament: Studies in Tools, Methods, and Practice.* Grand Rapids: Baker Academic, 2015.

Pöttner, Martin. "'Im Haus meines Vaters gibt es viele Aufenthaltsorte...': Erwägungen zur räumlichen Symbolik des johanneischen Sprechens in Joh 13,33–14,7." *MARG* 14 (1999): 141–50.

Powell, Mark Allan. "Characterization on the Phraseological Plane in the Gospel of Matthew." Pages 161–77 in *Treasures New and Old: Recent Contributions to Matthean Studies.* Edited by David R. Bauer and Mark A. Powell. Atlanta: Scholars Press, 1996.

———. *Chasing the Eastern Star: Adventures in Biblical Reader-Response Criticism.* Louisville: Westminster John Knox, 2001.

———. *What Is Narrative Criticism?* GBS. Minneapolis: Fortress, 1990.

Prince, Gerald. *Narratology: The Form and Functioning of Narrative.* Berlin: Mouton, 1982.

Procopius. *History of the Wars.* Translated by H. B. Dewing. 5 vols. LCL. Cambridge: Harvard University Press, 1914–1928.

Purves, Alex C. *Space and Time in Ancient Greek Narrative.* Cambridge: Cambridge University Press, 2010.

Quintilian. *The Orator's Education.* Edited and translated by Donald A. Russell. 5 vols. LCL. Cambridge: Harvard University Press, 2001.

Rabinowitz, Peter J. "Truth in Fiction: A Reexamination of Audiences." *CI* 4 (1977): 121–41.

Rahner, Johanna. *"Er aber sprach vom Tempel seines Leibes": Jesus von Nazareth als Ort der Offenbarung Gottes im vierten Evangelium.* BBB 117. Bodenheim: Philo, 1998.

Rand, Jan A. du. "Plot and Point of View in the Gospel of John." Pages 149–69 in *A South African Perspective on the New Testament: Essays by South African New Testament Scholars Presented to Bruce Manning Metzger during His Visit to South Africa in 1985.* Edited by J. H. Petzer and P. J. Hartin. Leiden: Brill, 1986.

Rehm, R. "Aeschylus." Pages in 307–24 in *Space in Ancient Greek Literature: Studies in Ancient Greek Narrative.* Edited by Irene J. F. de Jong. MnSup 339. Leiden: Brill, 2012.

———. "Sophocles. Pages 325–40 in *Space in Ancient Greek Literature: Studies in Ancient Greek Narrative.* Edited by Irene J. F. de Jong. MnSup 339. Leiden: Brill, 2012.

Reinhartz, Adele. "Anonymity and Character in the Books of Samuel." *Semeia* 63 (1993): 117–41.

———. *Befriending the Beloved Disciple: A Jewish Reading of the Gospel of John*. New York: Continuum, 2001.

———. "'Jews' and Jews in the Fourth Gospel." Pages 213–30 in *Anti-Judaism and the Fourth Gospel*. Edited by Reimund Bieringer, Didier Pollefeyt, and Frederique Vandecasteele-Vanneuville. Louisville: Westminster John Knox, 2001.

———. *"Why Ask My Name?": Anonymity and Identity in Biblical Narrative*. New York: Oxford University Press, 1998.

———. *The Word in the World: The Cosmological Tale in the Fourth Gospel*. SBLMS 45. Atlanta: Scholars Press, 1992.

Resseguie, James L. "The Beloved Disciple: The Ideal Point of View." Pages 537–49 in *Character Studies in the Fourth Gospel: Narrative Approaches to Seventy Figures in John*. Edited by Steven A. Hunt, D. Francois Tolmie, and Ruben Zimmermann. WUNT 314. Tübingen: Mohr Siebeck, 2013.

———. "Defamiliarization and the Gospels." *BTB* 20 (1990): 147–53.

———. *Narrative Criticism of the New Testament: An Introduction*. Grand Rapids: Baker Academic, 2005.

———. *The Strange Gospel: Narrative Design and Point of View in John*. BibInt 56. Leiden: Brill, 2001.

———. "The Woman Who Crashed Simon's Party: A Reader-Response Approach to Luke 7:36-50." Pages 7–22 in *Characters and Characterization in Luke-Acts*. Edited by Frank E. Dicken and Julia A. Snyder. LNTS 548. New York: Bloomsbury T&T Clark, 2016.

Rhoads, David. "Performance Criticism: An Emerging Methodology in Second Testament Studies, Part I." *BTB* 36 (2006): 1–16.

Rhoads, David, Joanna Dewey, and Donald Michie. *Mark as Story: An Introduction to the Narrative of a Gospel*. 3rd ed. Minneapolis: Fortress, 2012.

Richards, E. Randolph. "An Honor/Shame Argument for Two Temple Clearings." *TrinJ* 29 (2008): 19–43.

Richards, I. A. *The Philosophy of Rhetoric*. New York: Oxford University Press, 1936.

Richards, Jennifer. *Rhetoric*. London: Routledge, 2008.

Richardson, Brian. "General Introduction." Pages 1–7 in *Narrative Dynamics: Essays on Time, Plot, Closure, and Frames*. Edited by Brian Richardson. Columbus: Ohio State University Press, 2002.

———. "Singular Text, Multiple Implied Readers." *Style* 41 (2007): 259–74.

Richet, Pascal. *A Natural History of Time.* Translated by John Venerella. Chicago: University of Chicago Press, 2007.

Richter, David H. *Fable's End: Completeness and Closure in Rhetorical Fiction.* Chicago: University of Chicago Press, 1974.

Ricoeur, Paul. "Narrative Time." Pages 165–86 in *On Narrative.* Edited by W. J. T. Mitchell. Chicago: University of Chicago Press, 1981.

———. *The Rule of Metaphor: Multi-disciplinary Studies of the Creation of Meaning in Language.* Translated by Robert Czerny with Kathleen McLaughlin and John Costello, S. J. London: Routledge & Kegan Paul, 1977.

———. *Time and Narrative.* Translated by Kathleen McLaughlin and David Pellauer. 3 vols. Chicago: University of Chicago Press, 1984–1988.

Rimmon-Kenan, Shlomith. *Narrative Fiction: Contemporary Poetics.* 2nd ed. London: Routledge, 2002.

Roberts, Adam. *Get Started In: Writing Science Fiction and Fantasy.* London: Teach Yourself, 2014.

Rochais, Gérard. "Jean 7: Une construction littéraire dramatique, à la manière d'un scénario." *NTS* 39 (1993): 355–78.

Rodden, John. "How Do Stories Convince Us? Notes towards a Rhetoric of Narrative." *College Literature* 35 (2008): 148–73.

Ronen, Ruth. "Space in Fiction." *Poetics Today* 7 (1986): 421–38.

Rood, Tim. "Herodotus." Pages 121–40 in *Space in Ancient Greek Literature: Studies in Ancient Greek Narrative.* Edited by Irene J. F. de Jong. MnSup 339. Leiden: Brill, 2012.

———. "Polybius." Pages 179–97 in in *Space in Ancient Greek Literature: Studies in Ancient Greek Narrative.* Edited by Irene J. F. de Jong. MnSup 339. Leiden: Brill, 2012.

———. "Thucydides." Pages 141–59 in *Space in Ancient Greek Literature: Studies in Ancient Greek Narrative.* Edited by Irene J. F. de Jong. MnSup 339. Leiden: Brill, 2012.

———. "Xenophon." Pages 161–78 in *Space in Ancient Greek Literature: Studies in Ancient Greek Narrative.* Edited by Irene J. F. de Jong. MnSup 339. Leiden: Brill, 2012.

Rosenberg, Daniel, and Anthony Grafton. *Cartographies of Time: A History of the Timeline.* New York: Princeton Architectural Press, 2010.

Rosmarin, Adena. *The Power of Genre.* Minneapolis: University of Minnesota Press, 1985.

Rushton, Kathleen P. *The Parable of the Woman in Childbirth of John 16:21: A Metaphor for the Death and Glorification of Jesus*. Lewiston, NY: Mellen, 2010.

Russell, D. A. *Criticism in Antiquity*. London: Duckworth, 1981.

Rutherford, Ian. *Canons of Style in the Antonine Age: Idea-Theory in Its Literary Context*. Oxford: Clarendon, 1998.

Ryan, Marie-Laure. "Space." Pages 796–811 in vol. 2 of *Handbook of Narratology*. Edited by Peter Hühn, Jan Christoph Meister, John Pier, Wolf Schmid. 2nd expanded ed. 2 vols. Berlin: de Gruyter, 2014.

Sasse, Sylvia. "Poetischer Raum: Chronotopos und Geopoetik." Pages 294–308 in *Raum: Ein interdisziplinäres Handbuch*. Edited by Stephan Günzel. Stuttgart: Metzler, 2010.

Satlow, Michael L. " 'Try to Be a Man': The Rabbinic Construction of Masculinity." *HTR* 89 (1996): 19–40.

Saussure, Ferdinand de. *Course in General Linguistics*. Edited by Charles Bally and Albert Sechehaye with Albert Reidlinger. Translated by Wade Baskin. New York: McGraw-Hill, 1966.

Schelfer, Lochlan. "The Legal Precision of the Term 'παράκλητος.'" *JSNT* 32 (2009): 131–50.

Schenke, Gesa. "Das Erscheinen Jesu vor den Jüngern und der ungläubige Thomas: Johannes 20,19–31." Pages 893–904 in *Coptica—Gnostica—Manichaica: Mélanges offerts à Wolf-Peter Funk*. Edited by Louis Painchaud and Paul-Hubert Poirier. BCNHSE 7. Québec: University of Laval Press; Leuven: Peeters, 2006.

Schenke, Ludger. *Johannes: Kommentar*. Düsseldorf: Patmos, 1998.

Schneiders, Sandra M. *Written That You May Believe: Encountering Jesus in the Fourth Gospel*. New York: Crossroad, 1999.

Schnelle, Udo. "Das frühe Christentum und die Bildung." *NTS* 61 (2015): 113–43.

———. "Die Reihenfolge der johanneischen Schriften." *NTS* 57 (2013): 114–44.

Scholes, Robert. *Elements of Fiction*. New York: Oxford University Press, 1968.

Scholes, Robert, James Phelan, and Robert Kellogg. *The Nature of Narrative, Fortieth Anniversary Edition*. Rev. and expanded ed. New York: Oxford University Press, 2006.

Scholtissek, Klaus. " 'Geschrieben in diesem Buch' (Joh 20,30): Beobachtungen zum kanonischen Anspruch des Johannesevangeliums." Pages 207–26 in *Israel und seine Heilstradition im Johannesevangelium:*

Festgabe für Johannes Beutler SJ zum 70. Geburtstag. Edited Michael Labahn, Klaus Scholtissek, and Angelika Strottman. Paderborn: Schöningh, 2004.

Schuchard, Bruce G. *Scripture within Scripture: The Interrelationship of Form and Function in the Explicit Old Testament Citations in the Gospel of John.* SBLDS 133. Atlanta: Scholars Press, 1992.

Scobie, Charles H. "Johannine Geography." *SR* 11 (1982): 77–84.

Segovia, Fernando F. *The Farewell of the Word: The Johannine Call to Abide.* Minneapolis: Fortress, 1991.

———. "The Journey(s) of the Word of God: A Reading of the Plot of the Fourth Gospel." *Semeia* 53 (1991): 23–54.

Sellew, Philip. "Interior Monologue as a Narrative Device in the Parables of Luke." *JBL* 111 (1992): 239–53.

Sheridan, Ruth. "The Gospel of John and Modern Genre Theory: The Farewell Discourse (John 13–17) as a Test Case." *ITQ* 75 (2010): 287–99.

———. "Identity and Alterity in the Gospel of John." *BibInt* 22 (2014): 188–209.

———. *Retelling Scripture: "The Jews" and the Scriptural Citations in John 1:19–12:15.* BibInt 110. Leiden: Brill, 2012.

———. "The Testimony of Two Witnesses: John 8:17." Pages 161–84 in *Abiding Words: The Use of Scripture in the Gospel of John.* Edited by Alicia D. Myers and Bruce G. Schuchard. RBS 81. Atlanta: SBL Press, 2015.

Shklovsky, Viktor. "Art as Technique." Pages 3–24 in *Russian Formalist Criticism: Four Essays.* Edited by Lee T. Lemon and Marion J. Reis. Lincoln: University of Nebraska, 1965.

Siegert, Volker. *Das Evangelium des Johannes in seiner ursprünglichen Gestalt: Wiederherstellung und Kommentar.* SIJD 7. Göttingen: Vandenhoeck & Ruprecht, 2008.

Simplicius. *Corollaries on Place and Time.* Translated by J. O. Urmson. Ithaca, NY: Cornell University, 1992.

Skinner, Christopher W., ed. *Characters and Characterization in the Gospel of John.* LNTS 461. London: T&T Clark, 2013.

———. "Characters and Characterization in the Gospel of John: Reflections on the *Status Quaestionis.*" Pages xvii–xxxii in *Characters and Characterization in the Gospel of John.* Edited by Christopher W. Skinner. LNTS 461. London: T&T Clark, 2013.

———. *John and Thomas: Gospels in Conflict? Johannine Characterization and the Thomas Question.* PTMS 115. Eugene, OR: Wipf & Stock, 2009.

———. "Misunderstanding, Christology, and Johannine Characterization: Reading John's Characters through the Lens of the Prologue." Pages 111–27 in *Characters and Characterization in the Gospel of John.* Edited by Christopher W. Skinner. LNTS 461. London: T&T Clark, 2013.

———. *Reading John.* Cascade Companions. Eugene, OR: Cascade, 2015.

———. "'Son of God' or 'God's Chosen One'? (John 1:34): A Narrative-Critical Solution to a Text-Critical Problem." *BBR* 25 (2015): 341–58.

Smith, Barbara Herrnstein. *Poetic Closure: A Study of How Poems End.* Chicago: University of Chicago Press, 1968.

Smith, Craig A. "The Development of Style (Fifth Century BCE to Second Century CE) and the Consequences for Understanding the Style of the New Testament." *JGRChJ* 7 (2010): 9–31.

Smith, D. Moody. *John among the Gospels: The Relationship in Twentieth-Century Research.* Minneapolis: Fortress, 1992.

———. "When Did the Gospels Become Scripture?" *JBL* 119 (2000): 3–20.

Soja, Edward W. *Postmodern Geographies: The Reassertion of Space in Critical Social Theory.* New York: Verso, 1989.

Soskice, Janet Martin. *Metaphor and Religious Language.* Oxford University Press, 1987.

Staley, Jeffrey Lloyd. *The Print's First Kiss: A Rhetorical Investigation of the Implied Reader in the Fourth Gospel.* SBLDS 82. Atlanta: Scholars Press, 1988.

———. "Resurrection Dysfunction, or One Hundred Years of Cinematic Attempts at Raising a Stiff (John 11:1–46)." Pages 195–220 in *Anatomies of Narrative Criticism: The Past, Present, and Futures of the Fourth Gospel as Literature.* Edited by Tom Thatcher and Stephen D. Moore. RBS 55. Atlanta: Society of Biblical Literature, 2008.

Stamps, Dennis L. "Use of the Old Testament in the New Testament as a Rhetorical Device: A Methodological Proposal." Pages 9–37 in *Hearing the Old Testament in the New Testament.* Edited by Stanley E. Porter. Grand Rapids: Eerdmans, 2006.

Stein, Sol. *Solutions for Writers: Practical Craft Techniques for Fiction and Non-fiction.* London: Souvenir, 1998.

Stern, Sacha. *Calendars in Antiquity: Empires, States, and Societies.* Oxford: Oxford University Press, 2012.

Sternberg, Meir. *The Poetics of Biblical Narrative: Ideological Literature and the Drama of Reading.* Bloomington: Indiana University Press, 1985.

Stibbe, Mark W. G. "The Elusive Christ: A New Reading of the Fourth Gospel." *JSNT* 44 (1991): 20–38.

———. *The Gospel of John as Literature: An Anthology of Twentieth-Century Perspectives*. NTTS 17. Leiden: Brill, 1993.

———. "Hero." Pages 5–31 in *John's Gospel*. New Testament Readings. London: Routledge, 1994.

———. *John*. Readings: A New Biblical Commentary. Sheffield: JSOT Press, 1993.

———. *John as Storyteller: Narrative Criticism and the Fourth Gospel*. SNTSMS 73. Cambridge: Cambridge University Press, 1992.

———. *John's Gospel*. New Testament Readings. London: Routledge, 1994.

———. "Magnificent but Flawed: The Breaking of Form in the Fourth Gospel." Pages 149–66 in *Anatomies of Narrative Criticism: The Past, Present, and Futures of the Fourth Gospel as Literature*. Edited by Tom Thatcher and Stephen D. Moore. RBS 55. Atlanta: Society of Biblical Literature, 2008.

———. "'Return to Sender': A Structuralist Approach to John's Gospel." *BibInt* 1 (1993): 189–206.

Stoltzfus, Ben. "The Stones of Venice, Time and Remembrance: Calculus and Proust in *Across the River and into the Trees*." *The Hemingway Review* 22 (2003): 19–29.

Stroumsa, Guy G. *Hidden Wisdom: Esoteric Traditions and the Roots of Christian Mysticism*. 2nd ed. SHR 70. Leiden: Brill, 2005.

Tacitus, Cornelius. *Annals*. 3 vols. Translated by John Jackson. LCL. Cambridge: Harvard University Press, 1931–1937.

———. *Histories*. 2 vols. Translated by Clifford H. Moore. LCL. Cambridge: Harvard University Press, 1925–1931.

Talbert, Charles H. *Reading John: A Literary and Theological Commentary on the Fourth Gospel and the Johannine Epistles*. Rev. ed. Macon, GA: Smyth & Helwys, 2005.

Tannehill, Robert. "The Disciples in Mark: The Function of a Narrative Role." *JR* 57 (1977): 386–405.

Taschl-Erber, Andrea. "Erkenntnisschritte und Glaubenswege in Joh 20,1–11: Die narrative Metaphorik des Raumes." *Protokolle zur Bibel* 15 (2006): 93–117.

Taylor, George H. "Ricoeur's Philosophy of Imagination." *Journal of French Philosophy* 16 (2006): 93–104.

Temmerman, Koen de. "Chariton." Pages 483–502 in *Space in Ancient Greek Literature: Studies in Ancient Greek Narrative*. Edited by Irene J. F. de Jong. MnSup 339. Leiden: Brill, 2012.

Thatcher, Tom. "Anatomies of the Fourth Gospel: Past, Present, and Future Probes." Pages 1–35 in *Anatomies of Narrative Criticism: The Past, Present, and Futures of the Fourth Gospel as Literature*. Edited by Tom Thatcher and Stephen D. Moore. RBS 55. Atlanta: Society of Biblical Literature, 2008.

———. *Greater Than Caesar: Christology and Empire in the Fourth Gospel*. Minneapolis: Fortress, 2009.

———. *The Riddles of Jesus in John: A Study in Tradition and Folklore*. SBLMS 53. Atlanta: Scholars Press, 2000.

———. "Riddles, Repetitions, and the Literary Unity of the Johannine Discourses." Pages 357–77 in *Repetitions and Variations in the Fourth Gospel: Style, Text, Interpretation*. Edited by Gilbert Van Belle, Michael Labahn, and Petrus Maritz. BETL 223. Leuven: Peeters, 2009.

Thatcher, Tom, and Stephen D. Moore, eds. *Anatomies of Narrative Criticism: The Past, Present, and Futures of the Fourth Gospel as Literature*. RBS 55. Atlanta: Society of Biblical Literature, 2008.

Thompson, Marianne Meye. "'Every Picture Tells a Story': Imagery for God in the Gospel of John." Pages 259–77 in *Imagery in the Gospel of John: Terms, Forms, Themes, and Theology of Johannine Figurative Language*. Edited by Jörg Frey, Jan G. van der Watt, and Ruben Zimmermann. WUNT 200. Tübingen: Mohr Siebeck, 2006.

Thucydides. *History of the Peloponnesian War*. 4 vols. Translated by C. F. Smith. LCL. Cambridge: Harvard University Press, 1919–1923.

Thyen, Hartwig. "Johannes und die Synoptiker: Auf der Suche nach einem neuen Paradigma zur Beschreibung ihrer Beziehungen anhand von Beobachtungen an Passions-und Ostererzählungen." Pages 81–108 in *John and the Synoptics*. Edited by Adelbert Denaux. BETL 101. Leuven: Leuven University Press, 1992.

———. *Das Johannesevangelium*. HNT 6. Tübingen: Mohr Siebeck, 2005.

Tilborg, Sjef van. *Imaginative Love in John*. BibInt 2. Leiden: Brill, 1993.

Tolmie, D. Francois. *Jesus' Farewell to the Disciples: John 13:1–17:26 in Narratological Perspective*. BibInt 12. Leiden: Brill, 1995.

———. "The (Not So) Good Shepherd: The Use of Shepherd Imagery in the Characterisation of Peter in the Fourth Gospel." Pages 352–67 in *Imagery in the Gospel of John: Terms, Forms, Themes and Theology of Johannine Figurative Language*. Edited by Jörg Frey, Jan G. van der

Watt, and Ruben Zimmermann. WUNT 200. Tübingen: Mohr Siebeck, 2006.

Todorov, Tzvetan. *Introduction to Poetics*. Translated by Richard Howard. Sussex: Harvester, 1981.

———. "The Origin of Genres." *NLH* 8 (1976): 159–70.

Unnik, W. C. van. "The Quotation from the Old Testament in John 12:34." *NovT* 3 (1959): 174–79.

Uspensky, Boris. *A Poetics of Composition: The Structure of the Artistic Text and Typology of a Compositional Form*. Translated by Valentina Zavarin and Susan Wittig. Berkeley: University of California Press, 1973.

Utell, Janine. *Engagements with Narrative*. REL. London: Routledge, 2016.

Van Belle, Gilbert. *The Signs Source in the Fourth Gospel: Historical Survey and Critical Evaluation of the Semeia Hypothesis*. BETL 116. Leuven: Peeters, 1994.

———. "Style Criticism and the Fourth Gospel." Pages 291–316 in *One Text, A Thousand Methods: Studies in Memory of Sjef van Tilborg*. Edited by Patrick Chatelion Counet and Ulrich Berges. BibInt 71. Leiden: Brill, 2005.

Van Seters, John. *The Life of Moses: The Yahwist as Historian in Exodus-Numbers*. Louisville: Westminster John Knox, 1994.

Vanhoozer, Kevin J. *Is There a Meaning in this Text? The Bible, the Reader, and the Morality of Literary Knowledge*. Grand Rapids: Zondervan, 1998.

Vines, Michael E. *The Problem of Markan Genre: The Gospel of Mark and the Jewish Novel*. AcBib 3. Leiden: Brill, 2002.

Voorwinde, Stephen. *Jesus' Emotions in the Fourth Gospel: Human or Divine?* LNTS 284. London: T&T Clark, 2005.

Vorster, William S. "The Growth and Making of John 21." Pages 2207–21 in *The Four Gospels 1992: Festschrift Frans Neirynck*. Edited by Frans van Segbroek, Christopher M. Tuckett, Gilbert Van Belle, and Jos Verheyden. 3 vols. BETL 100. Leuven: Leuven University Press, 1992.

Wahlde, Urban C. von. "Archaeology and John's Gospel." Pages 523–86 in *Jesus and Archaeology*. Edited by James H. Charlesworth. Grand Rapids: Eerdmans, 2006.

———. *The Earliest Version of John's Gospel: Recovering the Gospel of Signs*. Wilmington, DE: Glazier, 1989.

———. "'The Jews' in the Gospel of John: Fifteen Years of Research (1983–1998)." *ETL* 76 (2000): 30–55.

Watt, Jan G. van der. *Family of the King: Dynamics of Metaphor in the Gospel according to John.* BibInt 47. Leiden: Brill, 2000.

Watts, James W. *Ritual and Rhetoric in Leviticus: From Sacrifice to Scripture.* Cambridge: Cambridge University Press, 2007.

Watty, William. "The Significance of Anonymity in the Fourth Gospel." *ExpTim* 90 (1979): 209–12.

Webb, Ruth. "The *Progymnasmata* in Practice." Pages 289–316 in *Education in Greek and Roman Antiquity.* Edited by Yun Lee Too. Leiden: Brill, 2001.

Wheaton, Gerry. *The Role of Jewish Feasts in John's Gospel.* SNTSMS 162. Cambridge: Cambridge University Press, 2015.

White, Hayden. *The Content of the Form: Narrative Discourse and Historical Representation.* Baltimore: Johns Hopkins University Press, 1987.

Whybray, R. N. *The Making of the Pentateuch: A Methodological Study.* JSOTSup 53. Sheffield: Sheffield Academic, 1987.

Wilcox, Donald J. *The Measure of Times Past: Pre-Newtonian Chronologies and the Rhetoric of Relative Time.* Chicago: University of Chicago Press, 1987.

Williams, Joel F. *Other Followers of Jesus: Minor Characters as Major Figures in Mark's Gospel.* JSNTSup 102. Sheffield: Sheffield Academic, 1994.

Williams, Rowan. *The Edge of Words: God and the Habit of Language.* London: Bloomsbury, 2014.

Williamson, Robert, Jr. "Pesher: A Cognitive Model of the Genre." *DSD* 17 (2010): 336–60.

Wilson, Brittany E. *Unmanly Men: Refigurations of Masculinity in Luke-Acts.* Oxford: Oxford University Press, 2015.

Wilson, Stephen G. *Related Strangers: Jews and Christians, 70–170 CE.* Minneapolis: Fortress, 1995.

Witherington, Ben, III. *John's Wisdom: A Commentary on the Fourth Gospel.* Louisville: Westminster John Knox, 1995.

Wittgenstein, Ludwig. *Preliminary Studies for the "Philosophical Investigations": Generally Known as the Blue and Brown Books.* 2nd ed. Oxford: Basil Blackwell, 1969.

Wright, Benjamin. "Joining the Club: A Suggestion about Genre in Jewish Texts." *DSD* 17 (2010): 288–313.

Wright, William M., IV. "Greco-Roman Character Typing and the Presentation of Judas in the Fourth Gospel." *CBQ* 71 (2009): 544–59.

Xenophon. *Anabasis*. Translated by Carleton L. Brownson. Revised by John Dillery. LCL. Cambridge: Harvard University Press, 1998.

Yamasaki, Gary. *Watching a Biblical Narrative: Point of View in Biblical Exegesis*. New York: T&T Clark, 2007.

Zeelander, Susan. *Closure in Biblical Narrative*. BibInt 111. Leiden: Brill, 2012.

Zimmermann, Ruben. "'Deuten' heißt erzählen und übertragen: Narrativität und Metaphorik als zentrale Sprachformen historischer Sinnbildung zum Tod Jesu." Pages 315–73 in *Deutungen des Todes Jesu im Neuen Testament*. Edited by Jörg Frey and Jens Schröter. 2nd ed. WUNT 181. Tübingen: Mohr Siebeck, 2012.

———. "Imagery in John: Opening Up Paths into the Tangled Thicket of John's Figurative World." Pages 1–43 in *Imagery in the Gospel of John: Terms, Forms, Themes, and Theology of Johannine Figurative Language*. Edited by Jörg Frey, Jan G. van der Watt, and Ruben Zimmermann. WUNT 200. Tübingen: Mohr Siebeck, 2006.

———. "Metaphoric Networks as Hermeneutic Keys in the Gospel of John: Using the Example of the Mission Imagery." Pages 381–402 in *Repetitions and Variations in the Fourth Gospel: Style, Text, Interpretation*. Edited by Gilbert Van Belle, Michael Labahn, and Petrus Maritz. BETL 223. Leuven: Peeters, 2009.

Zumstein, Jean. "Die Endredaktion des Johannesevangeliums (am Beispiel von Kapitel 21)." Pages 291–315 in *Kreative Erinnerung: Relecture und Auslegung im Johannesevangelium*. Edited by Jean Zumstein. 2nd ed. ATANT 84. Zurich: TVZ, 2004.

———. "The Mother of Jesus and the Beloved Disciple." Pages 641–45 in *Character Studies in the Fourth Gospel: Narrative Approaches to Seventy Figures in John*. Edited by Steven A. Hunt, D. Francois Tolmie, and Ruben Zimmermann. WUNT 314. Tübingen: Mohr Siebeck, 2013.

———. *L'Évangile selon Saint Jean (1–12)*. Genève: Labor et Fides, 2014.

CONTRIBUTORS

Harold W. Attridge (PhD, Harvard University) is Sterling Professor of Divinity at Yale University. He has written extensively on the Fourth Gospel, the New Testament, Hellenistic Judaism, and the early church, including numerous books, articles, essays, and edited volumes. One of his most recent books is *Essays on John and Hebrews* (Baker Academic, 2012). In 2001, Attridge served as the president of the Society of Biblical Literature. In 2015, he was inducted into the American Academy of Arts and Sciences.

Rekha M. Chennattu (PhD, Catholic University of America) is Professor of New Testament at Jnana-Deepa Vidyapeeth, Pontifical Institute of Philosophy and Religion, Pune, India. She is the author of the following books: *Johannine Discipleship as a Covenant Relationship* (Hendrickson, 2006); *The Bible and Indian Exegesis; A Biblia es az Indiai Exegezis* [translated by Prof. Fabiny Tibor] (Hermeneutikai Kutatokozpont, 2010). She was a participant (auditor) at the Synod of Bishops on New Evangelization in October 2012.

Douglas Estes (PhD, University of Nottingham) is Assistant Professor of New Testament and Practical Theology and the Director of the DMin Program at South University—Columbia. Previously he served in pastoral ministry for sixteen years. Douglas has written or edited six books, including a number of books and articles on the Fourth Gospel such as *The Temporal Mechanics of the Fourth Gospel* (Brill, 2008) and *The Questions of Jesus in John* (Brill, 2012). His next book is a Greek grammar resource, *Questions and Rhetoric in the Greek New Testament* (Zondervan, 2016).

Charles E. Hill (PhD, University of Cambridge) is John R. Richardson Professor of New Testament and Early Christianity at Reformed Theological Seminary in Orlando and is a Henry Luce III Fellow in Theology. He is the author of *The Johannine Corpus in the Early Church* (Oxford University Press, 2004) and *Who Chose the Gospels? Probing the Great "Gospel Conspiracy"* (Oxford University Press, 2010).

Edward W. Klink III (PhD, University of St. Andrews) is currently the Senior Pastor at Hope Evangelical Free Church in Roscoe, Illinois, after nearly a decade as Associate Professor of Biblical and Theological Studies at Talbot School of Theology, Biola University in southern California. He is the author of *The Sheep of the Fold: The Audience and Origin of the Gospel of John* (Cambridge University Press, 2007), *Understanding Biblical Theology* (with Darian R. Lockett; Zondervan, 2012), and *John* in the Zondervan Exegetical Commentary on the New Testament series.

Kasper Bro Larsen (PhD, University of Aarhus) is Associate Professor of New Testament Studies at the University of Aarhus. He has published on various topics related to early Christianity, including the Dead Sea Scrolls, Paul's Letter to the Romans, and the Gospel of John. His first book on the Fourth Gospel was *Recognizing the Stranger: Recognition Scenes in the Gospel of John* (Brill, 2008). Recently he edited *The Gospel of John as Genre Mosaic* (Vandenhoeck & Ruprecht, 2015).

Dorothy A. Lee (PhD, University of Sydney) is Head of the Theological School and Frank Woods Professor in New Testament at Trinity College, University of Divinity. She is the author of numerous books and articles on the Gospel of John and the New Testament, including *Hallowed in Truth and Love* (Wipf & Stock, 2014), *Transfiguration* (Continuum, 2004), and *Flesh and Glory* (Crossroad, 2002).

Susanne Luther (PhD, Friedrich-Alexander-University of Erlangen-Nuremberg, Germany) is Postdoctoral Research Assistant at Johannes Gutenberg University of Mainz, Germany. Her first book on speech-ethics in Matthew, James, and 1 Peter was published as *Sprachethik im Neuen Testament* (Mohr Siebeck, 2015). She has written several articles on hermeneutics and early Christian Apocrypha as well as on fictionality and factuality in early Christian literature. Her current research on the Fourth Gospel focuses on narrative historiography in the Gospel of John.

Francis J. Moloney (DPhil, University of Oxford) was born and educated in Melbourne Australia. A Salesian of Don Bosco since 1960, he has served as the Foundation Professor of Theology at Australian Catholic University (1994–1999) and as Professor of New Testament and Dean of the School of Theology and Religious Studies at the Catholic University of America (1999–2005). He is currently a Senior Professorial Fellow and a member of the Institute for Religion and Critical Inquiry at Australian Catholic University. He is a Member of the Order of Australia and a Fellow of the Australian Academy of the Humanities. He is the author of *The Gospel of John* in the Sacra Pagina series (Liturgical, 1998) and *Love in the Gospel of John: An Exegetical, Theological, and Literary Study* (Baker Academic, 2013).

Alicia D. Myers (PhD, Baylor University) is Assistant Professor of New Testament and Greek at Campbell University Divinity School. She is the author of *Characterizing Jesus: A Rhetorical Analysis on the Fourth Gospel's Use of Scripture in Its Presentation of Jesus* (T&T Clark, 2012), as well as coeditor with Bruce G. Schuchard of *Abiding Words: Perspectives on the Use of Scripture in the Gospel of John* (SBL Press, 2015). She has also written several journal articles and essays on the Gospel of John and is currently working on a monograph project exploring ancient expectations of motherhood and maternal imagery in the New Testament.

Dan Nässelqvist (PhD, Lund University) is currently a postdoctoral research fellow at the University of Gothenburg, Sweden. He has written several articles on John and stylistics. His first book on John is *Public Reading in Early Christianity: Lectors, Manuscripts, and Sound in the Oral Delivery of John 1–4* (Brill, 2015).

James L. Resseguie (PhD, Fuller Theological Seminary) is Distinguished Professor of the New Testament Emeritus, Winebrenner Theological Seminary. He has written five books on the New Testament, including *The Strange Gospel: Narrative Design and Point of View in John* (Brill, 2001), as well as numerous articles and essays related to point of view and the Fourth Gospel. His book, *Narrative Criticism of the New Testament: An Introduction* (Baker, 2005), has been translated into Italian (2008) and French (2009).

Ruth Sheridan (PhD, Australian Catholic University) is currently a postdoctoral research fellow at Charles Sturt University, Australia. Her first book, *Retelling Scripture: "The Jews" and the Scriptural Citations in John 1:19–12:15* (Brill, 2012) won the 2013 Manfred Lautenschlaeger Award for

Theological Promise (formerly the John Templeton Award). Ruth has published articles on the Gospel of John and its narrative rhetoric in a variety of academic journals and edited collections.

Christopher W. Skinner (PhD, Catholic University of America) is Associate Professor of New Testament in the Department of Theology at Loyola University, Chicago. In addition to numerous articles and essays, he has written or edited seven books, including *John and Thomas: Gospels in Conflict? Johannine Characterization and the Thomas Question* (Wipf & Stock, 2009), *Characters and Characterization in the Gospel of John* (T&T Clark, 2012), and *Reading John* (Cascade, 2015). He is currently coediting a book with Sherri Brown on the ethics of the Johannine literature (Fortress, forthcoming 2017).

Mark W. G. Stibbe (PhD, University of Nottingham) is the author of six books on John's Gospel, including *John as Storyteller* (Cambridge University Press, 1992) and a narrative critical commentary on John. He has also contributed chapters to volumes on John and written a number of articles in scholarly journals. Today he is a professional writer and published author, as well as a freelance editor and script doctor. He heads up a business dedicated to turning good writers into great authors and leads writers' workshops both in the UK and abroad. He is currently collaborating with New York Times bestselling author G. P. Taylor on a series of spy fiction novels featuring an English Vicar in the Napoleonic Wars.

Ancient Sources Index

Isaiah (*cont.*)
55:1 175
58:11 175
60:1 160
60:19–20 160

Jeremiah
52:4 46

Ezekiel
1:1–2 46
24:1 46
37:25 176
37:27 182

Daniel
7 178
7:14 176

Micah
5:2 178

Haggai
1:1 46
2:1 46

Zechariah
1:7 46
9:9 174, 178
13 178
14:8 175

DEUTEROCANONICAL AND PSEUDEPIGRAPHICAL BOOKS

Judith
2:1 46

Additions to Esther
1:1 46

Sirach
32:1–2 263

Baruch
1:2 46

1 Maccabees
1:54 46

4 Ezra
4:5–7 18
4:50 18
5:36 18

Jubilees
1:1 46
14:1 46

DEAD SEA SCROLLS

1QDM I, 1 46

4QCommGen A II, 1 46

4QCalDoc A I, 6 46

ANCIENT JEWISH WRITERS

Josephus, *Antiquitates judaicae*
4.219 277
12.248 46

Josephus, *Jewish War*
1.13–16 10

NEW TESTAMENT

Matthew
1:1–4:17 228
8:5–13 265
12:9–14 67
12:34 198
14:9 266
22:1–14 264
25:1–13 264
25:31–46 20

Modern Authors Index

Subject Index

temporal mechanics, 42
  as coordinates, 46–47
  as descriptors, 48, 53, 262
  as geodesic, 52–53
  as markers, 47–48, 53, 54, 262
  as process words, 54
  as value words, 54–55
tension, 18, 20, 21, 28, 39, 44–45, 74, 202, 233
Tertullian, 225, 264, 269, 271, 273, 275
testaments, 9, 16
testimony, 1, 17, 71, 153, 185, 186, 194, 201, 217, 229, 255, 268, 277
Thackeray, William Makepeace, 80
Theophilus of Antioch, 268, 276
Thomas, 17, 70, 104, 111, 116, 130, 157, 226, 229, 231, 232, 234, 235, 237, 254, 255, 276
Thucydides, 10, 47, 49, 192
Thunder: Perfect Mind, 18
time, 41–57, 64, 65, 82, 84–88, 232, 235, 239, 252, 262
  passing of, 50, 52, 53, 57, 82, 87, 88, 96, 231, 232
  restrictions on, 55, 56
Tolstoy, Leo, 80
topography, 59, 65–68, 76
  turn toward, 63
topology, 59, 60, 63
  turn toward, 63
topos, 62, 195, 198, 199, 201
torah, 160, 172, 192
tragedy, 10, 14, 18, 99, 116, 120
transformation, 2, 7, 11, 22, 64, 70, 74–77, 122, 151, 159, 165, 167, 168, 172
trial, 72, 73, 104, 106, 153, 154, 222, 228, 278
Troy, 108, 111
Twain, Mark, 138
Valentinus, 272, 273
verisimilitude, 47, 61, 259, 260, 262
vine, 16, 22, 32, 143, 159, 166, 173, 263
Walton, Jo, 136
warp, of narrative time, 53–55
watch, 43, 50–57

water, 153, 156, 157, 172, 175, 200, 217, 228, 262, 264, 271
wedding at Cana, 68, 153, 161, 228, 261, 263–65, 275, 278
whodunit, 106
Wikipedia, 98
witness, 17, 18, 56, 69, 95, 128, 145, 153, 156, 175, 177, 178, 217, 222, 226, 234, 236–38, 254–56, 276, 277
Wittgenstein, Ludwig, 9
woman in labor, 165
Woolf, Virginia, 93
Wordsworth, William, 207
world, 37, 55, 56, 59, 61, 70, 103, 105, 107, 120, 127, 134, 145, 159, 203, 205, 206, 209, 210, 212, 213, 221, 223, 231, 234, 236, 266, 277
Yeats, W. B., 207
Xenophon, 47
Zeno of Elea, 42

CPSIA information can be obtained
at www.ICGtesting.com
Printed in the USA
FFOW02n1518191116
29498FF